MW01482393

PASS TRAK®

65/66

License Exam Manual
Questions & Answers

Uniform Investment Adviser Law/Combined State Law Exam

5th Edition

Dearborn
Financial Institute, Inc.®

At press time, this 5th edition of PASSTRAK® Series 65/66 contains the most complete and accurate information currently available for the NASAA Series 65 and 66 license examinations. Owing to the nature of securities license examinations, however, information may have been added recently to the actual tests that does not appear in this edition.

Published by Dearborn Financial Institute, Inc.®

Printed in the United States of America.

98 99 00 10 9 8 7 6 5 4 3 2 1

PPN: 3665-01-05
ISBN: 0-7931-2584-7

Contents

Introduction ix

1. Regulation and Registration of Investment Advisers 1
Registration of Investment Advisers 2
Federal Registration of Investment Advisers 5
Exemptions from Federal Registration 5
SEC Registration Procedure 6
State Registration of Investment Advisers 8
Exemptions from State Registration 8
State Registration Procedure 8
Denial, Suspension or Revocation of Registration 10
Cancelation of Registration 11
Federal and State Laws Regarding Investment Advisers 12
Business Activities of Investment Advisers 14
Investment Adviser Brochure Rule 14
Recordkeeping and Reporting Requirements 15
Investment Advisory Contracts 17
Transactions 20
Discretionary Account Transactions 20
Agency Cross Transactions 20
Advertisements by Investment Advisers 21
Cash Payments for Client Solicitations 22
Disclosure of Financial and Disciplinary Information 23
SEC Release IA-1092 23
Enforcement of the Investment Advisers Act of 1940 25
Enforcement of the Uniform Securities Act 26

2. Regulation and Registration of Broker-Dealers and Agents 27
Overview of Securities Trading Regulation 28
Definitions 28
The Securities Exchange Act of 1934 31
Overview of the Uniform Securities Act 34
State Securities Laws 34
Administration of the Uniform Securities Act 34
Registration of Broker-Dealers and Agents 37
Federal Registration of Broker-Dealers 37
State Registration of Broker-Dealers 37
State Registration Procedures 38
Denial, Suspension or Revocation of Registration 41
Federal and State Laws Regarding Broker-Dealers 43

3. Regulation of New Issues 45
Overview of New Issue Regulation 46
Federal Registration of New Issues 47
Civil Liabilities under the Act of 1933 52
The Underwriting Process 53
Underwriting Corporate Securities 53
Participants in a Corporate New Issue 53
Types of Offerings 55
Time Line for an Underwriting 56
Exemptions from Federal Registration 60
Exempt Issuers and Securities 60
Exempt Transactions 60
Antifraud Regulations of the Acts of 1933 and 1934 63
State Registration of New Issues 65
Types of Securities Registrations 65
State Registration Provisions 67
Denial, Suspension or Revocation of Securities Registration 68
Exemptions from State Registration 68
Denial and Revocation of Exemptions 72
Unlawful Representations 73

4. Ethics in the Securities Industry 75
Ethical Behavior of Investment Advisers 76
Criminal Penalties 79

5. Investment Companies 81

Investment Company Offerings 82

Investment Company Purpose 82

Types of Investment Companies 82

Investment Company Registration 86

Registration of Investment Companies 86

Registration of Investment Company Securities 88

Restrictions on Operations 88

Management of Investment Companies 90

Board of Directors 90

Investment Adviser 90

Affiliated and Interested Persons 91

Custodian 93

Transfer Agent (Customer Services Agent) 93

Underwriter 94

Bonding of Directors and Employees 95

Information Distributed to Investors 95

6. Other Federal Legislation 99

Securities Investor Protection Act of 1970 100

Insider Trading and Securities Fraud Enforcement Act of 1988 100

Telephone Communications with the Public 103

7. Uniform Securities Act Review Exam 105

Answers & Rationale 124

8. Uniform Securities Act Exam One 135

Answers & Rationale 143

9. Uniform Securities Act Exam Two 147

Answers & Rationale 155

10. Uniform Securities Act Exam Three 159

Answers & Rationale 168

11. Uniform Securities Act Exam Four 173

Answers & Rationale 181

12. Series 65 Final Exam One 185

Answers & Rationale 201

13. Series 65 Final Exam Two 209
Answers & Rationale 225

14. Series 65 Final Exam Three 233
Answers & Rationale 249

15. Series 65 Final Exam Four 255
Answers & Rationale 269

16. Series 66 Final Exam 275
Answers & Rationale 295

Appendix: Form ADV, Part II 303

Glossary 311

Index 317

Acknowledgments

My thanks to each person who has contributed time and expertise for this 5th edition of *PASSTRAK® Series 65/66.* In particular, I wish to thank Marcia Burak, Phil Keener and the Answer Phone staff, who reviewed the text for technical accuracy; Stuart Egrin, who collaborated on the review, research and development of the material; and Thomas Drinkard, co-author, who participated in the overall research and development process of *PASSTRAK® Series 65/66,* 5th edition.

Joan M. McGillivray, Editor

Introduction

Welcome to PASSTRAK® Series 65/66. Because you probably have a lot of questions about the course and the exams, we have tried to anticipate some of them and provide you with answers to help you on your way.

The Course

How is the course structured?

PASSTRAK® Series 65/66 License Exam Manual and Questions & Answers consists of text chapters and exam sets. Chapter 1 addresses the regulation and registration requirements for investment advisers at both the federal and state levels. Chapter 2 details regulation and registration requirements for broker-dealers and agents at federal and state levels. Chapter 3 covers requirements for registration and regulation of new issues. Chapter 4 concentrates on the North American Securities Administrators Association's policies on unethical practices. Chapter 5 highlights the Investment Company Act of 1940 and applicable amendments. Chapter 6 focuses on those portions of other federal securities acts necessary to pass the Uniform Investment Adviser Law Exam (the Series 65) or the Uniform Combined State Law Exam (the Series 66). Each chapter of text is devoted to those study areas with which you need to become familiar.

The remaining chapters consist of a review exam (chapter 7) and final exams (chapters 8 through 16) composed of questions similar to those you will encounter on the Series 65 and Series 66 tests.

How much time should I spend studying?

You should plan to spend approximately 24 to 30 hours reading the material and working through the questions. Your actual time, of course, may vary from this figure depending on your reading rate, comprehension, professional background and study environment.

Spread your study time over the four to six days prior to the date on which you are scheduled to take the Series 65 or Series 66 exam. Select a time and place for studying that will allow you to concentrate your full attention on the material at hand. You have a lot of information to learn and a lot of ground to cover. Be sure to give yourself enough time to learn the material.

What is the best way to approach the exams?

Approach each review and final exam as if you were preparing to take the actual test. Read each question carefully and write down your answer. Then check your answers against the key and read the accompanying rationale. Making yourself go through all of these steps (rather than simply reading each question and skipping directly to the rationale) will greatly increase your comprehension and retention of the information in the book.

Do I need to take the final exams?

The final exams test the same knowledge you will need in order to answer the questions on the NASD Series 65 or Series 66 exam. Although the Series 65 and Series 66 exams differ in terms of emphasis and number of questions, they cover the same broad topic areas. Whether you are preparing for the Series 65 or the Series 66, you would be well advised to complete all of the final exams for additional practice in the topic areas.

By completing the exams and checking your answers against the rationale, you should be able to pinpoint any areas with which you are still having difficulty. Review any questions you miss, paying particular attention to the rationale for those questions. If any subjects still seem troublesome, go back and review the section(s) covering those topics. At the end of each rationale, you will find a page reference that directs you to the page in the text portion where the information is covered.

The Exam

Why do I need to pass the Series 65 exam?

The state in which you reside requires investment advisers to pass a qualification exam in order to become registered. To be compensated for providing investment advice in those states that require Series 65 qualification, you must pass the Series 65 exam.

Why do I need to pass the Series 66 exam?

The state in which you reside requires a qualification exam for investment advisers (the Series 65). Your state also requires a qualification exam in order to sell securities in the state (the Series 63). If your state accepts the Series 66 exam, you may fulfill both requirements at once.

What are the Series 65 and Series 66 exams like?

The Series 65 is a 120-minute, 75-question exam. The Series 66 is a 150-minute, 100-question exam. Both exams are administered by the NASD; they are offered as computer-based tests at various testing sites around the country. A pencil-and-paper exam is available to those candidates who apply to and obtain permission from the NASD to take a written exam.

What topics will I see covered on the exams?

This course covers the wide range of topics that the North American Securities Administrators Association (NASAA) has outlined as essential to the investment adviser and to the agent.

The Series 65 exam is divided into four broad topic areas:

Uniform Securities Act (as amended)	30%
Federal Securities Law	35%
Investment Advisers Act of 1940 and SEC Release IA-1092	15%
Unethical Business Practices of Investment Advisers	20%

The Series 66 exam is divided into two parts, which together cover four topic areas:

Part 1	Uniform Securities Act (as amended)	54%
Part 2	Federal Securities Law	26%
	SEC Release IA-1092	11%
	Unethical Business Practices of Investment Advisers	9%

What score must I achieve in order to pass?

Candidates for the Series 65 must answer at least 70% of the questions correctly to pass and become eligible for registration. Candidates for the Series 66 must score at least 70% *on each part* of the exam; failure on either part requires retaking the exam. Some states may require a higher score for principals and supervisory personnel.

How long does the exam take?

You will be allowed 120 minutes in which to finish the Series 65 exam. You will be allowed 150 minutes in which to finish the Series 66 exam. If you are taking the computerized version of the exam, you will be given additional time before the test to become familiar with the PROCTOR® terminal.

Are there any prerequisites I have to meet before taking the exam?

There are no prerequisite exams you must pass before sitting for the Series 65 or the Series 66.

How do I enroll for the exam?

To obtain an admission ticket to the Series 65 or Series 66 exam, your firm must file the proper application form with the NASD, along with the appropriate processing fees. The NASD will then send you a directory of Certification Testing Centers and a PROCTOR® enrollment valid for a stated number of days. To take the exam during this period, you must make an appointment with a Certification Testing Center as far in advance as possible of the date on which you would like to sit for the test.

What should I take to the exam?

Take one form of personal identification that bears your signature and your photograph as issued by a government agency. You are not allowed to take reference materials or anything else into the testing area. Calculators are available upon request; you will not be allowed to use your personal calculator.

Scratch paper and pencils will be provided by the testing center, although you will not be permitted to take them with you when you leave.

What is PROCTOR®?

The Series 65 and Series 66 exams, like many professional licensing examinations, are administered on the PROCTOR® computerized testing system. PROCTOR® is a nationwide, interactive computer system designed for the administration and delivery of qualifications examinations. Included with your PROCTOR® enrollment, you will receive a brochure describing how the exam is formatted and how to use the computer terminal to answer the questions.

When you have completed the exam, the PROCTOR® System promptly scores your answers and within minutes displays your grade for the exam on the terminal screen.

How well can I expect to do on the exam?

The examinations administered by the NASD are not easy. You will be required to display considerable understanding and knowledge of the topics presented in this course in order to pass the Series 65 or Series 66 exam and qualify for registration. If you study and complete all of the sections of the course, and consistently score at least 80% on the review and final exams, you should be well prepared to pass the Series 65 or Series 66 exam.

1 Regulation and Registration of Investment Advisers

Key Terms

agency cross transaction
assignment
bank
client solicitation
conditional exemption
contract
custody
de minimis exemption
disclosure brochure
fiduciary
foreign securities authority
Form ADV
impersonal advisory service
investment adviser
investment adviser representative
Investment Advisers Act of 1940
investment advisory contract
investment supervisory service
National Securities Markets Improvement Act of 1996
private investment company
qualified purchaser
supervised person
written disclosure statement

Overview

The regulation of investment advisers was deemed necessary when the growing profession became national in scope and grew to have far-reaching effects on the securities industry and its clientele's finances. Thus, the Investment Advisers Act of 1940 was enacted. Because investment advisers send their investment advice, reports, newsletters and other publications through the mails (that is, they use *instruments of interstate commerce*) and because their advice frequently involves the purchase and sale of securities traded on exchanges and in the national over-the-counter markets, a great part of their regulation falls under the SEC's jurisdiction.

Among the important aspects of the Investment Advisers Act of 1940 are (1) the requirement that persons in the business of giving investment advice on a regular basis and charging a fee for the advice must register as investment advisers, and (2) the establishment of standards of ethical business conduct.

The National Securities Markets Improvement Act of 1996 (NSMIA) amends sections of the act of 1940 on a state level. The act has two major themes: (1) the restructuring of the division of responsibilities between the federal regulatory authorities and state securities administrators and (2) the enhancement of mutual fund regulation.

In addition, the National Securities Markets Improvement Act of 1996 provides for the efficient regulation of investment advisers. An investment adviser is regulated either by the SEC or by the state in which it conducts business.

Registration of Investment Advisers

A familiarity with the terms established by the Investment Advisers Act of 1940, also known as the *advisers act,* and SEC Release IA-1092 is important to an understanding of the act itself. Most of the definitions used in the act are similar to those set forth in other securities acts.

Definitions

Person. Although most people think of an individual when they hear the word "person," throughout securities law and this text the term "person" refers to any:

- individual
- corporation
- partnership
- association
- joint stock company
- trust where a security evidences the beneficiaries' interests
- unincorporated organization
- government or political subdivision of a government

Investment adviser. Any person who (1) provides investment advice, (2) is in the business of providing investment advice and (3) is compensated for providing investment advice is considered an **investment adviser**. Investment advisory services may be direct, such as during face-to-face financial planning, or impersonal, such as through an investment newsletter, an analysis, a report or an online computer service. For example, a certified financial planner who is compensated for his investment advice during the regular course of business is regarded as an investment adviser.

If the person giving the advice holds himself out as an investment adviser or receives any compensation for giving investment advice, the person is considered to be "in the business" of giving investment advice and must register under the act. For example, an athlete's business manager is regarded as being "in the business" if he is compensated and provides investment advice to the athlete.

Compensation for investment advice can take the form of a(n):

- advisory fee
- total services fee
- commission
- any combination of the above

The payments may be considered compensation even if not paid directly by the person receiving the investment advice. Compensation can come from another source, such as commissions generated from sales of the products the investment adviser has recommended.

The definition of "investment adviser" does *not* include:

- banks and bank holding companies;
- publishers of any bona fide newspaper, newsmagazine or business or financial publication of general and regular circulation (such as *The Wall Street Journal* or *Business Week*);

- brokers or dealers (or their associated persons and registered reps) whose giving of investment advice is incidental to the conduct of the broker-dealer's business and who receive no special compensation for the advice;
- persons who advise on U.S. government securities; or
- persons whose giving of investment advice is incidental to their professions, such as:
  - lawyers
  - accountants
  - engineers
  - teachers

Investment adviser representative (supervised person). An investment adviser representative is any partner, officer, director or other individual directly or indirectly controlled by an investment adviser. An investment adviser rep is an individual who makes investment recommendations, manages customer accounts, solicits investment advisory services or supervises the employees who perform any of these duties. Clerical and ministerial personnel are not considered investment adviser reps.

Investment counsel. An investment adviser may use the term "investment counsel" to describe her business if her principal business consists of acting as an investment adviser and a substantial part of her business consists of rendering investment supervisory services.

Investment supervisory service. An investment adviser who gives continuous advice on the investment of funds on the basis of a customer's individual needs is said to be engaging in "investment supervisory services."

Impersonal advisory service. Any contract between an investment adviser and a client to provide investment advisory services that are not intended to meet directly the needs of a specific individual or account (such as an advisory newsletter or seminar) is considered a contract for "impersonal advisory services."

Administrator. The official or agency that administers the Uniform Securities Act in a state is known as the *administrator* or as the state securities *commissioner* or *secretary*.

Assignment. The term "assignment" signifies any direct or indirect transfer of an advisory contract or a controlling interest in an advisory contract. The term does not include a change in control based on the death of a partner or another member of an investment adviser. A transfer of control or ownership interest in an investment advisory contract is not considered an assignment if it does not result in an actual change in control or management.

Bank. A bank is any banking institution organized under the laws of the United States, any member of the Federal Reserve System or any other firm doing business as a bank under a state's laws.

Fiduciary. A person entrusted with the control of assets for another person (the beneficial owner) is considered a "fiduciary." The duties and responsibilities of fiduciaries are regulated by law in most states. In all cases, a fiduciary must act primarily for the benefit of his clients, exercise good faith and care in handling a beneficial owner's assets and make full and fair disclosure of all material facts.

One category of material facts that a fiduciary must disclose is any actual or potential conflicts of interest with a client. Conflicts of interest can take many forms, including:

- dual employment (such as an investment adviser who is also a registered representative of a broker-dealer or an associated person of an insurance company);
- personal transactions in securities that are affected by recommendations to clients (such as an investment adviser who holds options on a stock and who recommends that clients purchase that stock);
- any interest an investment adviser has in the securities about which he gives advice (such as being a controlling person of the issuer or receiving any form of compensation from the issuer for the recommendation of its securities); and
- any compensation that will be received from another source.

Private investment company. An unregistered investment company whose investment objective is to raise capital for business ventures is considered a private investment company. Investors in such a company are known as "qualified purchasers."

Foreign securities authority. Any foreign government, or any governmental body or regulatory organization empowered by a foreign government to regulate securities matters, is considered a "foreign securities authority."

Qualified purchaser. An investment sophisticate is considered a "qualified purchaser" if the investor is a(n):

- individual who owns $5 million or more in investments, including investments held jointly with a spouse;
- family-held business that owns $5 million or more in investments;
- business that has discretion over $25 million or more in investments; or
- trust sponsored by qualified purchasers.

North American Securities Administrators Association (NASAA). NASAA is a trade organization for state securities administrators of the United States, Canada and Mexico. Its purpose is to provide a medium for cooperation and coordination of state and international securities regulations.

Federal Registration of Investment Advisers

Any person who falls within the federal definition of "investment adviser" must register with the SEC under the Investment Advisers Act of 1940, which was amended by the NSMIA. SEC-registered investment advisers are known as *federally registered* investment advisers.

The following advisers must register with the SEC:

- persons managing $25 million or more in assets
- investment company advisers
- advisers not regulated under state law

An investment adviser that is not subject to federal registration requirements must register with the state in which it conducts business. For example, an investment adviser managing less than $25 million in assets must register with the state.

Federally registered investment advisers are exempt from state registration. While exempt from state registration, these investment advisers are still required to pay state filing fees and give notice.

State administrators are responsible for overseeing the business activities of all investment advisers that conduct business *within* the state and for enforcing the antifraud provisions under state and federal law.

Exemptions from Federal Registration

If an investment adviser meets one of the following conditions, he is exempt from the federal registration requirements of the Investment Advisers Act of 1940.

Local (intrastate) adviser exemption. The act of 1940 exempts from registration an investment adviser whose only clients are residents of the state in which the adviser is located and who does not give investment advice regarding securities that are listed, or admitted to unlisted trading privileges, on a national securities exchange.

De minimis exemption. Federal law also exempts a person whose investment advisory business is so small that the law considers it not worth regulating. (The term "de minimis" comes from a Latin phrase that means "the law does not concern itself with small things.") This exemption includes any investment adviser who has less than *15 clients* during the preceding 12 months and who does not hold himself out generally to the public as an investment adviser.

Insurance company advisory exemption. Exempt from registration under the act of 1940 are investment advisers whose only clients are insurance companies.

Burden of proof of exemption. The burden of proving an exemption from registration lies with the person claiming the exemption.

Federal registration of investment adviser representatives. A federally registered investment adviser must file information about its representatives (also called *supervised persons*) with the SEC. However, investment adviser representatives need not be registered individually with the SEC.

SEC Registration Procedure

A person who wishes to become a federally registered investment adviser must file an application for registration with the SEC on **Form ADV** and pay a nonrefundable fee. A copy of Form ADV Part II is reproduced in the Appendix, pages 303 through 310.

An application for registration as an investment adviser must include the following information on Form ADV:

- name of the adviser's business;
- education, business affiliations for the past 10 years and present business affiliations of the adviser and any partners, officers and controlling persons;
- manner of operation, including the manner in which advice will be given;
- balance sheet and any other financial statements the SEC requests, certified by an independent public accountant;
- scope of the adviser's authority with respect to clients' funds;
- basis on which the adviser will be compensated;
- whether the adviser or any associated person has a criminal record; and
- statement as to the anticipated percentage of the adviser's principal business of investment advice will constitute.

Within 45 days after the application is filed, the SEC either grants the registration or institutes proceedings to determine whether it should deny the application.

If a change occurs in its management, state of location or form of business organization, an investment adviser must file a new Form ADV and pay the fee.

Material misstatements. The registration application an investment adviser files must be accurate and free from misstatements and false information. The investment adviser is prohibited from willfully omitting information from a registration statement. If an investment adviser's registration documents contain a material misstatement, the SEC may impose a censure, suspension of up to 12 months, limitation on activities or revocation of registration.

Withdrawal from registration. If a registered investment adviser wishes to withdraw from registration, notification must be given to the SEC by filing **Form ADV-W**. The withdrawal becomes effective on the 60th day after filing, but the SEC may permit the withdrawal sooner. If any suspension or revocation action is pending against the investment adviser, the SEC can delay the withdrawal's effectiveness until it deems withdrawal necessary or appropriate in the public interest or for the protection of investors.

Investment adviser representative registration. Under federal law, representatives are typically exempt from state registration if they represent a federally registered (SEC) investment adviser. However, representatives who have places of business within the state may be required to register with the state. Federally registered investment advisers *may be required* to file information regarding their supervised persons with the SEC or states.

State Registration of Investment Advisers

The Uniform Securities Act (USA) is the model state law that governs the registration and regulation of investment advisers at the state level. Many, although not all, of the provisions of the Investment Advisers Act of 1940 have been adopted by the *North American Securities Administrators Association* **(NASAA)**, the trade organization for state securities administrators of the United States, Canada and Mexico. Under the USA, it is unlawful for *any* person to transact business in a state as an investment adviser or representative unless the person is registered with the state or exempt from registration. Investment advisers are exempt from state registration if they manage registered investment company portfolios or portfolios with $25 million or more in assets.

Exemptions from State Registration

Both the Investment Advisers Act of 1940 and the USA exempt from state registration any investment adviser that does minimal business in the state. This is known as the national *de minimis* exemption. The federal government also mandates a de minimis exemption from state registration. Under a provision of the National Securities Markets Improvement Act, a state may not require registration of an investment adviser if the adviser has directed business communications to fewer than six clients in the past 12-month period.

An exemption under the USA is also available to a person who has no place of business in the state and who limits his clientele to:

- other investment advisers;
- broker-dealers; and
- financial or institutional investors (such as banks, insurance companies or investment companies).

State registration of investment adviser representatives (supervised persons). An investment adviser representative who has a place of business in the state must register with the state. However, if the representative is a supervised person of a federally registered investment adviser, he is typically exempt from state registration, though, he must still pay filing fees. Under the USA, an individual need not register as an investment adviser representative if he acts in a clerical or an administrative capacity for the investment adviser.

State Registration Procedure

Application. An investment adviser or investment adviser rep may obtain an initial registration by filing (1) an application (Form ADV) with (2) the appropriate filing fee (as set by each state) and (3) a consent to service of process with the administrator (in the form the administrator requires).

A consent to service of process gives the administrator the irrevocable right to receive and process, as the applicant's attorney, any legal complaints that may arise in regard to an applicant's conduct as an investment adviser or an investment adviser rep. Once the applicant files the consent to service of process, any complaint presented to the administrator has the same force and validity as if it had been served personally on the applicant.

In addition to Form ADV, the adviser must file a balance sheet for the last fiscal year. If applicable, an investment adviser must furnish a copy of his surety bond and documentation that the appropriate licensing requirements were met.

The administrator may also require an applicant for initial registration to publish an announcement of the registration application in one or more specific newspapers in the state.

If the administrator does not deny the registration or is not in the process of denying the registration, that registration becomes effective at noon of the 30th day after the application is filed. The administrator may allow an earlier effective date. He also may defer the effective date until noon of the 30th day after the filing of any amendment.

Financial requirements. Under the USA, the state administrator may require, as a condition of registration, that an investment adviser meet minimum financial requirements. An investment adviser that has custody of customer assets must maintain a minimum net worth (assets minus liabilities) of $35,000. An investment adviser that has discretionary authority over customer accounts but that does not have custody must maintain a minimum net worth of $10,000.

Surety bonds. Investment advisers may be required by the administrator to post **surety bonds** if the person has custody of or discretionary authority over customer funds or securities. Typically, surety bonds are set in amounts of $35,000, although deposits of cash or securities may be permissible instead of the bonds. Compliance with minimum financial requirements releases the investment adviser from the surety bond requirement.

Registration Regulations and Restrictions

Qualification examinations. The administrator may require that one or more officers or representatives of an investment advisory firm take an examination that may be written, oral or both.

Successful completion of the Uniform Securities Agent State Law Examination (Series 63), the Uniform Investment Adviser Law Examination (Series 65), the Uniform Combined State Law Examination (Series 66) or any of the National Association of Securities Dealers (NASD), New York Stock Exchange (NYSE) or Municipal Securities Rulemaking Board (MSRB) examinations does not automatically constitute registration in a state. An applicant who has passed the exam does not have the right to transact business until the state administrator grants him registration.

Responsibilities of those who pass the examination. Successful completion of the Uniform Securities Agent State Law Examination, the Uniform

Investment Adviser Law Examination or the Uniform Combined State Law Examination does not relieve the agent of the following responsibilities:

- to know and abide by the specific requirements of the securities laws and the requirements of regulations of the states in which he will transact business;
- to understand that he does not have the right to transact business prior to being granted a license or registration; and
- to know that some states may require further certification to indicate that he has reviewed a state's blue-sky law and understands his responsibilities.

Denial, Suspension or Revocation of Registration

All registrations required by the Uniform Securities Act fall under the state administrators' jurisdiction. An administrator may deny, suspend or revoke any registration, or bar or censure any registrant, or restrict or limit any registrant's functions or activities if he finds that the:

- order is in the *public interest*; and
- the applicant, registrant or issuer of a security is guilty of any of a specified list of offenses.

Among these offenses are the following:

- filing of an incomplete, false or misleading application;
- willful violation of any Uniform Securities Act provision;
- conviction of a securities-related misdemeanor or felony within the past 10 years;
- permanent or temporary enjoinment (or injunction) by a court from investment-related activities;
- violation of any federal or state securities or commodities law within the past 10 years;
- engagement in dishonest or unethical securities practices;
- insolvency;
- willful violation of a foreign jurisdiction's securities or banking laws;
- denial, revocation or suspension of license by a foreign securities regulatory authority within the past five years;
- lack of qualification on the basis of training, experience or knowledge;
- failure to supervise registered employees; or
- failure to pay application filing fees.

Denial of registration due to lack of qualification. An individual's registration may be denied, revoked or suspended due to deficiencies in knowledge, training or experience. The administrator may not, however, deny registration solely on the lack of experience. Likewise, an investment adviser may not be denied licensing privileges based solely on the lack of its reps' experience.

The act authorizes the administrator to restrict a particular applicant's registration to that of a broker-dealer if the administrator finds the individual is not qualified as an investment adviser. Experience is a consideration, but lack of experience cannot be the sole factor for denying registration.

A representative need not meet the same level of qualification as the broker-dealer or investment adviser for which he works. A person registered and with experience as a broker-dealer or an agent is not necessarily qualified to be registered as an investment adviser. The broker-dealer may be prohibited from transacting business in any state as an investment adviser until such time as it does become registered.

Legal action. The Uniform Securities Act authorizes an administrator to proceed with legal action against an entire investment advisory firm if any one of that firm's officers has been disqualified, as long as this legal action is in the public interest. However, disqualification of an investment adviser rep, sometimes known as a *counselor*, may not be used automatically as a basis for taking legal action against the rep's entire firm unless further findings show that the firm's illegal actions (improper supervision, for example) were responsible for the rep's disqualification.

Withdrawal from registration. If a person or firm withdraws from registration, that withdrawal normally becomes effective 30 days after the administrator receives it, although the administrator may specify a shorter period of time if he so chooses. If a proceeding to revoke, deny or suspend the registration has begun, the effective date of the withdrawal will be delayed until whatever date the administrator determines is necessary to finalize the matter under consideration.

Notification requirements. The administrator must provide to any persons affected by an order under this section (1) advance notice of actions to deny, suspend or revoke registration to the persons affected and to the employer or prospective employer, (2) an opportunity for a hearing within 15 days of a written request and (3) a *written* statement of any findings, facts or conclusions.

Judicial review. A person who wishes to appeal the state administrator's decision or order may file a written petition in court within 60 days of the effective date of the order. The court may then decide whether to affirm or set aside the administrator's order.

Cancelation of Registration

An administrator may cancel any applicant's registration if he finds the applicant:

- is no longer in existence or has ceased to do business as an investment adviser;
- has been adjudged mentally incompetent or has been placed under the control of a guardian or conservator; or
- cannot be found after a reasonable search.

Federal and State Laws Regarding Investment Advisers

Table 1.1 compares federal and state registration requirements for investment advisers.

Table 1.2 compares federal laws and regulations to state laws under the Uniform Securities Act.

Forms Filed by Investment Advisers

Table 1.3 lists the forms that investment advisers must file and the purpose of each form.

Table 1.1 Summary of Revised Registration Requirements for Investment Advisers

Federally Registered	*State Registered*
Manage $25 million or more	Manage less than $25 million
State registration not required	Federal registration not required
Payment of federal and state filing fees required	Payment of state filing fee required
Federal registration of investment adviser reps not required; state registration may be required	State registration of investment adviser reps required

Table 1.3 Forms Investment Advisers File

Form	*Purpose*
ADV (Parts I and II)	Application for initial registration
ADV-E	Record of customer assets held in custody
ADV-W	Withdrawal of registration
Schedule H	Disclosure of wrap fee program

Table 1.2 Comparison of Federal and State Laws Regarding Investment Advisers

Item	*Federal Law*	*State Law*
Definition of "Investment Adviser" (IA)	Anyone who, for a fee, is "in the business of" advising others as to the worth of securities and who makes specific recommendations as part of his regular course of business, including issuing analyses and reports.	Same.
Exclusions	Bank; lawyer; accountant; engineer; teacher; broker-dealer; publisher of general news magazine; anyone whose advice is limited to U.S. government bonds.	Bank; lawyer; accountant; engineer; teacher; broker-dealer; publisher of general news magazine; IA representative.
Exemptions	All clients are residents of the adviser's state and no advice is rendered regarding exchange-listed securities; or all clients are insurance companies.	No place of business within the state and the only clients are institutions (investment companies, banks and insurance companies), broker-dealers, other IAs, employee benefit plans of $1 million or more, or government agencies.
	De minimis: Has had fewer than 15 clients (none of which are investment companies) during the previous 12 months and does not hold himself out to the public as an IA.	National de minimis: Has directed communications to fewer than six clients who are residents of the state during the previous 12 months.
Registration	File Form ADV with the SEC; effective within 45 days. No net capital requirement. No surety bonds. File for withdrawal on ADV-W.	File Form ADV with the administrator; effective at 12:00 pm on the 30th day. Net worth or surety bond required when IA has custody or discretion.
Criminal Penalties	Five years in jail and a $10,000 fine.	Three years in jail and a $5,000 fine.
Records	Must be readily accessible for 5 years; must be in the IA's main office for 2 of the years.	Same.
Assignment of Contract	Contract may not be assigned without the client's consent.	Same.
Change in Partnership Membership	The IA must notify the client of any change in partnership membership.	Same.
"Brochure Rule"	The "Brochure Rule" applies.	Same.
Use of Terms	The term "investment counsel" may not be used *unless:* the principal business is investment advice *and* a substantial portion is providing investment supervisory services (i.e., giving continuous advice on the investment of funds based on clients' individual needs).	An investment adviser representative is an associated person (not a clerk) of an adviser firm who makes recommendations; manages accounts; solicits advisory services; or supervises any of these activities.
Withdrawal of Registration	Takes effect 60 days after filing Form ADV-W.	Takes effect 30 days after filing Form ADV-W.
Insolvency	Not a cause for revocation.	Cause for revocation.

Business Activities of Investment Advisers

Investment Adviser Brochure Rule

Both federally registered and state-registered investment advisers must send a **written disclosure statement**, also known as a **disclosure brochure**, to each client.

Delivery. The adviser must deliver this brochure (1) *not less than 48 hours* before entering into a contract with a new client or (2) at the time of entering into the advisory contract *provided* the contract stipulates that the client has the right to terminate the agreement without penalty within five business days of signing the contract. The adviser must also send, or offer to send, each client a copy of the disclosure brochure at least annually (or more often if it has been changed or amended) at no cost or obligation to the client. If a client makes a written request for a copy of the brochure, it must be delivered or mailed within seven days of receipt of the request.

Contents. The brochure that the investment adviser delivers must contain substantially the same information required on Part II of Form ADV (and may, if the adviser wishes, be a copy of Part II). Form ADV is intended to provide investment advisory clients with information about the investment adviser and his advisory business. It includes such facts as:

- name and address of the investment adviser or the organization;
- nature of the business, including the manner in which advice will be given (for example, issuing periodicals, consulting or producing charts and graphs);
- advisory services and fees;
- types of clients;
- types of investments;
- methods of analysis, sources of information and investment strategies;
- education, business standards and business background of the adviser;
- other business activities of the adviser;
- other financial industry activities or affiliations;
- participation or interest in client transactions;
- conditions for managing accounts;
- review of accounts;
- investment or brokerage discretion;
- additional compensation; and
- balance sheet.

Exceptions. Two principal exceptions to the brochure delivery rule exist. The adviser need not deliver a brochure if the advisory client is (1) an investment company or (2) contracting for impersonal advisory services requiring a payment of less than $200.

Wrap Fee Brochure

Definition. According to the USA and the 1940 act, a wrap fee program is an arrangement under which the investment adviser, also called the *sponsor,* receives a flat fee for providing investment advisory services and executing client transactions. Investment advisory services may include recommending securities or recommending other investment advisers. The compensation the adviser receives under a wrap fee program is not directly related to the transactions executed for the client's account.

Disclosure. Information about an adviser's wrap fee program is filed with the regulators on Schedule H of Form ADV. At a minimum, the sponsor must provide to wrap fee clients a wrap fee brochure that contains the same information contained in the investment adviser brochure. If the sponsor provides further information regarding wrap fee programs, it must be specific to the program being offered to a client. The wrap fee brochure is subject to the same delivery requirements as the investment adviser brochure.

Sales and Advertising Materials

The administrator may require a state-registered investment adviser to file any informational materials or advertisements that are distributed to clients or prospective clients unless the security or transaction is exempted under the act. It is unlawful for any person subject to the act to file any misleading or fraudulent material.

Recordkeeping and Reporting Requirements

Both federally registered and state-registered investment advisers must keep and maintain any records, accounts, correspondences or papers as required. The state administrator or the SEC has the authority to examine all of an investment adviser's records at any time and place, without advance notice. These examinations may take the form of audits by the SEC or the state's administrator. These audits can be conducted in any state, as the administrator deems necessary or appropriate.

The records may be kept in any normally acceptable manner, including photographic (microfilm) and computer (disk) formats, as long as there exists the means to access (read) and make copies of the records as needed.

The USA and the 1940 act set requirements for investment adviser recordkeeping. The following records must be kept in an easily accessible place for five years (for the first two years, they must be kept in an office of the investment adviser):

- journals and other records of original entry;
- ledgers of assets, liabilities, reserves, capital, and income and expense accounts;
- order memorandums showing the following:
  - terms, conditions and special instructions of the order
  - identity of the person who recommended the transaction

    - account
    - date of entry
    - bank, broker or other party through whom the order was executed
    - whether discretionary power was exercised
- check books, bank statements, canceled checks and cash reconciliations;
- trial balances, financial statements and internal audit working papers;
- originals of all written communications received and copies of all written communications sent by the adviser relating to recommendations (if the advisory communication was sent to more than 10 persons, their names and addresses also must be recorded), receipts and disbursements of funds, and the placing of orders;
- list of accounts over which the adviser has discretionary power and copies of the powers of attorney for those accounts;
- written agreements between the adviser and each client;
- record of any transaction in which the adviser has a beneficial (ownership) or control interest;
- copies of written statements sent to clients;
- written acknowledgments from clients that they have received the required disclosure documents; and
- copies of any working papers relating to the calculation of performance or rates of return.

Advisers with custody of customer funds and securities. In addition to the records listed, an adviser who has custody of customer funds or securities must keep, and post at least daily, the following records:

- journal showing all purchases, receipts and deliveries of securities and cash;
- separate ledger for each customer showing all purchases, sales receipts and deliveries of securities, with dates and prices;
- copies of all confirmations; and
- securities records showing the names of clients who have positions in those securities.

Institutional investment managers who exercise discretion over accounts valued at more than $100 million must file quarterly and annual statements on Form 13F.

Business-related records. Under the act of 1940, partnership records, articles of incorporation, charters, minute books and other records relating to the investment adviser's business enterprise must be kept for three years after the termination of the business. It is the adviser's responsibility to make arrangements for the retention of these records after the firm ceases to do business, and he must inform the SEC in writing of these arrangements.

Advisers who operate investment supervisory or management services. If an investment adviser offers investment supervisory or management services, he must keep separate records for each client showing the securities purchased and sold, including the date, amount and price, and must be able to list clients' names by security position.

Financial Reports

Every registered broker-dealer and investment adviser must file all financial reports—including balance sheets, income statements, FOCUS reports and net capital reports—that the SEC or the administrator prescribes. The reports must be filed within 90 days of the end of the firm's fiscal year.

Prepayment of fees. If an investment adviser requires clients to pay fees exceeding $500 per client six months or more in advance, the adviser must file an audited balance sheet as of the end of the adviser's fiscal year.

Amendments to Records

If the information contained in any document filed with the SEC, the appropriate SRO (for example, the NASD) or the administrator is or becomes inaccurate or incomplete in any material respect, the registrant must file a correcting amendment promptly.

Custody of Customer Funds and Securities

The administrator may prohibit state-registered investment advisers from taking custody of customer assets. If custody is not prohibited, an investment adviser must notify the administrator if the adviser has or may have custody.

The Uniform Securities Act and the Investment Advisers Act of 1940 set out similar guidelines for the handling of customer funds and securities. Whether registered with the state or with the SEC, an investment adviser who has custody of customer funds and securities must ensure that the funds and securities are segregated and are marked to identify the owners. If the customer funds and securities are to be deposited in a bank, the bank accounts must contain only customer funds and must identify the investment adviser who acts as agent for the customers. The investment adviser must keep complete and accurate records of all such deposits and accounts on Form ADV-E. An independent public accountant must verify the accounts at least once each year without prior notice to the adviser.

Customers who have funds or securities in an investment adviser's possession must be sent at least once every three months an itemized statement showing these funds and securities as well as all transactions, debits and credits that have occurred or exist in an account.

Investment Advisory Contracts

The typical investment adviser's business is based largely on contracts between the adviser and potential clients for advisory services for which the adviser will receive compensation. Both federally registered advisers and state-registered advisers are subject to regulations governing the form and content of many parts of these contracts, including those regulations outlining the methods of compensation, methods of consent and notification of changes.

Contract terms. Before entering into, extending or renewing an investment advisory contract, the investment adviser must ensure that the following terms are written into the contract:

- services to be provided;
- contract duration;
- advisory fee;
- formula for computing the advisory fee;
- amount of any prepaid fee to be returned in the event of contract termination;
- whether the investment adviser has been granted discretionary power; and
- the fact that assignment of the contract by the investment adviser can occur only with the party's consent to the contract.

Compensation restrictions. An investment adviser is prohibited from entering into any contract that bases compensation on a share of the capital gains or capital appreciation (or any other measure of performance) that the client or the account achieves. This prohibition includes:

- waiving or refunding the client's advisory fee if the account underperforms (contingent fees);
- engaging in any form of profit-sharing arrangement; and
- rebating commissions on mutual fund sales.

An investment adviser is permitted to enter into a contract with an investment company or an account with *net assets* of more than $1 million basing compensation on a percentage of net assets as long as the compensation is:

- based on the fund's or account's average value over a specified time period; and
- proportional to the fund's or account's performance compared to a standard performance benchmark or an index.

An investment adviser may receive reimbursement for reasonable expenses related to handling customer accounts.

Conditional exemption. An investment adviser may enter into a contract with a client that provides for performance-based compensation if *all* of the following conditions are met:

- the client may be a **qualified purchasers pool** (private investment companies);
- the client is not an investment company;
- the client is an individual or a corporation with at least $500,000 under the investment adviser's management or is an individual with a net worth of at least $1 million;
- the formula by which the adviser's compensation is calculated (1) includes realized capital losses and unrealized depreciation and (2) bases the compensation on gains less losses for a period of not less than one year;
- certain disclosures are made before entering into the contract, including (1) that the performance compensation may create an incentive for the adviser to take greater risks, (2) that the compensation is based on realized as well as unrealized gains, (3) the periods that will be used, (4) the nature

of any index used as a comparative measure and (5) how any securities for which no readily available market quotations exist will be valued; and

- the investment adviser reasonably believes that an arm's-length arrangement has been made and that the client understands the basis for the compensation.

Validity of Investment Advisory Contracts

The Investment Advisers Act of 1940 voids any contract a federally registered investment adviser enters into that contains provisions or stipulations waiving compliance with any of the rules or regulations of the 1940 act.

Transactions

Discretionary Account Transactions

An adviser may direct transactions for a discretionary account to any broker-dealer, as long as the charges for services performed are reasonable and are disclosed in the client brochure. Clients must provide written permission before the adviser handles transactions on a discretionary basis.

Agency Cross Transactions

Definition. According to the USA and the 1940 act, an agency cross transaction is a transaction in which the investment adviser arranges a trade, acting either as agent or principal, on behalf of both the advisory client and the party on the other side of the transaction. For a state-registered investment adviser to effect an agency cross transaction, the adviser must also be registered as a broker-dealer in the state. For a federally registered investment adviser to effect an agency cross transaction, the person may be registered as an investment adviser or as a broker-dealer.

Conditions. An investment adviser may make an agency cross transaction if:

- the investment adviser has provided disclosure in advance that an agency cross transaction provides commissions to the adviser from both parties and thus causes a potential conflict of interest;
- after receiving the disclosure, the client gives written consent to such transactions;
- the adviser provides the client with a confirmation at or before the transaction's completion, stating the details of the transaction, the date and the source and amount of compensation the adviser received;
- the customer's account statements summarize the total number of agency cross transactions effected during the preceding period and the total amount of commissions received; and
- the client is notified that the written consent may be revoked at any time.

Restrictions. An investment adviser may not effect an agency cross transaction if the adviser has recommended the transaction to both the buyer and the seller. An adviser executing an agency cross transaction is still obligated to provide the best executions to his clients and must disclose whether he is acting as an agent or as a principal.

Advertisements by Investment Advisers

In general, every communication from an investment adviser to the public must be based on principles of fair dealing and good faith. Such communication should provide a sound basis for evaluating the facts in regard to the product, service or industry promoted. Exaggerated, unwarranted or misleading statements or claims are strictly prohibited.

The definition of "advertisement" includes any notice, circular, letter or other written communication addressed to more than one person, or any other announcement (whether in a publication, over the radio, on television or through another medium) that offers any report, chart, formula or other service to be used in making investment decisions.

To guide advisers in creating and producing advertising and sales literature, the following specific requirements apply.

Identification. In general, sales literature must identify the following:

- name of the member firm;
- person or firm that prepared the material if copy was prepared outside;
- date the material was first used; and
- whether any price or market performance data or other pertinent information cited in the literature is not current.

Using past stock selection records. It is acceptable to use lists of stock and other security recommendations the investment adviser made in the past provided that the following conditions are met:

- The list of recommendations and any accompanying text must not imply that comparable future performance can be expected.
- The list must include all recommendations made (gainers and losers) over the selected period of time (at least the previous one year).

Claims and opinions couched as facts and conclusions. It is both unprofessional and a violation of the regulations to pass off opinions, projections, charts, graphics, formulas and forecasts as guarantees of performance or as scientific evidence.

Testimonials. The use by celebrities and influencers of public opinion of testimonials and endorsements related to specific recommendations, results, advice, analyses, reports or other services is strictly prohibited. This prohibition does not, however, prevent an investment adviser from hiring a well-known spokesperson for an advertisement or a campaign, as long as that person does not imply that she uses the investment adviser's services.

Offers of free service. It is unprofessional to offer free services or free investment reports and topical news if, in fact, the respondent must assume obligations of some sort. Reports, analyses or other services offered to the public as "free" must be furnished entirely without condition or obligation.

Other Communication Prohibitions

The following lists other unprofessional practices as they relate to investment adviser advertisements:

- stating or implying that research facilities are more extensive than they actually are;
- using hedge clauses, caveats and disclaimers if they are misleading or inconsistent with the content of the material;
- making ambiguous references to the SEC, an SRO or another organization, with the aim of leading people to believe that the adviser acts with the sponsorship, recommendation, endorsement or approval of the SEC, SRO or other organization, or that any of these has passed on the adviser's merits or qualifications;
- using the initials "RIA" after the adviser's name with the aim of implying he has attained a certain level of education or qualification (the description "registered investment adviser" may be used); and
- in the case of advertisements or sales literature that includes price performance information in the form of charts, graphs or statistical tables prepared by or obtained from outside sources, not disclosing the source of the data used.

Cash Payments for Client Solicitations

A federally registered investment adviser is limited in its ability to pay another person (a solicitor) to solicit clients for investment advisory services. To do so, the investment adviser must be registered as such under the act of 1940; furthermore, an adviser may pay a solicitor a cash fee for soliciting clients only if a written agreement exists between the solicitor and the adviser. Solicitations are limited to those for impersonal advisory services unless the solicitor is a partner, a director, an officer or a controlling person of the investment adviser.

The written agreement must contain the following information and provisions:

- description of the solicitation activities;
- agreement to conduct the solicitation activities in a manner consistent with the regulations of the act of 1940; and
- agreement that the solicitor will provide any potential clients with a copy of both the adviser's disclosure brochure and the solicitor's disclosure brochure.

The solicitor's disclosure brochure must contain the following information:

- name of the solicitor;
- name of the investment adviser;
- nature of the relationship and any affiliation between the two parties;
- statement that the solicitor is being compensated for solicitation services;
- terms (such as amount) of the compensation arrangement; and
- any amount the client will be charged to cover the costs of soliciting his account.

It is the investment adviser's responsibility to ascertain that the solicitor has met the terms and conditions of the agreement.

Disclosure of Financial and Disciplinary Information

Both state-registered advisers and federally registered advisers must disclose to clients any financial information that could have an impact on the type or quality of the advisory services offered. They are also required to disclose any legal or disciplinary actions—including civil, criminal and SRO—against them that could have a bearing on a client's capability to evaluate an adviser's integrity or ability to meet contractual commitments.

SEC Release IA-1092

Persons Considered Investment Advisers

SEC Release IA-1092 was issued to clarify the application of the Investment Advisers Act of 1940 to persons who provide investment advice as part of other financial services. The SEC and NASAA developed Release IA-1092 to provide uniform interpretation and application of federal and state advisers laws, as well as to define "in the business" with respect to investment advisers. The release identifies the following three groups that are included in the act's definition of "investment adviser":

- financial planner who gives financial advice to individuals or families based on their needs and objectives (the advice might include general or specific recommendations as to insurance, savings, investments, retirement, taxes or estate planning);
- pension consultant who offers administrative services to employee benefit plans and their fiduciaries, and who may also offer general or specific advisory services; and
- sports or entertainment representative who manages the career of an athlete or entertainer. The representative may negotiate contracts, organize promotions and provide tax planning and money management services and often has discretion over the client's money (for example, the representative may pay the client's bills).

Investment Adviser Status

Release IA-1092 discusses the 1940 act's three tests for determining whether a person is an investment adviser. All three tests must be met to fit the definition of "investment adviser."

Advice or analyses concerning securities. A person who limits advice to general categories of investments without recommending securities by name is considered an investment adviser. This includes a person who provides a comparison of securities with insurance or other nonsecurities products.

The "business standard." The degree of advisory activities determines whether a person is "in the business of" providing investment advice. If the person holds herself out to the public as an adviser, receives separate compensation for advice or gives advice on anything other than rare and isolated occasions, she meets the requirements of this test. A person who makes a simple recommendation that a client diversify his assets is not considered to be in the business of giving investment advice.

Compensation. A person who receives any economic benefit as a result of providing investment advice is considered an investment adviser. This includes compensation received from insurance-based products. The compensation may be direct or indirect; for example, the adviser may receive a fee from the firm executing the recommended transaction rather than from the client.

Disclosing Conflicts of Interest

The antifraud provisions of the Investment Advisers Act of 1940 require advisers to disclose material facts, especially those concerning a conflict of interest. SEC Release IA-1092 includes the following illustrations of such disclosures:

- If an adviser is associated with a broker-dealer or an insurance company through which the adviser's plans will be implemented, the adviser must disclose that she is acting as an agent for the broker-dealer or insurance company.
- If a registered representative provides investment advice outside of the scope of his employment with a broker-dealer, the rep must disclose that he is making recommendations independently from the firm.
- If an investment adviser recommends that a client execute transactions through a broker-dealer associated with the adviser, the adviser must also inform the client that the transactions may be executed by another broker-dealer.
- If an investment adviser recommends only those products available through a broker-dealer associated with the adviser, the adviser must disclose that the recommendations are limited.
- If at any time an adviser's personal interests conflict with a client's, he must disclose that his personal transactions are inconsistent with the recommendations he's given to the client.

Enforcement of the Investment Advisers Act of 1940

Both the state administrator and the SEC are required to enforce antifraud provisions for all investment advisers, whether the advisers are federally registered or state-registered.

SEC enforcement. The SEC reserves the right to enforce the provisions of the act of 1940 either upon receiving a complaint or if it appears to the SEC that a violation of the act has occurred or could occur. As part of its jurisdiction, the SEC has the right to require any federally registered investment adviser to file with it a written, sworn statement covering all of the relevant facts and circumstances relating to the incident(s). The SEC has the right to fully investigate the incident, including the circumstances surrounding or contributing to it and any persons involved.

In exercising its enforcement rights, the SEC may bring an action in a district court against a person believed to be (or about to be) in violation of the act, and a restraining order or temporary injunction may be granted.

Civil penalties. If it appears to the SEC that a person has violated a rule under the act of 1940, it may seek civil penalties against that person. A violation can be placed into one of three "tiers." Depending on how the violation is classified, the penalty can range up to $100,000 for a natural person (individual), $500,000 for any other person, or the amount of the gain that resulted from the violation (for a third-tier violation). SEC-imposed penalties are payable directly to the U.S. Treasury.

Criminal penalties. If the violation cannot be classified into the three-tier system, the SEC can impose a criminal penalty of up to $10,000, imprisonment for not more than five years, or both. (The Uniform Securities Act allows for a maximum fine of $5,000, imprisonment for not more than three years, or both.) The SEC or state administrator will refer the case to the criminal courts if there is evidence of criminal activity.

Availability of Information

Public access to investment adviser registration form. Information filed by an investment adviser in a registration form is considered public domain information and, as such, is available to the public on request (and on payment of a reasonable charge to cover the costs of search, photocopies and so on).

Confidentiality of investigations. If an investigation, an examination or a similar action is under way at the time of a request for information, this fact and any information produced by the investigation need not be disclosed to anyone who is not an SEC member, officer or employee.

Enforcement of the Uniform Securities Act

A state administrator has full jurisdiction over *only* those investment advisers registered with the state. The administrator enforces the USA provisions with regard to state-registered investment advisers. However, the state administrator is also required to enforce all antifraud provisions as they pertain to *any* adviser that conducts business in the state.

2 Regulation and Registration of Broker-Dealers and Agents

Key Terms

administrator
advertising
agent
blue-sky laws
broker-dealer
institutional investor
Investment Company Act of 1940
offer
person
rescission
sales representative
Securities Act of 1933
Securities Exchange Act of 1934
securities information processor
security
surety bond
transfer agent
underwriter
Uniform Securities Act (USA)

Overview

The securities industry is regulated at both the federal and the state levels. These regulations govern how securities are issued, registered, sold and traded, as well as who may perform these activities. At the federal level, the principal acts that regulate the industry are the Securities Act of 1933 and the Securities Exchange Act of 1934. The focus of the National Securities Markets Improvement Act of 1996 regarding broker-dealers and agents is the prevention of abuse of the public trust in sales and trading practices. These provisions were adopted under the Uniform Securities Act.

The basis for industry regulation at the state level is the Uniform Securities Act (USA); this is model legislation that each state may adopt in its entirety or may, within certain limits, adapt to suit its needs. Each state appoints a state securities administrator, who is vested with certain powers under the USA.

This chapter describes both state and federal regulation of broker-dealers and agents.

Overview of Securities Trading Regulation

Definitions

Accredited investor. As defined in Rule 502 of Regulation D of the Securities Act of 1933, an accredited investor is any institution (such as a bank, a broker-dealer or an investment company) or any individual meeting minimum net worth requirements for the purchase of securities qualifying under the Regulation D registration exemption.

An accredited investor, also called a *professional*, a *sophisticated* or an *institutional investor*, generally is accepted to be one who has:

- a net worth of $1 million or more; or
- had an annual income of $200,000 or more in each of the two most recent years (or $300,000 jointly with a spouse) and who has a reasonable expectation of reaching the same income level in the current year.

Agent. An agent, also called a *sales representative*, is an individual who acts for the accounts of others. The Uniform Securities Act gives the term "agent" special meanings. "Agent" is defined as an individual who represents a broker-dealer or an issuer when selling or trying to sell securities to the investing public. This individual is considered an agent whether he actually receives or simply solicits orders. In other words, an agent is anyone who accepts an order and receives compensation while representing a broker-dealer or an issuer.

Associated person. An associated person includes any partner, branch manager, officer or director of a broker-dealer, including outside directors. It also includes employees such as sales representatives who are not clerks or ministerial personnel, as well as anyone who controls, is controlled by or is under common control with the broker-dealer.

Broker-dealer. A broker-dealer is any person with an established place of business who engages in the business of effecting securities transactions for the accounts of others or for his own account. Broker-dealers must be licensed (registered) in a state to transact business in that state.

Equity security. An equity security is any kind of stock—common or preferred, for example—or any security that allows someone to acquire stock, either through a right or warrant to purchase stock or through a conversion privilege. Bonds are not equity securities, but if they are issued with a warrant to purchase stock or are convertible into stock, they fall under the definition of an equity security in the 1934 act.

Government security. The 1934 act defines government securities as those issued or guaranteed by the U.S. government or one of its agencies. Securities issued or guaranteed by a state, county or city or any agency of a nonfederal governmental unit are municipal securities.

Government securities dealer. A government securities dealer is any dealer that effects transactions in government securities exclusively.

Guaranteed. Under the USA, the term "guarantee" indicates that a person (such as an insurance company or the U.S. government) has assumed responsibility for the payment of a security's principal, interest or dividends, as specified by the guarantee.

Institutional investor. An institutional investor is a person or an organization that trades for itself or for others in a fiduciary capacity and typically trades securities in large enough share quantities or dollar amounts that it qualifies for preferential treatment and lower trade costs (commissions). However, no minimum investment amount is set for institutional transactions. Institutional investors are covered by fewer protective regulations because it is assumed that they are more knowledgeable and better able to protect themselves.

Institutional investors include:

- investment companies
- insurance companies
- investment advisers
- broker-dealers
- banks
- trust companies
- savings and loan associations
- employee benefits programs with assets of at least $1 million
- government agencies

Issuer (underwriter). Any person who issues or proposes to issue a security is considered an issuer under the USA.

Market maker. A dealer willing to accept the risk of holding securities to facilitate trading in a particular security(ies) is a market maker.

Offer and sell. To understand the rules relating to the sale and purchase of securities, it is important to understand the difference between *offering to sell* a security and *selling* a security. An offer is an indication by an investor, a trader or a dealer of a willingness to sell a security or commodity. Under the Uniform Securities Act, every attempt to solicit a purchase or sale in a security *for money or other value* constitutes an offer. The term "sell," on the other hand, means the act of conveying ownership of a security or other property for money or other value and includes every contract to sell a security or an interest in a security. In addition to the everyday usage of the term "sell," sales also include the following:

- Any security given or delivered with or as a bonus for any purchase of securities is considered to have been offered and sold for value.
- A gift of assessable stock is considered to involve an offer and a sale.
- Every sale or offer of a warrant or right to purchase or subscribe to another security is considered to include an offer of the other security.

The definition of "sale" does not include a stock dividend if nothing of value is given by the stockholders for the dividend. The definition also does not include a bona fide pledge or loan, such as a broker-dealer's loan of securities to a customer.

Securities information processor. The 1934 act defines a securities information processor as a person who is in the business of providing information about securities transactions or quotations on a current and continuing basis. The information may be published on paper (such as in the *Pink Sheets*), or it may be disseminated through a computer network (such as the Dow Jones Wire News) or another communications system. However, persons who handle such information on a regular basis in the course of their business activities—such as a radio or television station—but who are not "in the business" of doing so are specifically excluded from the definition of "securities information processor."

Security. Under the USA and the acts of 1933 and 1934, any note, stock, bond, investment contract, debenture, certificate of interest in a profit-sharing or partnership agreement, certificate of deposit, collateral trust certificate, preorganization certificate, option on a security, or other instrument of investment commonly known as a *security* is considered a security.

The accurate determination of what is a security is crucial to registered representatives conducting their activities in compliance with state securities laws. In general, "security" can be defined as any piece of securitized paper that can be traded for value.

As established by the federal courts, the basic test for determining whether a specific investment falls within the definition of a security is whether the person invests her money in a common enterprise and is led to expect profits from the managerial efforts of the promoter or a third party. Thus, the definition of "security" also includes interests in the following: oil and gas drilling programs, real estate condominiums and cooperatives, farmland or animals, commodity option contracts (but not the underlying futures contracts), whiskey warehouse receipts, insurance company separate accounts, multilevel distributorship arrangements and merchandising marketing programs.

Exemptions from the definition of "security" are insurance policies; endowment contracts; fixed annuities; retirement plans that serve as vehicles for other investments; checking, savings or passbook accounts; and preliminary or final prospectuses.

Transfer agent. A transfer agent is a person or an organization responsible for recording the names of registered stockholders and the number of shares owned, seeing that the certificates are signed by the appropriate corporate officers, affixing the corporate seal and delivering the securities to the transferee. A firm that effects shareholder requests to convert mutual fund shares on behalf of the mutual fund would be considered a transfer agent. Clearing agencies performing the functions of a transfer agent with respect to contracts they issue and insurance companies are specifically excluded from the act of 1934 definition of "transfer agent."

The Securities Exchange Act of 1934

After the Securities Act of 1933 was enacted regulating primary issues of securities, attention turned to the need for regulating secondary trading. One purpose of the Securities Exchange Act of 1934 is to maintain a fair market for the investing public. It seeks to attain this goal by regulating the securities exchanges and the over-the-counter (OTC) markets. Commonly called the **Exchange Act**, it formed the SEC and gave the Commission authority to oversee the securities markets and to register and regulate the exchanges.

The Securities Exchange Act of 1934, which has much greater breadth than the act of 1933, addresses the:

- creation of the SEC;
- registration and regulation of the exchanges and their members;
- regulation of credit (through the margin requirements set by the Federal Reserve Board—FRB);
- registration of broker-dealers that trade securities on national exchanges or OTC;
- registration of persons who effect securities transactions with the public;
- regulation of insider transactions, short sales and proxies;
- regulation of trading activities;
- regulation of client accounts;
- customer protection rule;
- regulation of the self-regulatory organizations (SROs)—for example, the National Association of Securities Dealers, the New York Stock Exchange and the Municipal Securities Rulemaking Board;
- regulation of the OTC market; and
- net capital requirements for broker-dealers.

The Securities and Exchange Commission

The SEC, created by the act of 1934, was given responsibility and authority to regulate the securities markets. The SEC is made up of five commissioners appointed by the President of the United States and approved by the Senate. SEC commissioners appointed under the act of 1934 may have no business or employment other than their commission's, and may not engage in securities trading during their terms. One of the group's primary responsibilities is to enforce the act of 1934.

The SEC has established rules regarding net capital requirements for broker-dealers, hypothecation (pledging) of customers' securities, commingling (mixing) of broker-dealer securities with those of customers, the use of manipulative and deceptive devices and broker-dealer recordkeeping. The SEC enforces the Securities Exchange Act of 1934 and others by providing rules and prescribing penalties for violations.

The SROs, such as the NASD, are required to assist the SEC by establishing rules and trade practices that member firms must follow. The SROs are empowered by law to enforce both federal law and their own rules.

Expansion of the SEC's Role

The National Securities Markets Improvement Act of 1996 enhanced the SEC's role to include improvement and oversight of (1) market efficiency, (2) competition in the securities industry, (3) capital formation and (4) elimination of regulations that no longer serve the public interest.

Jurisdiction of the SEC

As discussed earlier, the 1934 act formed the SEC and gave the Commission authority to oversee the securities markets and self-regulatory organizations such as the NASD, the MSRB and the NYSE. The SEC has the power to administer federal and SRO laws relating to the securities industry, and to investigate violations of those laws. The SEC's jurisdiction does not extend to violations of banking rules. The Commission has preemptive authority over the rules established by the Uniform Securities Act or state securities administrators.

The jurisdiction of the SEC was greatly enhanced by changes to federal securities law enacted as the National Securities Markets Improvement Act of 1996.

Registration of Exchanges and Corporations

Under the 1934 act, a "securities exchange" is any entity in the business of providing the facilities and means for buyers and sellers to transact business in securities. The national securities exchanges must file registration statements with the SEC. When they register, the exchanges agree to comply with and help enforce the rules of this act. Registered broker-dealers are prohibited from effecting transactions on any exchange that is not registered with the SEC.

Each exchange gives the SEC copies of its bylaws, constitution and articles of incorporation. Any amendment to rules must be disclosed as soon as it is adopted. The exchange must also institute and enforce disciplinary procedures for members who do not use just and equitable practices. Small local exchanges are exempt from registration.

The SEC may suspend all trading on an exchange if it has cause to believe that the suspension would be in the public good and if it notifies the President of the United States.

In addition to the registration of exchanges, the act of 1934 requires companies that list securities on those exchanges to register with the SEC. Each listed company must file quarterly statements on Form 10Q and annual statements on Form 10K informing the SEC of its financial status as well as other information.

Many firms with securities traded OTC must also register. Those firms with 500 or more stockholders and assets of $5 million or more are required to do so. Exchange members who do business with the public also must register with the SEC, as well as broker-dealers that do business OTC or that use the mail or other *instruments of interstate commerce* (telephone, television, radio, etc.) to conduct OTC business.

The Maloney Act, an amendment to the Securities Exchange Act of 1934, permitted the establishment of a national securities association of broker-dealers transacting business in the OTC market. According to the act, SROs such as the NASD could be established and registered with the SEC.

Extension of Credit in the Securities Industry

The Federal Reserve Board, established by Congress in 1913, is composed of seven members appointed by the President of the United States and confirmed by the Senate to serve 14-year terms.

The FRB regulates the extension of credit (**margin**) in the industry through **Regulation T (Reg T)**. To prevent the excessive use of credit to buy securities, the FRB sets the minimum margin a customer must deposit (expressed as a percentage of purchase price) when purchasing securities from a broker-dealer or when selling securities short. Currently, the required minimum deposit is 50 percent of the securities' market value at the time of purchase.

Reg T requires that a customer pay for purchases in a cash account or make deposits in a margin account within two business days after the end of the regular way settlement cycle unless an SRO has granted an extension. (Currently, regular way settlement takes place on the third day after the trade date.)

Certain securities are exempt from the Reg T initial margin requirement, including U.S. government securities and municipal bonds. Other securities are not eligible for purchase on margin—for example, new issues of securities (within the first 30 days of issuance) and over-the-counter securities that the FRB has not designated as marginable.

Changes to federal securities law enacted under the National Securities Markets Improvement Act of 1996 eased restrictions regarding the financing of new issues (primary offerings) by loans from commercial banks to broker-dealers acting as underwriters.

Overview of the Uniform Securities Act

State Securities Laws

In addition to federal securities regulations, each state has laws that pertain to the trading of securities in the secondary market. State securities laws are known as **blue-sky laws**. The term "blue-sky" was first used by a Kansas Supreme Court justice, who referred to "speculative schemes that have no more basis than so many feet of blue sky." The Uniform Securities Act serves as model legislation that each state may follow or adapt to its own needs.

Kansas was the first state in the Union to adopt a comprehensive licensing system pertaining to securities and individuals engaged in the securities business. That law passed in 1911. Within two years, 23 states had followed this state's leadership and had enacted similar laws. By 1933, the blue-sky movement had spread to 47 of the 48 states then in the Union, as well as to the territory of Hawaii.

Through the years, many attempts were made to devise a uniform act to regulate the sale of securities. In 1954, the National Conference of Commissioners on Uniform State Laws commissioned an examination of the problem and a detailed analysis of the numerous existing laws and judicial decisions. The result, after two years of intensive study, was the **Uniform Securities Act** (**USA**).

This act has gained wide acceptance throughout the nation, simplifying and improving greatly the functioning of professionals within the securities industry.

Administration of the Uniform Securities Act

Scope of the act. The Uniform Securities Act gives each state's state securities administrator (sometimes known as the *state securities commissioner* or *state securities secretary*) the power to enforce the act in that state. The administrator has jurisdiction over any offer to buy or sell and any acceptance of an offer to buy or sell securities if the offer is:

- originated in the administrator's state
- directed to that state
- accepted in that state

This regulation means that any offer of a security is subject to the rules of the state administrator of the state in which the offer was made and of the state to which the offer was directed or in which the offer was accepted. The state from which payment is made or to which securities are delivered is not considered important.

A distinction must be made here, however. An advertisement of an offer that is placed in a newspaper or magazine, or that is broadcast on radio or television, is considered an offer *only in the state of publication or broadcast*. This interpretation of the act provides some protection for the offeror under those circumstances where the offeror's control over who receives the offer is limited. As an example, a person may advertise an offer in the *Chicago Tribune* and not be liable for subscriptions mailed to residents of states where the security is not registered. Also, an advertisement placed in a national publication is not considered an offer in the state where the newspaper or magazine is published if more than two-thirds of its circulation is outside the state. The offeror would, however, be responsible for determining whether an offer to purchase that comes from another state meets that state's requirements before it is accepted.

State Securities Administrators

The Uniform Securities Act sets forth the requirements for appointing state securities administrators. The act provides for minimum official behavior and conduct requirements, such as prohibitions against an administrator's using his position for personal benefit, disclosing confidential information and so on.

Administrators are permitted to establish broker-dealer and agent registration, testing, filing and fee regulations as would be appropriate to their states' requirements. In addition to mandating the registration of firms and associated persons, most states require that securities be registered in those states before they can be sold to the public. The Uniform Securities Act gives administrators the right to deny, suspend or revoke the registrations of broker-dealers, agents, investment advisers and securities if the administrators have just reason to do so under the rules of the act.

The USA also provides for criminal penalties and civil liabilities for persons involved in illegal securities transactions and prescribes the limits of a state's jurisdiction.

Investigations and Subpoenas

The administrator has the authority to inspect a broker-dealer and to conduct investigations to determine whether persons have violated or are about to violate the provisions of the Uniform Securities Act. These investigations may be private or public, and they may take place in the administrator's state.

The administrator also has the power to administer oaths, subpoena persons to testify, compel them to produce records or to attend hearings in connection with investigations. The administrator may delegate another official to carry out these functions only. Should a person who has been subpoenaed demonstrate *contumacy* (contempt for the administrator's order), or if a person ignores a subpoena, the administrator may ask a court to enforce the order. A person demonstrating contumacy risks punishment for contempt of court.

The Fifth Amendment—refusal to give information or assistance in an administrator's investigation because of possible self-incrimination—cannot be applied under the USA.

Penalties under the USA

If the administrator suspects that a person has engaged in or is about to engage in an activity that violates the act, the administrator may issue a cease and desist order without a prior hearing or may bring an action against that person in an appropriate court.

Criminal penalties. Persons found guilty of willful violations of the Uniform Securities Act are subject to criminal penalties. Upon conviction, a person may be fined up to $5,000, imprisoned not more than three years or both. In criminal matters, the statute of limitations runs for five years. The Investment Advisers Act of 1940 allows for a maximum fine of $10,000, imprisonment for not more than five years or both.

Civil liabilities. If a sale of a security has violated the provisions of the Uniform Securities Act, the buyer may sue to:

- recover the money he paid for the security from the person who sold that security to him; and
- receive interest on his money from the date of the purchase. (Any income the buyer received while he owned the security is deducted from the interest the seller paid.)

Under the Uniform Securities Act, the seller is not necessarily the only person held liable for a fraudulent sale of securities.The seller's supervisor or employer, who directly or indirectly controls the seller's activities, may also be subject to civil penalties, and liability may also extend to any other employee who assisted the seller materially. In addition, the seller may be held liable for court costs and reasonable attorney's fees.

Right of rescission. If the seller discovers that he has made an illegal sale, he may offer to repurchase the security from the buyer. To satisfy the buyer's rights of rescission, the amount paid to the buyer must include the purchase price and interest, as set by the administrator.

Statute of limitations. The buyer of a security or the receiver of investment advice may not sue for compensation more than two years after discovering the violation or three years after the act or transaction that constituted the violation, whichever occurs first. The buyer may not sue either if, when he still owned the security, he received a written offer from the seller to refund the money and interest and failed to accept the offer within 30 days. The act also contains settlement provisions for buyers who already have disposed of the stock before a settlement is offered.

Registration of Broker-Dealers and Agents

Federal Registration of Broker-Dealers

According to the Securities Exchange Act of 1934, exchange members and broker-dealers that trade securities OTC and on exchanges and individuals who effect securities trades with the public must register with the SEC.

Exemptions. Exemptions from registration include any broker-dealer that deals only on an intrastate basis. The intrastate exemption is available to a broker-dealer whose business is conducted exclusively in one state and that does not make use of national securities exchanges. An *intra*state firm, however, cannot use the mail or other instruments of *inter*state commerce and still qualify for the exemption from registration.

Statutory disqualification from registration. Administrative sanctions, court injunctions and findings of criminal wrongdoing are causes for statutory disqualification from registration with the SEC and association with any SRO.

State Registration of Broker-Dealers

Most states require broker-dealers that do business in a particular state to register with that state's securities commission or administrator. Agents associated with a broker-dealer also must be registered in the state(s) where they do business. The state securities administrator has the power to revoke a broker-dealer's registration or an agent's license if the firm or representative has violated any of the state's securities laws.

The Uniform Securities Act establishes specific licensing and registration requirements and procedures for broker-dealers and agents. The act also prescribes certain post-licensing provisions.

Under the USA, it is unlawful for any person to transact business in a state as a broker-dealer or an agent unless the person is registered under the Uniform Securities Act or is exempt from registration.

Exemptions from state registration. Agents, issuers, banks, savings institutions and trust companies are exempt from registering as broker-dealers in the states where they conduct business. The definition of "broker-dealer" also exempts persons who transact business exclusively with issuers, depository institutions, trust companies, insurance companies, investment companies, pension or profit-sharing plans, financial institutions or institutional buyers.

A broker-dealer is not subject to state registration requirements if it conducts business in a state with an existing client who has less than 30 days' temporary residence in the state. The exemption allows a broker-dealer to serve the needs of an existing client who is vacationing in a state where the broker-dealer is not registered. This registration exemption was adopted from the National Securities Markets Improvement Act (NSMIA).

Agent Registration

A broker-dealer may not employ a person as an agent unless that person is registered (or exempt). It is unlawful for any person to transact business in any state as an agent unless that person is registered under the Uniform Securities Act or is exempt from registration. The person must be registered as an agent even if the securities or the transactions involved in a particular offer or sale are exempt from registration requirements.

Exemptions from state registration. Agents must be licensed (registered) in a state to transact business there. However, certain classes of agents are exempt from the registration requirements.

An agent is not required to register if he represents (is employed by) only the following exempt *issuers*:

- U.S. government;
- municipality;
- Canadian government, province or municipality (but not a Canadian corporation);
- any foreign government with which the United States maintains diplomatic relations; or
- depository institution, savings institution or trust company.

An agent is not required to register if he represents only the following exempt *securities*:

- promissory note, draft or banker's acceptance with a maturity of nine months or less; or
- investment contract issued in connection with an employee's stock purchase, savings, pension, profit-sharing or similar benefit plan.

Finally, an agent is not required to register if:

- he represents an issuer in an exempt *transaction*; or
- as a partner, an officer or a director of a brokerage firm, he limits his activities to managerial functions and does not attempt to effect purchases or sales. (He is not considered an agent merely because he is a partner, an officer or a director of a brokerage firm.)

Length of Registration

Every registration of a broker-dealer or an agent expires annually on December 31st unless renewed.

State Registration Procedures

Application. A broker-dealer or an agent may obtain an initial or a renewal registration by filing (1) an application with (2) the appropriate filing fee, as set by each state, and (3) a consent to service of process with the administrator in the form the administrator requires.

A consent to service of process gives the administrator the irrevocable right to receive and process, as the applicant's attorney, any legal complaints that may arise in regard to an applicant's conduct as an agent or a broker-dealer. Once the applicant has filed the consent to service of process, any complaint presented to the administrator has the same force and validity as if it had been served personally on the applicant.

An application for any registration must contain whatever information the administrator requires concerning such matters as the applicant's:

- form and place of business organization;
- proposed method of doing business;
- qualifications and business history, including those of any partner, director or similar person of a broker-dealer;
- history of injunctions, conviction of any felony or conviction of any misdemeanor involving any aspect of the securities business; and
- financial condition and history.

The administrator may also require an applicant for initial registration to publish an announcement of the registration application in one or more specific newspapers in the state.

If the administrator does not deny the registration or is not in the process of denying the registration, that registration becomes effective at noon of the 30th day after the application is filed. The administrator may allow an earlier effective date. He also may defer the effective date until noon of the 30th day after the filing of any amendment.

Financial requirements. The administrator may set minimum capital requirements for broker-dealers registered in the state. Broker-dealers in compliance with the SEC's net capital requirements are exempt from the USA's minimum capital requirements.

Surety bonds. Broker-dealers and agents may be required by the administrator to post **surety bonds** if the person has custody of or discretionary authority over customer funds or securities. Typically, surety bonds are set in amounts of $35,000, although deposits of cash or securities may be permissible instead of the bonds. Compliance with minimum capital requirements releases the person from the surety bond requirement.

Qualification examinations. The administrator may require that one or more officers or agents of the broker-dealer take an examination that may be written, oral or both.

Successful completion of the Uniform Securities Agent State Law Examination (Series 63), the Uniform Investment Adviser Law Examination (Series 65), the Uniform Combined State Law Examination (Series 66) or any of the NASD, New York Stock Exchange (NYSE) or Municipal Securities Rulemaking Board (MSRB) examinations does not automatically constitute registration in a state. An applicant who has passed the exam does not have the right to transact business until the state administrator has granted his registration. Before granting an agent's initial registration, some states may require that the applicant, his firm or both provide additional certification showing that the applicant has reviewed his state's blue-sky laws and understands his responsibilities.

Responsibilities of those who pass the examination. Successful completion of the Series 63, Series 65 or Series 66 does not relieve the agent of the following responsibilities:

- to know and abide by the specific requirements of the securities laws and requirements of regulations of the states in which he will transact business;
- to understand that he does not have the right to transact business before a state grants his license or registration; and
- to know that some states may require further certification to indicate that he has reviewed his state's blue-sky laws and understands his responsibilities.

Employment. No broker-dealer or issuer can lawfully employ an agent unless that agent is registered. Conversely, an agent is not effectively registered unless he is employed by a registered broker-dealer or issuer. This means that an agent's registration is not considered to be in effect during any period when the agent is not employed by a broker-dealer, even if the agent's nonassociation is temporary, such as when the agent is between employers.

Changes in employment. Whenever an agent begins or terminates employment with an employer, the agent as well as the employer must promptly notify the administrator.

When an agent transfers his employment from one broker-dealer or issuer to another, all three persons—the agent, the former employer and the new employer—must notify the administrator.

A termination becomes effective 30 days after the state administrator receives the notice, but may be postponed if a suspension or revocation proceeding is pending. After the termination becomes effective, the administrator retains the right to suspend or revoke registration for one year.

Firm registration. At the time a broker-dealer is registered, anyone who is then a partner, an officer or a director of the broker-dealer is automatically registered as an agent if that person acts in the capacity of an agent and not otherwise. Silent partners are not considered agents because they do not act in the capacity of agents.

If a person becomes a partner, an officer or a director of a broker-dealer after the broker-dealer's registration date, that individual is not automatically registered as an agent, even if he acts as one. If an individual is an officer of a broker-dealer at the time the broker-dealer is registered, and if that individual acts in the capacity of an agent and therefore is considered registered as an agent, he need not take an additional examination.

If a registered broker-dealer intends to cease doing business as such and to pass its registration on to a successor firm, such as in the event of a merger, an acquisition or a sale of the business, it must file an application for registration of the successor firm, even if the successor firm is not yet in existence. The term of the new registration begins on the date the original firm ceases to do business. The filing fee is waived for the successor's initial registration application.

Denial, Suspension or Revocation of Registration

All registrations required by the Uniform Securities Act fall under the state administrators' jurisdiction. An administrator may deny, suspend or revoke any registration, or bar or censure any registrant, or restrict or limit any registrant's functions or activities if he finds that the:

- order is in the public interest; *and*
- the applicant, registrant or issuer of a security is guilty of any of a specified list of offenses.

Among these offenses are the following:

- filing an incomplete, false or misleading application for registration;
- willfully violating any provision of the Uniform Securities Act;
- being convicted of a misdemeanor involving any aspect of the securities business or being convicted of any felony within the past 10 years;
- being temporarily or permanently enjoined from engaging in the securities business by a court of law;
- being subject to an order of the administrator denying, suspending or revoking registration;
- violating any federal or state securities or commodities law within the past 10 years;
- engaging in dishonest or unethical securities practices;
- insolvency;
- having willfully violated securities or banking laws of a foreign jurisdiction or, within the past five years, being subject to an action of a foreign securities regulator denying, suspending or revoking the right to conduct securities business;
- being discovered not to be qualified on the basis of training, experience or knowledge;
- being in a supervisory position and failing to supervise registered employees; or
- failing to pay application filing fees.

Denial of registration due to lack of qualification. The administrator may deny, revoke or suspend any applicant's registration because that person is not qualified due to lack of knowledge, training or experience. However, the administrator may not base the decision solely on lack of experience. In the same way, the administrator may not deny, revoke or suspend the registration of a firm (broker-dealer or investment adviser) based solely on its representatives' lack of experience.

The act authorizes the administrator to restrict a particular applicant's registration to that of a broker-dealer if the administrator finds the individual is not qualified as an investment adviser. Experience is a consideration, but lack of experience cannot be the sole factor for denying registration.

A representative is not required to meet the same level of qualification as the broker-dealer or investment adviser for which he works. A person registered and with experience as a broker-dealer or an agent is not necessarily qualified to be registered as an investment adviser. The broker-dealer may be prohibited from transacting business in any state as an investment adviser until such time as it does become registered.

Canadian Firms and Agents

Registration exemption. A Canadian broker-dealer may conduct business in a state without registering under the USA if it has an office in Canada, has no office in the state and conducts business exclusively with established customers or with financial institutions. The same registration exemption applies to Canadian agents.

Simplified registration. If a Canadian broker-dealer or agent is not exempt from registration, the USA provides a simplified registration process. If it is registered in Canada and is a member of a Canadian self-regulatory organization, a broker-dealer may register by filing an application and a consent to service of process. An agent registered in Canada may register by filing the same materials. The registrations become effective 30 days after filing.

Additional requirements. Each Canadian broker-dealer must maintain its Canadian registration and exchange membership in good standing; provide its books and records to the state administrator upon request; inform the administrator of any sanction or regulatory action entered against it; and disclose to its customers in the state that it is not subject to all USA requirements.

A Canadian broker-dealer or agent registered under the USA must file annual renewal applications and pay the appropriate filing fees. It is subject to all of the USA's antifraud provisions.

Federal and State Laws Regarding Broker-Dealers

Table 2.1 compares the federal and state laws and regulations regarding broker-dealers.

Table 2.1 Comparison of Federal and State Laws Regarding Broker-Dealers

Item	*Federal Law*	*State Law*
Definition	A person engaged in the business of effecting securities transactions for the accounts of others or for its own account.	A person who effects transactions for the accounts of others or for its own account.
Exclusions	Bank.	Agent; issuer; bank; savings institution; trust company.
Exemptions	Business is exclusively in one state and does not make use of any national securities exchange.	No place of business within the state and directs an offer in the state to an existing customer who has less than *30 days'* temporary residency in the state. Clients are limited to issuers, other broker-dealers, depository institutions, trust companies, investment companies, employee benefit plans, other financial institutions.
Registration	File application on Form BD with the SEC; effective 45 days after filing.	File application, consent to service of process and fee; effective on the 30th day after filing.
Length of Registration	Effective until withdrawn, revoked or canceled.	Expires every December 31st unless renewed.
Withdrawal of Registration	Takes effect 60 days after filing Form BDW with the SEC.	Takes effect 30 days after filing.
Insolvency	Not cause for revocation.	Cause for revocation.
Records	Must be maintained for 3 years, 6 years or the life of the firm, depending on the type of record.	Must maintain records prescribed by administrator for 3 years.
Criminal Penalties	10 years in jail or $1 million fine; for other than a natural person, $2.5 million fine.	$5,000 fine or 3 years in jail.
Statute of Limitations	3 years after act or 1 year after discovery.	3 years after act or 2 years after discovery.

3 Regulation of New Issues

Key Terms

- ask
- bid
- cooling-off period
- covered security
- due diligence
- Glass-Steagall Act of 1933
- hot issue
- indication of interest
- initial public offering (IPO)
- investment banker
- Maloney Act
- new issue market
- nonaccredited investor
- omitting prospectus
- preliminary prospectus
- primary offering
- private placement
- public offering
- red herring
- registration statement
- secondary offering
- Securities Act of 1933
- Securities Exchange Act of 1934
- selling group
- shelf offering
- split offering
- standby offering
- syndicate
- tombstone
- underwriting

Overview

Securities industry legislation at both the federal and the state levels is designed to protect investors by requiring proper disclosure of information and establishing procedures that safeguard against fraud and misrepresentation. Securities laws at the state level are known as *blue-sky laws;* they deal with issues such as the state registration requirements for securities, broker-dealers, investment advisers and representatives. The Uniform Securities Act is model legislation that most states have adopted or have adapted to meet specific state requirements.

This chapter also describes the major pieces of federal securities legislation: the Securities Act of 1933 and the Securities Exchange Act of 1934, with the subsequent acts that expanded or amended these basic regulations.

Overview of New Issue Regulation

The Crash of 1929

During the early 1900s, America enjoyed a long-term bull market that promised to last forever. Attracted by the dream of easy money, Americans turned en masse to Wall Street, poring over stock price tables and learning the language of trading operations. For the first time, the general public became a significant factor in the market; but often they purchased securities knowing little or nothing about the issuing companies or their plans for spending the money.

Investors borrowed heavily; that is, they bought securities *on margin*. Doing so was an act of faith in the perpetual bull market and an outcome of generous credit policies that allowed investors to borrow most of the purchase price of stock. By the summer of 1929, more than a million Americans held stock on margin.

The rest is familiar history. Stock prices reached new heights in early September 1929. Then things fell apart. By the third week of September, tumbling prices brought the Dow Jones averages down 19 points. A month later, averages were 50 points below the September high mark. The downward spiral of prices gained momentum, breaking through crumbling layers of anticipated buying support.

Rapidly declining prices meant investors' stocks were no longer adequate security for the loans they had taken out to buy them. Securities purchased on very low margins, therefore, were sold to raise money, and this caused even deeper drops in market prices. Stock dumping destroyed grassroots investors and wealthy traders alike, including those supposedly safe investment trusts, which unloaded their holdings for whatever they could bring.

The Legislative Reaction

After the crash, the market continued to decline for several years. During that time, Congress examined the causes of the debacle and passed several laws meant to prevent its recurrence. This legislation included, among other acts, the Securities Act of 1933, the Glass-Steagall Act of 1933 and the Securities Exchange Act of 1934.

The Securities Act of 1933. The Securities Act of 1933 requires securities issuers to provide sufficient information for investors to make fully informed buying decisions. This information must be registered with the federal government and published in a prospectus. The act outlaws fraud committed in connection with the underwriting and issuing of all securities, including exempt securities.

The Glass-Steagall Act (Banking Act) of 1933. Securities firms were not the only financial companies to go belly-up in the early 1930s. Banks, too, went broke in vast numbers. Congress concluded that one factor in the general financial collapse was the fact that commercial bankers engaged in investment banking. In their role as commercial bankers, they took deposits and financed commercial enterprises. As investment bankers, they underwrote stocks, using deposits to finance their securities ventures. Losses on a bank's investment side, therefore, affected the health of its commercial operations.

With the Glass-Steagall Act, Congress attempted to erect a wall between commercial banking and investment banking. The act forbids commercial banks to underwrite securities (except municipal general obligation bonds) and denies investment bankers the right to open deposit accounts or make commercial loans.

The Securities Exchange Act of 1934. The Securities Exchange Act of 1934 addresses secondary trading of securities, personnel involved in secondary trading and fraudulent trading practices. It also created the Securities and Exchange Commission (SEC), a government agency, to oversee the industry.

In 1938, the act was broadened when it was amended by the **Maloney Act**, which provides for the establishment of a self-regulatory body to help police the industry. Under the provisions of the Maloney Act, the National Association of Securities Dealers (NASD) regulates over-the-counter (OTC) trading in much the same way as the exchanges regulate their members.

The Trust Indenture Act of 1939. The Trust Indenture Act of 1939 was created, in part, to provide the same sort of protection to the purchasers of debt securities as investors in equities receive. The term "debt securities" includes all notes, bonds, debentures and other similar evidences of indebtedness. The term "trust indenture" covers any mortgage, trust or other indenture, or any similar instrument or agreement.

As its major focus and means of protecting the public interest, the act prohibits the sale of any corporate debt security unless it has been issued under a **trust indenture**. In addition to full disclosure about the nature of the debt issue and the issuer, the trust indenture identifies the trustee's responsibilities, rights and powers.

The trust indenture is the contract that gives the appointed trustee the powers necessary to enforce the issuer's obligations and the debt holders' rights. Among the trustee's responsibilities is to represent future investors in the indenture's preparation.

Federal Registration of New Issues

The Legislation

The Securities Act of 1933 regulates new issues of corporate securities sold to the public. The act also is referred to as the *Full Disclosure Act*, the *New Issues Act*, the *Truth in Securities Act* and the *Prospectus Act*. It requires the registration of new issues (debt and equity) before they may be sold to the public. The main purpose of the act is to ensure that the investing public is fully informed about a security and its issuing company when the security is first sold to the public. The act requires registration of new issues of nonexempt securities with the SEC. It also requires that a **prospectus** (a written offer to sell a security), which contains information derived from the registration statement, be given to buyers.

The 1933 act protects the investor considering purchase of new issues by:

- requiring registration of new issues that are to be distributed interstate;
- requiring each issuer to provide full and fair disclosure about itself and the offering;
- requiring each issuer to make available all material information necessary for the investor to judge the issue's merit;
- regulating the underwriting and distribution of primary and secondary issues; and
- providing *criminal penalties* for fraud in the issuance of new securities.

When a corporation wants to issue its securities to the public, the SEC requires it to supply:

- detailed information about itself and its securities to the SEC; and
- the relevant portion of that information to the general investing public.

A **registration statement** disclosing material information must be filed with the SEC by the issuer. Part of the registration statement is a prospectus, which must be provided to all purchasers of the new issue. A prospectus contains much of the same information included in the registration statement, but without the supporting documentation. The registration statement must contain:

- a description of the issuer's business;
- the names and addresses of corporate officers and directors, their salaries and a five-year business history of each;
- the amount of corporate securities owned by these key people and by owners of 10 percent or more of the company;
- the company's capitalization, including its equity and amount of funded debt;
- a description of how the proceeds will be used; and
- whether the company is involved in any legal proceedings.

The Prospectus

The preliminary prospectus. After an issuer files a registration statement with the SEC, a **cooling-off** period begins. This period lasts 20 days, during which the SEC reviews a security's registration statement and can issue a **stop order** if the prospectus does not contain all of the required information. During the cooling-off period, a registered rep may discuss the new issue with clients and provide them with a **preliminary prospectus**, also known as a **red herring**. A registered rep *may not* send any other material to potential customers with the preliminary prospectus, including research reports, *Value Line* sheets, marketing letters and so on.

A red herring need not include the securities' final price, commissions, dealer discounts or net proceeds to the company, although pricing formulas and other information are often included. The document must carry a legend to the effect that a registration statement has been filed with the SEC, but is not yet effective. By law, this disclaimer message must be printed in red ink.

SEC rules prohibit the sale of public offering securities other than by prospectus, which means that no sales are allowed unless and until the buyer is furnished with a final prospectus; that is, securities may be *sold by prospectus only*.

However, the SEC does allow the use of preliminary prospectuses (essentially all the same information found in a final prospectus, but with only a POP range or no price at all) as prospecting tools. The underwriters and selling group members thus have a document to use as they test for investor receptivity and gather **indications of interest.**

An indication of interest is just that—a broker-dealer's or investor's declaration that it might be interested in purchasing some of the security from the underwriter after the security comes out of registration. An indication of interest is *not* a commitment to buy because sales are prohibited until after the registration becomes effective (the *effective date*).

The final prospectus. When the registration statement becomes effective, the issuer amends the preliminary prospectus and adds information, including the final offering price and the underwriting spread. This revised report becomes the final prospectus. Registered representatives may then take orders from those customers who indicated an interest in buying during the cooling-off period.

A copy of the final prospectus must precede or accompany all sales confirmations. The prospectus should include all of the following information:

- description of the offering
- price of the offering
- selling discounts
- date of the offering (effective date)
- use of the proceeds
- description of the underwriting, but not the actual contract
- statement of the possibility that the issue's price may be stabilized
- history of the business
- risks to the purchasers
- description of management
- material financial information
- legal opinion concerning the formation of the corporation
- SEC disclaimer

SEC review. The SEC reviews the prospectus to ensure that it contains whatever material facts the SEC deems necessary, but it does not guarantee the accuracy of the disclosures. Furthermore, the SEC does not approve the issue, but simply clears it for distribution. Implying that the SEC has approved the issue violates federal law. Finally, the SEC does not pass judgment on the issue's investment merit. The front of every prospectus must contain a clearly printed SEC disclaimer clause specifying the limits of the SEC's review procedures. A typical SEC disclaimer clause reads as follows:

> These securities have not been approved or disapproved by the Securities and Exchange Commission nor has the Commission passed upon the accuracy or adequacy of this prospectus. Any representation to the contrary is a criminal offense.

The information supplied to the SEC becomes public information, accessible to anyone, once a registration statement is filed. (This is one of the reasons issuers look for ways to sell securities to the public without having to file registration statements.)

Delivery of Prospectus by Dealers

Preliminary prospectus. A preliminary prospectus must be made available to any customer who expresses interest in the securities about to be distributed in a public offering from the SEC registration filing date to the effective date.

The 48-hour rule. If the issuer is *not* an SEC-reporting company, a preliminary prospectus must be sent to all interested customers and must arrive at least 48 hours prior to the mailing of a customer purchase confirmation.

Aftermarket sales by prospectus. SEC rules require that all sales of public offering stock listed on an exchange or traded on Nasdaq be accompanied by a prospectus during the period beginning with the public offering date (normally the registration statement's effective date) through to a specified date following the public offering date. During this period, a broker-dealer must furnish a final prospectus with every sale of the newly issued security. This restriction extends from the effective date to:

- 90 days for an initial public offering;
- 40 days for an additional issue not listed on an exchange or quoted on Nasdaq; and
- 25 days for an additional issue listed on an exchange or quoted on Nasdaq.

If offering securities remain unsold beyond this end date, the sale-by-prospectus requirement continues. The 25-day sale-by-prospectus requirement applies to underwriters and anyone else who participates in the public distribution (i.e., selling group members). It also applies to broker-dealers that play a part in the public offering.

An exemption under the 1933 act covers sales by nonparticipants and underwriters that no longer act as underwriters—that is, all public offering stock has been sold and the syndicate is closed. If additional issue stock is involved (not new issue stock) and the issuer is an SEC-reporting company, meaning it files quarterly—10Q—and annual—10K—information reports, no prospectus requirement applies.

Prospectus in use after nine months (Rule 427). Rule 427 requires that any prospectus in use *more than nine months* must be updated so it provides potential purchasers with current, relevant financial information. Financial statements included in a prospectus may not have been issued *more than 16 months* before the current use date.

Advertising a New Issue

Advertising and sales literature, as defined by Rule 134, include any notice, circular, advertisement, letter or other communication published or transmitted to any person. The only advertising allowed during the cooling-off period is commonly referred to as a **tombstone (omitting prospectus)**, defined by SEC Rule 482; it is a simple statement of facts without embellishment. The tombstone announces a new issue, but does not offer the securities for sale (an offer for sale can be made only by prospectus) and is not distributed with an application form of any sort.

Advertising copy and other sales materials will qualify as tombstones and will not be deemed a prospectus—which means they need not be filed with the SEC as part of the registration statement—if the body copy is limited to the following:

- name of the issuer of the securities being offered (or the name of the person or company whose assets are to be sold in exchange for the securities being offered);
- brief description of the business of the person making the offer;
- date, time and place of the meeting at which stockholders are to vote on or consent to the proposed transaction (exchange of securities or sale of assets);
- brief description of the planned transaction (material facts and financial information); and/or
- any legend or disclaimer statement required by state or federal law.

Any advertising copy in a tombstone *must* contain the following disclaimers:

- that the issuer has filed the registration statement, but it is not yet effective;
- that the communication does *not* represent an offer to sell the securities described—securities are **sold by prospectus only**;
- name and address of the person or firm to contact for a prospectus; and
- that a response to this advertisement does not obligate the prospect to a buying commitment of any kind (i.e., that it represents only an *indication of interest*).

Rule 482 also covers advertisements and other promotional materials created in support of open-end investment company securities being sold on a continuous new issue offering basis.

The tombstone may appear before or after the effective date. Its publication may be simply a matter of record—that is, an indication that the new issue has already been sold. Federal law does not require issuers to publish tombstones.

Underwriter and selling group member prohibitions. Previously produced research materials and sales literature on a stock in registration must be pulled off the shelves 20 days prior to the effective date, which means at the time of filing.

If a stock in registration is included in an underwriter's or a selling group member's recommended list, the opinion given and quality rating assigned must not be upgraded—for example, from "hold" to "buy"—or emphasized in any fashion. These restrictions continue in force until the underwriter—or selling group member—has completed its participation in the public offering.

If an underwriter pays an investment advisory newsletter a fee to publish a report on the security, the report must disclose the amount and existence of the payment.

Civil Liabilities under the Act of 1933

Untruths in Registration Statements

If a registration statement contains untrue statements of material fact or omits material facts, any person acquiring the security may sue any or all of the following:

- those who signed the registration statement;
- directors and partners of the issuer;
- anyone named in the registration statement as being or about to become a director or partner of the company;
- accountants, appraisers and other professionals who contributed to the registration statement; and
- the underwriters.

Statute of limitations. A civil lawsuit to recover damages incurred owing to untrue statements or omissions of material facts in a registration statement must be filed within three years after the sale of the security.

Untruths in Prospectuses and Communications

The seller of any security being sold by prospectus—which includes oral communications based on information contained in a security's prospectus—will be liable to the purchaser if the prospectus contains misstatements or omissions of material facts. For example, an issuer states in its prospectus that it has made consistent repayment of bond principal and interest to its bondholders. However, if in fact its outstanding bonds carry a rating that indicates a high risk of default, the issuer's prospectus contains a misstatement of this material fact. To avoid civil liability, the seller must prove that he did not know of the misstatements or omissions and that he exercised reasonable care at the time of the sale to prevent communicating any untrue or misleading information of a material nature.

Misrepresentations

It is unlawful for a seller to tell a purchaser of a security that the information contained in the registration statement (and, therefore, in the prospectus) must be 100 percent true and complete as evidenced by the fact that the SEC has not issued a stop order.

The Underwriting Process

Underwriting Corporate Securities

The first successful securities underwriting in the United States is attributed to Jay Cooke. During the Civil War, he and his force of bond salesmen placed more than $2 billion in U.S. government bonds with private investors throughout the North. By fostering these financial ties between government and investors, Cooke's sales force reinforced the loyalty and patriotism of many investors.

After the war ended, securities underwriting continued to be critical to the economic development of the United States. Today, publicly owned and financed corporations dominate U.S. business. Each year, the underwriting activities of investment bankers provide billions of dollars in new equity and debt financing.

Investment Banking

A business or branch of municipal government that plans to issue securities usually works with an **investment banker**, a securities broker-dealer that may also specialize in underwriting new issues by helping to bring securities to market and sell them to investors.

An investment banker's functions may include:

- advising corporations on the best ways to raise long-term capital
- raising capital for issuers by distributing new securities
- buying securities from an issuer and reselling them to the public
- distributing large blocks of stock to the public and to institutions

Participants in a Corporate New Issue

Securities and Exchange Commission. When a corporation issues new securities, the SEC is responsible for the following:

- reviewing the registration statement filed for the offering (accomplished during the cooling-off period between the filing date and the effective date);
- sending a deficiency letter to the issuer if the review uncovers problems, thus halting the review until deficiencies are corrected, at which point the cooling-off period continues; and
- declaring the registration statement effective—that is, releasing the securities for sale.

The issuer. The issuer is the party selling the securities to raise money. The issuer's duties may include:

- filing the registration statement with the SEC;
- filing a registration statement with the states in which it intends to sell securities (also known as *blue-skying the issue*); and
- negotiating the securities' price and the amount of the spread with the underwriter.

National Association of Securities Dealers. The NASD Committee on Corporate Financing reviews the underwriting spread to determine fairness and reasonableness of underwriting compensation.

The individual states. State securities laws, also called **blue-sky laws**, may require state registration of new issues, broker-dealers and registered reps. As mentioned above, registering securities with the state is called **blue-skying the issue**. The issuer or investment banker may blue-sky an issue by one of the following three methods:

- **Coordination**. The issuer registers simultaneously with the state and the SEC. Both registrations become effective on the same date.
- **Filing**. Certain states allow some new issues to blue-sky by having the issuers notify the state of registration with the SEC. In this case, no registration statement is required by the state, although certain other information must be filed.
- **Qualification**. The issue is registered with the state independent of federal registration, meeting all state requirements.

The underwriter. The underwriter not only assists with registration, but also may advise the corporate issuer on the best way to raise capital. The underwriter considers at least the following matters:

- **Whether to offer stock or bonds**. If stocks currently sell at depressed prices, bonds may seem the more attractive alternative. If bonds currently sell at high interest rates, the company may choose to issue stock.
- **Tax consequences of the offering**. The interest a corporation must pay on its bonds is tax deductible. The stock dividends it pays investors are paid out of aftertax profits.
- **Whether to go to the money market for short-term funds or to the capital market for long-term funds**. If the corporation decides to go to the capital market, it will issue one of the following types of securities: secured bonds, debentures, preferred stock or common stock.

Under the provisions of the Securities Act of 1933, offering such securities normally requires registration with the SEC unless a specific exemption applies.

Types of Offerings

Securities Markets

The **new issue market** consists of companies "going public"—privately owned businesses raising capital by selling common stock to the public for the first time. New issue securities are also known as **initial public offering (IPO)** securities.

The **additional issue market** is made up of new securities issues from companies that are already publicly owned; that is, they currently have stock outstanding with the public. These companies increase their equity capitalization by issuing more stock. This is accomplished when an underwriter either distributes the stock in a public offering or arranges for the shares to be sold in a private placement.

In addition to being classified by whether they represent initial or additional issues of new securities, offerings can be distinguished by the final distribution of their proceeds.

Primary Offering

In a primary offering, the underwriting proceeds go to the **issuing corporation**. The corporation increases its capitalization by selling stock, either a new issue or previously authorized but unissued stock. It may do this at any time and in any amount, provided the total stock outstanding never exceeds the amount authorized in the corporation's bylaws.

Secondary Offering

In a secondary offering, one or more major stockholders in the corporation sell all or a major portion of their holdings. The underwriting proceeds are paid to the stockholders rather than to the corporation itself. Typically, secondary offerings occur in situations where the founder of a business, and perhaps some of the original financial backers, determines that the company has more to gain by going public than by staying private.

Table 3.1 compares primary and secondary offerings.

Table 3.1 Offerings and Markets

	New Issue (IPO) Market	*Additional Issue Market*
Primary Offering	Company goes public; underwriting proceeds go to the company.	Company is already public; underwriting proceeds go to the company.
Secondary Offering	Company goes public; underwriting proceeds go to the selling stockholders.	Company is already public; underwriting proceeds go to the selling stockholders.

Split Offering (or Combined Distribution)

A split offering is a combination of a primary and a secondary offering. Some of the stock offered will be issued by the corporation, and the rest represents shares held by present corporate stockholders.

Shelf Offering (Rule 415)

Normally, an issuer sells all of the securities it has registered in a new issue as soon as it can. By doing so, the issuer brings in a large sum of money in a short amount of time. Faced with an immediate need for such a large sum, the issuer should not have a problem handling or investing the money. However, what if the issuer needs the same amount of cash, but in smaller portions over a year or two? A normal issue would provide all of the cash up front, but much of it would have to be invested elsewhere until the investor actually needed it. Delaying the issue could result in cash flow problems.

As an alternative, an issuer can register a new issue security without selling the entire issue at once through a **shelf offering**. The issuer can sell limited portions of a registered shelf offering over a two-year period without having to reregister the security or incurring penalties, but it must file a supplemental prospectus prior to each sale. Shelf offerings provide issuers and their investment bankers with flexibility—money can be raised and expenses incurred only as needed.

Time Line for an Underwriting

Forming the Syndicate

The syndicate and selling group may be assembled before or after the issue is awarded to the underwriter. In competitive bidding, the syndicate is assembled first and syndicate members work together to arrive at the bid. In a negotiated underwriting, the syndicate may be formed after the issuer and underwriting manager have negotiated the terms of the offering.

Preparing Documents

The underwriter may help the issuer prepare and file the registration statement and prospectus. The registration statement must be signed by the issuer's chief executive officer, chief financial officer and chief accounting officer, as well as a majority of the issuer's board of directors.

Cooling-off Period

After the issuer (with the underwriter's assistance) files with the SEC for registration of the securities, a cooling-off period ensues before the registration becomes effective. The registration can become effective as soon as the 20th calendar day following the date the SEC receives it. In practice, however, the cooling-off period is seldom 20 days; the SEC usually takes longer to clear registration statements. If it finds that the registration statement needs revision or expansion, the SEC may suspend the review and issue a *deficiency letter*. The 20-day cooling-off period resumes when the issuer submits a corrected registration statement.

Because of the time it takes to make additions and corrections, the cooling-off period can, in fact, last several months. The SEC sometimes issues a *stop order*, which demands that all underwriting activities cease. This may be done if requirements of the 1933 act have not been met or if fraud is suspected.

During the cooling-off period, underwriters may use the preliminary prospectus (the red herring) to tell investors about the new issue that will be available after the registration's effective date. Though the underwriter cannot sell the securities at this time, it can collect indications of interest (that is, indications from customers that if and when the issue comes to market, they might be interested in acquiring shares or units) and perform final due diligence.

Due Diligence

Near the end of the cooling-off period, the underwriter holds a **due diligence meeting**. The preliminary studies, investigations, research, meetings and compilation of information about a corporation and a proposed new issue that go on during an underwriting are known collectively as **due diligence**. The underwriter, primarily through the syndicate manager, is expected to exercise due diligence (reasonable effort and care) in obtaining all of the information it needs and in verifying its accuracy.

Underwriters are required to conduct a formal due diligence meeting for the benefit of brokers who want information about the issue, the issuer's financial background and the intended use of the proceeds. For issues expected to attract national interest, several meetings might be scheduled at different locations around the country. Representatives of the issuer and the underwriter attend these meetings and provide answers to questions from brokers, securities analysts and top institutional accounts.

In theory, the due diligence meeting provides a last chance for the underwriters to abandon the underwriting if it seems ill-advised. As part of this process, the investment banker must:

- examine the use of the proceeds
- perform financial analysis and feasibility studies
- determine the company's stability
- determine whether the risk is reasonable

Under the full and fair disclosure requirements of the Securities Act of 1933, the underwriter is responsible for making sure the company is doing all it claims. Due diligence includes a:

- preliminary study;
- letter of intent; and
- general examination of other factors, including the industry data (major trends, major competitors, etc.), operational data (company history, major products, etc.), management and employee relations, financial stability and legal status of the issuer.

Pricing the New Issue

An issue's price is determined by the effective date of the registration. It is based on such factors as:

- indications of interest from the underwriter's book
- prevailing market conditions
- price the syndicate members will accept
- price-earnings ratios of similar companies
- company's dividend payment record and financial health

Price is always the great equalizer in the securities business. In the new issue market, the underwriter counsels and advises the issuing corporation on the best price at which to offer shares to the public. Although pricing new issues is largely an art form, the following factors are some of those considered.

Company's present PE. Based on the number of shares to be sold to the public and the issuing company's most recent earnings report, the underwriter decides the price at which shares should be offered so that the price-earnings (PE) ratio will be in line with the PEs on other stocks of similar quality already issued and publicly traded.

Recent offerings. The underwriter determines the prices at which other new issue stocks similar in quality were issued and whether they proved to be hot issues or the open market showed them to be overpriced.

Hot issues. A hot issue is any security that sells at an immediate premium in the public offering aftermarket, indicating that demand outstrips supply. As an extension of this definition, any security that a syndicate manager can *reasonably expect* will sell at a premium after the offering period is also considered a hot issue. The syndicate manager can tell which issues might and which might not become hot from the number of shares for which brokers have entered *indications of interest* in the underwriter's book.

In the additional issue market, pricing the offering is far less of a problem because stock previously issued by the company is publicly traded. The POP for additional issue stock normally is priced off the open market price, which may or may not be stabilized to accommodate the public offering.

Effective Date

An issue's effective date is the first date on which the securities can be sold to the public. The syndicate members can then contact clients who had indicated interest in the issue and confirm orders.

Final Prospectus

The final prospectus must be delivered with each sale of a newly issued security. It must contain all the information found in Part I of the registration statement. Documentation of facts need not be included in the prospectus, but all information in this document must be up to date.

Selling the Securities

After the final due diligence meeting and the passing of the cooling-off period, the syndicate sells the securities to the public. This process may take a few hours or several weeks.

Stabilizing and Sticky Issues

The opposite of a hot issue is called a *sticky issue*. Sticky issues are those for which supply considerably outweighs demand and for which the price in the public offering aftermarket is falling or is likely to fall when the offering closes. At this point, the underwriter has the option of *stabilizing* the security by bidding for shares in the open market. The managing underwriter can enter stabilizing bids for the security until the end of the offering period. At that point, the security's price is allowed to float and find its own level.

Stabilizing bids must *not* be made at a price higher than the public offering price. This is called *pegging* (or *fixing*) and is prohibited by the SEC. If public buying interest does not increase, the managing underwriter may have no choice but to abandon the POP and let the stock find its own level by pulling the stabilizing bid.

With a sticky issue on the underwriter's hands, not only is some of the public offering stock still on the shelf, but the manager also holds a pile of stock reacquired in stabilizing purchases. If the manager sets the price free, the underwriters will have to face losses—losses on the value of their underwriting allotments, plus losses the manager will prorate to each underwriter on the stock bought back in stabilizing purchases.

The syndicate manager also has the option of increasing the selling concession (at the expense of the underwriting fee) if the issue is selling poorly.

Customer Payment

Purchasers of public offering securities are requested to pay for the securities on the transaction settlement date, which is normally the third business day from the public offering date (usually the same as the registration statement's effective date).

Disbursing Proceeds

When the offering has been completed, the underwriting manager allocates underwriting profits and commissions. A final accounting must be given to syndicate members for the disbursement of underwriting proceeds.

Exemptions from Federal Registration

Exempt Issuers and Securities

With certain exceptions, the Securities Act of 1933 requires the registration of new issues with the SEC. Certain securities are exempt from the registration statement and prospectus requirements of the 1933 act, either because of the issuer's creditworthiness or because another government regulatory agency has jurisdiction over the issuer. The following issuers and securities are not required to be registered with the SEC:

- U.S. government securities
- state and municipal bonds
- commercial paper and bankers' acceptances (maturities under 270 days)
- insurance policies and fixed annuity contracts (but not variable annuities)
- national and state bank securities (except bank holding companies)
- building and loan (S&L) securities
- common carrier (e.g., trucking, airline and railroad) securities
- farmers' cooperative securities
- small business investment company (SBIC) securities
- charitable, religious, educational and nonprofit association issues

Banks are exempted from SEC registration of securities because they file information on new issues with bank regulators, and that information is available to investors. This exemption applies only to the securities of banks, not to those of bank holding companies. Private transactions in securities are not covered by the 1933 and 1934 acts if they do not involve the use of the U.S. mail or other means of interstate commerce.

Insurance policies are not included in the definition of "security"; however, variable annuities, variable life insurance and variable universal life insurance are funded by *separate accounts* and must be registered as securities with the SEC.

Exempt Transactions

Even though neither the issuer nor the type of security is exempt, the manner of sale may qualify an offering for exemption. Securities offered by industrial, financial and other corporations may qualify for exemption from the registration statement and prospectus requirements of the 1933 act under one of the following exclusionary provisions:

- Regulation A: corporate offerings of less than $5 million
- Regulation D: private placements
- Rule 144: control and restricted securities
- Rule 147: securities offered and sold exclusively intrastate

Regulation A: Small Offerings

The Regulation A (Reg A) exemption permits issuers to raise up to $5 million capital in a 12-month period without full registration. This allows a small company access to the capital market to raise a small amount of money without incurring prohibitive costs.

In a Reg A offering, instead of filing a full registration statement with the SEC in Washington, the issuer files an abbreviated notice of sale (offering circular) with the regional SEC office. Purchasers are provided with an **offering circular** rather than a full prospectus. The cooling-off period is 20 days between filing date and effective date, and the issuer need not provide audited financial information. The Regulation A exemption is not available for investment companies or for oil and gas limited partnerships.

Regulation D: Private Placements

Rule 506. Rule 506 under Regulation D specifically provides an exemption from registration if the issue is sold to no more than 35 **nonaccredited investors**. An unlimited number of sales may be made to accredited investors (financial institutions or wealthy individuals, as defined by the rule).

The SEC does not require registration of an offering privately placed with:

- officers or other insiders of the issuer;
- financial institutions or other similar investors that do not need SEC protection (accredited investors); or
- a maximum of 25 individual (nonaccredited) investors.

An **accredited investor** is generally accepted to be one who:

- has a net worth of $1 million or more; or
- has had an annual income of $200,000 or more in each of the two most recent years (or $300,000 jointly with a spouse) and who has a reasonable expectation of reaching the same income level in the current year.

The purchasers must have access to the same type of information they would receive if the securities were being sold under prospectus in a registered offering. A private placement memorandum is supplied in place of a prospectus. The SEC must be notified of the private placement on Form D. Rule 506 does not limit the amount of capital that can be raised.

The purchaser in a private placement must sign a letter stating that she intends to hold the stock for investment purposes only. Private placement stock is referred to as **lettered stock** due to this investment letter. The certificate may bear a legend indicating that it cannot be transferred without registration or exemption. Thus, private placement stock is also referred to as **legended stock**.

Rule 144: Control and Restricted Securities

Rule 144 regulates the sale of two types of securities: control and restricted. It stipulates the holding period, quantity limitations, manner of sale and filing procedures for both types of stock.

Control securities are owned by directors, officers or persons who own 10 percent or more of any type of outstanding securities of the company (or financially dependent relatives of such individuals). Persons who have a control relationship with an issuer are considered **affiliated persons**.

Restricted securities are those acquired through some means other than a registered public offering. A security purchased in a private placement is a restricted security. (Most restricted securities are acquired through private placements.)

Sales volume restrictions. Securities may not be sold by a control person until they have been held fully paid for two years. To prevent control persons from dumping stock and upsetting normal market equilibrium, Rule 144 limits the amount of stock they can sell. Total sales over any 90-day period must not exceed the greater of:

- 1 percent of the total outstanding shares of the same class at the time of sale, as reported by the issuing corporation; or
- the average weekly trading volume in the stock over the past four weeks on all exchanges (all markets), or as reported through Nasdaq.

Sales by control persons in amounts not exceeding 500 shares or $10,000 in sale proceeds are permitted without filing a Form 144. Current information about the company must be made available to the buyer. This can be accomplished by verifying that the company is a reporting company that regularly files 10K and 10Q reports with the SEC.

Rule 144a: Nonregistered Foreign Securities

Rule 144a covers nonregistered foreign securities sold to institutional investors in the United States. To qualify under a Rule 144a exemption, the seller must determine that the purchaser is a qualified institutional buyer, such as an insurance company, an investment company, a trust or a similar business group or plan. No time limit is enforced if an institutional investor makes the sale. Securities acquired in a Rule 144a transaction are considered restricted securities.

Rule 145: Reorganization

Rule 145 of the 1933 act is intended to protect stockholders of companies that propose to reorganize their internal ownership structures, acquire other companies or merge with other companies. Or it might be that a stockholder's company is the target of another company's takeover ambitions. The SEC views these propositions as possible ways of victimizing stockholders who may lack the necessary knowledge to reach a decision and vote for or against a specific proposition.

As with new issue public offerings, these propositions require the stockholders' approval. The stockholders need information to vote intelligently; thus, they need a full-disclosure document similar to a prospectus. This document is called a **proxy statement**.

Transactions covered by Rule 145. The transactions covered by Rule 145 are categorized as reclassifications, mergers or consolidations and transfers of assets.

- **Reclassification**. When one class of securities will be exchanged internally for another class, which shifts ownership control in the process, this is considered a reclassification and is covered by Rule 145.
- **Merger or consolidation**. This is when the stockholders in a target company are offered securities in another company—or an assortment of different securities held by either an individual or a consortium of private investors—in exchange for the surrender of their stock.
- **Transfer of assets**. This occurs when all or a portion of one company's business assets (physical property and tangibles) are exchanged for another company's securities. The stockholders thus solicited are being asked to approve their company's dissolution.

Rule 147: Intrastate Offerings

Under Rule 147, offerings that take place entirely in one state do not fall under the SEC's jurisdiction. They are, instead, the responsibility of the state commissioner of securities. SEC Rule 147 exempts such offerings from registration under the following conditions:

- The securities issuer has its principal office and receives at least 80 percent of its income within that state.
- At least 80 percent of its assets are located within that state.
- At least 80 percent of the offering proceeds are used within that state.
- The broker-dealer acting as underwriter is a resident of that state and has an office in the state.
- All of the purchasers are residents of that state, as verified by voter registration or driver's licenses.

Purchasers of an intrastate issue may not resell the stock to any resident of another state for at least nine months after the underwriting is completed.

Antifraud Regulations of the Acts of 1933 and 1934

Although a security might be exempt from the registration requirement and regulations regarding disclosure of information, *no offering is exempt from the antifraud provisions* of the Securities Act of 1933. The antifraud or antimanipulation provisions of the 1933 act apply to all new securities offerings, whether exempt from registration or not. Issuers must provide accurate information regarding any securities offered to the public.

Exemptions from the act of 1934. Securities exempt from registration under the act of 1933 are not subject to most of the Securities Exchange Act of 1934's rules and regulations regarding trading, proxy solicitation, insider trading or margin requirements. As with the act of 1933, however, no security is exempt from the act of 1934's antifraud and market manipulation regulations.

State Registration of New Issues

Agents and broker-dealers must be registered before they can offer or sell any security in a state. However, registration of the persons involved in the offer or the sale often is not enough to make the transaction legal. The security itself must be registered, too, unless that type of security or the transaction involved is exempt from the registration requirement.

According to the Uniform Securities Act, no person can offer or sell any security in a state lawfully unless the:

- security is registered under the Uniform Securities Act;
- security is designated by the act as exempt from the registration requirement; or
- transaction is designated by the act as exempt from the registration requirement.

If a security is not exempt from the registration requirement, the security is called a *nonexempt security.*

Types of Securities Registrations

The Uniform Securities Act provides for three types of registrations for nonexempt securities: registration by coordination, registration by filing and registration by qualification.

Registration by Coordination

Registration by coordination involves coordinating a state registration with a federal registration. Coordination is the state registration of an initial public offering. If an application to register a security with the SEC under the Securities Act of 1933 currently is pending, the security may be registered simultaneously with the state administrator of the Uniform Securities Act.

Registration by coordination is accomplished by filing a registration statement containing the following information:

- three copies of the latest prospectus;
- if the administrator requires it, copies of the articles of incorporation or bylaws, any agreements among underwriters, any indenture, a specimen of the security and any other necessary information; and
- any amendments to the prospectus that are filed with the SEC.

The registration statement must reveal the amount of the securities to be offered in the state and list the other states in which the offering will be filed. Any amendments made in the federal registration also must be made in the state registration.

If the administrator does not rule to the contrary and if the registration statement has been on file for 10 days and no stop orders are in effect, the registration becomes effective at the same time as the federal registration.

Registration by Filing

To be eligible to register securities by filing, the corporation must be an established issuer and must meet stringent financial requirements. Therefore, registration by filing is available for the registration of an issuer's additional shares. The issuer may use registration by filing to coincide with the effective date of a federal registration statement or to extend into an additional state its legal sales territory for an offering that the SEC has already cleared. The issuer notifies the administrator of its intent to offer and sell the securities in the state and supplies documents demonstrating that the issuer:

- has been in continuous operation for at least 36 consecutive calendar months;
- has previously registered an equity offering with the SEC (currently, the stock must be held by at least 500 persons, and at least 400,000 shares must be held by members of the public, not insiders);
- has a minimum total net worth of $4 million;
- has filed all material the SEC requires for at least 36 months;
- has at least four market makers for the securities (if the registration is of equity securities);
- has not defaulted on a debt payment or failed to pay a preferred dividend within the past fiscal year; and
- is offering securities at a price of at least $5 per share.

Registration by filing also requires that each participating underwriter be a member of an association of securities dealers, contract to purchase the securities as a principal and receive a commission or discount of not more than 10 percent of the securities' aggregate offering price. Registration by filing is accomplished by filing a registration statement containing the following information:

- statement as to the firm's eligibility for registration
- description of the security being offered
- issuer's name, address and form of organization
- copy of the offering circular or prospectus

Unless the administrator or the SEC issues a stop order, a registration by filing becomes effective concurrently with the effectiveness of the federal registration statement (or after five days, if the federal registration is already effective).

Registration by Qualification

Registration by qualification is the most complex means of registering an issue in a state and involves the filing of all required registration statements with a state administrator to qualify an issue of securities. Any security may be registered by this method, and all nonexempt securities not eligible for registration by some other procedure must be registered by qualification. A security that needs to be registered in only one state (an *intrastate* security) most likely will be registered by qualification.

Registration by qualification is accomplished by filing a registration statement containing the following information:

- issuer's name, address and form of organization;
- general character and nature of its business;
- description of its physical properties and equipment;
- statement of conditions of the industry or business in which it intends to engage;
- name, address and occupation of every director and officer of the issuer and every owner of 10 percent or more of the issuer's securities, the amount of the issuer's securities the person owns and the amount of remuneration paid him during the last 12 months;
- issuer's capitalization and long-term debt;
- kind and amount of securities to be offered, the proposed offering price and the aggregate selling and underwriting discounts;
- estimated cash proceeds and purpose for which the proceeds will be used;
- copies of any prospectus, pamphlet, circular, form letter, advertisement or other sales literature intended to be used with the offering;
- specimen of the security being registered;
- balance sheet from within four months of the filing; and
- any additional information the administrator requires.

The administrator has the power to require any information he decides is necessary before registering the security.

A registration by qualification becomes effective whenever the administrator so orders.

State Registration Provisions

A number of general provisions apply to all forms of state securities registration. Among these provisions are the following:

- The state administrator sets filing fees for registrations of securities. If a security is withdrawn from registration before it becomes effective, the administrator normally retains a specified amount of the fee paid.
- If the issuer has filed a registration for a similar security within the previous five years, the issuer may reference the previously filed documents in the current registration statement if the documents are still current and accurate. The administrator has the power to permit the issuer to omit any item of information from the required registration documentation.
- A securities registration is effective for one year from its effective date unless the underwriters are still attempting to distribute unsold shares, in which case the registration's effectiveness will be extended until the shares are sold.

- While the registration is effective, the administrator may require the persons who filed the registration to file reports not more often than quarterly, to keep the registration statement current and to disclose the offering's progress.

Under the provisions of the National Securities Markets Improvement Act of 1996, the states no longer exercise certain controls over securities registration. The SEC regulates:

- securities registration of investment companies
- disclosure documents (such as prospectuses)
- proxies
- annual reports

This provision was adopted under the USA.

Although states no longer exercise control over those activities or communications, they still must enforce all applicable antifraud laws and regulations. The states also continue to receive filing fees from the issuers.

Denial, Suspension or Revocation of Securities Registration

An administrator may issue a stop order denying, suspending or revoking the effectiveness of any securities registration, whether by filing, coordination or qualification, if he finds it in the public interest to do so and he finds that:

- the registration statement is misleading or incomplete
- any officer of the issuer has been convicted of a securities crime
- the security is subject to court injunction
- the offering is fraudulent
- offering expenses or promoter's fees are excessive or unreasonable

Exemptions from State Registration

Covered Securities

The Securities Act of 1933 now exempts "covered securities" from state registration. This exemption was established under the NSMIA and adopted under the USA. To avoid duplicate registration of securities that are deemed to have a national interest, covered securities must be registered with the SEC only. States are not permitted to require registration of these securities. Covered securities include the following:

- securities listed on an exchange or quoted on the Nasdaq National Market System;
- shares of registered investment companies;
- securities sold to qualified purchasers; and
- offerings and transactions exempt from federal registration.

Exempt Securities

Some securities are exempt from both the registration requirements and the advertising filing requirements of the Uniform Securities Act. However, no security is exempt from the antifraud provisions of the USA or any other federal act. Securities issued by the following issuers are considered exempt under this act. (For purposes of this section, "guaranteed" means guaranteed as to payment of principal, interest or dividends.)

- **U.S. government securities**. All securities issued or guaranteed by the government of the United States, including Series EE and Series HH savings bonds and certificates of deposit (CDs), are exempt from the registration requirements of the Uniform Securities Act.
- **Municipal securities.** Securities issued or guaranteed by any state or political subdivision of any state or any agency of a state or a subdivision are exempt.
- **Any recognized foreign government securities.** All securities issued by a recognized foreign government—that is, a government with which the United States currently maintains diplomatic relations—are exempt. In addition, all securities issued not only by the national government of Canada, but also by any of the Canadian provinces or any political subdivision (such as a town), are exempt.
- **Certain financial institutions' securities.** All securities issued by and representing an interest in or a debt of any national bank or federal savings and loan association, including CDs, are exempt. Securities issued by banks, savings institutions or trust companies organized under the laws of any state also are exempt, as are securities issued by credit unions and industrial loan associations.
- **Insurance company securities.** Any security that represents an interest in or a debt of or is guaranteed by an insurance company is exempt. Variable annuities, investment contracts and similar securities with payments dependent on the performance of a segregated fund or account invested in securities are not exempt.
- **Public utility and common carrier securities.** Any security issued or guaranteed by a railroad, a trucking company or another common carrier that is subject to the jurisdiction of the Interstate Commerce Commission (ICC), or by a public utility or a holding company subject to the jurisdiction of the Public Utility Holding Company Act of 1935, is exempt.
- **Religious and charitable organization securities.** Any security issued by a religious or charitable not-for-profit organization is exempt. Individual state statutes vary widely, but educational, benevolent, fraternal and reformatory associations are other types of organizations usually included in this category.

Certain other classes of securities are exempt from the act's registration requirements.

Securities listed on national stock exchanges. All securities listed on the NYSE, the American Stock Exchange (AMEX), the Chicago Stock Exchange or another approved regional U.S. securities exchange are exempt. This exemption is sometimes referred to as the *blue chip exemption*. Securities that are unlisted but that are admitted to unlisted trading privileges on a national exchange are also exempt.

Nasdaq-quoted securities. Certain Nasdaq-quoted (National Association of Securities Dealers Automated Quotation system-quoted) securities are now exempt in 26 states. Nasdaq is the electronic quotation system for OTC securities. To qualify for quoting on the Nasdaq system, an OTC security must meet specific standards. For example, the company issuing the security must have total assets of $2 million or more, and at least 100,000 shares of the company's stock must be publicly held. Two states do not require registration of Nasdaq securities, and one state automatically registers Nasdaq securities.

Commercial paper. Promissory notes, bankers' acceptances, drafts and other types of short-term notes with one of the top three ratings, maturities of nine months (270 days) or less and denominations of at least $50,000 are exempt.

Employee pension and profit-sharing or savings plans. Investment contracts issued in connection with employee profit-sharing, savings or similar benefit plans are exempt if the state administrator is notified in writing at least 30 days before the commencement of such a plan.

Exempt Transactions

The following transactions are exempt from the registration and advertising filing requirements of the Uniform Securities Act, but not from its antifraud provisions.

Isolated nonissuer transactions. All isolated nonissuer transactions, whether effected through a broker-dealer or not, are exempt. A nonissuer transaction is any transaction that does not directly or indirectly benefit an issuer; that is, the securities are traded between members of the public through a broker-dealer. Initial (primary) offerings are considered issuer transactions. Transactions in the secondary market are considered nonissuer transactions.

"Isolated" means one or very few transactions within the state per broker-dealer per year. The exact number varies by state. Agents should be cautioned that the philosophy that "an occasional sale is OK for me" is very dangerous. The agent must check carefully the firm's compliance authority before entering an order on the premise that it is an isolated transaction.

Nonissuer transactions in outstanding securities. Nonissuer transactions in outstanding securities (securities already publicly held) are exempt if either of the following two conditions is met:

- A recognized securities manual (such as Moody's, Standard & Poor's, Fitch's or Best's) contains certain information about the issuer. This exemption is commonly referred to as a *manual exemption*. The manual must contain the names of the issuer's officers and directors, a balance sheet of the issuer dated within the last 18 months and an income statement for the most recent calendar or fiscal year.

- The security has a fixed maturity or a fixed interest or dividend provision and has not defaulted during the preceding four years (including the current year) or for the life of the issuer, whichever is less.

For example, an individual who purchases IBM shares would be effecting a nonissuer transaction in outstanding securities.

Unsolicited orders. Unsolicited nonissuer transactions effected through a broker-dealer are exempt. State laws or a state administrator may dictate what securities transactions an agent may or may not solicit. This same limitation cannot be placed on the general public; however, a client may purchase any security she chooses.

How does an agent legally fill an order for a client who wishes to purchase a security that is nonexempt, does not appear in a recognized manual and does not qualify under isolated sales provisions? It is a good business practice to have the client acknowledge in writing the order's unsolicited status. Under the USA, the state administrator may require the client to sign an acknowledgment that the order was unsolicited. Unsolicited orders are exempt transactions, but the agent must be prepared to carry the burden of proof.

Issuer transactions. Transactions between issuers and underwriters are exempt.

Transactions by certain persons. "**Fiduciary**" refers to a person responsible for something held in trust for another person. Any transaction by a fiduciary is exempt from state security regulations. Fiduciary transactions include those by an executor, an administrator, a sheriff, a marshall, a receiver, a trustee in bankruptcy, a guardian or a conservator.

Pledges. A margin account transaction in which the investing customer's securities are *pledged* by the broker-dealer to a lending bank for the funds necessary to complete the trade. This process is known as *hypothecation.*

Transactions with financial institutions. This exemption is known as the *sophisticated* (or *professional*) *investor transaction exemption.* The Uniform Securities Act is designed to protect the general public, not to limit the activities of informed professional investors, institutional buyers and broker-dealers, including:

- banks
- savings institutions
- trust companies
- insurance companies
- registered investment companies
- pension or profit-sharing trusts
- broker-dealers

Transactions with these financial institutions are exempt whether the institutions act for their own accounts or for the accounts of others.

Private placements. A private placement is simply a sale of nonexempt securities that is not made to the general public. In a private placement, registration of the security is not necessary. However, the Uniform Securities Act does stipulate the following requirements for private placements:

- The number of people receiving offers, other than financial or institutional investors or broker-dealers, must be restricted to 10 in any 12-month period.
- All sales must be made to buyers who purchase for the purpose of investment.
- No commissions or fees may be paid directly or indirectly for soliciting noninstitutional buyers.

Preorganization certificates. A preorganization certificate is an agreement to purchase shares of stock in a company not yet in existence, but to be incorporated. An offer or a sale of a preorganization certificate (or subscription) is exempt if it meets *all* of the following conditions:

- No commission or other remuneration is provided for soliciting prospective subscribers.
- The number of subscribers does not exceed 10.
- No payment is made by any subscriber.

Other exempt transactions. Other transactions are exempted under the act, including:

- underwriting transactions;
- offers to existing securities holders, including holders of convertible securities, nontransferable warrants and transferable warrants exercisable within 90 days of their issuance, provided:
  - no commission is paid for soliciting the securities holders; and
  - the issuer files with the administrator a notice of the offer that the administrator does not disallow within five full business days; and
- indications of interest.

Denial and Revocation of Exemptions

The administrator may deny or revoke an exemption if he discovers that the security's or transaction's exemption is based on fraudulent, misleading or unethical business practices and if he finds that doing so would be in the public's best interest. In any event, the burden of proving eligibility for an exemption falls to the person claiming the exemption. The administrator may, without prior notice, issue a summary order denying or revoking the exempt status of a security issued by a religious or charitable organization, or denying or revoking the exempt status of any exempt transaction, such as a private placement or a transaction with a financial institution.

Unlawful Representations

It is unlawful to make misleading statements to customers concerning the status of a security's or transaction's registration or exemption, including:

- telling customers that exchange listing of a security is anticipated, without knowing the truth about such a statement;
- telling customers that a security registered with the SEC or a state securities administrator has been approved by such regulators; and
- implying to customers that regulation by any authority, including listing on a registered stock exchange, enhances a security's safety or performance.

4 Ethics in the Securities Industry

Key Terms

breakpoint sale
churning
excessive trading
painting the tape
private securities transaction
selling dividends
shared account

Overview

The USA's antifraud provisions apply to anyone involved in a securities transaction or anyone who receives compensation for investment advice. The antifraud provisions of the Investment Advisers Act of 1940 apply to both registered investment advisers and to any person who fits the definition of an investment adviser, whether or not that person is registered.

The Uniform Securities Act lists specific fraudulent or prohibited practices, but with the notation that the list is not all-inclusive. Each person has the responsibility of determining whether his business practices are dishonest or unethical. Some acts that would be considered fraudulent are easy to identify as such, but many are not. "Fraud" is defined as the deliberate concealment, misrepresentation or omission of material information or truth to deceive or manipulate another party for unlawful or unfair gain, whether or not the act results in a sale.

This chapter describes specific acts that constitute unethical business practices in the securities industry.

Ethical Behavior of Investment Advisers

Because of the nature of their business and the amount of trust a client must put into an advisory relationship, the standard of business ethics to which investment advisers are expected to conform is very high. As is the case with any investment or securities professional, investment advisers are prohibited from:

- employing any device, scheme or artifice to defraud;
- engaging in any fraudulent or deceitful practice or course of business;
- failing to disclose in writing the capacity in which the investment adviser acts (agent or principal) in a transaction for a client and failing to obtain the client's written consent before the transaction's completion;
- making any untrue statement of material fact or omitting a material fact; or
- engaging in any other practices the administrator defines by rule as dishonest or unethical.

Disclosure of Capacity

If the investment adviser acts as a principal in a transaction—that is, she buys securities from or sells securities to a client from her own account—she must make a written disclosure to the client of her capacity and obtain the client's consent before any such transaction. The same disclosure and consent are required if the investment adviser acts as a broker, arranging the transaction on behalf of a client.

A broker-dealer acting as an investment adviser is exempt from the disclosure of capacity requirement if it is engaged in (1) offering impersonal advisory services or (2) distributing written materials to 35 or more persons who are paying for those materials, *always provided* that the broker-dealer includes a statement in any communication to clients that, depending on the transaction and the circumstances, it *may* act as either a principal for its own account or an agent for another person.

Disclosure of Legal Action

Any material legal or disciplinary action must be disclosed to clients and prospective clients not less than 48 hours prior to entering into an investment advisory contract.

The Uniform Securities Act considers a legal or disciplinary action to be material if the finding was handed down within the past 10 years and:

- resulted in the adviser being restricted from conducting an investment-related business;
- took place in a criminal or civil court of law or was the result of a hearing with a state securities administrator, the SEC or a self-regulatory organization; and
- involved the investment adviser or a person associated with the firm who has the power to exercise influence over the firm's policies or the investment advice given.

Suitability and Investment Recommendations

Investment recommendations must be in keeping with customer needs, financial capability and objectives. Customers should be guided to investments that make sense for them, not for the broker. The investment adviser should explain each investment fully, including its risks. At no time should customers own an investment which could put them at risk beyond their financial capacity.

Dishonest or Unethical Business Practices

Investment advisers are prohibited from engaging in any business practice or behavior that is dishonest, unethical or fraudulent. "Fraud" is commonly understood to mean making a statement while knowing it to be false and having the intention to deceive.

The state administrator in each state is authorized by the Uniform Securities Act to define unethical and dishonest behavior in whatever way is necessary to protect the interests of the investors in that state. The Uniform Securities Act also codifies NASAA's *Statement of Policy on Unethical Business Practices of Investment Advisers* and sets forth specific business practices that constitute fraudulent or deceitful methods for taking unfair advantage of customers.

Suitability. An investment adviser may not recommend a transaction to a customer without having a basis for believing the transaction to be suitable. An adviser must consider each customer's individual financial situation and investment objectives whenever he recommends a transaction. Failure to make reasonable inquiry about the customer's needs and objectives is unethical and prohibited.

Discretionary authority. Discretion is the authority to decide the security, the number of shares or units and whether to buy or sell, but not the timing or price of a transaction only. An investment adviser must not carry out discretionary transactions for or on behalf of a customer without first obtaining the customer's written authority.

Third-party authority. An investment adviser may not accept orders on behalf of a customer from individuals other than the customer without first obtaining third-person trading authority. The adviser may accept only those orders placed by the account owner or by another party who has been granted trading authorization in writing.

Excessive trading. An investment adviser must not induce trading in a client's account that is excessive in terms of size or frequency. This is a prohibited practice known as *churning*. Inducing transactions solely to generate commissions without regard to the customer's best interest or investment objectives is a form of churning.

Borrowing. An investment adviser is prohibited from borrowing money or securities from a customer, even if the customer agrees or signs a written contract, except in a few circumstances. An adviser may borrow from a customer that is an affiliate, a broker-dealer, or a bank or some other institution in the business of lending money.

Commingling. An investment adviser may not commingle (mix) a customer's funds with the adviser's own funds. The Uniform Securities Act does not prohibit an adviser or investment adviser rep from having a personal joint account with a customer or another person.

Material facts. An investment adviser may not misrepresent or omit a material fact regarding an investment or regarding the adviser's qualifications or fees. For example, an adviser may not state that the state administrator has approved his business. With regard to a particular transaction, the adviser must accurately state the amount of commission or markup or markdown to be charged. An investment adviser is also responsible for informing the customer if a certain transaction involves larger than ordinary commissions or costs.

Sources. If someone other than the investment adviser prepares a report or recommendation, the adviser or rep must disclose that fact.

Fees. An investment adviser cannot charge unreasonable fees for advisory services—that is, fees out of line in relation to fees charged by other advisers offering similar services.

Conflicts of interest. An investment adviser must disclose any material conflict of interest that could impair his objectivity. For example, an adviser must disclose an arrangement whereby the adviser receives compensation from an outside source in addition to compensation from the client receiving advisory services. Also, an adviser must disclose if he receives both a fee for investment advice and a commission for executing securities transactions based on that advice.

Customer protection. An investment adviser must comply with safekeeping requirements that protect customer funds and securities. These requirements are set forth in the Uniform Securities Act's custody rule.

Contracts. Each investment advisory contract must be in writing, disclose terms and fees, specify whether discretionary power is granted and prohibit the contract from being assigned—that is, sold or transferred to another firm—without the customer's permission.

Market Manipulation

Another type of violation is an action intended to influence the price of securities in the market. Securities industry personnel are responsible for upholding the integrity of the markets and must not engage in activities that illegally manipulate market values.

Other Unethical Practices

Regardless of whether a particular course of action of a broker-dealer, an investment adviser or a representative is specifically prohibited, these persons are always held to high ethical standards. Other business practices not specified in the Uniform Securities Act but generally agreed to be dishonest or unethical include:

- deliberately failing to follow a customer's instructions;
- effecting transactions with a customer who is not recorded on the books of the rep's employer, unless the transactions are approved in writing in advance;
- failing to bring a customer's written complaint to the attention of the rep's employer;
- soliciting orders for unregistered nonexempt securities;
- sharing in the profits or losses of a customer's account, unless the customer and the employer have given written consent and the percentage of profit or loss is the same as the percentage of the registered person's personal funds invested in the account;
- misrepresenting to customers the status of their accounts;
- promising to perform certain services for customers without intending to perform those services or being qualified to do so; and
- disseminating inaccurate or phony market quotations—any quotation that an adviser, a broker-dealer or a rep provides to a customer must be bona fide.

Criminal Penalties

The criminal penalties for violations of securities laws were increased through an amendment to the act of 1934. If a person is convicted of willfully violating federal securities regulations, or of *knowingly* making false or misleading statements in a registration document, that person can be fined up to $1 million, sentenced to prison for not more than 10 years or both; the maximum fine is $2.5 million for other than a natural person.

Assistance to Foreign Authorities

The SEC is pledged to assist foreign regulatory authorities in the investigation of any person who has violated, is violating or is about to violate any laws or rules relating to securities matters.

5 Investment Companies

Key Terms

advertising prospectus
affiliated person
face amount certificate
investment company
management company
private investment company
qualified purchaser
underwriting
unit investment trust

Overview

During the early decades of this century, Congress directed the Securities and Exchange Commission (SEC) to study investment trusts and investment companies, their corporate structures, their investment policies and their influence on the companies in which they invest. This study led to the passage of the Investment Company Act of 1940, providing for SEC regulation of investment companies and their activities. This act was amended under the National Securities Markets Improvement Act and adopted under the USA.

This chapter describes the registration and regulation requirements set forth by the Investment Company Act of 1940 and the amendments to the act.

Investment Company Offerings

Investment Company Purpose

Like corporate issuers, investment companies raise capital by selling shares to the public. Investment companies must abide by the same registration and prospectus requirements imposed by the Securities Act of 1933 on every other issuer, plus more. Because of what investment companies do with the capital they raise, they are subject to stringent regulations regarding the manner, means, methods and conditions under which their shares are sold to the public, which is the subject of the Investment Company Act of 1940, as amended.

Investment companies have one thing in common: they are all **portfolio intermediaries** in the business of pooling the public's money and investing it for them. One of the reasons people invest in investment companies is that they believe a professional money manager should be able to outperform the average investor in the market.

Types of Investment Companies

The Investment Company Act of 1940 classifies investment companies into three broad types: face-amount certificate companies (FACs); unit investment trusts (UITs); and management investment companies, which are the most common. The various investment company classifications are shown in Figure 5.1.

Face-amount Certificate Companies

A face-amount certificate is a contract between an investor and an issuer in which the issuer guarantees payment of a **stated** (or **fixed**) sum to the investor at some set date in the future. In return for this future payment, the investor agrees to pay the issuer a set amount of money either as a lump sum or in periodic installments. If the investor chooses to pay for the certificate in a lump sum, the investment is known as a **fully paid face-amount certificate**. Issuers of these investments are called, naturally enough, **face-amount certificate companies**.

Face-amount certificates may be backed by specific assets, such as U.S. government issues, VA and FHA mortgages, corporate debt issues or preferred stock. Usually, however, they are backed by bonds that mature when the certificates mature. In either case, principal and interest are guaranteed. When the certificates' value is paid to the investor at maturity, the investment fund is exhausted.

Face-amount certificate companies continuously offer their shares, or investment contracts. A typical face-amount certificate contract requires the investor to make 20 semiannual payments of $1,000 each over a period of 10 years for a total investment of $20,000. In return, the company guarantees that at the end of

Figure 5.1 Classification of Investment Companies

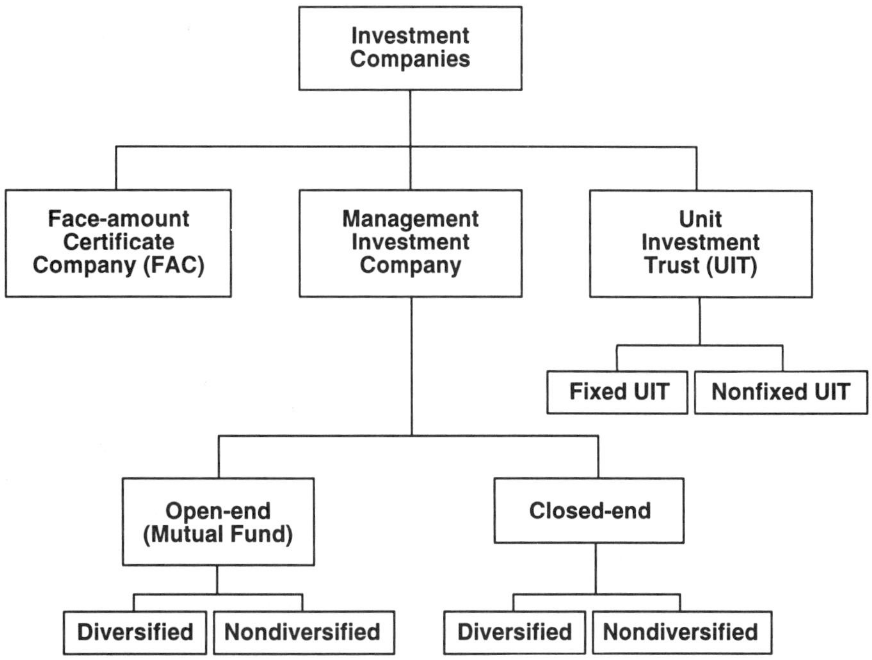

10 years, it will return to the investor $25,000. Very few face-amount certificate companies operate today because of tax code changes.

Unit Investment Trusts

A **unit investment trust** is an investment company organized under a trust indenture. The primary characteristics that set UITs apart from other types of investment companies are that UITs:

- do not have boards of directors
- do not employ investment advisers
- do not actively manage their own portfolios (trade securities)

A UIT functions basically as a holding company for its investors. UIT managers typically purchase an investment portfolio, consisting of other investment company shares or of fixed-income securities such as government or municipal bonds. They then sell redeemable shares, also known as *units* or *shares* of beneficial interest, in this portfolio of securities. Each share represents the ownership of an undivided interest in the underlying portfolio. Because UITs are not managed, once any securities in the portfolio are sold, mature or are otherwise liquidated, the proceeds must be distributed. UITs are organized without boards of directors and investment advisers; therefore, they cannot reinvest proceeds or otherwise manage the trusts' portfolios.

A UIT may be fixed or nonfixed. A typical fixed UIT may purchase a portfolio of bonds. When the bonds in the portfolio have matured, the trust is terminated. The nonfixed UIT is often used by investors interested in purchasing units on a contractual basis (a contractual plan). The trust may purchase shares of an underlying mutual fund for the nonfixed UIT portfolio.

Under the act of 1940, a UIT trustee must maintain a secondary market in the units, thus guaranteeing a measure of liquidity to the shareholders.

Management Investment Companies

To many people, the most familiar type of investment company is the **management investment company**, which actively manages a portfolio of securities in accordance with the investment objectives stated in its prospectus. The single most important distinction between different types of management investment companies is their status as either closed-end or open-end. Both closed- and open-end companies sell shares to the public; the difference between them lies in the types of securities they sell and where investors buy and sell their shares.

Closed-end Investment Companies

As with many corporations, when a **closed-end** investment company wants to raise capital for investments, it conducts a stock offering. For the initial offering, the company registers a fixed number of shares with the SEC and makes these shares available to the public for a limited time through an **underwriting group** composed of the broker-dealers chosen to handle the distribution. When the underwriters have distributed all of the shares that the investment company has registered to sell, the public offering period comes to a close. The fund's capitalization is basically fixed unless an additional issue public offering is made. Closed-end investment companies may issue both common stock and senior securities such as preferred stock and bonds within certain limits. Closed-end funds do not redeem their securities.

Closed-end investment companies are more commonly known as **publicly traded funds**. After the stock is distributed, anyone who wants to buy or sell shares does so in the secondary market either on an exchange or OTC. Supply and demand determine the price the investor receives or pays for shares. For the shares of many larger investment companies, the **bid** price (or price at which an investor can sell) and the **ask** price (or price at which an investor can buy) are published daily in the financial pages of most major newspapers. These bid and ask prices reflect the open market's current valuation of the shares.

Open-end Investment Companies

An **open-end** investment company (or **mutual fund**), unlike the closed-end company, does not specify the exact number of shares it intends to issue; rather, it registers an open offering with the SEC. With this type of registration, the open-end investment company can raise an unlimited amount of investment capital by continuously issuing new shares in its portfolio of investments. By the same token, when investors liquidate their holdings in a mutual fund, the fund's capital shrinks. Because the number of shares the company can offer is not limited, the offering in effect never "closes." Any person who wants to invest in—or increase his holdings in—the company buys shares directly from the company or its underwriters at the public offering price (net asset value plus a sales charge).

The shares that an open-end investment company sells fall into a special category known as **redeemable securities**. Instead of buying and selling shares on the open market, as do the investors in a closed-end company, mutual fund investors place their orders directly with the investment company's underwriters (broker-dealers). When investors sell their shares, the company itself redeems them at their net asset value (NAV). For each share an investor sells back (or redeems), the company sends the investor her proportionate share of the company's net assets.

Diversified and Nondiversified

Diversified. In the mutual fund business, advertising the fact that a fund is an open-end diversified investment company is an important selling point. Diversification is a combination risk management technique and investment approach that makes mutual funds popular with many investors. But not all investment companies feature diversified portfolios.

Under the Investment Company Act of 1940, an investment company qualifies as a diversified investment company if it meets the following **75-5-10** test:

- *75 percent* of total assets must be invested in securities issued by companies *other than the investment company itself* or its affiliates. Cash on hand and cash equivalent investments (short-term government and money market securities) count as part of the 75 percent required investment in outside companies.
- No more than *5 percent* of total assets can be invested *in any one corporation's* securities.
- No more than *10 percent* of an outside corporation's *voting class securities* (common stock) can be owned by the investment company.

Nondiversified. A nondiversified investment company, on the other hand, is any company that fails to meet one or more of these criteria. Some investment companies choose to invest their assets in such a way as to concentrate (or specialize) in a geographic area or industry. Investors may be familiar with investment companies specializing in natural resources, precious metals or gold mining stocks, to name a few.

Investment Company Registration

A company must register as an investment company with the SEC if:

- the company is in the business of investing in, reinvesting in, owning, holding or trading securities; or
- 40 percent or more of the company's assets are invested in securities. (Government securities and securities of majority-owned subsidiaries are not used in calculating the 40 percent limitation.)

Under the NSMIA, the regulation and registration of investment companies have been concentrated under the SEC's jurisdiction. States may no longer impose registration or reporting requirements. This provision has been accepted under the USA.

Registration of Investment Companies

Before a company may register as an investment company with the SEC, it must meet certain minimum requirements. A management company, or any other type of investment company, is not allowed to issue securities to the public unless it has:

- private capitalization (seed money) of at least $100,000
- 100 investors
- clearly defined investment objectives

If the open-end investment company does not have 100 shareholders and $100,000 in assets, it can still register a public offering with the SEC provided that it can meet these requirements within 90 days of registration.

The company must clearly define an investment objective under which it plans to operate. Once defined, the objective, whether growth, income or whatever, may be changed only with a majority vote of the company's outstanding shares.

Open-end companies. In addition, the act of 1940 requires open-end companies to have the following:

- no more than one class of security
- a minimum asset-to-debt ratio of 300 percent

Open-end investment companies can issue only one class of voting equity (common stock). Open-end companies may not issue senior securities (such as preferred stock and bonds) but may borrow from lending institutions such as banks as long as a company maintains a 3-to-1 asset-to-debt ratio, sometimes described as a *300 percent coverage ratio.*

SEC Registration and Public Offering Requirements

Investment companies must file registration statements with the SEC, provide full disclosure and generally follow the same public offering procedures that other corporations and noninvestment companies follow when issuing securities. In filing for registration as an investment company with the SEC, a corporation must provide the following information in its registration form:

- type of investment company it intends to be (open-end or closed-end);
- any plans the company has to raise money by borrowing;
- company's intention (if any) to concentrate its investments in a single industry;
- any plans for investing in real estate or commodities;
- conditions under which investment policies may be changed by a vote of the shareholders;
- full name and address of each affiliated person; and
- description of the business experience of each officer and director during the preceding five years.

The investment company is considered registered when the SEC receives its notification of registration. Once a corporation has met the above tests for registration as an investment company, the SEC allows it certain rights and places certain prohibitions on its activities. While operating as an investment company, a corporation is strictly prohibited from:

- seeking to gain control of other companies
- acting in the capacity of a broker by trading securities for a commission
- acting as a bank, an insurance company or a savings and loan
- operating with fewer than 100 shareholders or less than $100,000 in assets

Exceptions to these guidelines exist. Under the act, the following corporations are exempt from registration as investment companies with the SEC, even if more than 40 percent of their assets are invested in securities:

- underwriters and brokers;
- banks, insurance companies and bank investment advisory accounts;
- mortgage bankers;
- security holders protective committees;
- real estate investment trusts (REITs); and
- investment pools (private investment companies) whose securities are held exclusively by qualified purchasers.

Deceptive or misleading names. An investment company may not use as its name, or as part of its name, any words that are misleading. A name is prohibited if it might cause an investor to be confused about the investment company's relative safety or investment objective.

Continuous Public Offering Securities

The SEC treats the sale of open-end investment company shares as a continuous public offering of shares, which means that the shares must be sold by prospectus only. All sales must be accompanied by a prospectus, and the financial information contained in the prospectus must be dated not more than 16 months prior to the sale. With publicly traded closed-end funds, only the initial public offering stock is sold with a prospectus.

Purchasing mutual fund shares on margin. Because a mutual fund continually issues new shares and is considered a *continuous primary offering*, Regulation T prohibits the purchase of mutual fund shares on margin. Mutual fund shares may be used as collateral in a margin account, however, if they have been held fully paid for 30 days.

Registration of Investment Company Securities

In addition to filing as an investment company under the act of 1940, the investment company, like any other corporation, must register with the SEC any securities it intends to issue. The registration of shares takes place under the Securities Act of 1933.

Registration Statement—Prospectus

The registration statement a corporation must file consists of two parts: part 1 is the prospectus, a copy of which the corporation must furnish to every person to whom it offers the securities; and part 2 is the document containing information that need not be furnished to every purchaser, but that must be made available for public inspection. In general, the prospectus must contain any information that the SEC decides should be revealed in the public's best interest. The fact that all publicly issued securities must be registered with the SEC does not mean that the SEC in any way approves the securities. For that reason, every prospectus must contain on its front cover a disclaimer similar to the following:

> These securities have not been approved or disapproved by the Securities and Exchange Commission nor has the commission passed upon the accuracy or adequacy of this prospectus. Any representation to the contrary is a criminal offense.

Restrictions on Operations

Functions and Activities of Investment Companies

The act of 1940 sets out rules, restrictions and regulations under which investment companies must operate. These rules and regulations were written to protect the investor and have been amended and updated frequently. Unless a fund meets stringent disclosure and financial responsibility requirements, the SEC has been granted authority under the act of 1940 to prohibit the mutual fund from:

- making securities purchases on margin
- selling securities short
- participating in joint investment or trading accounts
- acting as distributor of its own securities, except through an underwriter

The fund must specifically disclose these activities and the extent to which it plans to engage in these activities in its prospectus.

Changes in the Registration Statement

Shareholders' Right to Vote

Whatever is stated in the prospectus as the management company's purpose for existence, investment objectives, capital formation methods, organizational structure and shareholder services can be changed only by a *majority of shares outstanding* being voted in favor of the change.

Before any change can be made to the fund's published bylaws or objectives, shareholder approval is mandatory. In voting matters, it is the *majority of shares voted* for or against a proposition that counts, *not the majority of people voting.* Thus, one shareholder holding 51 percent of all shares outstanding can determine a vote's outcome.

A majority vote of the shares outstanding would be required for changes in:

- **borrowing** by open-end companies (open-end investment companies can borrow cash from banks; closed-end companies cannot);
- **issuing or underwriting** other securities (closed-end companies can raise capital by issuing senior securities, either debt or preferred stock; open-end companies cannot);
- purchasing or underwriting **real estate**;
- making **loans**;
- **subclassification** (for example, from open-end to closed-end or from diversified to nondiversified);
- **sales load policy** (for example, from a no-load fund to a load fund);
- **nature of the business** (for example, ceasing business as an investment company); and
- **investment policy** (for example, from income to growth or from bonds to small capitalization stocks).

In addition to the right to vote on these items, shareholders retain all rights normally accorded to the holders of any corporate stock.

Management of Investment Companies

Board of Directors

Like publicly owned corporations in general, a management investment company has a CEO, a team of officers and a board of directors, all in place to serve the interests of the investors. The officers and directors concern themselves with investment objectives, long-term strategy, portfolio funding and cash flow matters, accounting and business administration duties. But they themselves do not manage the investment portfolio. As with any other type of corporation, the shareholders of a management investment company elect the board of directors to make decisions and oversee operations. Management investment company shareholders must approve the election of the fund's board members, as well as any additions or replacements to the board.

The only exception to this rule is that any vacancies occurring after the initial election may be filled in any legal manner as long as the shareholders have elected at least two-thirds of the directors. The board may be divided into classes, provided that no one class of directors is elected for a period shorter than one year or longer than five years.

The act of 1940 restricts those persons eligible to sit on an investment company's board of directors. A section of the act, called **interlocking directorate**, requires that at least 40 percent of the directors be independent (noninterested persons). This means that no more than 60 percent of the board members may be interested persons, including attorneys on retainer, accountants and any persons employed in similar capacities with the company. For example, if a fund has 10 directors, at least four of them can hold no other position within the fund.

The second restriction is that no one may serve on a board of directors who has been convicted of either a felony of any type or a misdemeanor involving the securities industry.

The third restriction is that no person who has been either temporarily or permanently enjoined from acting as an underwriter, a broker, a dealer or an investment company by any court can be elected to a term on a board.

Investment Adviser

Once an investment company is registered as such and has elected its board of directors, the board contracts with an outside **investment adviser** (portfolio manager). The fund's investment adviser may be an individual or an investment advisory company. Once hired, the adviser is responsible for investing the cash and securities held in the fund's portfolio, implementing investment strategy, clearly identifying the tax status of any distribution made to shareholders as a result of activity in the fund's portfolio, and managing the portfolio's day-to-day trading. Naturally, the adviser must adhere to the objective as stated in the fund's prospectus; only a majority vote of the shares can alter the objective. The adviser cannot transfer the responsibility of portfolio management to anyone else. The simple fact that an investment adviser is elected does not relieve the directors of their responsibility of adhering to the fund's objective.

An investment adviser earns a management fee for his services, typically a set annual percentage, such as .5 percent of the portfolio asset value he manages. This management fee is paid from the fund's net assets. In addition, if an investment adviser consistently outperforms a specified market performance benchmark, he typically earns an incentive bonus. But, the sword is double-edged; if the adviser underperforms, his management contract may not be renewed.

In choosing an investment adviser, the company must select the best, most qualified adviser it can find without regard to former, current or future ties or business the adviser might have with the company. To protect investment company shareholders, the act of 1940 requires that:

- the contract is in writing and approved initially by a vote of the shareholders; and
- the advisory contract has a *maximum life of two years*, after which time it may be extended on a year-to-year basis by the annual approval of the directors and/or a majority vote of the shares.

The **contract** must also include:

- a precise description of all compensation to be paid the investment adviser;
- a provision that the contract may be terminated by the board of directors or by a majority vote of the shares with 60 days' notice;
- the stipulation that the contract will be terminated if the investment adviser assigns its contract to another person (*assignment* means any transfer of a controlling interest in the management group, of which the investment adviser is a part);
- the requirement that the investment company shareholders approve any such assignment; and
- the requirement that a majority of the noninterested (independent) directors approve any amendment or renewal of the advisory contract.

An investment company is prohibited from contracting with an investment adviser who has been convicted of a securities-related felony unless it has received an exemption from the SEC. In addition, an investment company is prohibited from lending money to its investment adviser.

Affiliated and Interested Persons

The act of 1940 and subsequent amendments identify certain categories of individuals and entities that have control over or may influence an investment company's operations. The identification of these persons is critical, as the act regulates and restricts their activities. The act broadly defines two classes of persons: affiliated and interested.

An **affiliated person** is in a *control* position within the company; in general, an affiliated person controls the investment company's operations. An **interested person** is in a position to *influence* the operations of the investment company.

Affiliated Persons

Anyone who could have any type of control over an investment company's operations is an affiliated person. The act has set forth a series of regulations that effectively prohibit affiliated persons from using the control they have for their personal benefit. Those persons considered affiliated include:

- anyone with 5 percent or more of the investment company's outstanding voting securities;
- any corporation in which the investment company holds 5 percent or more of its outstanding securities;
- any person (individual or corporate entity) controlled in whole or in part by the investment company;
- all officers, directors, partners and employees of the investment company;
- the investment adviser; and
- in the absence of a board of directors, the individual who deposits the UIT's assets into the account at the custodial bank, also known as the *depositor*.

Interested Persons

Introduced by the 1970 amendments to the act, the designation "interested person" broadens the category of people whose actions the SEC restricts or regulates. The list of restricted persons now includes broker-dealers, legal counsels and immediate family of affiliated persons, as well as anybody else whom the SEC wishes to designate as such. All of the following are considered interested persons:

- person associated with the investment company, its investment adviser or its principal underwriter, including the immediate family of any affiliated person;
- person employed by the investment company, the investment adviser or the principal underwriter;
- person who, within the last two years, has acted as legal counsel to any affiliated person;
- broker-dealer registered under the Securities Exchange Act of 1934; and
- any other person the SEC deems to be interested because of business dealings with the company, its investment adviser or its principal underwriter.

Investment company directors are specifically excluded from the definition of an interested person. The directors are, however, affiliated persons.

Restrictions

In addition to any other restrictions, an affiliated or interested person is prohibited from:

- borrowing money from the investment company; or
- selling any security or other property to the investment company or to any company the investment company controls.

Custodian

As a means of safeguarding investors' assets, the act of 1940 requires each investment company to place its securities in the custody of a bank with assets of at least $500,000 or a stock exchange member broker-dealer. The bank or broker-dealer performs an important safekeeping role as custodian of the company's securities and cash and receives a fee for its services. This fee, like the adviser's fee, is paid from the fund's net assets. Often, the custodian handles most of the clerical functions the investment company needs. The custodian may, with the investment company's consent, deposit the securities it is entrusted to hold in one of the systems for the central handling of securities established by the National Association of Securities Dealers (NASD) or the New York Stock Exchange (NYSE). These systems make it easier to transfer or pledge securities. Once securities are placed in the systems, most such transfers can be accomplished with a simple bookkeeping entry rather than actual physical delivery of the securities.

Once an investment company designates a custodian and transfers assets into its safekeeping, the custodian must follow certain rules and regulations as specified by the act, including:

- keeping the investment company's assets physically segregated at all times;
- allowing withdrawal only under SEC rules; and
- restricting access to the account to certain officers and employees of the investment company.

The board of directors designates, by majority vote, which employees it wishes to have access to the account. As a further safeguard, the act specifies that at least two of these designated employees must be present each time the account is opened. The only other people the custodian can allow access to the account are the independent public accountants verifying the securities and any authorized SEC employees.

The securities in the account must be verified by an independent public accountant at least three times a year. One accounting is performed for the annual report; the other two are held at the accountant's request without advance notice to the company.

Transfer Agent (Customer Services Agent)

The functions of the transfer agent are manifold; they include, among other duties, issuing and redeeming fund shares, handling name changes for the fund, sending out customer confirmations and sending out fund distributions.

The transfer agent can be the fund custodian or a separate service company. The fund pays the transfer agent a fee for these services.

Underwriter

The underwriter, often called the *sponsor* or *distributor*, markets fund shares, prepares sales literature and, in return, receives a percentage of the sales charge paid by the client. The underwriter's compensation is part of the sales load paid by the customer when shares are purchased. Sales fees are not part of the fund's expenses.

In general, open-end investment companies (issuers) may not also act as the distributors (underwriters). For example, the distributor for the JH Mutual Fund must be a separate and distinct entity from the JH Mutual Fund, even though it may be called JH Distributors. Section 12b-1 of the 1940 act provides an exception to this prohibition and allows a fund to charge a fee to cover its expenses for acting as its own distributor.

The underwriter (distributor) of funds receives a fee for selling and promoting the fund shares to the public. This fee is in the form of a sales charge. Except for offerings defined as *contractual plans*, sales charges cannot exceed 8.5 percent. The underwriter is hired as the head salesperson for the investment company. Obviously, this is an ongoing and important position. The board of directors appoints an underwriter (sponsor, or distributor) to sell fund shares to the public. The open-end investment company sells its shares to the underwriter at the current NAV, but only as the underwriter needs the shares to fill customer orders. The underwriter is prohibited from maintaining an inventory in open-end company shares. The underwriter is compensated by adding a sales charge to the share's NAV when it makes sales to the public.

Under the 1940 act, the contract between the investment company and the underwriter must be in writing and must have a maximum term of two years, after which time it may be extended on a year-to-year basis by the annual approval of the board of directors and/or a majority vote of the outstanding shares.

Organization of a Mutual Fund

Table 5.1 illustrates how a typical mutual fund is organized.

Table 5.1 Organization of a Mutual Fund

Manager	*Custodian/Transfer Agent*	*Underwriter*
Makes investment decisions	Holds assets	Distributes shares
Paid a percentage of NAV	Issues and redeems shares	Paid from sales charges
Two-year initial contract	Clerical duties	Two-year initial contract
Contract renewed annually	Paid a fee by the fund	Contract renewed annually

Bonding of Directors and Employees

An investment company, as well as each officer or employee of the investment company who has access to the company's cash or securities, must be bonded. The company may purchase separate bonds for each individual to be covered, or it may purchase a single bond that lists by name each employee to be covered within the company.

The amount of the bond must be determined by a majority of the noninterested directors at least once every 12 months. The SEC has set forth a schedule of minimum bonding requirements, determined by the investment company's gross assets at the end of the most recent fiscal quarter. A copy of the bond must be filed with the SEC. If a claim is made under the bond, the investment company must notify the SEC in writing of the nature and amount of the claim. The SEC must also be notified within five business days of the terms of a settlement of any such claim.

Officers and directors may be covered by the bond only for negligence. No bond protects an officer or a director from acts of willful malfeasance, bad faith or gross negligence or reckless disregard of his duties in the conduct of his office.

Information Distributed to Investors

Prospectus

In an effort to simplify and enhance its readability, the prospectus distributed to investors may come in two parts: the prospectus (called an *N1-A prospectus* or a *summary prospectus*) and a statement of additional information. The prospectus must be distributed to an investor before or during any solicitation for sale. The investor may obtain the statement of additional information from the fund upon request.

The prospectus contains information on the fund's objective, investment policies, sales charges, management expenses and services offered, as well as a 10-year history of per-share capital changes (performance). The statement of additional information typically contains the fund's consolidated financial statements, including the balance sheet, statement of operations, income statement and portfolio list at the time the statement was compiled.

Advertising Prospectus

The National Securities Markets Improvement Act of 1996 includes an amendment to the 1940 act that allows an investment company to distribute an *advertising prospectus*. An advertising prospectus offers considerably more flexibility than other permitted forms of advertising. The advertising prospectus is not restricted to the information disclosed in the summary prospectus, and it may include historical performance data. Unlike the summary prospectus, the advertising prospectus need not be filed as part of the registration statement.

Financial Reports

The act of 1940 requires that shareholders receive financial reports at least semiannually (every six months). Under the NSMIA, the SEC may now require reports to be provided more frequently to keep the information reasonably current. Investment companies are no longer required to state reporting requirements. These reports must contain:

- the investment company's balance sheet;
- a valuation of all securities in the investment company's portfolio on the date of the balance sheet (a portfolio list);
- the investment company's income statement;
- a complete statement of all compensation paid to the board of directors and to the advisory board; and
- a statement of the total dollar amount of securities purchased and sold during the period.

It is the principal's responsibility to see that each of these reports is current and accurately reflects the state of the company at the end of the reporting period. In addition, the company must send a copy of its balance sheet to any shareholder who makes a written request for one at any time between semiannual reports.

The investment company must be audited at least annually and distribute an audited annual report to every investor once a year.

Additional Disclosure Requirements

The SEC, in a continuing effort to give investors more information on which to evaluate the performance of mutual funds, requires a fund to include in its prospectus or annual reports:

- a discussion of those factors and strategies that materially affected its performance during its most recently completed fiscal year;
- a line graph comparing its performance to that of an appropriate broad-based securities market index; and
- the name(s) and title(s) of the person(s) primarily responsible for the day-to-day management of the fund's portfolio.

Fund performance. Fund management is required to discuss what happened to the fund during the previous fiscal year and why it happened. In its review, management is not obligated to evaluate the effectiveness of its strategies or the investment techniques used to achieve its performance.

Financial highlights. The prospectus must provide a simplified per-share table of condensed financial information. The table enables an investor to track the fund's operating performance on a per-share basis from its beginning net asset value to its ending net asset value. A line graph comparison of the fund's per-share performance to an appropriate broad-based securities market index must be provided. For example, a broadly diversified common stock fund touting an 18 percent rise in share value may lose some of its appeal when compared to the S&P 500, which has risen 26 percent during the same time frame.

Disclosure of advisers. Many investment advisers who have achieved stellar returns have attained celebrity status. A fund marketing its portfolio often advertises itself as being managed by the adviser "star," when in fact the fund is managed by a committee that may or may not include the personality advertised. To clarify and eliminate the potential for abuse, the prospectus must disclose the person(s) responsible for the day-to-day management of the fund's portfolio. Money-market and index funds are excluded from this requirement.

6 Other Federal Legislation

Key Terms

Chinese Wall Doctrine
contemporaneous traders
Insider Trading Act of 1988
Securities Investors Protection Act of 1970
Telephone Consumer Protection Act of 1991

Overview

The preceding chapters describe the registration and regulation requirements for securities, broker-dealers, agents and investment advisers on both the state and federal levels. The major acts addressed were the Uniform Securities Act, the Securities Exchange Act of 1933, the Securities Act of 1934 and the acts of 1940. Amendments to federal legislation were enacted under the National Securities Markets Improvement Act of 1996.

This chapter covers additional legislation that affects participants in the U.S. securities markets.

Securities Investor Protection Act of 1970

The Securities Investor Protection Corporation (SIPC) was established in 1970 with the passage of the Securities Investor Protection Act. The purpose of the act is to protect the customers of securities firms that go bankrupt. SIPC is a nonprofit corporation, not a government-sponsored corporation such as the Federal Deposit Insurance Corporation (FDIC).

Members include all broker-dealers registered under the Securities Exchange Act of 1934, all members of national securities exchanges and most NASD members.

Each separate customer at a broker-dealer firm is covered for a maximum of $500,000 in securities and cash. Of that amount, up to $100,000 in cash is covered. Equity in margin accounts is covered up to $500,000. Commodities accounts are not covered. Customers with claims beyond $500,000 are treated as general creditors on the excess amount.

A person who has several accounts in her own name at one broker-dealer firm still has maximum coverage of $500,000 because the protection is $500,000 *per separate customer, not per account*. That customer could, however, have several accounts at one broker-dealer firm in different forms of ownership.

When a member firm is in financial trouble, SIPC requests that a federal district court appoint a trustee, whose responsibilities include:

- supervising the SIPC member's orderly liquidation
- notifying clients of the liquidation
- returning clients' identifiable securities

When notified, clients file claims with the trustee to receive any monies or securities due them.

Insider Trading and Securities Fraud Enforcement Act of 1988

Policies and procedures. The Insider Trading and Securities Fraud Enforcement Act of 1988 expanded the definition of, and the liabilities and penalties for, the illicit use of nonpublic information established by the Securities Exchange Act of 1934. Insiders, including officers, directors and 10 percent shareholders, may be held liable for more than just transactions in their own accounts. The act recognizes the insider's fiduciary responsibility to the issuer, to the stockholders and to others who might be affected by trades made with insider knowledge. Investors who have suffered monetary damage because of insider trading have legal recourse against the insider and against any other party who had control over the misuse of nonpublic information.

An insider is any person who has access to nonpublic information about a corporation. Insiders may not use inside information as a basis for personal trading until that information has been made public. The SEC can levy a civil penalty of up to three times the amount of profit made or loss avoided if inside information is used. Any individual who is a corporate insider and owns securities in that corporation must file a statement of ownership with the SEC. Inside information is any information that has not been disseminated to, or is not readily available to, the general public. To determine whether information is nonpublic, the SEC considers the method by which the information is released to the public and the timing of trades relative to when other people also have the information.

Chinese Wall Doctrine

The Chinese Wall Doctrine is a descriptive name for the restrictions against sharing potentially material information between departments of a firm. Those departments or branches of a broker-dealer that have access to material nonpublic information, such as the legal department, the investment banking division and the various security analysts, may not disseminate this information to anyone who could conceivably trade on it. Firms must erect a "wall" between those who have information and those who do not in order to prevent possible violations of the law.

Written supervisory procedures. All broker-dealers must establish written supervisory procedures specifically prohibiting the use of material nonpublic information by all persons interested in, affiliated with or in any way engaged in the broker-dealers' securities-related activities. Once these procedures are established, broker-dealers must actively maintain and enforce them.

SEC investigations. The SEC has the right to investigate any person who has violated or is suspected of violating any of the provisions of the Insider Trading Act. The Commission also has the right to require anyone who has violated the act or is suspected of a violation to file a written statement with the SEC covering all of the facts and circumstances relating to the suspected violation.

The Commission also has the right to exempt anyone involved in a violation of the act from prosecution if it decides that it would be in the public interest to do so or that it would be necessary for the protection of investors.

Insider Trading Rules

The key elements of tipper and tippee liability under the insider trading rules are as follows:

- Does the tipper owe a fiduciary duty to a company or its stockholders, and has he breached it?
- Does the tipper meet the personal benefits test, even something as simple as enhancing a friendship or reputation?
- Does the tippee know or should the tippee have known that the information was inside or confidential?
- Is the information material and nonpublic?

Given these elements, a "slip of the tongue" by a corporate insider could leave that person liable under the rules, and anyone who trades on information that she knows or should know is not public is also liable.

Civil Penalties

Profits gained and losses avoided. When determining how much profit was made (or loss avoided) by the inside trader, the Commission looks at the security's market price a reasonable period after the information becomes general public knowledge. The difference between this price and the price the trader obtained is the profit or loss against which penalties are set.

Control. It is important to establish who had control over the violation or the person who committed the violation. A controlling person who knew of the violation is just as liable as the person who actually committed the misuse of nonpublic information.

Limitations to this liability exist. The simple fact that a person normally has control over another, such as the control a branch manager has over a registered rep, does not imply guilt. The Commission establishes the full extent of a person's control and involvement before it exacts any penalties.

Disgorging short-swing profits. Insiders may not retain short-swing profits (those occurring in six months or less) in securities; any short-swing profit must be repaid (disgorged) by the insider. Insiders are prohibited from establishing short-against-the-box positions and entering short sales. Any trading of insider-owned securities must be reported to the SEC within 10 days of the trade.

Criminal Penalties

The criminal penalties for violations of securities laws were increased through an amendment to the act of 1934. If a person is convicted of willfully violating federal securities regulations or of knowingly making false or misleading statements in any registration document, that person can be fined up to $1 million, sentenced to prison for up to 10 years or both. The maximum fine is $2.5 million for other than a natural person.

Contemporaneous Traders

Any person who has entered trades that have violated the insider trading regulations or who has communicated material nonpublic information to someone who has violated these regulations may be liable to contemporaneous traders and may be sued in a court of law. The concept of **contemporaneous traders** is a relatively recent addition to federal securities regulation. A contemporaneous trader is any person who enters a trade at or near the same time and in the same security as a person who has inside information.

Statute of limitations. A lawsuit can be brought in court by anyone who, at the same time, bought (if the insider sold) or sold (if the insider bought) securities of the same class. The suit may be initiated up to five years after the violation, and the damages imposed under a lawsuit of this kind can go up to the profits the insider made or the losses he avoided.

Procedures for collection. If the Commission imposes a monetary penalty for violations of the 1988 act, the penalty is payable directly to the Treasury of the United States. The U.S. attorney general has been given the authority and responsibility to collect any penalties imposed and may do so through the U.S. district courts if necessary.

Misuse of Nonpublic Information

The Investment Advisers Act of 1940 established strict regulations concerning the use and misuse of nonpublic information. Every investment adviser must establish, maintain and enforce written policies and procedures devoted to preventing violations of the rules covering nonpublic (inside) information.

Telephone Communications with the Public

The Telephone Consumer Protection Act of 1991 (TCPA), administered by the Federal Communications Commission (FCC), was enacted to protect consumers from unwanted telephone solicitations. A telephone solicitation is defined as a telephone call initiated for the purpose of encouraging the purchase of or investment in property, goods or services. The act governs commercial calls, recorded solicitations from autodialers, and solicitations and advertisements to facsimile machines and modems (E-mail). The act requires any organization that performs telemarketing (in particular, cold calling)—including a broker-dealer—to:

- maintain a "do-not-call list" of customers who do not want to be called and keep a customer's name on the list for 10 years from the time the request is made;
- institute a written policy (available on demand) on maintenance procedures for the "do-not-call list";
- train reps on using the list;
- ensure that reps acknowledge and immediately record the names and telephone numbers of customers who ask not to be called again;
- ensure that anyone making cold calls for the firm informs the customer of the firm's name and telephone number or address;
- ensure that telemarketers do not call customers within 10 years of a do-not-call request; and
- ensure that telephone solicitations occur between the hours of 8:00 am and 9:00 pm of the time zone in which a customer is located.

The act exempts calls made:

- to parties with whom the caller has an established business relationship or where the caller has prior express permission or invitation;
- on behalf of a tax-exempt nonprofit organization;
- for no commercial purpose; and
- for legitimate debt collection purposes.

7 Uniform Securities Act Review Exam

In questions 1 through 21, write "T" (true) if the phrase fits the definition of a security and write "F" (false) if it does not.

1. ______ U.S. Treasury bond
2. ______ Annuity that pays the same amount of money each month
3. ______ Annuity that pays a varying amount of money each month
4. ______ Certificate of interest in a profit-sharing agreement
5. ______ Keogh (HR-10) plan
6. ______ Collateral trust certificate
7. ______ Preorganization certificate
8. ______ Savings and loan account passbook
9. ______ Interest in an oil and gas drilling program
10. ______ Interest in a real estate condominium
11. ______ Term insurance policy
12. ______ Interest in farmland or animals
13. ______ Final prospectus for an oil and gas corporation
14. ______ Option contract for wheat
15. ______ Interest in a whiskey warehouse receipt
16. ______ Evidence of indebtedness, such as an interest in a condominium pool
17. ______ American Express money order
18. ______ Written confirmation of a sale of AT&T common stock
19. ______ Interest in a multilevel distributorship arrangement
20. ______ Interest in a merchandise marketing plan
21. ______ Interest in an oil, gas or mining title or lease, or in payments out of production under such a title or lease

In questions 22 through 27, write "T" (true) if the phrase fits the definition of a person and write "F" (false) if it does not.

22. ______ Unincorporated investment club
23. ______ Canadian national government

24. ______ State of New York

25. ______ Microscam, Inc.

26. ______ Individual investor

27. ______ Securities brokerage firm

In questions 28 through 31, write "T" (true) if the phrase fits the definition of a nonissuer transaction and write "F" (false) if it does not.

28. ______ Primary transaction

29. ______ Transaction between persons on a stock exchange

30. ______ Stock offering by Kelptek, Inc.

31. ______ Trade between two OTC brokers

In questions 32 through 36, write "T" (true) if the person described must register as a broker-dealer and write "F" (false) if not.

32. ______ Person who has no place of business in the state and deals exclusively with 10 institutional clients

33. ______ Person who has no place of business in the state and deals exclusively with other broker-dealers

34. ______ Person who has no place of business in the state and effects transactions exclusively with issuers of securities

35. ______ Person who has no place of business in the state and directs an offer to an existing customer with less than 30 days' temporary residency.

36. ______ Brokerage firm doing retail business in the state

In questions 37 through 44 concerning agents as defined by the Uniform Securities Act, write "T" if the statement is true and write "F" if the statement is false.

37. ______ An agent is a broker-dealer.

38. ______ The term "agent" includes an individual who effects transactions in municipal securities for a broker-dealer.

39. ______ The term "agent" includes an individual who represents an issuer in effecting transactions in six-month commercial paper.

40. ______ An agent can only be an individual.

41. ______ The term "agent" includes an individual who effects transactions in common stocks.

42. ______ An agent who represents an issuer in effecting transactions with savings institutions or trust companies is not an agent and does not have to register.

43. ______ A partner of a broker-dealer is an agent if she attempts to effect securities transactions, but is not successful at the attempts.

44. ______ The term "agent" includes a person who represents an issuer in a transaction with an underwriter.

In questions 45 through 49, write "T" (true) if the security could be sold to the public legally by an individual who represents the issuer but who is not a registered agent and write "F" (false) if the security could not be sold to the public legally by such an individual.

45. ______ Common stock issued by Mountain Brewing of Canada

46. ______ Bonds issued by the Canadian government

47. ______ Debentures issued by Worthmore, Moola Savings and Loan

48. ______ Commercial paper with a six-month maturity

49. ______ Preferred stock listed on stock exchanges

In questions 50 through 56, write "T" (true) if the phrase fits the definition of an investment adviser as defined under the USA and write "F" (false) if it does not.

50. ______ Bank that specifically sells portfolio and investment advice

51. ______ Accountant who designs a portfolio approach for a client to include tax strategies, and charges for this service

52. ______ Broker-dealer that helps a client construct a suitable portfolio and charges a small fee for this service

53. ______ Person who sells to subscribers his own investment advice letter on specific investments and who has no direct contact with the subscribers

54. ______ Publisher of a business news magazine with national circulation

55. ______ Person who sells investment advice regarding U.S. government securities

56. ______ Person acting as an investment adviser who has not been designated by the state administrator as exempt

In questions 57 through 59 concerning issuers, write "T" if the statement is true and write "F" if it is false.

57. ______ In a new offering of shares of Acme Sweatsocks, Inc., the company itself would be considered the issuer.

58. ______ The term "issuer" does not distinguish between persons who issue and persons who propose to issue securities.

59. ______ When Kelptek, Inc. issues bonds, the president of the corporation is considered an issuer.

60. What is a transaction called when there is no benefit to the issuer?

A. Primary transaction
B. Nonprofit transaction
C. Issuer transaction
D. Nonissuer transaction

61. What is the official designation of the person or agency that enforces the Uniform Securities Act in each state?

A. Transfer agent
B. Registrar
C. Issuer
D. Administrator

62. What does "guaranteed" mean when the word is used to describe a security?

A. The broker-dealer will buy the security back at the same price or higher.
B. The security has been cleared and is backed by the SEC.
C. The security has a backer that guarantees the payment of principal and interest.
D. The security is an annuity product that guarantees a retirement income.

63. What is the difference between an offer and a sale?

A. An offer is the attempt to sell, and a sale is a binding contract to transfer a security for value.
B. An offer is a binding proposal to sell, and a sale is a nonbinding proposal to sell.
C. An offer can be made only by a customer, and a sale can be made only by a broker-dealer.
D. An offer must be approved by a branch manager, and a sale needs no approval.

64. What is the smallest order that can be placed for an institutional account?

A. $50,000 or 1,000 shares
B. $100,000 or 2,500 shares
C. $100,000 or 5,000 shares
D. There is no limit on institutional order sizes.

In questions 65 through 67 concerning the registration of broker-dealers, write "T" if the statement is true and write "F" if it is false.

65. ______ The administrator may require minimum net capital for broker-dealers.

66. ______ The administrator may require a surety bond.

67. ______ Officers of a broker-dealer may be required to take registration examinations after the broker-dealer is registered in a state.

In questions 68 through 72 concerning the registration of agents, write "T" if the statement is true and write "F" if it is false.

68. ______ When an agent changes his place of employment, only the new employer is responsible for notifying the administrator.

69. ______ The Uniform Securities Agent State Law Examination is accepted by most states, which means that the administrators will have no further examination requirements for agents.

70. ______ An agent's license is effective only while the agent represents a registered broker-dealer.

71. ______ The registration of a broker-dealer automatically registers every partner, officer and director of the same firm as an agent.

72. ______ An agent representing a broker-dealer lives in one state and would like to do business in another state. No registration is necessary in the other state as long as the agent's activities are limited exclusively to effecting transactions in certain securities exempted under the Uniform Securities Act.

73. Under the national de minimis, investment advisers are exempt from state registration if they solicit how many clients within the year?

A. Less than 6
B. Less than 10
C. Less than 25
D. Less than 30

In questions 74 through 75, write "T" (true) if the person may transact business legally as an investment adviser in that state and write "F" (false) if he may not.

74. ______ The person is not registered, and his clientele is limited to banks and individuals.

75. ______ The person is registered as a broker-dealer only, and gives investment advice for special compensation beyond the scope of her broker-dealer practice.

In questions 76 through 79 concerning registration procedures, write "T" if the statement is true and write "F" if it is false.

76. ______ An application is the only document that needs to be filed if a broker-dealer, an agent or an investment adviser is to be granted registration by the state administrator.

77. ______ An application must contain whatever information the administrator requires.

78. ______ An applicant's financial condition and history are not registration considerations.

79. ______ An applicant's proposed method of doing business is a registration consideration.

In questions 80 and 81 concerning post-licensing requirements, write "T" if the statement is true and write "F" if it is false.

80. ______ Unless the administrator rules otherwise, the investment adviser of a registered investment company must maintain records for three years.

81. ______ Sales materials and advertisements for registered investment companies must be filed with the administrator before they are used.

82. The National Securities Markets Improvement Act of 1996 affected federal and state laws in which of the following ways?

    A. The Uniform Securities Act will now supersede the Investment Advisers Act of 1940.
    B. Federal law will preempt state law.
    C. State law will preempt federal law.
    D. Federal law and state law will remain the same.

83. Which of the following is a type of security registration that allows the administrator to require any information he decides is necessary?

    A. Coordination
    B. Filing
    C. Qualification
    D. Modulation

84. Which of the following is a type of state security registration that is used when a security is being registered simultaneously with the SEC under the Securities Act of 1933?

    A. Coordination
    B. Qualification
    C. Implementation
    D. Integration

85. Which of the following require(s) no specific response from the state administrator before the securities registration becomes effective?

    I. Coordination
    II. Filing
    III. Qualification
    IV. Conjugation

    A. I
    B. I and II
    C. II, III and IV
    D. II and IV

In questions 86 through 100, write "E" if the security is exempt and write "NE" if the security is nonexempt.

86. ______ Over-the-counter call option

87. ______ Security issued by the national government of Germany

88. ______ Security issued by a province of Canada

89. ______ Security issued by a political subdivision of Mexico

90. ______ U.S. Treasury note

91. ______ Church bond

92. ______ Commercial paper

93. ______ U.S. Treasury bill

94. ______ First offering of stock issued by a manufacturing company

95. ______ Stock issued by Madre Merryl Federal Savings and Loan Association

96. ______ Common stock in Seven Seas Freightways

97. ______ Stock listed exclusively on the London Stock Exchange

98. ______ Preferred stock issued by Amalgamated Featherbedders of Canada and listed on the NYSE

99. ______ Certain Nasdaq securities in certain states

100. ______ Interest in warehouse receipts

In questions 101 through 111 concerning exempt transactions under the Uniform Securities Act, write "T" if the statement is true and write "F" if it is false.

101. ______ An agent is not required to be registered in a state if the transaction he solicits is exempt.

102. ______ A private placement is a method of selling nonregistered securities.

103. ______ A sale to a sophisticated investor, such as an insurance company, is an exempt transaction whether or not the security sold is exempt.

104. ______ An agent may solicit orders in unregistered securities if his clients will sign statements that orders are unsolicited.

105. ______ An agent may execute secondary trades in nonexempt unregistered securities if he limits the number of transactions to no more than 10 in any 12-month period.

106. ______ A manual exemption allows a security to be offered even if it is not registered in a state.

107. ______ A manual exemption provides for an exempt transaction. It does not make the security itself exempt.

108. ______ Unsolicited orders are exempt transactions.

109. ______ All executor transactions are exempt.

110. ______ No commissions may be charged in a private placement if the transaction is to qualify as an exempt transaction.

111. ______ A private placement involves the sale of exempt securities.

In questions 112 through 125, indicate whether you think the action described is lawful or unlawful and explain your decision.

112. ALFA Enterprises paid four quarterly dividends of $.25 each during the last calendar year. In addition, it paid a special $1 year-end dividend because of an extraordinary item of income. An agent informs his client that owning ALF shares should provide an ever-increasing income in the form of dividends because of the dramatic increase authorized by the board at year-end.

____

____

Use the following information to answer questions 113 through 116. Three years ago, General Gizmonics, Inc. earned $2 per share. Two years ago, earnings dropped to $1 per share. Last year, the earnings per share were $2. Analysts have projected earnings of $3 per share this year.

	EPS	% Change
Estimate for this year	$3	50%
Actual, last year	$2	100%
Actual, two years ago	$1	– 50%
Actual, three years ago	$2	0%

113. An agent tells his client that earnings have increased at an average rate of 75 percent.

____

____

114. An agent tells his client that earnings dropped 50 percent two years ago, increased 100 percent last year and are expected to rise another 50 percent this year. Earnings, he states, thus show an average increase of 33 1/3 percent a year.

____

____

115. An agent tells his client that earnings were $2 per share three years ago and are expected to reach $3 per share this year. He says a 50 percent increase over a four-year period averages to 12.5 percent per year.

____

____

116. An agent tells his client that he likes the potential of General Gizmonics over the long term, but points out that there is quite a bit of risk associated with buying the stock. He explains the risk of using simple averages when discussing the company's earnings and illustrates his point by showing the client that there was a 50 percent reduction in earnings two years ago and that the 100 percent increase in earnings last year offset the earlier reduction.

____

____

117. An agent tells his client that the net earnings figure is the best indicator of a particular company's progress because recent stock offerings distort comparisons on a per-share basis.

____

____

118. An agent tells his client that a company has finally "graduated" to the level of quality acceptable to the New York Stock Exchange. He recommends the stock to the client based on the Exchange's stringent earnings requirements for listing.

____

____

119. An agent informs his client that he thinks the common stock of a company will be listed on a national securities exchange. The agent is basing his prediction on his "feel" for the market.

____

____

120. An agent offers a stock to a client with no markup or commission. The current quote is 14–14 1/2. The client's order is filled at 14 3/4.

____

____

121. An agent informs his client that SEC and state approval finally have been received on a new issue so that an offering now can be released.

____

____

122. The credit department of a broker-dealer calls one of the agents to inform him that margin requirements dictate that one of his clients deposit $2,000. Knowing that the client does not have $2,000 excess cash at this time, the agent calls the client and suggests that the client sell shares of one of his securities in the margin account. The agent thinks this sale would meet the margin call and at the same time make it unnecessary to worry the customer by informing him of the margin call.

____

____

123. As a standard part of his prospecting presentation, an agent promises each of his prospects that he will supply him with copies of each item he sees in all of the major financial publications that have to do with the client's security positions. Normally, the agent does not have time for this, but every few months, when business is slow, he sends out a few items.

____

____

124. As a standard part of his prospecting presentation, an agent promises to perform all tax services and portfolio analysis for a client. He took a tax course in college, but knows he is not always up on current laws and generally tries to avoid filling out clients' forms unless they really push for it.

____

____

125. An agent offers a security to his client, and the offer is accepted. The trade is executed at $27 per share. One week later, the stock is trading at $20 per share and the agent does not want to inform his client of this fact. He tells the client that the price of the stock is still in the $27 area, but circumstances have changed and the client should liquidate now to avoid a loss. When the liquidation is executed at $20, the agent calls the client and apologizes for the precipitous drop in price just prior to the client's taking advantage of the agent's astute advice.

____

____

In questions 126 and 127 concerning what constitutes the fraudulent or misleading omission of material facts, indicate whether you think the action described is lawful or unlawful and explain your decision.

126. An agent wants to make a short but efficient presentation to a number of clients, but realizes that he cannot cover everything. To save time, he deliberately "sorts out" material facts regarding a company he is recommending.

____

____

127. At a time of a 50 percent margin, a client buys $20,000 worth of securities with a deposit of $10,000 cash. When he makes the purchase, the client informs the agent that he cannot afford a loss that would exceed $4,000. Later, trading is halted in the stock owing to an influx of sale orders. When the stock reopens, the market value has dropped in half and a margin call is sent to the client in the amount of $3,000. When informed that he is down $10,000 on paper, the client is stunned. He cannot understand how he has lost all of his money and still needs to pay an additional $3,000.

____

____

In questions 128 and 129 concerning the fraudulent or deceitful use of material inside information, indicate whether you think the action described is lawful or unlawful and explain your decision.

128. While visiting a publicly held corporation, an agent overhears that the company has just lost its largest client to a competitor. Because of this knowledge, the agent decides to discontinue his efforts to sell the common stock of this corporation.

____

____

129. An agent hears from a friend that a publicly held company has just lost its largest client to a competitor. He decides to sell the stock short in his brother's account.

____

____

In questions 130 through 134 concerning the requirement that agents' recommendations and transactions be suitable for individual clients, indicate whether you think the action described is lawful or unlawful and explain your decision.

130. An 80-year-old man with limited resources wants to purchase shares of a speculative new company. Before his agent asks any questions, the man informs him that he will buy the stock either from him or from another agent across the street. The agent opens a new account and enters the order marked "unsolicited."

____

____

131. An agent with a large clientele of individual investors decides to recommend that each client purchase shares of stock in a new company that has expertise in the area of solar power.

____

____

132. An agent sells 1,000 shares of a $50 security to a new account. One week later, he finds that the customer does not have enough funds to make the full payment.

____

____

133. One agent has been following the recommendations of another agent in the office because each of the other agent's recommendations has had an impressive performance. Therefore, as soon as the second agent begins selling a new investment idea, the first agent picks up the phone and offers it to all of his clients, too.

____

____

134. In the last week of the commission month, an agent recommends the sale of FLB and purchase of DOH to clients who own FLB. To clients who own DOH, he recommends the sale of DOH and the purchase of FLB.

____

____

In questions 135 through 137, use the following information and indicate whether you think the action described is lawful or unlawful; explain your decision.

An agent hears from another agent a rumor about a possible buyout of Greater Health, Inc. at book value. The book value of the company is $15 per share and the current market value is $10 per share.

135. The agent calls several clients and suggests purchase because of an impending buyout at $15 per share.

____

____

136. The agent discusses the rumor with his branch manager to determine what action, if any, could be taken.

____

____

137. The agent takes a careful look at Greater Health, Inc. He decides the investment merit of GHI is good regardless of a buyout and begins recommending it to some of his clients. He does not include any reference to the potential buyout and feels that, if it does happen, it would be a pleasant surprise for the clients who own the stock.

____

____

In questions 138 through 149 concerning prohibited business practices, indicate whether you think the action described is lawful or unlawful and explain your decision.

138. An agent opens an individual account for Randy Bear. By way of a referral from Randy, the agent also opens an individual account for Hugh Heifer, who is Randy's partner. Both Randy and Hugh purchase identical portfolios from the agent. In a telephone conversation, Randy informs the agent that one particular security should be liquidated from each individual account. The agent does this.

____

____

139. An agent receives an unsolicited order from a client to purchase shares of an obscure foreign merchant bank. After days of toil and transatlantic telephone calls, the exhausted trader triumphantly reports an execution. In addition to the usual commission charge, the broker-dealer adds the cost of the telephone calls. The client balks, feeling that the charges should be absorbed by the broker-dealer as a cost of doing business.

____

____

140. Ada Bullwether, a lifelong friend and neighbor of an agent, also happens to be that agent's largest client. During one particularly bad downturn in the market, the agent is faced with a margin call he cannot meet without liquidating some of the securities in his account. Mrs. Bullwether offers to transfer cash and securities from her own account into the agent's account. Rather than accept this offer, the agent has a legal and binding loan agreement drawn up and borrows $10,000 from Mrs. Bullwether.

____

____

141. An agent has a good client who is on vacation in Europe. While the client is gone, two limit orders fill, resulting in a net amount due from the client of $750. The agent knows the client is not a poor credit risk, but is unable to contact him. The agent deposits his own check for $750 so that the client is not sold out because of Federal Reserve Board regulations. Later, when the client returns from Europe, he gives the agent his check for $750.

____

____

142. A customer calls his agent and informs him that he must liquidate a security today. The customer has to have the funds available to him a week later, when an important business transaction is to be completed. The agent, rather than entering the sell order immediately, holds the order off until later in the day to get his customer a better price. As luck would have it, trading activity is suspended in the stock during the afternoon because of an impending news announcement. Several days later, it is learned that the stock probably will never open again because of bankruptcy proceedings.

____

____

143. An agent frantically tries to reach his customer regarding bad news about one of the customer's security positions. Finally, even though he cannot contact the customer, the agent enters an order to liquidate the security because he knows it is in the customer's best interest.

____

____

144. An agent enters an order from a person who, until now, has not been a client. He writes "new account" on the order form and turns in the new account information at the end of the trading day.

____

____

145. A client writes a blistering letter to an agent regarding stocks that the agent had recommended and that subsequently have performed very poorly. The agent decides not to forward the letter to his supervisor because he knows the analyst involved already is aware that he misread the market.

____

____

146. A client informs his agent that he wants to buy one share of each of the 30 companies that make up the Dow Jones Industrial Average. The client is shocked when he discovers that the agent's employer has charged $25 commission per share. He does not feel any better when he finds out that it is the employing broker-dealer's policy to charge a minimum of $25 commission on each order.

____

____

147. An agent sells his client 10 U.S. government bonds due to mature in 30 years. The agent tells the client that he has chosen these securities because there is "no way you can lose money on the safest security on earth."

____

____

148. An agent with extensive personal resources knows that a particular technical analyst is waiting for 20,000 shares of Quantum Rapid Search, Inc. stock to trade in one day before he recommends the security. Just for the fun of it, the agent buys 10,000 shares in the morning and sells 10,000 shares in the afternoon of the same day. Seeing the volume of the stock finally hitting 20,000 shares, the technical analyst promptly issues his buy recommendation.

____

____

149. An agent actively solicits orders for a new underwriting in his home state. The next day, he learns that the underwriting is not registered in his home state. Now, feeling lucky that his sales efforts have gone unrewarded, he ceases soliciting orders in this nonexempt security.

____

____

In questions 150 through 155, write "Y" (yes) if the action is in compliance with the Uniform Securities Act and write "N" (no) if it is not.

150. ______ An investment adviser assigns an advisory contract after providing written notice to the client.

151. ______ An adviser notifies his client that the president of the advisory corporation has left to start his own business.

152. ______ An investment adviser and his client enter into a contract that calls for the adviser to receive a fee of $10,000 plus 30 percent of any profits or less 40 percent of any losses.

153. ______ An investment adviser and his client enter into a contract that calls for the adviser to receive a fee of $10,000 or 1/2 percent of the average annual assets, whichever is greater.

154. ______ An investment adviser takes custody of a client's securities and money with no further action on the adviser's part. There is no rule against such activity and he has a written contract with the client.

155. ______ A new investment adviser that as of yet has no customers notifies the administrator that it intends to have custody of customer assets. There is no rule against such activity.

156. Which of the following would justify an administrator's denial of a security's registration?

I. The order is in the public interest.
II. The company has not been paying dividends.
III. The underwriter's compensation is excessive.

A. I
B. I and II
C. I and III
D. III

157. Which of the following would justify an administrator's suspension of an agent's registration?

I. The order is in the public interest.
II. The agent has been found guilty of a felony.
III. The agent is being sued by a client.

A. I only
B. I and II only
C. II only
D. I, II and III

In questions 158 through 162, write "T" if the statement is true and write "F" if it is false.

158. ______ The administrator must give notice of his orders to persons negatively affected.

159. ______ Any person negatively affected by an order of an administrator must be offered a hearing.

160. ______ Suspension of an agent is reason enough for an administrator to suspend automatically the agent's entire firm.

161. ______ Suspension of an officer or a director of a brokerage firm does not authorize the administrator to proceed against the entire firm.

162. ______ If the administrator finds that it is in the public interest to do so, he may deny an investment adviser's registration on the grounds of lack of experience.

163. Which of the following would exonerate the seller from civil suit resulting from an illegal sale made in a state?

A. The seller offers to buy back the security sold.
B. The security sold pays income that exceeds 6 percent.
C. The buyer already has disposed of the security.
D. The seller reimburses the buyer for any losses incurred within one year.

164. An agent works for a brokerage firm in Illinois, and his client lives in Illinois. The agent makes an offer to the client by phone while the client is vacationing in California. The client accepts the offer while still in California. The client travels to Texas before returning home and sends payment for the security from there. He makes his payment by sending a check from a money-market fund based in Ohio. The administrator(s) of which state(s) have authority over the sale?

I. Illinois
II. California
III. Texas
III. Ohio

A. I only
B. I and II only
C. II, III and IV only
D. I, II, III and IV

165. Which of the following statements is(are) true regarding civil liabilities when a sale violates provisions of the Uniform Securities Act?

I. A buyer may not sue for compensation later than three years after the sale.
II. A rescission offer must include interest.
III. A rescission offer must be at a current price.

A. I only
B. I and II only
C. II only
D. I, II and III

166. Registration statements are effective

A. for a period of time determined by the administrator for each issue
B. for one year from the effective date
C. for one year from the date of issue
D. until the next registration statement is filed

167. Which of the following statements are true regarding registration of securities by coordination?

I. The cooling-off period for the SEC is 20 days.
II. The registration statement must be on file with the state administrator for 10 days.
III. The registration becomes effective in the state only after the state's cooling-off period.
IV. The registration becomes effective at the state level in conjunction with the SEC if the administrator has not entered an order to deny it.

A. I, II and IV only
B. II and III only
C. III and IV only
D. I, II, III and IV

168. All of the following are exempt securities EXCEPT

I. U.S. government securities
II. unsolicited transactions
III. transactions between issuers and underwriters
IV. securities of credit unions

A. I, II and IV
B. I and IV
C. II and III
D. IV

169. An agent finds out from his uncle, an office manager at Microscam, that Microscam is going to acquire Datawaq. The agent should

A. call all of his customers and tell them to buy Datawaq
B. call all of his customers and tell them to sell short Microscam
C. inform his supervisor or principal
D. buy the stock in his mother's account

170. An agent has a good customer with a margin account. The customer informs the agent that he is taking a business trip for a month. He tells the agent to handle the account. While the customer is gone, the stock market goes down and the customer receives a margin call for $1,000. The agent should

A. pay the $1,000 on behalf of his good customer and collect at a later date
B. arrange a loan from a local bank to cover the margin call
C. sell some securities in the account and use the proceeds to cover the margin call
D. try to make contact with the customer and, failing that, inform his principal and do nothing until instructed

171. An agent and his sister open a special cash account at the agent's broker-dealer. Both parties contribute $5,000 to the account and purchase $10,000 worth of securities. The agent

A. can open the account, but cannot share in any profits
B. can share in the profits to the extent of his proportional contribution with written employer and customer consent
C. needs only the employer's consent to open the account and can share in the profits
D. cannot share in any profits

172. An agent gets a phone call from the wife of a customer. The wife wants to sell $25,000 worth of securities and use the proceeds as a down payment on a house. The account is in her husband's name, but she says he told her to sell the securities. The agent knows the couple to be happily married. He should

A. call the husband immediately and confirm the order
B. sell as instructed
C. get permission from his principal
D. tell the couple that the purchase of a house is a bad investment

173. A customer asks an agent for advice in choosing a balanced mutual fund for an IRA. The agent may state which of the following?

A. "Last year, ArGood Mutual Fund was up 40 percent. Based on this past performance, I expect the trend to continue, thus making it suitable for an IRA."
B. "I guarantee that you will make money in ArGood Mutual Fund over a long period of time based on past performance, making it a good investment for an IRA."
C. "Last year, ArGood Mutual Fund was up 40 percent. However, over the last 10 years, ArGood had both up and down periods. The potential for gain does exist; however, there is no guarantee as to how much gain or loss will take place."
D. "ArGood Mutual Fund is such a good buy that I will guarantee against any losses personally."

174. The net asset value in NavCo Mutual Fund is $9 per share. Currently, the fund pays $.60 per share in annual dividends and $2 in capital gains distributions. The projections for the next year are $.75 per share in annual dividends and $2.50 per share in capital gains distributions. The agent could state which of the following to the customer?

A. "Currently, the NavCo Mutual Fund has paid $.60 per share in dividends and guarantees to pay $.75 per share this year."
B. "The current yield in NavCo Mutual Fund is 6.7 percent. However, the research report on NavCo Mutual Fund projects the possibility of a higher current yield next year."
C. 'The fund is yielding 29 percent currently, and the expectation is for a higher rate of return for next year."
D. "The projected yield on the fund this year would be in the neighborhood of 36 percent."

175. A customer is upset with her agent for not servicing her account properly and sends him a complaint letter about his actions. The agent should

A. call the customer and apologize, promising to do a better job
B. tell the customer he is willing to make rescission
C. do nothing and hope that he doesn't hear any more about it
D. bring the customer complaint to his employer immediately

176. Which of the following would NOT be considered a market manipulation?

A. Three market markers intentionally start buying and selling the same security simultaneously in their own accounts.
B. A specialist buys and sells stock for his own account.
C. A principal in a broker-dealer allows a rumor to leak out that Kelptek is going to acquire Consolidated Codfish. After a few days, the broker-dealer sells short Consolidated Codfish for its own account.
D. All of the above are examples of market manipulation.

177. In order to get a sale of $10,000 worth of bonds, an agent promises to balance a customer's checkbook each month for as long as the customer remains an account of his, even though the agent is in line for a promotion and an office transfer. This is considered a(n)

A. acceptable practice
B. unacceptable practice
C. practice that is not a violation; however, it is not a wise practice
D. acceptable practice if it is in accordance with house rules

178. According to the Uniform Securities Act, which of the following statements regarding state registration of securities is true?

A. Registration by filing is effective when so ordered by the administrator.
B. Registration by coordination is effective concurrently with federal registration.
C. Registration by qualification is effective after 30 days.
D. Registration by coordination is effective when so ordered by the administrator.

179. All of the following are examples of prohibited sales practices EXCEPT

A. buying on one exchange and selling on another
B. withholding a material fact from the buyer
C. buying and selling intentionally to show market activity
D. giving a phony quote

180. A customer has a discretionary account. The objective of the account is current income. The agent purchases a speculative growth stock. This is considered a(n)

A. wash sale
B. unauthorized transaction
C. acceptable transaction
D. matching activity

181. Under the Uniform Securities Act, if an investment adviser has custody of customer funds and securities, how often must the adviser send the customer a statement of account activity?

A. Annually
B. Quarterly
C. Monthly
D. With every transaction

182. Which of the following are examples of fraudulent practices?

I. Matched orders
II. Phony quotes
III. Material misrepresentations
IV. Wash sales

A. I and II only
B. I, II and III only
C. III and IV only
D. I, II, III and IV

183. Which of the following is an example of market manipulation?

A. Creating the illusion of active trading
B. Buying on one exchange and selling on another
C. Fictitious quotes to customers
D. Transactions in excess of customers' financial capabilities

184. As defined in the Uniform Securities Act, which of the following is NOT considered a security?

A. Fixed annuity
B. Stock option
C. Limited partnership unit
D. Commodity option

185. An agent fails to state facts in which a prudent investor would be interested. This action

A. is fraudulent under the USA for nonexempt securities only
B. is fraudulent under the USA for exempt securities only
C. is fraudulent under the USA for both exempt and nonexempt securities
D. does not constitute fraud if there was no willful intent to omit the information

186. A customer living in one state receives a phone call from an agent in another state. A transaction between the two occurs in yet another state. Under whose jurisdiction does the transaction fall?

A. Administrator of the state in which the customer lives
B. Administrator of the state in which the agent's office is located
C. Administrator of the state in which the transaction took place
D. Administrators of all three states involved

187. An agent who willfully violated state securities law is subject to which of the following?

I. Civil liabilities
II. Criminal penalties
III. Denial, suspension or revocation of registration as an agent by the administrator

A. I only
B. I and II only
C. III only
D. I, II and III

188. A person who sells securities in violation of state securities laws is civilly liable for which of the following?

I. Principal
II. Interest
III. Court costs
IV. Attorney's fees

A. I, II and IV only
B. I and III only
C. II, III and IV only
D. I, II, III and IV

189. An agent's license could be revoked if he were

A. convicted of a securities-related misdemeanor
B. declared insolvent
C. either convicted of a securities-related misdemeanor or declared insolvent
D. Once issued, an agent's license cannot be revoked.

190. Which of the following would subject an agent to a possible denial of registration?

I. Engagement in fraud in selling to an insurance company
II. Conviction of a security misdemeanor eight years ago
III. Insolvency
IV. Failure to pay filing fees

A. I only
B. I, II and III only
C. II, III and IV only
D. I, II, III and IV

191. Which of the following is a securities information processor?

A. Television channel that provides up-to-the-minute information on the current prices of specific stocks
B. Brokerage firm that provides its customers with securities prices on a continuing basis
C. Provider of a ticker tape service
D. Daily newspaper that includes a comprehensive financial section, listing prices of both stocks and mutual funds

192. According to the Uniform Securities Act, from which of the following customers may an investment adviser borrow money?

I. Affiliate of the investment adviser
II. Broker-dealer
III. Bank
IV. Issuer of blue chip stock

A. I, II and III
B. I and IV
C. II and III
D. III

193. Under the Uniform Securities Act, all of the following persons may provide investment advice incidental to their normal business without requiring registration as an investment adviser EXCEPT a(n)

A. teacher
B. economist
C. lawyer
D. engineer

194. Under the Uniform Securities Act, all of the following are excluded from the definition of broker-dealer EXCEPT a(n)

I. investment adviser
II. bank
III. issuer
IV. financial planner

A. I and III
B. I and IV
C. II and III
D. IV

◆ Answers & Rationale

1. **True**. U.S. government issues are securities.

2. **False**. Fixed annuities (those that pay a guaranteed, unchangeable amount each month) are specifically exempted from the definition of "securities."

3. **True**. The return of variable annuities is tied to the return on the underlying separate account, and because that account is generally invested in securities, the variable annuity is considered a security.

4. **True**. Certificates representing interests in pension and profit-sharing plans are included in the definition of "securities."

5. **False**. A Keogh plan is a retirement plan in which securities can be purchased or placed, but it is not a security itself.

6. **True**. Collateral trust certificates are included in the definition of "securities."

7. **True**. Preorganization certificates are included in the definition of "securities."

8. **False**. A passbook is not transferable and is not a security. Withdrawals may be made only by a person whose signature is on file for that specific account.

9. **True**. Interests in oil and gas drilling programs are included in the definition of "securities."

10. **True**. Interests in real estate condominiums are included in the definition of "securities."

11. **False**. Term policies are specifically exempted from the definition of "securities."

12. **True**. Interests in farmland or animals (racehorses, prize bulls, ostriches and so on) are included in the definition of "securities."

13. **False**. A prospectus is a document that constitutes an offer to sell specific securities. The prospectus itself has no monetary value and is not transferable.

14. **True**. Option contracts for wheat and other commodities (such as corn, natural gas and currencies) are included in the definition of "securities."

15. **True**. Whiskey warehouse receipts represent interests in a security and are included in the definition of "securities."

16. **True**. Evidences of indebtedness (such as an interest in a condominium pool or another type of collateralized note) are included in the definition of "securities."

17. **False**. A money order has a set value and is not an investment that could be transferable for a profit to a third party.

18. **False**. A confirmation of a securities transaction is used to confirm the particulars of the transaction (name of the security, number of shares and so on), but it is not itself a security.

19. **True**. Certificates representing interests in multilevel distributorship or marketing plans are included in the definition of "securities."

20. **True**. Certificates representing interests in merchandise marketing plans are included in the definition of "securities."

21. **True**. Certificates representing interests in oil and gas or mining titles and leases are included in the definition of "securities."

22. **True**. Unincorporated and incorporated investment clubs are included in the broad legal definition of "person."

23. **True.** All national and municipal governments are included in the broad legal definition of "person."

24. **True.** Legal entities such as the State of New York are included in the broad legal definition of "person."

25. **True.** Corporations, partnerships and sole proprietorships are all included in the broad legal definition of "person."

26. **True.** Individual investors are included in the broad legal definition of "person."

27. **True.** A securities brokerage firm, an investment adviser, an issuer and all others in the financial industry are included in the broad legal definition of "person."

28. **False.** Any transaction involving the primary offering of securities is considered an issuer transaction.

29. **True.** Any transactions in the secondary market, such as trades on an exchange, are considered nonissuer transactions.

30. **False.** An initial offering of stock from a corporation is considered an issuer transaction.

31. **True.** Any transactions in the secondary market, such as trades between over-the-counter broker-dealers or market makers, are considered nonissuer transactions.

32. **False.** A person who has not established a place of business in the state and who has a client base consisting exclusively of financial institutions need not register as a broker-dealer.

33. **False.** A person who deals only with other broker-dealers and who has no place of business in a state is not considered a broker-dealer.

34. **False.** A person who deals only with issuers and who has no place of business in a state is not considered a broker-dealer.

35. **False.** A broker-dealer with no place of business in a state is permitted to direct an offer into the state without being registered in the state if it meets certain conditions. The broker-dealer must be registered in another state where it has a place of business, and the offer must be directed to an existing customer who has less than 30 days' temporary residency.

36. **True.** A person (including a retail broker-dealer) who has established a place of business in a state must register as a broker-dealer.

37. **False.** An agent represents a broker-dealer.

38. **True.** Any individual who effects transactions in exempt securities for a broker-dealer is considered an agent. An individual who effects transactions in exempt securities, such as municipal or government securities, for an *issuer* is not considered an agent.

39. **False.** If the person had been effecting the transactions in commercial paper for a broker-dealer rather than an issuer, the individual would be considered an agent.

40. **True.** An agent is an individual person other than a broker-dealer who represents a broker-dealer or an issuer in effecting transactions in securities.

41. **True.** An agent is an individual person other than a broker-dealer who represents a broker-dealer or an issuer in effecting transactions in securities, including common stock.

42. **True.** An individual who effects exempt transactions does not have to register. Transactions with financial institutions are exempt transactions.

43. **True.** The Uniform Securities Act does not distinguish between attempting to effect a transaction and successfully effecting a transaction. If a partner, an officer or a director of a broker-dealer attempts to effect transactions for securi-

ties, she must be registered as an agent in that state.

44. **False**. An individual who effects transactions with an underwriter on behalf of an issuer is not considered an agent.

45. **False**. The securities of a foreign corporation could not be handled legally by a representative of an issuer who is not a registered agent.

46. **True**. A person representing an issuer in a transaction for an exempted security, such as bonds issued by the Canadian government, could handle the transaction legally without registering as an agent.

47. **True**. A person representing an issuer in a transaction for an exempted security, such as the securities issued by banks, savings and loans and trust companies, could handle the transaction legally without registering as an agent.

48. **True**. A person representing an issuer in a transaction for an exempted security, such as commercial paper, could handle the transaction legally without registering as an agent.

49. **False**. Exchange-listed securities of a corporation could not be handled legally by a representative of an issuer who is not a registered agent.

50. **False**. Banks, savings and loans and trust companies are not included in the definition of "investment adviser."

51. **False**. Lawyers, accountants, engineers and other professionals who advise others on investments incidentally to the practice of their own professions are not included in the definition of "investment adviser."

52. **True**. Anyone who engages in the business of giving investment advice for a fee is considered an investment adviser.

53. **True**. Impersonal advisory services include statistical information on specific investments which is made available to a specific group.

54. **False**. The publishers of a general circulation, business and financial newspaper or magazine that does not provide individualized advice are not included in the definition of "investment adviser."

55. **True**. Under the Uniform Securities Act, persons whose investment advice relates solely to exempt securities, such as U.S. government and municipal securities, are included in the definition of "investment adviser."

56. **True**. In addition to the standard exemptions from the definition of "investment adviser," the state administrator may designate any other person as exempt, as he sees fit.

57. **True**. A company that raises capital by issuing shares in itself is considered an issuer of securities.

58. **True**. The Uniform Securities Act does not distinguish between a proposed issue and an actual issue of securities in defining "issuer."

59. **False**. The president is not considered an issuer because it is the corporate person, Kelptek, Inc. that is issuing the securities.

60. **D.** Nonissuer transactions are any transactions that do not directly benefit an issuer.

61. **D.** The Uniform Securities Act specifies that the state's administrator (who also may be called the commissioner or secretary) has the authority to enforce the act in that state.

62. **C.** The security has a backer (such as an insurance company or a parent company) that has guaranteed the payment of principal, interest or dividends.

63. **A.** An offer is made in an attempt to sell. A sale is the binding contract to sell.

64. **D.** Although institutional investors typically trade very large blocks of securities, there is no upper or lower limit placed on the size of their trades.

65. **True.** The administrator in a state may require that broker-dealers seeking registration in that state have and maintain a certain minimum net capital.

66. **True.** An administrator may require a surety bond.

67. **True.** The administrator in a state has the right to require officers or executive officers of a broker-dealer to qualify by written or oral exam.

68. **False.** The agent, the new employer and the former employer all must notify the administrator.

69. **False.** The administrator may require other exams in addition to the Uniform Securities Agent State Law Examination (USASLE) of any reasonably defined class of persons (such as broker-dealers, state-registered investment advisers or representatives).

70. **True.** Licensing begins and ends with employment by a registered broker-dealer. Registration is not transferable and must be canceled and renewed when an agent changes employment.

71. **False.** Only those persons who are officers at the time the broker-dealer is registered and who act in the capacity of agents are registered automatically.

72. **False.** The person must be registered as an agent in any state in which she wishes to transact securities business, even if the securities or the transactions involved in any offer or sale are exempt from registration requirements.

73. **A.** Under the amended act, investment advisers are now exempt from registration in any one state if they solicit less than six clients within the year.

74. **False.** A person whose clients are individuals must be registered as an investment adviser in that state before transacting business.

75. **False.** If a broker-dealer receives special compensation for investment advice, she must be registered as an investment adviser.

76. **False.** A consent to service of process and a filing fee also must be filed to obtain a registration.

77. **True.** The administrator may ask for any information from the broker-dealer that he deems necessary.

78. **False.** Registered broker-dealers and state-registered investment advisers must file regular financial reports with the state administrator.

79. **True.** Broker-dealers and state-registered investment advisers must file with the state administrator a complete business methods proposal. Federally-registered investment advisers must give notice only to state administrators and pay filing fees.

80. **False.** The investment adviser of a registered investment company must register with the SEC only. Recordkeeping and reporting requirements are established by the SEC. State administrators have no jurisdiction over federally registered investment companies.

81. **False.** Under the NSMIA and the USA, registered investment companies are exempt from state registration and reporting requirements.

82. **B.** The National Securities Markets Improvement Act of 1996 defines the SEC's function and responsibilities as well as the state

securities administrators' authority level. Federal law now overrides state law.

83. **C.** In order to register a security by qualification, the issuer must file with the state administrator any registration documents and other information the administrator requires.

84. **A.** A registration by coordination is used when the issuer is registering the offering with the SEC at the same time. Copies of the registration documents filed with the SEC also are filed with the administrator of the state.

85. **B.** Registration by filing and by coordination become effective concurrently with the federal registration.

86. **Nonexempt**

87. **Exempt**

88. **Exempt**

89. **Nonexempt.** The only political subdivisions that are granted exempt status are in Canada.

90. **Exempt**

91. **Exempt**

92. **Exempt**

93. **Exempt**

94. **Nonexempt**

95. **Exempt**

96. **Exempt.** This corporation is a common carrier subject to the ICC.

97. **Nonexempt.** Securities listed on a U.S. securities exchange are exempt.

98. **Exempt**

99. **Exempt** or **nonexempt.** Some Nasdaq securities are exempt, and others are not.

100. **Nonexempt**

101. **False.** An agent must be registered to make solicitations in a state, whether the security is exempt or nonexempt. For example, to sell municipals in another state, the agent must be registered in that state.

102. **True.** Registration is not required if the securities are not distributed by means of public offering.

103. **True**

104. **False.** The key word is "solicit." One cannot solicit orders and then claim they were unsolicited.

105. **False.** The number of nonexempt unregistered secondary (nonissuer) transactions that can be made varies from state to state. For example, one state might permit only one transaction in any one 12-month period. Do not confuse this regulation with the rules governing private placements, which limit offerings to no more than 10 nonaccredited investors in any 12-month period. Private placements are primary (issuer) transactions.

106. **True**

107. **True**

108. **True.** The burden of proof that a transaction is unsolicited lies with the agent.

109. **True.** Executors are fiduciaries; therefore, the transactions are exempt.

110. **True.** Under the USA, no commissions may be paid for soliciting nonaccredited investors.

111. **False**. A private placement is an exempt transaction of nonexempt securities.

112. **Unlawful.** Implying that the $1 year-end special dividend was part of a normal dividend-paying procedure is misleading.

113. **Unlawful.** The earnings have increased at the rate of 75 percent for the last two years (100 percent and 50 percent). However, because this limited information does not tell the complete story of recent years' earnings, it is misleading.

114. **Unlawful.** The three percentages do average out to a 33 1/3 percent increase in earnings, but the statement is materially misleading. The 100 percent increase in the middle year simply offsets the 50 percent decrease of the previous year. This is a good example of the misuse of numbers that constitutes fraud.

115. **Unlawful.** This calculation is misleading because it does not inform the client of the decline that occurred in earnings per share. Leaving out material information constitutes fraud.

116. **Lawful**. Clearly, the agent is attempting to cover the material facts when discussing the earnings per share. No fraud is involved here.

117. **Unlawful.** Stock offerings bring in more capital. The additional capital usually produces additional earnings, so examining net earnings without offering a per-share comparison is misleading and fraudulent.

118. **Unlawful.** This agent should have pointed out that the Exchange listing requirements are, in many cases, quantitative, not qualitative. Acceptance for listing by the New York Stock Exchange does not necessarily reduce the risk of loss to the client. The agent's statement is misleading and, therefore, prohibited.

119. **Unlawful.** An agent's telling clients that exchange listing of a security is anticipated when he has no knowledge of the truth of such a statement is prohibited.

120. **Unlawful.** An execution price of 14 3/4 constitutes a markup of a quarter of a point. The agent has indicated there would be no markup.

121. **Unlawful.** Neither the SEC nor the state approves the accuracy or the adequacy of information regarding a new issue.

122. **Unlawful.** The agent misrepresents the status of the account to the client. He also induces the client to make a transaction that might not be suitable at that time.

123. **Unlawful**. An agent's promising to perform certain services on a client's behalf when he has no intent to perform those services is a prohibited activity.

124. **Unlawful.** With rare exception, this action constitutes promising to perform certain services on a client's behalf without any intent to perform those services or without being properly qualified to perform those services.

125. **Unlawful.** Misrepresenting to clients the status of their accounts is prohibited.

126. **Unlawful.** Obviously, an agent cannot give every fact in his sales presentation, but he must give all material facts.

127. **Unlawful.** The agent failed to describe sufficiently the important facts and risks concerning a transaction or set of transactions.

128. **Lawful.** Because the agent has material nonpublic information, he is considered an insider and cannot take advantage of the information. On the other hand, this agent's continuing to recommend the stock would not be in the best interest of his clients and would mean he would have to withhold material facts.

129. **Unlawful.** An agent must not take advantage of inside information.

130. **Unlawful.** This agent failed to make a reasonable inquiry as to the customer's needs and

objectives. Refusing to do business may be the only good business practice available to an agent in certain situations.

131. **Unlawful.** This action constitutes recommending security transactions to clients without regard to their individual financial situations. It is highly unlikely that shares of stock in a new company would be a suitable investment for every one of any agent's clients.

132. **Unlawful.** The agent either did not make a reasonable inquiry as to the customer's financial situation or he induced a transaction that was excessive in size in relation to the customer's financial resources. Either action is prohibited.

133. **Unlawful.** The agent is recommending the purchase of a security without reasonable grounds for the recommendation. The agent is probably also guilty of recommending security transactions without regard to clients' individual financial situations or investment objectives.

134. **Unlawful.** This action is called *churning* and is prohibited.

135. **Unlawful.** This action constitutes recommending the purchase of a security without reasonable grounds for the recommendation.

136. **Lawful.** This action is not fraudulent or prohibited.

137. **Lawful.** The agent is making a recommendation based on reasonable grounds.

138. **Unlawful.** Accepting orders on behalf of customers from individuals other than the customers without first obtaining third-party trading authority is a prohibited business practice.

139. **Unlawful.** Failing to inform a client that certain transactions involve larger than ordinary commissions, taxes or other costs is prohibited.

140. **Unlawful.** Borrowing money or securities from a client is a prohibited business practice.

141. **Unlawful.** The agent cannot commingle his funds with a client's funds.

142. **Unlawful.** Deliberately failing to follow a customer's instructions is prohibited.

143. **Unlawful.** The agent effected a transaction on behalf of a customer without the specific authority to do so.

144. **Unlawful.** Effecting transactions with a client not recorded on the regular books or records of the agent's employing broker-dealer is not allowed, unless those transactions are authorized in writing by the broker-dealer before the execution of the transactions.

145. **Unlawful.** The agent has failed to bring a client's written complaints to the attention of his employing broker-dealer.

146. **Unlawful.** The agent failed to inform the client that certain transactions involve higher than ordinary commissions, taxes or other costs.

147. **Unlawful.** Assuring clients that they will make a profit is a prohibited practice. Besides, it is all too possible to lose money (interest rate risk) on fixed-income securities when interest rates go up.

148. **Unlawful.** This transaction is a wash sale, which may reasonably be expected to distort the trading in a security. This prohibited activity is sometimes referred to as *painting the tape.* Do not confuse this activity with an arbitrage transaction, which is legal. (An arbitrage transaction is the simultaneous purchase and sale of the same security on different exchanges to take advantage of a price difference.)

149. **Unlawful.** Soliciting orders for unregistered nonexempt securities is illegal whether or not this effort results in an order.

150. **No.** Written consent is required from the client.

151. **No**. Notification is necessary when the adviser is a participant in a partnership, but not when the adviser is a participant in a corporation.

152. **No**

153. **Yes**

154. **No.** An investment adviser must provide notice to the administrator if he has or may have custody of customer funds or securities.

155. **Yes.** If an adviser has (or may have in the future) custody of customer funds or securities, the administrator must be notified.

156. **C.** Answers A and D are incorrect because neither choice I nor choice III by itself justifies an action for denial.

157. **B.** Choices I and II would be grounds for the suspension of an agent's registration by the state administrator.

158. **True**

159. **True**

160. **False**

161. **False**

162. **False**. The administrator cannot use lack of experience alone to determine qualification.

163. **A.** The seller can offer to buy back the security at the purchase price plus an interest rate set by the state administrator.

164. **B.** The offer was made from Illinois to a person in California, and so the state administrators of both states would have jurisdiction. The state from which payment was mailed and the state in which the checking account or money-market fund is based are unimportant.

165. **B.** Rescission must occur by the earlier of two years after the discovery of the facts or three years after the occurrence.

166. **B.** Registration statements are effective for one year from the effective date.

167. **A.** The federal 1933 securities act requires that securities offered to the public be registered with the SEC. The registration statement becomes effective on the 20th calendar day following the date the statement is received by the SEC (assuming the SEC does not find any deficiencies or misrepresentations). During the 20-day cooling-off period between the filing date and the effective date, indications of interest from the public for shares may be taken. When the registration becomes effective, shares in the new issue may be reconfirmed and actual orders taken. Note that on the federal level, the registration must be on file with the SEC for 20 days, while on the state level it must be on file with the administrator for 10 days.

168. **C.** Take care to distinguish between an exempt security and an exempt transaction.

169. **C.** Making recommendations on the basis of material inside information is a fraudulent or deceitful business practice.

170. **D.** For margin accounts falling below the minimum maintenance amount required, and if the customer cannot be reached, the agent should inform his principal, who will then determine which and how many securities must be sold to maintain the margin requirement as set by Regulation T. The agent may not take further action or execute any transactions without a written trading authorization.

171. **B.** The agent may share in proportion to his contribution, assuming he has written consent of the broker-dealer and the customer.

172. **A.** The agent may accept orders only from the customer, unless third-party trading authorization has been obtained.

173. **C.** The agent has the responsibility to describe sufficiently the risks and to state all important facts. Offering a guarantee is obviously misleading.

174. **B.** Misrepresenting yields is clearly fraudulent.

175. **D.** Failure to bring customers' written complaints to the attention of the agent's broker-dealer is prohibited.

176. **B.** The function of the specialist normally is to act as a broker for orders left with him by other members and to act as a dealer in buying and selling for his own account.

177. **B.** An agent may not make promises that probably cannot be kept.

178. **B.** Coordination is frequently used to register a security simultaneously under the Securities Act of 1933 and in a state. If the security's federal registration is pending and the administrator has received all of the required material, the two registrations can be declared effective at the same time.

179. **A.** Buying on one exchange and selling on another is a perfectly acceptable market arbitrage.

180. **B.** The customer authorized the agent to buy income-producing securities only. Wash sale and matching activity refer to creating the impression of activity in the stock by buying and selling the same stock at the same price without a change in beneficial ownership. These activities may cause others to buy or sell the security.

181. **B.** An investment adviser in possession of customer assets must send a statement to the customer every three months; the statement must list the securities held by the adviser and must show all transactions in the account since the last statement date.

182. **D.** All of the activities listed are fraudulent practices.

183. **A.** Creating the illusion of trading activity is a manipulation of the market. Arbitrage (choice B) is not market manipulation. Giving fictitious quotes is prohibited because they are untrue statements; however, it is not market manipulation. Trades that are too large for a customer also are prohibited because they are not suitable, but they are not considered market manipulation.

184. **A.** A fixed annuity is an insurance contract that cannot be traded for value. Commodity options (although not the underlying futures contracts) and stock options are considered securities, as are interests purchased in a limited partnership enterprise.

185. **C.** The omission of a material fact in the sale, purchase or offer of a security is fraudulent. This applies whether the security being offered is exempt or nonexempt.

186. **D.** The Uniform Securities Act gives the state administrator jurisdiction over offers to buy or sell when the offers originate in the administrator's state or are directed to or accepted in that state.

187. **D.** Violations of securities laws are subject to criminal penalties, civil liabilities and denial, suspension or revocation of registration.

188. **D.** The person illegally selling the securities is liable for the purchase price of the securities plus interest from the date of purchase, costs and reasonable attorney's fees.

189. **C.** If you missed this, review the list in the text on offenses leading to denial, suspension or revocation of registration.

190. **D.** Fraud, conviction of a felony or misdemeanor involving a security and insolvency are grounds for denial.

191. **C.** A provider of a ticker tape service is included in the definition of a securities information processor; all of the other choices are excluded from the definition.

192. **A.** An investment adviser may not borrow money from a customer unless the customer is an affiliate of the investment adviser, a broker-dealer, or a bank or another institution in the business of lending money.

193. **B.** The Uniform Securities Act exempts from registration teachers, engineers, lawyers and accountants providing investment advice that is incidental to the performance of their normal business. Economists are not granted an exemption under the act.

194. **B.** The USA excludes issuers and banks from the definition of broker-dealer, as well as agents. Investment advisers and financial planners are not granted exclusions from the definition.

8 Uniform Securities Act Exam One

1. As defined in the Uniform Securities Act, which of the following is NOT a security?

   A. Interest in a real estate condominium
   B. Commercial paper issued with an eight-month maturity
   C. Variable annuity
   D. $100,000 whole life insurance policy

2. Which of the following persons is defined as an agent by the Uniform Securities Act?

   A. Silent partner
   B. Secretary of a sales manager
   C. Clerk who is authorized to take orders
   D. Executive who does not solicit or transact business

3. As defined in the Uniform Securities Act, which of the following are considered securities?

   I. Commodity option contract
   II. Treasury stock
   III. Keogh plan

   A. I and II only
   B. I and III only
   C. II and III only
   D. I, II and III

4. According to the Uniform Securities Act, an investment adviser is all of the following EXCEPT a

   I. broker who charges for investment advice
   II. publisher of a financial newspaper
   III. person who sells security analysis
   IV. CPA who charges for constructing a portfolio of tax-sheltered investments

   A. I and II
   B. II and III
   C. II and IV
   D. III and IV

5. Interests in which of the following are considered securities under the Uniform Securities Act?

   I. Merchandising marketing scheme
   II. Multilevel distributorship arrangement
   III. Oil and gas drilling program

   A. I and II only
   B. I and III only
   C. II and III only
   D. I, II and III

6. Under the Uniform Securities Act, an individual is required to register as an "agent" if she represents an issuer in which of the following transactions?

   A. Sale of six-month commercial paper
   B. Sale of Canadian corporation's common stock
   C. Transaction with an underwriter
   D. Transaction in municipal securities

7. Under the Uniform Securities Act, the definition of "issuer" includes which of the following?

   A. Seller in a transaction on the floor of an exchange
   B. Officer or director of a company that is offering new shares to the public
   C. Person proposing to issue a security
   D. Market maker for a new issue

8. Under the Uniform Securities Act, the definition of "broker-dealer" includes a(n)

   A. person in the business of making trades in his own account or for the accounts of others
   B. agent handling principal transactions
   C. trust company when executing transactions in accounts in which it does NOT act in a fiduciary capacity
   D. authorized representative of the issuer

9. According to the Uniform Securities Act, a sale is a(n)

   A. attempt to transfer ownership of a security
   B. solicitation of an offer to buy
   C. contract to transfer ownership of a security for value
   D. offer equivalent contract

10. Under the Uniform Securities Act, all of the following are considered securities EXCEPT

    A. warehouse receipts
    B. fixed-annuity contracts
    C. preorganization certificates
    D. commercial paper

11. An employee of a large publicly held company effects transactions with existing employees for the purchase of company debentures. Under the Uniform Securities Act, which of the following statements is true?

    A. He must register as an agent of the issuer.
    B. He never need register as an agent of the issuer.
    C. He may receive commissions without registration.
    D. He must register as an agent if he will receive commissions or remuneration, directly or indirectly.

12. According to the Uniform Securities Act, which of the following is NOT considered a person?

    A. Custodian
    B. Minor
    C. Municipality
    D. Corporation

13. Under the Uniform Securities Act, a person who has passed the Uniform Securities Agent State Law Examination but whose license has not yet been issued can participate in which of the following activities?

    A. Prospecting in person
    B. Prospecting by mail
    C. Accepting unsolicited orders
    D. None of the above

14. According to the Uniform Securities Act, a consent to service of process must accompany which of the following?

    I. Agent's registration application
    II. Civil complaint against a broker-dealer
    III. Broker-dealer's initial registration application

    A. I only
    B. I and III only
    C. II and III only
    D. I, II and III

15. An agent representing a broker-dealer lives in one state and would like to do business in another state. Under the Uniform Securities Act, which of the following statements is true?

    A. No registration is necessary in the other state as long as the agent's activities are limited exclusively to effecting transactions in certain exempted securities.
    B. No registration is necessary if no commission or other remuneration is paid or given directly or indirectly.
    C. If the agent is a partner, an officer or a director and held that position at the time the broker-dealer was registered, the individual need not register separately.
    D. Registration is required only if an offer is directed, accepted and paid for in that state.

16. Persons who have less than $25,000,000 in assets under management must register at what level?

    A. Federal
    B. State
    C. Both federal and state
    D. Neither federal nor state

17. According to the Uniform Securities Act, which of the following may be required by an administrator prior to issuing an agent's license?

    A. Oral or written examination or both
    B. Completed application or evidence of a completed and current registration with the SEC or an SRO
    C. Consent to service of process
    D. All of the above

18. Under the Uniform Securities Act, for what period of time is a broker-dealer's agent's license in effect?

    A. It depends on the renewal dates in the various states.
    B. Until December 31st unless renewed
    C. Until withdrawn by the agent or revoked by the administrator
    D. Length of the agent's employment by all broker-dealers

19. According to the Uniform Securities Act, which of the following is responsible for notifying the administrator when an agent changes his place of employment?

    A. Agent
    B. Former employer
    C. New employer
    D. The agent, the former employer and the new employer

20. Which of the following statements is true regarding an agent's license issued under the Uniform Securities Act?

    A. Upon issuance, it is valid for a predetermined length of time that varies by state.
    B. It is valid immediately after the agent passes an examination.
    C. It is not valid if the agent terminates employment with a broker-dealer.
    D. It is valid for 30 days after termination of employment with a broker-dealer if new employment is pending.

21. Under the Uniform Securities Act, which of the following types of transactions can be entered into legally with unregistered nonexempt securities?

    A. Public offering
    B. Private placement
    C. Rights offering
    D. Offering to employees of the issuer

22. Which of the following securities is(are) exempt from the registration provisions of the Uniform Securities Act?

    I. Issue of a savings and loan association
    II. General obligation municipal bond
    III. Bond issued by a company that has common stock listed on the American Stock Exchange

    A. I only
    B. II only
    C. II and III only
    D. I, II and III

23. Which of the following activities would violate the Uniform Securities Act?

    I. Buying and selling the same stock on the same day on different exchanges
    II. Offering shares of an unregistered non-exempt security to customers
    III. Offering a Canadian government bond to a resident of a state in which the agent of a broker-dealer is not registered

    A. I only
    B. II only
    C. II and III only
    D. I, II and III

24. Which of the following exemptions under the Uniform Securities Act applies to the sale of securities to institutions that are regarded as professional investors?

    A. Blue chip exemption
    B. Manual exemption
    C. Exempt transaction
    D. Exempt security

25. Which of the following statements is true regarding the antifraud provisions of the Uniform Securities Act?

    A. The only securities exempt from the provisions are those regulated by federal authority.
    B. The only exempt securities are those issued by national governments or political subdivisions of countries that maintain diplomatic relations with the United States.
    C. The only exempt securities are those that are properly registered under blue-sky laws.
    D. No securities are exempt from the antifraud provisions of the act.

26. The Uniform Securities Act prohibits which of the following?

    I. Agents exercising discretion in discretionary accounts
    II. Charging larger than ordinary commissions on certain transactions
    III. Soliciting orders for unregistered non-exempt securities

    A. I only
    B. II and III only
    C. III only
    D. I, II and III

27. An agent is asked by a customer to open an account and buy stock for the customer's spouse. According to the Uniform Securities Act, which of the following statements about this action is true?

    A. The agent could be liable if the stock declines in value.
    B. This practice is ordinary and acceptable.
    C. This action is prohibited unless the spouse signs a trading authorization.
    D. This action is prohibited unless the customer signs a trading authorization on behalf of his spouse.

28. A customer who wishes to retire in three years informs his agent that he wants to use the equity in his house to make enough money in the market to fund his retirement. According to the Uniform Securities Act, the agent should

A. help meet the customer's needs by constructing a high-quality, growth-oriented portfolio
B. urge the customer to reconsider because the time allotted is not consistent with his means
C. suggest that the customer invest in an ultraconservative portfolio of municipal bonds
D. invest the money in stocks because of their unlimited potential

29. An agent hears that the chairman of a large manufacturing firm may be ousted because of erratic social behavior. The agent decides to call all of his customers who own shares of the manufacturing corporation and tell them to liquidate their positions. Under the Uniform Securities Act, which of the following statements is true?

A. The agent may have made an error as to the effect of the rumor, so he should wait until he has a better feel for the situation.
B. This action is based on material inside information, so he must inform all of his customers of this fact.
C. This action constitutes a prohibited use of rumor to induce a purchase or sale.
D. This action is legal and legitimate as long as the agent limits the exposure to 12 customers or fewer.

30. An agent hears material inside information regarding a company that is publicly held. Which of the following actions would NOT violate the Uniform Securities Act?

A. Soliciting orders based on this information
B. Trading for the agent's personal account based on this information
C. Discussing the situation with a superior or compliance officer in the agent's firm
D. Discussing the information at a seminar, but not making an investment recommendation

31. Under the Uniform Securities Act, which of the following may have custody of customer funds?

I. Investment adviser who maintains $35,000 net worth
II. Investment adviser who maintains $35,000 surety bond
III. Broker-dealer who maintains $10,000 surety bond
IV. Broker-dealer in compliance with SEC net capital rules

A. I and III
B. I and IV
C. I, II and IV
D. III and IV

32. According to the Uniform Securities Act, which of the following would be an unlawful activity for an investment adviser?

    A. Entering into an investment advisory contract that does not mention the compensation arrangements
    B. Taking custody of a customer's securities or funds without notifying the administrator, even though the administrator has no rule that prohibits such custody
    C. Entering into an investment advisory contract that provides specifically for compensation based on a share of capital appreciation of the customer's funds
    D. All of the above

33. Which of the following actions would NOT be considered unlawful under the Uniform Securities Act?

    A. An agent makes an untrue statement of a material fact
    B. An agent omits a material fact because she knew she did not have time to cover everything in a short presentation
    C. An agent deliberately fails to follow a customer's instructions
    D. An agent actively solicits orders in unregistered exempt securities

34. The Uniform Securities Act permits excessive trading activity that generates high commissions and low returns in a customer's account

    A. in discretionary accounts
    B. with written permission of the customer
    C. when it is consistent with the customer's needs
    D. under no circumstances

35. Under the Uniform Securities Act, which of the following statements is true regarding the use of material facts?

    A. To omit them is fraudulent and unethical.
    B. Because all material facts cannot be presented, it is up to the sales rep to decide which to use.
    C. Restrictions apply only to sales, not solicitations.
    D. The agent is the final arbiter on what is material and what is not.

36. Persons with $5,000,000 or less under management who act in an advisory capacity in states that do not require registration must do which of the following?

    A. Register with the SEC.
    B. Register with the NASD.
    C. Pass the Series 7 General Securities Representative Examination.
    D. Pass the Series 65 Uniform Investment Adviser Law Examination.

37. An agent receives a letter from an irate customer. This letter is the fourth in the last four months and is very abusive. The agent decides against a reply, and discards the letter. Under the Uniform Securities Act, which of the following statements is correct?

    A. The agent is entitled to decide how to handle such situations.
    B. The administrator may, by rule, dictate how this should be handled.
    C. All material complaints must be forwarded to the administrator.
    D. The agent's behavior is prohibited. He must forward all written complaints to his employer.

38. Which of the following are considered investment adviser representatives (supervised persons) under the Uniform Securities Act?

    I. Vice-president of the firm
    II. Temporary employee hired to solicit clients
    III. Employee who performs only clerical tasks
    IV. Employee who supervises the management of customer accounts

    A. I only
    B. I, II and IV only
    C. III and IV only
    D. I, II, III and IV

39. According to the Uniform Securities Act, to determine whether an investment adviser is trading excessively in a customer's account, regulators examine whether the

    A. adviser received compensation for the trades
    B. transactions matched the investor's objectives
    C. customer approved the transactions in writing
    D. adviser acted as a principal or an agent

40. Under the Uniform Securities Act, which of the following statements is true of an agent who deliberately gives a fictitious quote to a customer?

    A. He is guilty of a felony.
    B. He has committed a fraudulent and misleading act.
    C. He must execute at that price.
    D. He is committed to selling or buying 100 shares at that price.

41. State securities administrators are required to enforce which of the following with respect to investment advisers who practice within their state?

    A. Rules of Fair Practice
    B. Conduct Rules
    C. Antifraud regulations
    D. Fraud regulations

42. Which of the following is a fraudulent or prohibited activity under the Uniform Securities Act?

    A. Using the dividends paid in the last 12 months to determine the current yield of a common stock
    B. Implying that registration of a security means approval of the security
    C. Selling common stock to a customer with income objectives
    D. Stating that zero-coupon bonds pay no current interest

43. Which of the following practices violates the Uniform Securities Act?

    A. Deliberately not charging a commission
    B. Failing to charge a markup
    C. Failing to state every fact
    D. Failing to follow a customer's instructions

44. An investment adviser ignores a state administrator's subpoena of records. Under the Uniform Securities Act, the adviser may be subject to

    A. a court injunction
    B. a registration revocation
    C. a probationary period
    D. all of the above

45. Under the Uniform Securities Act, the state administrator may revoke or deny an investment adviser's registration for which of the following reasons?

    A. Conviction for a securities felony 15 years ago
    B. Conviction for a securities misdemeanor 15 years ago
    C. Violation of another state's securities law five years ago
    D. Lack of experience as an investment adviser

46. Which of the following statements regarding licensing and registration under the Uniform Securities Act is(are) true?

    I. When an agent's license is suspended, the broker-dealer's also is suspended.
    II. When a broker-dealer's license is suspended, the agent's registration is suspended.
    III. The administrator may suspend or revoke registrations whenever the public good is the sole consideration.
    IV. If a principal's license is suspended, the broker-dealer's license is suspended.

    A. I and II
    B. II and III
    C. II and IV
    D. III and IV

47. If it is in the public interest to do so, the Uniform Securities Act provides that the state administrator may deny the registration of a person for all of the following reasons EXCEPT

    A. the applicant is not qualified owing to lack of experience
    B. a willful violation of the Uniform Securities Act has taken place
    C. the applicant is financially insolvent
    D. the applicant is temporarily enjoined from engaging in the securities business

48. According to the Uniform Securities Act, which of the following would rectify an inadvertent sale of an unregistered nonexempt security?

    I. Offering to buy the security back from the customer
    II. Asking the customer to sign a customer agreement
    III. Registering the stock by notification
    IV. Offering to pay interest as set by the administrator, less income paid, from the date the security was purchased

    A. I and III only
    B. I and IV only
    C. II and III only
    D. I, II, III and IV

49. Which of the following statements is true regarding a state administrator's authority under the Uniform Securities Act?

    A. The administrator has authority over any transaction made in his state.
    B. The administrator may criminally prosecute an agent.
    C. The administrator may suspend an agent's license based solely on the public good doctrine.
    D. The administrator must determine the state from which payment is made and to which securities are delivered.

50. An agent in Alabama directs a solicitation to a customer who lives in Connecticut while the customer is temporarily in Indiana. The customer does not accept the offer until he arrives back in Connecticut. According to the Uniform Securities Act, the administrators of which states have jurisdiction?

    A. Alabama and Connecticut
    B. Alabama and Indiana
    C. Indiana and Connecticut
    D. Alabama, Connecticut and Indiana

◆ Answers & Rationale

1. **D.** "Security" can be defined as any piece of paper that can be traded for value. An investment is considered a security if a person invests her money in a common enterprise with the expectation of profit from the managerial efforts of a third party. Insurance policies and fixed annuities are not considered securities. (Page 30)

2. **C.** Anyone who solicits or receives an order while representing a broker-dealer is an agent. (Page 28)

3. **A.** An IRA or a Keogh plan is a vehicle for an investment, not a security itself. Note that a commodity option contract is considered a security, while a commodity futures contract is not a security. (Page 30)

4. **C.** Investment advisers are persons in the business of selling investment advice. Professionals such as lawyers, accountants and teachers whose performance is incidental to the practice of their profession are not considered investment advisers. (Page 2)

5. **D.** All of the investments mentioned fall into the definition of "security." (Page 30)

6. **B.** An individual is not considered an agent when representing an issuer in such securities as municipal securities, Canadian government securities or commercial paper maturing in 270 days or less. Also, an individual is not considered an agent when representing an issuer in exempt transactions, such as between the issuer and underwriter. However, an individual representing a Canadian issuer of common stock is included in the Uniform Securities Act's definition of "agent." (Page 38)

7. **C.** The term "issuer" includes any person who issues or proposes to issue any security. (Page 29)

8. **A.** "Broker-dealer" is defined as any individual or firm in the business of making trades in its own account or for the accounts of others. (Page 28)

9. **C.** "Sale" is defined as every contract to sell a security or an interest in a security, including a security given as a bonus with the purchase of another security, or a gift of assessable stock. "Offer to sell" is defined as an attempt to solicit a purchase or sale in a security. (Page 29)

10. **B.** Fixed annuities are not considered securities. (Page 30)

11. **D.** An individual is not considered an agent when effecting transactions with an issuer's employees only if no commission is paid. (Page 38)

12. **B.** Minors cannot enter into contracts and are therefore not considered legal persons. (Page 2)

13. **D.** A person who has passed the exam cannot transact business until the state administrator grants registration, which normally is on the 30th day after the application is filed. (Page 39)

14. **B.** A broker-dealer, an agent or a state-registered investment adviser may obtain registration by filing an application and a consent to service of process with the administrator. The consent to service of process gives the administrator the irrevocable right to process legal complaints against the applicant. Federally registered advisers must give notice only and pay filing fees in the states in which they conduct business. (Page 39)

15. **C.** Both the broker-dealer and the agent must be registered in the state where business is to be transacted, even if the securities or the transactions are exempt from registration. At the time the broker-dealer is registered, officers of the firm who act as agents will be registered automatically as agents. (Page 37)

16. **B.** Persons who have less than $25 million in assets under management must register on a state basis. These advisers will be referred to as "state-registered" investment advisers. (Page 5)

17. **D.** As a condition of registration, the state administrator may require that an agent pass a written or an oral examination or both. Most states also may require applicants, their firms or both to provide a completed application and a consent to service of process. (Page 39)

18. **B.** Registrations expire on December 31st of each year unless renewed. (Page 42)

19. **D.** All three parties must notify the administrator. (Page 40)

20. **C.** After passing the exam, the agent must be granted registration by the state administrator. If the administrator does not deny registration, it becomes effective 30 days following the application. (Page 39)

21. **B.** Private placements involve the sale of nonexempt securities to qualified public investors. Private placement transactions are exempt from registration. The Uniform Securities Act stipulates that no more than 10 nonaccredited investors receive offers in any 12-month period; that the purchase be made for the purpose of investment; and that no commissions be paid for solicitation of non-institutional buyers. (Page 72)

22. **D.** Each of the securities listed is exempt from registration under the Uniform Securities Act. (Page 70)

23. **C.** Buying a security on one exchange and selling it on another is a proper market arbitrage. Broker-dealers and agents must be registered in each state where offers or sales occur. Also, every security must be registered unless it is an exempt security or an exempt transaction. (Page 79)

24. **C.** The Uniform Securities Act is designed to protect the general public, not to limit the activities of informed professional investors, such as banks, insurance companies and pension or profit-sharing trusts. Transactions with institutions are exempt. (Page 70)

25. **D.** Neither exempt securities nor exempt transactions are exempt from the antifraud provisions. (Page 63)

26. **C.** The Uniform Securities Act prohibits soliciting orders for unregistered nonexempt securities. (Page 78)

27. **C.** Effecting transactions without specific authority to do so is prohibited. (Page 77)

28. **B.** Making unsuitable recommendations to customers is prohibited. (Page 77)

29. **C.** Repeating rumors is both misleading and prohibited under the Uniform Securities Act. (Page 78)

30. **C.** Disseminating and acting on inside information is prohibited. (Page 78)

31. **C.** If an investment adviser or broker-dealer has custody of customer assets, the state administrator may set a minimum capital or surety bond requirement of $35,000. A broker-dealer in compliance with federal net capital rules is exempt from the state's requirements. (Page 9)

32. **D.** Each of the answers listed is an example of an unlawful activity by an investment adviser. (Page 77)

33. **D.** Securities that do not require registration under the Uniform Securities Act are exempt securities. Although the securities are exempt, the agent who makes the solicitation and his broker-dealer must be registered. (Page 79)

34. **D.** Excessive trading activity in an account is called *churning* and is a prohibited practice. (Page 77)

35. **A.** Material facts are facts essential for making an investment decision. To omit them is fraudulent or deceitful. (Page 78)

36. **A.** Those persons who act in an advisory capacity in states that do not require registration must register with the SEC. (Page 5)

37. **D.** The Uniform Securities Act requires an agent to forward any written complaints received to his employer. (Page 79)

38. **B.** Clerical and ministerial personnel are not included in the definition of investment adviser representatives (supervised persons). Any other person associated with an investment adviser, including an officer of the firm, is generally considered to be an investment adviser representative. (Page 3)

39. **B.** Trading in a customer's account must not be excessive in terms of size or frequency with respect to the customer's investment objectives and financial ability. Whether the adviser acted as principal or agent, or received compensation, is not a consideration. The customer's approval of the transactions does not release the adviser from abiding by suitability requirements. (Page 77)

40. **B.** Disseminating phony or misleading quotes is a prohibited practice. (Page 79)

41. **C.** Under the NSMIA (National Securities Markets Improvement Act), state administrators are no longer able to exercise full jurisdiction over federally registered advisers. However, administrators must enforce all antifraud regulations for investment advisers practicing within their states. (Page 26)

42. **B.** Registration of a security with the SEC or the state implies neither approval nor disapproval. (Page 77)

43. **D.** If it seems illegal, it probably is a violation. (Page 79)

44. **A.** If an investment adviser demonstrates contempt (contumacy) for an administrator's order or subpoena, a court may be asked to enforce it. The adviser's registration or ability to conduct business may not be affected. (Page 35)

45. **C.** A violation of any state or federal securities or commodities law is grounds for denial, suspension, revocation or cancellation of registration. Convictions are grounds for administrator action if they occurred within the past 10 years. Lack of experience is not sufficient cause for revoking or denying registration. (Page 10)

46. **C.** An administrator may suspend or revoke any registration if he finds that the order is in the public interest *and* he finds guilt of any of the listed offenses. (Page 40)

47. **A.** An administrator may not deny, suspend or revoke registration solely on the basis of lack of experience. (Page 41)

48. **B.** The rescission right of the buyer is to recover the purchase price and interest. If the seller discovers the illegal sale, the seller may offer to repurchase the security. The buyer has 30 days to accept after receiving the rescission letter offering to refund the money and interest; otherwise, the sale stands. (Page 36)

49. **A.** The Uniform Securities Act gives the state administrator jurisdiction (the scope of the act) over transactions originated in, directed to or accepted in the administrator's state. An administrator may suspend any registration if two things are true: (1) it is in the public interest and (2) one of the specific offenses listed has been committed. An administrator must turn over to the court system any cases which suggest criminal penalties. (Page 68)

50. **D.** The administrator in any state to or from which an offer is made has jurisdiction over the offer. (Page 34)

9 Uniform Securities Act Exam Two

1. According to the Uniform Securities Act, a person would be required to register as a broker-dealer in a state under which of the following circumstances?

   I. The person has no place of business in the state, but has directed offers to clients with more than 30 days' temporary residency.
   II. The person has no place of business in the state and deals exclusively with broker-dealers in that state.
   III. The person has no place of business in the state and effects transactions exclusively with issuers of securities in that state.
   IV. The person has a place of business in the state.

   A. I, II and IV only
   B. I and IV only
   C. II and III only
   D. I, II, III and IV

2. Under the Uniform Securities Act, a person representing an issuer of which of the following securities would NOT have to be registered as an agent?

   I. Banker's acceptance
   II. Municipal bond
   III. U.S. bank issue
   IV. Investment contract issued in connection with an employee's stock purchase, savings, pension, profit-sharing or similar benefit plan

   A. I and II only
   B. I, III and IV only
   C. III and IV only
   D. I, II, III and IV

3. Under the Uniform Securities Act, an individual would NOT be considered an agent if he engages in which of the following types of transactions?

   I. Between an issuer and an insurance company
   II. Between an issuer and unsophisticated investors
   III. Between an issuer and the underwriters
   IV. Between an issuer and savings institutions or trust companies

   A. I, III and IV only
   B. II and III only
   C. II and IV only
   D. I, II, III and IV

4. An issuer employs its officers and directors to sell newly issued shares of the company. The officers and directors are compensated for the sales. According to the Uniform Securities Act, the officers and directors would have to be registered as agents of the

   A. issuer
   B. broker-dealer
   C. broker-dealer and issuer
   D. state administrator

5. A nonissuer corporation has its employees sell nonexempt securities. The corporation receives a commission on the sale of the securities, and some of the commission is then paid to the employees. According to the Uniform Securities Act, the corporation is a

   A. broker-dealer that must be registered
   B. corporation selling only to sophisticated investors
   C. broker-dealer engaging in exempt transactions
   D. corporation selling to an employee pension fund

6. Under the National Securities Markets Improvement Act, a person with $25,000,000 or more in assets under management must register with the

   A. NASD
   B. NASAA
   C. SEC
   D. NYSE

7. As defined by the Uniform Securities Act, an example of an investment adviser is a

   A. lawyer
   B. publisher of a magazine
   C. person who is paid a fee for advising customers on securities
   D. person who is paid a commission for advising customers on securities

8. An issuer uses its directors to sell stock to employees, for which the directors receive commissions. According to the Uniform Securities Act, which of the following describe the directors?

   I. Agents of the issuer
   II. Agents of a broker-dealer
   III. Need not be licensed
   IV. Must be licensed

   A. I and III
   B. I and IV
   C. II and III
   D. II and IV

9. A corporate officer of an issuer sells securities of that corporation to a bank for a commission. What is his status under the Uniform Securities Act?

   A. He is a broker-dealer.
   B. He is an agent of a broker-dealer.
   C. He must be licensed as an agent.
   D. He need not be licensed as an agent.

10. Under the Uniform Securities Act, which of the following statements about a sale, an offer or an offer and sale is true?

   I. Any security given or delivered with or as a bonus for any purchase of securities is considered to have been offered and sold for value.
   II. A gift of assessable stock is considered to involve an offer and sale.
   III. Every sale or offer of a warrant or stock right to purchase or subscribe to another security is considered to include an offer of the other security.
   IV. Every bona fide pledge is considered an offer and sale.

   A. I, II and III only
   B. I and III only
   C. II and IV only
   D. I, II, III and IV

11. According to the Uniform Securities Act, an offer or a sale does NOT exist if it is a(n)

    I. act as a result of a class vote by stockholders regarding a merger or consolidation
    II. bona fide pledge or loan
    III. act incident to a judicially approved reorganization in which a security is issued in exchange for one or more outstanding shares
    IV. act as a result of a judicially approved reorganization in which one security is issued in exchange for an outstanding security

    A. I and II only
    B. I, II and III only
    C. IV only
    D. I, II, III and IV

12. An interest in which of the following can be defined as a security under the Uniform Securities Act?

    I. Merchandising marketing scheme
    II. Multilevel distributorship arrangement
    III. Oil and gas drilling program

    A. I only
    B. II and III only
    C. III only
    D. I, II and III

13. According to the Uniform Securities Act, the administrator has the power to require the agent licensee to

    A. have minimum net capital, post a surety bond and pass an exam
    B. post a surety bond and pass an exam
    C. post a surety bond, pay filing fees and pass an exam
    D. have minimum net capital, pay filing fees, pass an exam and post a surety bond

14. According to the Uniform Securities Act, after an agent passes the Series 63 exam and an NASD/NYSE licensing exam, when can she begin to sell?

    I. Immediately
    II. When she is affiliated with a broker-dealer
    III. When she has been granted a registration from the state administrator
    IV. When she gets permission from the principal in the office

    A. I
    B. I and IV
    C. II and III
    D. II and IV

15. An agent representing a broker-dealer in Utah wishes to do business in California exclusively in the trading of certain exempt securities. Under the Uniform Securities Act, the agent would

    A. not have to register in California
    B. have to register in California
    C. not have to register if the broker-dealer is registered in California
    D. be allowed to do business because the securities are exempt

16. According to the Uniform Securities Act, under what circumstances is an employee of a licensed broker-dealer firm allowed to sell exempt securities as an unregistered agent?

    A. The securities are exempt.
    B. The transaction is exempt.
    C. The employee is not paid any commission or salary.
    D. Under no circumstances

17. If it is in the public interest to do so, the Uniform Securities Act provides that the state administrator may deny the registration of a person for all of the following reasons EXCEPT

    A. the applicant is not qualified owing to lack of experience
    B. a willful violation of the act has taken place
    C. the applicant is financially insolvent
    D. the applicant is enjoined temporarily from engaging in the securities business

18. If a person is exempt from state registration but is a federally registered investment adviser, what must be done in order to practice within a particular state?

    I. Pay state filing fees
    II. Pass an oral or written examination
    III. Give notice to the state
    IV. Become licensed as a broker-dealer

    A. I and II
    B. I and III
    C. II and III
    D. II and IV

19. Under the Uniform Securities Act, an agent's license is effective for what period of time?

    A. Until December 31st
    B. Eighteen months, of which the first six months is a probationary period
    C. Twenty years
    D. Term of the agent's employment, unless withdrawn or revoked

20. Under the Uniform Securities Act, the administrator may require the filing of which of the following documents?

    I. Prospectus
    II. Pamphlet
    III. Circular
    IV. Advertisement

    A. I, III and IV only
    B. I and IV only
    C. II and III only
    D. I, II, III and IV

21. All of the following are part of the Uniform Securities Act's registration by filing procedure EXCEPT that

    A. companies must have attained a specific level of earnings for the prior three-year period
    B. a copy of the offering circular or prospectus must be filed
    C. if not denied, registration becomes effective after 30 days
    D. a statement must list the name(s) of the underwriter(s) and describe the terms of the offering

22. Under the Uniform Securities Act, an initial public offering registered simultaneously with the state and the SEC will MOST likely be registered by

    A. coordination
    B. qualification
    C. filing
    D. representation

23. Under the Uniform Securities Act, no specific response is required from the state administrator before which of the following types of securities registration becomes effective?

  I. Coordination
  II. Qualification
  III. Filing
  IV. Consanguination

  A. I and II only
  B. I and III only
  C. II, III and IV only
  D. I, II, III and IV

24. According to the Uniform Securities Act, the administrator may require an issuer that has an effective registration statement to file reports NOT more than

  A. quarterly
  B. semiannually
  C. annually
  D. biennially

25. All of the following statements are true regarding the selling of private placements under the Uniform Securities Act EXCEPT that

  A. they cannot be offered to more than 10 persons in 12 consecutive months
  B. they cannot be offered to more than 35 persons in 12 consecutive months
  C. the seller must reasonably believe that all buyers are purchasing for investment purposes only
  D. no commission or other remuneration may be paid for soliciting noninstitutional buyers

26. Registration statements for securities under the Uniform Securities Act are effective for

  A. a period of time determined by the administrator for each issue
  B. one year from the effective date
  C. one year from the date of issue
  D. one year from the previous January 1st

27. According to the Uniform Securities Act, which of the following statements are true regarding the registration of securities by coordination?

  I. The cooling-off period for the states is 10 days.
  II. The cooling-off period for the SEC is 20 days.
  III. The registration becomes effective in the state only after the state's cooling-off period.
  IV. The registration becomes effective at the state level in conjunction with the SEC if the administrator has not entered an order to deny it.

  A. I, II and IV only
  B. I and III only
  C. IV only
  D. I, II, III and IV

28. All of the following are considered exempt securities under the Uniform Securities Act EXCEPT

  I. U.S. government securities
  II. unsolicited transactions
  III. transactions between issuers and underwriters
  IV. securities of credit unions

  A. I, II and IV
  B. I and IV
  C. II and III
  D. IV

29. Investment advisers who manage private investment company portfolios may be compensated by

  A. performance-based fees
  B. flat fees established by written contract
  C. total services fee
  D. fees based upon a percentage of net assets under management

30. Which of the following are exempt from state registration as covered securities?

    A. Sales to qualified purchasers
    B. Federally exempt offerings and transactions
    C. Registered investment company securities
    D. All of the above

31. According to the Uniform Securities Act, under which of the following circumstances may an administrator cancel a person's registration?

    A. The person is adjudged to be mentally incompetent.
    B. The administrator determines it would be in the public interest.
    C. The person is the subject of an insider trading lawsuit.
    D. The person has been terminated from employment at an investment adviser firm.

32. According to the Uniform Securities Act, the investment adviser brochure must include the business background of

    A. the investment adviser
    B. employees of the adviser
    C. an affiliated broker-dealer
    D. institutional clients

33. Under the Uniform Securities Act, the state securities administrator may revoke an exemption claimed by which of the following securities issuers?

    A. Nonprofit charitable organization
    B. Canadian province
    C. Common carrier subject to the Interstate Commerce Commission
    D. Federal savings and loan association

34. Under the Uniform Securities Act, which of the following constitutes an offer of a security?

    A. Stock dividend distributed to current shareholders
    B. Agreement between an issuer and an underwriter
    C. Prospectus
    D. Tombstone advertisement

35. A customer is upset with her agent for not servicing her account properly and sends him a complaint letter about his actions. Under the Uniform Securities Act, the agent should

    A. call the customer and apologize, promising to do a better job
    B. tell the customer he is willing to make rescission
    C. do nothing and hope the customer forgets to send the letter
    D. bring the customer complaint to the employer immediately

36. Which of the following would NOT be considered a market manipulation under the Uniform Securities Act?

    A. Three market makers start buying and selling the same security simultaneously in their own accounts.
    B. A specialist buys and sells stock for his own account.
    C. A principal in a broker-dealer allows a rumor to leak out that Microscam is going to acquire Datawaq; after a few days, the broker-dealer sells short for its own account Microscam.
    D. A broker sells a customer's stock at the bid price and makes up the difference with a personal check.

37. In order to get a sale of $10,000 worth of bonds, an agent promises to balance a customer's checkbook each month for as long as the customer lives, even though the agent is in line for a promotion and an office transfer. Under the Uniform Securities Act, this is considered a(n)

   A. acceptable practice
   B. unacceptable practice
   C. practice that is not a violation; however, it is not a wise practice
   D. acceptable practice if it is in accordance with house rules

38. The state administrator revokes the registration of an agent. Under the Uniform Securities Act, the agent may file for a review of the revocation order within how many days of revocation?

   A. 30
   B. 60
   C. 90
   D. 270

39. According to the Uniform Securities Act, market manipulation includes all of the following EXCEPT

   A. buying on one exchange and selling on another
   B. withholding a material fact from a buyer
   C. buying and selling intentionally to show market activity
   D. giving a false quote

40. A customer has a discretionary account with his agent. The objective of the account is current income. The agent purchases a speculative growth stock. Under the Uniform Securities Act, this is considered a(n)

   A. wash sale
   B. unauthorized transaction
   C. acceptable transaction
   D. matching activity

41. Under the Uniform Securities Act, which of the following is responsible for proving that a securities issue is exempt from registration?

   A. Underwriter
   B. Issuer
   C. State administrator
   D. There is no need to prove eligibility for an exemption.

42. According to the Uniform Securities Act, which of the following are fraudulent or deceitful business practices?

   I. Matched order
   II. Phony quote
   III. Material misrepresentation
   IV. Wash sale

   A. I and II only
   B. I, II and III only
   C. III and IV only
   D. I, II, III and IV

43. According to the Uniform Securities Act, which of the following is an example of market manipulation?

   A. Creating the illusion of active trading
   B. Buying on one exchange and selling on another
   C. Guaranteeing performance of a security
   D. Transactions in excess of a customer's financial capability

44. A famous tennis player offers to record a testimonial for an investment adviser for use in a television commercial. Under the Uniform Securities Act, the investment adviser may

   A. use the testimonial as long as the athlete receives no compensation
   B. use the testimonial and may pay the athlete
   C. use the testimonial with the approval of the state administrator
   D. not use the testimonial under any circumstances

45. An agent omits to state facts in which a prudent investor would be interested. Under the Uniform Securities Act, this action is

A. fraudulent for nonexempt securities only
B. fraudulent for exempt securities only
C. fraudulent for both exempt and nonexempt securities
D. not fraudulent if there was no willful intent to omit the information

46. A customer living in one state receives a phone call from an agent in another state. A transaction between the two occurs in yet another state. According to the Uniform Securities Act, under whose jurisdiction does the transaction fall?

A. Administrator of the state in which the customer lives
B. Administrator of the state in which the agent's office is located
C. Administrator of the state in which the transaction took place
D. Administrators of all three states involved

47. Under the Uniform Securities Act, an agent who willfully violates state securities law is subject to which of the following?

I. Civil liabilities
II. Criminal penalties
III. Suspension, revocation or barring from registration as an agent by the administrator

A. I only
B. I and II only
C. III only
D. I, II and III

48. According to the Uniform Securities Act, a person who sells securities in violation of state securities laws is civilly liable for which of the following?

I. Principal
II. Interest
III. Court costs
IV. Attorney's fees

A. I, III and IV only
B. I and IV only
C. II and III only
D. I, II, III and IV

49. Under the Uniform Securities Act, an agent's license could be revoked if

I. he was convicted of a security misdemeanor
II. he was insolvent
III. he was judged mentally incompetent

A. I
B. I or II
C. II
D. III

50. As a result of which of the following would an agent possibly be subject to denial of registration under the Uniform Securities Act?

I. She has engaged in fraud in selling to an insurance company.
II. She was convicted of a security misdemeanor eight years ago.
III. She is insolvent.
IV. She has failed to pay filing fees.

A. I only
B. I, II and III only
C. II, III and IV only
D. I, II, III and IV

◆ Answers & Rationale

1. **B.** The term "broker-dealer" does not include a person who has no place of business in the state and who (1) effects transactions exclusively through issuers, other broker-dealers or institutions or (2) directs an offer in the state to an existing customer who has more than 30 days temporary residency within the state where the offer is received. (Page 37)

2. **D.** An individual is not considered an agent when representing the issuer in each of the cases cited. Note that for purposes of the exam, unless otherwise stated, all commercial paper is considered to mature in 270 days or less. (Page 38)

3. **A.** An individual who effects securities transactions for compensation is defined as an agent. A person representing an issuer in an exempt transaction does not fall under the definition, nor does a person who represents an issuer in effecting transactions with existing employees in which no commissions are paid. (Page 38)

4. **A.** The definition of "agent" would include an individual representing the issuer in a transaction for the benefit of the issuer unless the individual does not receive compensation. (Page 38)

5. **A.** A broker-dealer is in the business of effecting transactions in securities for its own account or for the accounts of others. Under the Uniform Securities Act, the broker-dealer must register in the state where business is transacted. (Page 28)

6. **C.** Under current law, persons who have $25 million or more in assets under management must register exclusively with the SEC. These persons are referred to as federally registered investment advisers. (Page 5)

7. **C.** An investment adviser is any person who is in the business of selling investment advice. (Page 2)

8. **B.** Registration as an agent of the issuer is necessary because commissions are paid. (Page 38)

9. **D.** The definition of "agent" does not include an officer of the issuer selling the issuer's securities to a bank (institutional investor). (Page 39)

10. **A.** The term "sale" does not include a bona fide pledge. (Page 29)

11. **D.** The Uniform Securities Act specifically excludes these four choices from the definition of "offer and sale." (Page 30)

12. **D.** Any investment contract entered into for profit where management is performed by someone other than the investors can be considered a security. (Page 30)

13. **C.** The administrator *may* require that, as a condition of registration, the agent post a surety bond, pay filing fees and pass an examination that may be written, oral or both. (Page 39)

14. **C.** Passing an NASD or NYSE licensing exam qualifies an individual to solicit security sales on a federal level. The state administrator must grant registration and the individual must be associated with a broker-dealer before she may engage in securities transactions. (Page 40)

15. **B.** Although the securities are exempted from registration, typically, the agent must register in every state where business is attempted. (Page 38)

16. **D.** It is unlawful for a person to transact business unless that person is registered, even if the securities are exempt. (Page 38)

17. **A.** Registration may be denied if the applicant willfully violates the Uniform Securi-

ties Act, is financially insolvent or has been enjoined from engaging in the securities business. If the person qualifies by virtue of training or knowledge, registration cannot be denied for lack of experience only. (Page 41)

18. **B.** While exempt from state registration, federally registered investment advisers must "give notice" (written) and pay state filing fees to practice within the given states. (Page 9)

19. **A.** An agent's license is not valid immediately after the agent passes the Uniform Securities Examination; rather, it is issued 30 days after he meets all registration requirements. Once the agent terminates employment with a broker-dealer, his license is no longer valid. Registration must be renewed annually or it will expire on December 31st. (Page 38)

20. **D.** The administrator may require the filing of any advertising or sales literature. Prospectuses, pamphlets, circulars and advertisements can fall under the definition of "advertising and sales literature." However, registered investment companies are exempt from state registration and filing requirements. (Page 67)

21. **C.** Registration by filing becomes effective concurrently with federal effectiveness. (Page 66)

22. **A.** Both registration by filing and registration by coordination become effective when the security is released by the SEC. However, an initial public offering may not be registered by filing; the security will therefore be registered by coordination. (Page 66)

23. **B.** Registration by coordination and by filing do not require a specific response from the state administrator. (Page 66)

24. **A.** As long as the registration is effective, the administrator may require the person who filed the registration statement to file quarterly reports. The reports update information contained in the registration statement and disclose the progress of the offering. (Page 68)

25. **B.** This question distinguishes the differences in federal and state requirements for private placements. Under state law, a private placement can be offered to no more than 10 non-accredited investors. (Page 72)

26. **B.** Securities registration statements are effective for one year from the effective date. (Page 67)

27. **A.** The federal 1933 securities act requires that securities offered to the public be registered with the SEC. The registration statement becomes effective on the 20th calendar day following the date the statement is received by the SEC (assuming the SEC does not find any deficiencies or misrepresentations). During the 20-day cooling-off period between the filing date and the effective date, indications of interest from the public for shares may be taken. When the registration becomes effective, shares in the new issue may be reconfirmed and actual orders taken. Note that on the federal level, the registration must be on file with the SEC for 20 days, while on the state level it must be on file with the administration for at least 10 days. (Page 66)

28. **C.** You must be able to distinguish between an exempt security and an exempt transaction. (Page 69)

29. **A.** Investment company advisers are typically prohibited from accepting performance-based compensation. However, advisers who manage private investment company portfolios can now accept compensation in the form of performance-based fees. (Page 18)

30. **D.** Covered securities are exempt from state registration. These securities include listed securities, registered investment company securities (funds), private investment company sales, and offerings and transactions exempt on a federal level. (Page 68)

31. **A.** Registration may be canceled by the administrator if the registered person has been adjudged mentally incompetent. Merely being the subject of a lawsuit, without being convicted of the crime, is not grounds for cancellation. A person's registration is not in effect any time when the person is no longer associated with an employing firm. However, the registration has not been canceled. (Page 11)

32. **A.** The business background of any person who will be responsible for making investment recommendations must be included in Part II of the Form ADV filed for registration; substantially the same information must be provided in the disclosure brochure. (Page 15)

33. **A.** The state administrator has the authority to deny or revoke the exempt status of a security issued by a religious or charitable organization or by an employee benefit plan; he may also deny or revoke the exempt status of any exempt transaction. (Page 68)

34. **C.** A prospectus is the document that offers a security for sale. A tombstone advertisement is not considered an offer of the security; it is used to solicit indications of interest. An agreement between an issuer and an underwriter is not considered an offer to purchase or sell the security; and the definition of offer and sale specifically excludes stock dividends. (Page 29)

35. **D.** Failure to bring customers' written complaints to the attention of the agent's broker-dealer is prohibited. (Page 79)

36. **B.** The function of the specialist normally is to act as a broker for orders left with him by other members and to act as a dealer in buying and selling for his own account. (Page 78)

37. **B.** An agent may not make promises that probably cannot be kept. (Page 79)

38. **B.** If a person wishes to appeal a final order of the state administrator, a written petition may be filed with the appropriate court within 60 days of the entry of the order. The court may then affirm or set aside the revocation order. (Page 40)

39. **A.** Buying on one exchange and selling on another is known as "arbitrage." This is an accepted trading practice. (Page 77)

40. **B.** The customer authorized the agent to buy income-producing securities only. Wash sale and matching activity refer to creating the impression of activity in a stock by buying and selling the same stock at the same price without a change in beneficial ownership. These activities may cause others to buy or sell the security. (Page 77)

41. **B.** The burden of proof for claiming eligibility for an exemption falls to the person claiming the exemption. (Page 69)

42. **D.** Both matched orders and wash sales distort the actual trading activity in a security. Phony quotes and material misrepresentations are untrue statements of fact and are therefore prohibited. (Page 77)

43. **A.** Creating the illusion of trading activity is a manipulation of the market. Arbitrage (choice B) is not market manipulation. Guaranteeing performance of a security is prohibited because they are untrue statements; however, it is not market manipulation. Trades that are too large for a customer also are prohibited because they are not suitable, but they are not considered market manipulation. (Page 78)

44. **D.** Under the Uniform Securities Act, advertising materials are deemed to be misleading if they are in violation of the Investment Advisers Act's advertising requirements. Testimonials are specifically prohibited under both state and federal law. (Page 21)

45. **C.** The omission of a material fact in the sale, purchase or offer of a security is fraudulent. This applies whether the security being offered is exempt or nonexempt. (Page 78)

46. **D.** The Uniform Securities Act gives the state administrator jurisdiction over offers to buy or sell when the offers originate in or are directed to the administrator's state or are accepted in that state. (Page 34)

47. **D.** Violations of securities laws are subject to criminal penalties, civil liabilities and denial, suspension or revocation of registration. (Page 41)

48. **D.** The person illegally selling the securities is liable for the purchase price of the securities plus interest from the date of purchase, costs and reasonable attorney's fees. (Page 36)

49. **B.** A license may be revoked if it is in the public interest and the administrator ascertains that the agent is insolvent or has a criminal record. (Page 41)

50. **D.** Fraud, conviction of a felony or misdemeanor involving a security and insolvency are grounds for denial. (Page 41)

10 Uniform Securities Act Exam Three

1. You are a broker having lunch with your grandfather, who is head of Datawaq. He tells you that the government did not approve a large contract, which will hurt Datawaq's profits next year. According to the Uniform Securities Act, you should

   A. tell your best customers to sell their holdings of the corporation
   B. inform your broker-dealer of this promptly
   C. call the "60 Minutes" team
   D. sell Datawaq short so you do not get left out of the trading

2. A financial contract can best be defined as which of the following?

   A. The purchase of a whole life insurance policy
   B. The purchase of exchange-listed stock shares
   C. A negotiated transaction with lawful consideration
   D. The signing of an investment adviser's agreement with an investment company

3. According to the Uniform Securities Act, which of the following are considered securities?

   I. HR-10 or Keogh accounts
   II. Commercial paper
   III. IRAs
   IV. Voting trust certificates

   A. I and II
   B. I, III and IV
   C. II
   D. II and IV

4. Under the Uniform Securities Act, a state administrator may appoint another officer to

   A. serve subpoenas
   B. grant registration exemptions
   C. issue a cease and desist order
   D. set recordkeeping requirements

5. Which of the following is an example of a nonissuer transaction as defined by the Uniform Securities Act?

   A. Private placement
   B. Secondary offering
   C. Primary issue of a corporation
   D. Preemptive offering

6. Violations of the Uniform Securities Act can be punishable by

   A. civil liabilities
   B. criminal penalties
   C. license suspension
   D. all of the above

7. Under the Uniform Securities Act, which of the following is(are) considered a sale(s)?

   I. Gift of an assessable stock
   II. Gift of an ordinary stock
   III. Security given as a bonus for purchasing a bond
   IV. Offer of securities

   A. I
   B. I and II
   C. I and III
   D. II, III and IV

8. If convicted of a willful violation of the Uniform Securities Act, an agent may be subject to a maximum of

   A. imprisonment for five years
   B. a fine of $5,000 and/or imprisonment for three years
   C. a fine of $10,000
   D. disbarment

9. As defined by the Uniform Securities Act, secondary trades are also known as

   A. private placements
   B. issuer transactions
   C. nonissuer transactions
   D. exempt transactions

10. Under the Uniform Securities Act, which of the following can be distributed if an issuing company has applied for registration by qualification, but the security has not yet been cleared for sale?

    I. Tombstone advertising
    II. Red herring
    III. Application with down payment
    IV. Registration statement

    A. I
    B. I, II and IV
    C. II and III
    D. II and IV

11. According to the Uniform Securities Act, all of the following are violations of suitability requirements EXCEPT failing to

    A. identify customer objectives
    B. identify terms and fees on the customer's contract
    C. make reasonable inquiry of the customer's security holdings
    D. determine the customer's ability to take on risk

12. An agent tells a customer that one of the customer's stocks is worth $10 more per share than it is really worth. Under the Uniform Securities Act, this activity is

    A. allowed if the agent explains that the difference is a service charge
    B. allowed if the customer makes a profit from the end result
    C. misrepresentation and a fraudulent act
    D. misrepresentation without written permission from the branch

13. Under the Uniform Securities Act, which of the following activities are market manipulations?

    I. Disseminating false information
    II. Giving market quotes that can be misinterpreted easily
    III. Selling securities in large amounts to help keep prices down
    IV. Entering matched buy and sell orders to attract attention to the security

    A. I and II only
    B. I, III and IV only
    C. II and III only
    D. I, II, III and IV

14. As defined by the Uniform Securities Act, which of the following activities is an example of churning?

    A. Frequent purchases one day and sales of the same stock the next day in order to align with a customer's investment objectives
    B. Bond swaps
    C. Frequent purchases and sales of load mutual fund shares in a single account
    D. Day trading

15. Under the Uniform Securities Act, which of the following are NOT considered securities?

    I. Commodity futures contract
    II. Commodity options contract
    III. Voting trust certificate
    IV. Insurance contract

    A. I and II
    B. I and IV
    C. II, III and IV
    D. II and IV

16. Of the following, which are violations of the Uniform Securities Act?

    I. Arbitrage
    II. Soliciting investors for unregistered nonexempt securities
    III. Selling bonds of a foreign government to residents of a state other than the one in which the agent of a broker-dealer is registered and is paid a commission
    IV. Selling T bonds without being registered as an agent of a broker-dealer and not receiving a commission

    A. I and IV only
    B. II and III only
    C. II, III and IV only
    D. I, II, III and IV

17. A customer placed an order with an investment adviser to sell 100 shares of ALF in order to have cash for an urgent purchase the next day, and instructed the adviser to limit any losses. The adviser did not have discretionary authority over the account. The adviser waited to sell the shares, hoping to get a better price for the customer. The price of the shares went down, so the adviser sold 50 ALF shares to limit the customer's losses. According to the Uniform Securities Act, this is a

    A. violation because the adviser acted without discretionary authority
    B. permissible activity because the adviser is obligated to get the best price for the customer
    C. violation because the adviser is required to execute sell transactions immediately after the order is placed
    D. permissible activity because the adviser is not permitted to guarantee a price to a customer

18. An investment adviser is a subsidiary of a broker-dealer. The adviser is the subject of a civil lawsuit alleging a fraudulent sale of securities to a customer. Under the Uniform Securities Act, the brokerage firm may be held jointly liable for the violation EXCEPT if the firm

    A. received payment or another benefit from the transaction
    B. has a record of similar violations
    C. could not have reasonably known about the transaction
    D. discussed the purchase with the customer

19. A sole proprietor incorporates and then sells stock in his company. Under the Uniform Securities Act, the company would be considered a(n)

    A. broker-dealer
    B. exempted proprietorship
    C. issuer
    D. agent

20. A customer is retired, in a low tax bracket and living on a fixed income. An agent recommends and sells to the customer a portfolio of municipal bonds. Under the Uniform Securities Act, what can the administrator do about this?

    A. Force the agent to offer rescission
    B. Revoke the agent's license for selling an unsuitable investment
    C. Suspend the agent's license until the bonds mature
    D. Nothing, because the customer agreed to the purchase

21. Karen Kodiak works for a broker-dealer that is registered in all 50 states. Karen is a registered representative in Nebraska. Klaus Bruin is a customer living and registered to vote in Florida. Klaus calls Karen at her office in Nebraska and offers to purchase securities. Under the Uniform Securities Act, Karen should

    A. accept the order because her broker-dealer is registered in all 50 states
    B. accept the order because she received it in Nebraska
    C. reject the order because she is not registered in Florida
    D. reject the order because it was not a wire order

22. An agent executes a trade in a customer's individual account for the customer. Three days later, when the security is trading three points higher, the customer's husband calls and tells the agent to liquidate the account because the customer has lost her job. Under the Uniform Securities Act, the agent can

    A. write the customer a personal check for the original amount and keep the appreciation as commission
    B. cancel the trade, but retain the commission
    C. cancel the trade
    D. do nothing

23. A millionaire wants to invest in an income portfolio. An agent, acting with discretionary power, invests the customer's money in a portfolio of stock stressing appreciation and little, if any, income. Under the Uniform Securities Act, this activity is

    A. ethical because the customer will make more money
    B. illegal because the customer must make the investment decision
    C. unsuitable
    D. all of the above

24. An agent hears a rumor concerning an investment and uses the information to influence a customer who has hesitated to make the purchase. Under the Uniform Securities Act, which of the following statements is true?

 A. Because the agent made it clear that it was a rumor, this is not a violation.
 B. Because the customer knew it was a rumor and therefore could not be reliable, this is not a violation.
 C. Because rumors are not considered to be inside information, this is not a violation.
 D. Under no circumstances would this be allowed.

25. Under the Uniform Securities Act, an agent may NOT make which of the following statements to a customer?

 A. "This security is registered with the state."
 B. "This security is cleared by the administrator."
 C. "This security is approved for sale by the administrator."
 D. "This security is exempt from registration."

26. An agent receives inside information concerning the possibility of an impending merger. Under the Uniform Securities Act, the agent may divulge the information to

 A. his best customers three days prior to a public announcement
 B. anyone three days prior to a public announcement
 C. the broker-dealer three days after public notice
 D. anyone after public notice

27. When a broker-dealer's registration under the Uniform Securities Act is revoked, which of the following occur(s)?

 I. The registrations of agents of that firm are no longer in effect.
 II. The registrations of agents of that firm are still in effect.
 III. The agent's registration is held in escrow until the broker-dealer gets out of jail.
 IV. One of the agents must be appointed the new broker-dealer.

 A. I
 B. I and III
 C. II
 D. II and IV

28. Which of the following stocks qualifies for the blue chip exemption provided by the Uniform Securities Act?

 A. Stock of a corporation with $10 million in net worth
 B. Stock of a corporation that is listed on the NYSE
 C. Stock of a bank holding company
 D. Stock of a municipal issuer

29. Under the Uniform Securities Act, a registered agent could offer securities for purchase during the underwriting period and before the effective date of registration in which of the following circumstances?

 I. Never
 II. With the use of a red herring
 III. If the securities are not exempt
 IV. Only if a bona fide registration statement has been properly filed with the state administrator and the SEC

 A. I
 B. II
 C. II, III and IV
 D. II and IV

30. According to the Uniform Securities Act, which of the following are considered securities?

    I. Condominium project with a rental pool agreement
    II. U.S. Treasury bill
    III. Limited partnership in an oil and gas exploration program
    IV. Contract in soybean futures

    A. I and II only
    B. I, II and III only
    C. III only
    D. I, II, III and IV

31. If an agent receives a commission from both a broker-dealer and an issuer, under the Uniform Securities Act she is considered an agent of

    A. the issuer
    B. the broker-dealer
    C. both the issuer and the broker-dealer
    D. neither the issuer nor the broker-dealer

32. A president of a bank sells shares of the bank and receives a commission. Under the Uniform Securities Act, he is

    A. a broker-dealer for the bank
    B. an agent of the issuer
    C. an investment adviser
    D. none of the above

33. Which of the following are defined as "supervised persons"?

    I. Partner of an investment advisory firm
    II. Officer of an investment advisory firm
    III. Director of an investment advisory firm
    IV. Investment adviser representative

    A. I and IV only
    B. II, III and IV only
    C. I, II and III only
    D. I, II, III and IV

34. Under the Uniform Securities Act, which of the following is(are) NOT considered a security(ies)?

    I. Secondary sale of a bank mortgage as a pass-through certificate
    II. Limited partnership unit in a cattle-breeding program
    III. Purchase of a condominium as a vacation home
    IV. Franchise agreement where a profit has been promised in the agreement

    A. I and II
    B. I, II and III
    C. I, II and IV
    D. III

35. Which of the following would fall under the Uniform Securities Act's definition of "person"?

    I. Government subdivision
    II. Closely held corporation
    III. Individual
    IV. Parent and child in a custodial account

    A. I only
    B. I and II only
    C. III and IV only
    D. I, II, III and IV

36. According to the Uniform Securities Act, all of the following can provide manual exemptions for a nonissuer distributor of an outstanding security EXCEPT

    A. *Moody's Public Utility Manual*
    B. *Best's Life Insurance Manual*
    C. the Dow Jones Industrial Average
    D. *Fitch's Manual*

37. All of the following practices are prohibited by the Uniform Securities Act EXCEPT

    I. borrowing money from a customer without the customer's written permission
    II. failing to determine adequately the suitability of an investment for a customer
    III. offering rescission
    IV. telling a customer that past history of an investment is not indicative of future results

    A. I and II
    B. I, II and IV
    C. II, III and IV
    D. III and IV

38. An investment adviser may not have custody of a customer's funds and securities under the Uniform Securities Act if

    A. there is a rule barring such custody
    B. the adviser fails to tell the customer that he has custody
    C. the adviser is not a registered broker-dealer
    D. the customer is not a registered adviser recipient

39. According to the Uniform Securities Act, a person representing an issuer of which of the following securities would have to be registered as an agent?

    I. Commercial paper
    II. Municipal bonds
    III. Securities of a U.S. bank
    IV. Investment contracts issued in connection with an employee stock purchase, savings, pension, profit-sharing or similar benefit plan

    A. I and II
    B. I, III and IV
    C. II and IV
    D. None of the above

40. An issuer employs its officers and directors to sell newly issued shares of the company and compensates them for the sales. To comply with the Uniform Securities Act, the officers and directors would have to be registered as agents of

    A. the issuer
    B. the broker-dealer
    C. the broker-dealer and the issuer
    D. neither the broker-dealer nor the issuer because the transactions are exempt

41. The purpose of a private investment company is to

    A. raise capital for business ventures
    B. raise capital for publicly traded corporations
    C. attract capital that will be managed by fee-based advisers
    D. allow advisers to have another product to offer clients

42. An issuer uses its directors to sell stock to employees, for which the directors receive commissions. Under the Uniform Securities Act, the directors

    I. are agents of the issuer
    II. are agents of a broker-dealer
    III. need not be licensed
    IV. must be licensed

    A. I and III
    B. I and IV
    C. II and III
    D. II and IV

43. According to the Uniform Securities Act, which of the following are considered sales, offers or offers and sales?

    I. Any security given or delivered with or as a bonus for any purchase of securities
    II. Any gift of assessable stock
    III. Every sale or offer of a warrant or stock right to purchase or subscribe to another security
    IV. Bona fide pledge

    A. I, II and III only
    B. I and III only
    C. II and IV only
    D. I, II, III and IV

44. Advisers of private investment companies may be compensated by which of the following fee structures?

    A. Commission
    B. Hourly rate
    C. Performance fee
    D. Trading stamps

45. According to the Uniform Securities Act, after an agent passes the Series 63 exam and a Series 6, 7 or 22 exam, when can she begin to sell?

    I. Immediately
    II. When she is affiliated with a broker-dealer
    III. When she has been granted a registration from the state administrator
    IV. When she gets permission from the principal in the office

    A. I
    B. I and IV
    C. II and III
    D. II and IV

46. Under the Uniform Securities Act, an employee of a licensed broker-dealer firm is allowed to sell exempt securities as an unregistered agent in which of the following cases?

    A. The securities are exempt.
    B. The transactions are exempt.
    C. The employee is not paid any commission or salary.
    D. Under no circumstances

47. Which of the following requirements are common to the registration of agents, state-registered investment advisers and broker-dealers under the Uniform Securities Act?

    I. The person must file, along with the application, a consent to service.
    II. The person's registration is two years in length.
    III. The person may be required to pass a written exam.
    IV. The person may be required to post a surety bond.

    A. I and III only
    B. I, III and IV only
    C. II and IV only
    D. I, II, III and IV

48. Qualified purchasers include all of the following EXCEPT

    A. individual with $5 million in investments
    B. family-owned business with $5 million in investments
    C. business with $5 million in investments
    D. trust sponsored by qualified purchasers

49. A registered broker-dealer gives investment advice as part of its business. One of its registered representatives gives investment advice outside the scope of his employment at the firm. Under SEC Release IA-1092, which of the following statements is(are) true?

    I. The broker-dealer must register as an investment adviser.
    II. The rep must register as an investment adviser.
    III. The rep need not register as an investment adviser.
    IV. The broker-dealer need not register as an investment adviser.

    A. I and II
    B. I and III
    C. II and IV
    D. III

50. Broker-dealers are exempt from state registration under which of the following circumstances?

    A. The broker-dealer is federally registered.
    B. The broker-dealer is also an investment adviser.
    C. The broker-dealer's client has less than 30 days' temporary residency within the state.
    D. The broker-dealer's client has less than 60 days' temporary residency within the state.

◆ Answers & Rationale

1. **B.** If you receive inside information, you should inform your supervisor immediately so that he may take the appropriate steps to avoid any transaction that may be construed to violate the Uniform Securities Act. (Page 78)

2. **C.** A financial contract is a binding agreement entered into to meet the objectives of both parties. (Page 17)

3. **D.** Individual retirement accounts and Keogh plans are types of customer accounts, not types of securities. (Page 30)

4. **A.** An official designated by the administrator may carry out the functions of the administrator with regard to investigating violations of the USA. The other activities described are responsibilities of the administrator and may not be delegated. (Page 35)

5. **C.** "Nonissuer transaction" is defined as any transaction that does not benefit the issuer. Choices I, III and IV would provide the issuer with capital and, therefore, a benefit. In a secondary offering, the seller, not the issuer, receives the benefit. (Page 70)

6. **D.** Violations of securities law will come under the scrutiny of both state and federal jurisdictions, the SEC and the NASD. (Page 36)

7. **C.** A "sale" is defined as a contract or transaction for value. Because an assessable stock may have value, the gift is considered a sale. A warrant is both an offer and a sale. Gifts of stock are not sales, and choice IV is an offer, not a sale. (Page 29)

8. **B.** Under the act, the maximum penalty is a fine of $5,000 and/or three years in jail. These penalties may be in addition to other penalties. (Page 36)

9. **C.** Secondary transactions are transactions that do not benefit the issuer. Issuer transactions and private placements are primary offerings. (Page 70)

10. **B.** Prior to clearance, a red herring may be distributed to estimate or gauge customer interest. Additionally, the registration statement may be distributed (although normally it is not). A tombstone advertisement is also allowed. (Page 57)

11. **B.** Failure to identify objectives or to obtain corresponding financial information is considered contrary to the know-your-customer rule. (Page 77)

12. **C.** In this situation, aside from misrepresenting the value of the stock, the agent has committed a fraudulent act. Fraudulent acts are not part of selling. (Page 79)

13. **D.** Any action to influence the price of a security is considered market manipulation. Stating falsehoods, misrepresenting prices, matching and placing orders to influence prices are all examples of manipulation. (Page 78)

14. **C.** "Churning" is defined as excessive activity in a customer's account for the sole purpose of generating commissions. As long as the trading is sanctioned by the customer, churning does not occur. Because mutual funds carry a front-end load and are considered long-term investment vehicles, frequent trades constitute churning. (Page 77)

15. **B.** Commodity futures contracts are not securities, but options are. The other items that are not securities are life insurance contracts, endowment contracts, fixed annuities and IRA and Keogh plans. A voting trust certificate is issued in place of a stock certificate to stockholders of a corporation that is temporarily managed by a voting trust. (Page 30)

16. **B.** Arbitrage is not a violation. An individual selling exempt securities such as government securities, both foreign and domestic, is not

considered an agent and does not have to register as such as long as no commission is collected. If a commission is collected, that individual would have to be registered. (Page 78)

17. **A.** An investment adviser may determine the price and timing of a transaction without discretionary authority. In this situation, the adviser acted without authority when he changed the amount of the security sold. (Page 77)

18. **C.** In general, supervisors and employers may be held jointly liable for violations committed by any person under their direct or indirect control. This includes a firm that is in a position to manage or influence the activities of a subsidiary firm. The controlling firm may be released from liability if it establishes that it did not know of the violation and could not reasonably have known of it. (Page 36)

19. **C.** Under the USA, any person who issues or proposes to issue any security is an issuer. The company is considered an issuer. (Page 29)

20. **B.** The keys here are "low tax bracket" and "fixed income." A portfolio of municipal bonds is an unsuitable investment. The customer would be better off to buy bonds that pay a higher rate of return. Because the agent failed to make a suitable recommendation, the administrator could revoke the agent's license. (Page 77)

21. **C.** Typically, both the broker-dealer and the agent must be registered in each state in which they plan to do business. In order for the agent to accept the order, either she would have to be registered in Florida or the customer would have to be present in her office in Nebraska. (Page 37)

22. **D.** The key here is "individual account." The only individual who can place an order is the person who has the account. The customer's husband can tell the agent to sell until he is blue in the face, but the agent cannot do so. (Page 77)

23. **C.** This investment is unsuitable because the investor wants income only. The agent has discretionary power over the account; therefore, the transaction is not illegal. (Page 17)

24. **D.** The use of information that has no basis in fact is strictly prohibited. The use of rumors is misrepresentation and a violation of the Uniform Securities Act. (Page 78)

25. **C.** The state administrator does not *approve anything*. The other statements are statements of fact and are permitted. (Page 78)

26. **D.** After the information has become public, it is no longer considered inside information and may be disseminated. (Page 78)

27. **A.** An agent's license is effective only as long as that agent is associated with a registered broker-dealer. (Page 40)

28. **B.** Companies whose securities are listed on a national exchange, such as the NYSE or AMEX, qualify for the blue chip exemption. Companies that are listed must provide periodic reports concerning their firms, and the reports must be available to prospective investors. (Page 70)

29. **A.** During the cooling-off period, indications of interest may be solicited with the use of a red herring. No offers or sales can be made prior to the registration's effective date. (Page 79)

30. **B.** Except for those items specifically exempted from the definition of "security" (such as life insurance), almost anything can be a security. However, certain items, such as futures contracts, are not securities; therefore, choice IV is incorrect. (Page 30)

31. **C.** For securities purposes, it is necessary only that the individual represent the broker-dealer or the issuer. Receiving a commission from the sale of securities from either the broker-dealer or the issuer satisfies the basic definition of "agent." (Page 38)

32. **D.** Securities of a bank are exempt securities, and a person who transacts business only in exempt securities is, by definition, not an agent or a broker-dealer. (Page 38)

33. **D.** A "supervised person" is an individual who provides investment advice and services on the investment adviser's behalf. This individual is subject to the supervision and control of the investment adviser. (Page 3)

34. **D.** A vacation home is not a security; however, if the condominium had been purchased to rent out, it may be a security. (Page 30)

35. **D.** All of these are "persons" in law. The legal definition of "person" does not include a minor, a deceased individual or a mentally incompetent individual. (Page 2)

36. **C.** *Moody's Public Utility Manual, Fitch's Manual* and *Best's Life Insurance Manual* are all recognized manuals that provide the information necessary for an investor to make an informed investment choice, thus qualifying for the manual exemption. Dow Jones is a market average, not a manual. (Page 70)

37. **D.** The exceptions are offering rescission and explaining that performance is not necessarily guaranteed. (Page 78)

38. **A.** If there is a rule barring custody, under no circumstances may the adviser have custody of customer funds or securities. (Page 17)

39. **D.** An individual is not considered an agent when representing the issuer in each of the cases cited. Note that, for purposes of the exam and unless otherwise stated, all commercial paper is considered to mature in 270 days or less. (Page 38)

40. **A.** The definition of "agent" would include an individual representing the issuer in a transaction for the benefit of the issuer unless the individual does not receive compensation. (Page 38)

41. **A.** Private investment companies represent an unregistered form of investment companies. Their purpose is to raise capital for business ventures. (Page 4)

42. **B.** Registration as an agent of the issuer is necessary because commissions are paid. (Page 38)

43. **A.** The term "sale" does not include a bona fide pledge or loan. (Page 29)

44. **C.** Advisers of private investment companies may be compensated on a performance-fee basis. (Page 18)

45. **C.** Passing the Series 6 (mutual funds and variable annuities), Series 7 (general securities) or Series 22 (direct participation programs) qualifies an individual to solicit security sales on a federal level. The state administrator must grant registration and the individual must be associated with a broker-dealer before the individual may engage in securities transactions. (Page 39)

46. **D.** It is unlawful for a person to transact business unless that person is registered, even if the securities are exempt. (Page 38)

47. **B.** Broker-dealers, agents and state-registered investment advisers must file consent to service of process forms with initial applications for registration. The consent to service gives the administrator rights over the applicants. Each applicant may be required to pass an exam and post a surety bond. Federally registered investment advisers must give notice and pay a filing fee in any state in which they conduct business. (Page 39)

48. **C.** Qualified purchasers are eligible to invest in private investment companies. These persons fall into four categories: (1) individuals with $5 million in investments, (2) trusts sponsored by qualified purchasers, (3) family businesses with $5 million or more invested and (4) business with no less than $25 million invested. (Page 4)

49. **C.** Broker-dealers and registered reps who give advice as part of their normal business are not required to register as investment advisers. However, if a registered rep provides investment advice outside the scope of employment at the broker-dealer, the rep must be registered. Thus, both choice II and choice IV are true statements. (Page 11)

50. **C.** Broker-dealers with no office in the state and clients with less than 30 days' temporary residency are exempt from state registration. (Page 37)

11 Uniform Securities Act Exam Four

1. Under the Uniform Securities Act, an investment adviser may select which of the following to execute customer transactions?

   I. Full-service broker-dealer
   II. Discount broker-dealer
   III. Broker-dealer associated with the investment adviser
   IV. Another investment adviser

   A. I only
   B. II only
   C. II and III only
   D. I, II, III and IV

2. Under the Uniform Securities Act, which of the following persons is included in the definition of "investment adviser"?

   A. Antiques dealer who receives a fee for advising customers as to the value of antiques and rare coins
   B. Registered representative of a broker-dealer who receives a flat fee for analyzing a customer's investment objectives and recommending a portfolio of securities
   C. Publisher that receives a yearly subscription fee for a newsletter that provides nonspecific investment advice
   D. Bank that offers investment counseling to its high net worth customers

3. An agent discovers that he has sold to a customer an unregistered nonexempt security that he thought was exempt. The agent offers to buy it back. Under the Uniform Securities Act, which of the following statements is(are) true?

   I. The customer may accept the offer, but still may sue.
   II. This is legal and is called *rescission.*
   III. The offer also must include interest.
   IV. This cannot be done under any circumstances.

   A. I
   B. II
   C. II and III
   D. IV

4. A customer living in one state receives a phone call from an agent in another state. A transaction between the two occurs in yet another state. Under the Uniform Securities Act, under whose jurisdiction does the transaction fall?

   A. Administrator of the state in which the customer lives
   B. Administrator of the state in which the agent is registered
   C. Administrator of the state in which the transaction took place
   D. Administrators of all three states involved

5. According to the Uniform Securities Act, the sale of a security to an insurance company is
   A. an exempt security
   B. an exempt transaction
   C. always a private placement
   D. illegal

6. Under the NSMIA, issuers are required to pay
   A. federal filing fees
   B. state filing fees
   C. both state and federal filing fees
   D. none of the above

7. All of the following are prohibited practices under the Uniform Securities Act EXCEPT
   I. borrowing money or securities from a customer's account without express written permission
   II. failing to identify a customer's financial objectives
   III. selling rights
   IV. guaranteeing a customer's account against losses

   A. I and II
   B. I, II and III
   C. I, II and IV
   D. III

8. According to the Uniform Securities Act, which of the following statements regarding state registration of securities is true?
   A. Registration by filing is effective when so ordered by the administrator.
   B. Registration by coordination is effective concurrently with federal registration.
   C. Registration by qualification is effective after 30 days.
   D. Registration by coordination is effective when so ordered by the administrator.

9. According to the Uniform Securities Act, under which of the following circumstances is an agent allowed to tell a customer that, when dividends are reinvested in a mutual fund, the customer always will be able to sell at a profit?
   A. The agent does not use the word "guaranteed."
   B. The agent further explains that dividends reinvested are not taxable income.
   C. The fund is a no-load fund.
   D. This is not permitted under any circumstances.

10. What information may be contained in the advertising prospectus of a management investment company?
    A. Management fees
    B. Sales charges
    C. Investment risks
    D. Performance figures

11. According to the Uniform Securities Act, when an agent leaves one broker-dealer to join another broker-dealer, the agent's license must be changed over
    A. immediately
    B. within 45 days
    C. at the agent's next license renewal date
    D. The agent's license cannot be changed.

12. Which of the following would be defined as a qualified purchaser?
    A. Stuart and Carol, who invest jointly and own $5.5 million in securities
    B. Stuart, who owns $1 million in securities
    C. Adam, who owns a $100,000 house and $1 million in securities
    D. Allison, who is the beneficiary of a $1 million variable life insurance policy and owns $4.9 million in securities

13. States may require a surety bond as a prerequisite to registration under the Uniform Securities Act for which of the following persons?

    I. Broker-dealer
    II. Agent
    III. State-registered investment adviser

    A. I only
    B. I and II only
    C. II and III only
    D. I, II and III

14. The SEC's role now includes

    A. improvement and oversight of market efficiency
    B. competition in the securities industry
    C. capital formation
    D. all of the above

15. According to the Uniform Securities Act, the investment adviser (with the exception of a private investment company's adviser) must be careful not to

    A. receive performance-based fees
    B. enter into a contract with a customer that does not specifically spell out the compensation agreement
    C. refund commissions on mutual fund sales
    D. engage in any of the above activities

16. Which of the following fits the definition of "sale," according to the Uniform Securities Act?

    A. Solicitation of an offer to buy a security for value
    B. Attempt to dispose of a security for value
    C. Contract to dispose of a security
    D. Issuing a prospectus

17. Under the National Securities Markets Improvement Act and the Uniform Securities Act, if an investment adviser has custody of customer funds and securities, how often must the adviser send the customer a statement of account activity?

    A. Annually
    B. Quarterly
    C. Monthly
    D. With every transaction

18. Microscam wants to sell stock to the public. Six of Microscam's full-time employees sell the stock for Microscam. Under the Uniform Securities Act, these people would be considered

    A. broker-dealers
    B. agents of the issuer
    C. issuers
    D. agents of the broker-dealer

19. Under the Uniform Securities Act, which of the following is an example of a cease and desist order?

    A. Order that can be issued only by a federal agency to a brokerage firm to stop an advertising campaign
    B. Order by any administrative agency to refrain from a practice of business found by that agency to be unfair
    C. Order that can be issued only by the courts, requiring a business to stop an unfair practice
    D. Order from one brokerage firm to another brokerage firm to refrain from unfair business practices

20. The SEC can deny a person a license if the person

    I. has a criminal record
    II. has served jail time of one year or more
    III. has lost a civil lawsuit within the last year
    IV. was convicted of a crime but was given probation

    A. I and II
    B. I and III
    C. II and III
    D. III and IV

21. According to the Uniform Securities Act, if the registration of an agent is revoked by the administrator, the administrator can deny future registration of that agent as a(n)

    A. agent
    B. broker-dealer
    C. broker-dealer or agent
    D. The administrator has no authority to deny future registration.

22. Under the NSMIA, registered investment companies are required to file reports with the SEC

    A. more frequently
    B. quarterly
    C. semiannually
    D. annually

23. An elderly widow with no other income wishes to invest the proceeds from her husband's life insurance. According to the Uniform Securities Act, which of the following would be a suitable recommendation?

    A. Call options
    B. Municipal bonds
    C. Oil and gas exploration program that you know is going to strike
    D. Blue chip income stocks

24. You would be exempt from state registration as an investment adviser under the NSMIA and the USA if you had no place of business in the state and if, in any consecutive 12-month period, you executed trades for fewer than how many customers?

    A. Six
    B. Ten
    C. Fifteen
    D. Unlimited

25. Under the Uniform Securities Act, all of the following persons may provide investment advice incidental to their normal business without requiring registration as an investment adviser EXCEPT a(n)

    A. teacher
    B. economist
    C. lawyer
    D. engineer

26. As defined in the Uniform Securities Act, which of the following is NOT considered a security?

    A. Fixed annuity
    B. Stock option
    C. Limited partnership unit
    D. Commodity option

27. According to the Uniform Securities Act, from which of the following customers may an investment adviser borrow money?

    I. Affiliate of the investment adviser
    II. Broker-dealer
    III. Bank
    IV. Issuer of blue chip stock

    A. I, II and III
    B. I and IV
    C. II and III
    D. III

28. All of the following are exempt securities under the Uniform Securities Act EXCEPT

I. U.S. government securities
II. unsolicited transactions
III. transactions between issuers and underwriters
IV. securities of credit unions

A. I, II and IV
B. I and IV
C. II and III
D. IV

29. Under the Uniform Securities Act, which of the following is considered a broker-dealer?

I. Agent
II. Issuer
III. Corporation selling interests in an oil and gas limited partnership
IV. Credit union selling its own stock

A. I
B. I and III
C. II and IV
D. III

30. A partner in an issuing corporation effects transactions in the issuer's registered, non-exempt securities and receives a commission. Under the Uniform Securities Act, the partner is considered a(n)

A. agent
B. broker-dealer
C. investment adviser
D. issuer

31. With regard to the Uniform Securities Act, which of the following persons does NOT have to register as an investment adviser?

I. Broker-dealer who gives advice and charges a specific fee for that advice
II. Agent of a broker-dealer who gives investment advice within the course of his duties and charges a fee for that advice
III. Broker-dealer who gives investment advice that is incidental to the course of her business
IV. Attorney who writes a legal opinion of counsel for a municipal bond

A. I, II and IV only
B. III only
C. III and IV only
D. I, II, III and IV

32. According to the Uniform Securities Act, an investment adviser may have custody of a customer's funds and securities in which of the following circumstances?

A. If he has received the permission of the administrator
B. If custody is prohibited by the administrator
C. If he does not share in the capital gains of the account
D. If the administrator has been informed of the custody

33. Which of the following acts outlines the procedure for registering securities by coordination?

A. Securities Act of 1933
B. Securities Coordination Act of 1933
C. Uniform Securities Act
D. Trust Indenture Act of 1939

34. Which of the following statements are true?

    I. States cannot enforce recordkeeping and reporting responsibilities for state-registered investment advisers.
    II. States regulate investment advisers with less than $25 million in assets under management whose activity is largely concentrated within their boundaries.
    III. The SEC regulates investment advisers with $25 million or more in assets under management.
    IV. Only the SEC can enforce antifraud regulations against investment advisers.

    A. I and III
    B. II and III
    C. III and IV
    D. I, II and IV

35. An agent's registration under the Uniform Securities Act must be renewed how frequently?

    A. Every 90 days
    B. Every December 31st
    C. Each state varies.
    D. Registration is effective until it is revoked, is withdrawn or expires.

36. According to the Uniform Securities Act, what must broker-dealers, state-registered investment advisers and agents provide the administrator as requirements for registration?

    I. Financial statements
    II. Consent to service of process
    III. Surety bonds
    IV. Updates of information during registration

    A. I and II only
    B. I and III only
    C. II only
    D. I, II, III and IV

37. According to the Uniform Securities Act, an agent could share in the profits of a customer's account in which of the following situations?

    I. The agent has written permission from the customer.
    II. The agent has written permission from the broker-dealer.
    III. The participation is proportional to the commission the agent receives.
    IV. The participation is proportional to the agent's investment in the account.

    A. I, II and IV only
    B. I and III only
    C. II and III only
    D. I, II, III and IV

38. According to the Uniform Securities Act, a person would be required to register as a broker-dealer in a state under which of the following circumstances?

    I. Person has no place of business in the state, but has directed offers to 25 residents of that state
    II. Person has no place of business in the state and deals exclusively with broker-dealers in that state
    III. Person has no place of business in the state and effects transactions exclusively with issuers of securities in that state
    IV. Person has a place of business in the state

    A. I, II and IV only
    B. I and IV only
    C. II and III only
    D. I, II, III and IV

39. An individual would NOT be considered an agent under the Uniform Securities Act if she engages in which of the following transactions?

I. Isolated nonissuer transactions
II. Transactions between an issuer and ordinary investors
III. Transactions between an issuer and the underwriters
IV. Transactions between an issuer and savings institutions or trust companies

A. I, III and IV only
B. II and III only
C. II and IV only
D. I, II, III and IV

40. A nonissuer corporation uses its employees to sell nonexempt securities. The corporation receives a commission on the sale of the securities. Some of the commission is then paid to the employees. According to the Uniform Securities Act, the corporation is a

A. broker-dealer that must be registered
B. corporation selling only to sophisticated investors
C. broker-dealer engaging in exempt transactions
D. corporation selling to an employee pension fund

41. According to the Uniform Securities Act, an example of an investment adviser is a

A. lawyer
B. publisher of a magazine
C. person who is paid a fee for advising customers on securities
D. person who is paid a commission for advising customers on securities

42. The definition of "investment company" excludes an investment pool

A. that offers its securities to no more than 35 accredited investors
B. that makes a public offering of its securities
C. that purchases more than 25 percent of any registered investment company's securities
D. whose securities are held exclusively by qualified purchasers (sophisticated investors)

43. As outlined in the Uniform Securities Act, an offer and sale does NOT exist if it is a(n)

I. act as a result of a class vote by stockholders regarding a merger or consolidation
II. bona fide pledge or loan
III. act incident to a judicially approved reorganization in which a security is issued in exchange for one or more outstanding shares
IV. act as a result of a judicially approved reorganization in which one security is issued in exchange for an outstanding security

A. I and II only
B. I, II and III only
C. IV only
D. I, II, III and IV

44. Under the Uniform Securities Act, the administrator has the power to require an agent licensee to

A. have minimum net capital, post a surety bond and pass an exam
B. post a surety bond and pass an exam
C. post a surety bond, pay filing fees and pass an exam
D. have minimum net capital, pay filing fees, pass an exam and post a surety bond

45. An agent representing a broker-dealer in Arkansas wishes to do business in Tennessee exclusively in the trading of certain exempt securities. Under the Uniform Securities Act, the agent would

    A. not have to register in Tennessee
    B. have to register in Tennessee
    C. not have to register if the broker-dealer were registered in Tennessee
    D. be allowed to do business because the securities are exempt

46. If it is in the public interest to do so, the Uniform Securities Act provides that the state administrator may deny the registration of a person for all of the following reasons EXCEPT that

    A. the applicant is not qualified owing to lack of experience
    B. a willful violation of the Uniform Securities Act has taken place
    C. the applicant is financially insolvent
    D. the applicant is enjoined temporarily from engaging in the securities business

47. Under the Uniform Securities Act, an agent's license is effective for

    A. one year, although each state may determine its own schedule for renewal
    B. 18 months, of which the first six months is a probationary period
    C. 20 years
    D. one year, with all registrations expiring on December 31st

48. All of the following are part of the registration by filing procedure under the Uniform Securities Act EXCEPT that

    A. companies must have attained a specific level of earnings for the prior three-year period
    B. a copy of the offering circular or prospectus must be filed
    C. if not denied, registration becomes effective after 30 days
    D. a statement must list the name(s) of the underwriter(s) and describe the terms of the offering

49. Under the Uniform Securities Act, no specific response is required from the state administrator before which of the following types of securities registration become effective?

    I. Coordination
    II. Qualification
    III. Filing
    IV. Mastication

    A. I and II only
    B. I and III only
    C. II and III only
    D. I, II, III and IV

50. All of the following statements are true regarding the selling of private placements under the Uniform Securities Act EXCEPT that

    A. they cannot be offered to more than 10 people in 12 consecutive months
    B. they cannot be offered to five people or more in 12 consecutive months
    C. the seller must reasonably believe that all buyers are purchasing for investment purposes only
    D. no commission or other remuneration is paid

◆ Answers & Rationale

1. **D.** An investment adviser may execute transactions through any firm, provided that the fee charged the customer is reasonable in comparison to the services provided. Potential conflicts of interest, such as when a transaction is executed through an affiliated broker-dealer, are subject to disclosure requirements. (Page 24)

2. **B.** Answer B outlines the conditions under which a broker-dealer is considered an investment adviser. The antiques dealer provides advice on objects that are not considered securities; he therefore is not providing investment advice. Publishers may provide generic investment advice without being considered an investment adviser, and banks are excluded from the definition. (Page 2)

3. **C.** As long as the agent sold the security with no intent to defraud, rescission may be offered. Rescission is the return of the customer's money, plus interest, less any income received from the investment. (Page 36)

4. **D.** Under the scope of the Uniform Securities Act, if any part of a transaction occurs in a state, the entire transaction is under the jurisdiction of the state administrator. (Page 34)

5. **B.** Sales of securities to financial institutions or accredited investors are exempt transactions. (Page 71)

6. **B.** The states continue to receive filing fees from exempt issuers. (Page 68)

7. **D.** The exception is selling rights. Choice I is stealing, choice II is failure to follow suitability standards and choice IV is fraudulent. (Page 78)

8. **B.** Coordination is frequently used to register a security simultaneously under the Securities Act of 1933 and in a state. If the security's federal registration is pending and the administrator has received all of the required material, the two registrations can be declared effective at the same time. (Page 65)

9. **D.** This statement is misleading under any circumstances. Under no circumstances can an agent promise profit in a security transaction. (Page 73)

10. **D.** The advertising prospectus may now include performance data on the fund and would be subject to the SEC's reporting requirements. This data is added to the standardized information placed in a summary prospectus. (Page 95)

11. **A.** An agent's license must be transferred immediately. Additionally, both the new and the old broker-dealer, as well as the agent, must notify the administrator of the transfer in writing. (Page 40)

12. **A.** A qualified purchaser falls into one of the following categories: (1) individuals with $5 million in investments, (2) trusts sponsored by qualified purchasers, (3) family businesses with $5 million or more invested or (4) business with no less than $25 million invested. (Page 4)

13. **D.** The common requirements are to pay filing fees, post a surety bond and consent to service of process for all three of these designations. For broker-dealers and state-registered investment advisers, an additional net worth requirement has to be met. (Page 9)

14. **D.** Under the NSMIA, the SEC will now be responsible for the improvement and oversight of market efficiency, competition in the securities industry and capital formation. The SEC is still responsible for acting in the public's best interest. (Page 32)

15. **D.** All of these are violations under the Uniform Securities Act. Fees must be spelled out and can be either a flat fee or a percentage of the assets managed. Investment advisers of private

investment companies may receive performance-based fees. (Page 18)

16. **C.** Solicitations and attempts to dispose are offers. Sales involve any contract or disposition for value. (Page 29)

17. **B.** An investment adviser in possession of customer assets must send a statement to the customer every three months; the statement must list the securities held by the adviser and must show all transactions in the account since the last statement date. (Page 17)

18. **B.** Microscam is the issuer. The definition of "agent" is any individual who works for others. If the employees are working for Microscam, they would be considered agents of the issuer. (Page 38)

19. **B.** A cease and desist order is nothing more than an administrative agency telling you to stop what you are doing. The order can come from a federal, state or judicial body; it is not exclusive to any one. (Page 36)

20. **A.** The SEC will now deny licensure to those persons with a criminal record who have served jail sentences of one year or more. (Page 10)

21. **C.** Once registration has been revoked, the administrator can bar the registrant from ever again working in the securities business in any capacity. (Page 35)

22. **A.** Management investment companies are now open to more frequent reporting requirements as deemed necessary by the SEC. (Page 96)

23. **D.** This customer needs income. Of the answers given, the blue chip stocks would provide the highest level while still maintaining safety. The municipal bonds could be recommended if she had a tax problem, but she does not. (Page 77)

24. **A.** Under the NSMIA and the USA, an investment adviser would be exempt from state registration requirements if he directed business communications in the state to fewer than six customers in a 12-month period. This is referred to as the "national de minimis." (Page 8)

25. **B.** The Uniform Securities Act exempts from registration teachers, engineers, lawyers and accountants providing investment advice that is incidental to the performance of their normal business. Economists are not granted an exemption under the act. (Page 3)

26. **A.** A fixed annuity is an insurance contract that cannot be traded for value. Commodity options (although not the underlying futures contracts) and stock options are considered securities, as are interests purchased in a limited partnership enterprise. (Page 30)

27. **A.** An investment adviser may not borrow money from a customer unless the customer is an affiliate of the investment adviser, a broker-dealer, or a bank or another institution in the business of lending money. (Page 77)

28. **C.** Government securities and securities of financial institutions are exempt securities. Unsolicited transactions and transactions between issuers and underwriters are exempt transactions, not exempt securities. (Page 69)

29. **D.** "Broker-dealer" is defined as any person that invests for others or for his own account. A broker-dealer is not an issuer or an agent. (Page 28)

30. **A.** Being a partner of an issuer does not automatically make you an agent unless you actively participate in the underwriting process and receive a commission for sales efforts. (Page 38)

31. **C.** The key is "charges a fee" for the advice. Remember, attorneys are exempt from the definition of "investment adviser." (Page 3)

32. **D.** As long as retaining custody of funds is not prohibited, he may have custody of a customer's account after providing notice to the administrator. (Page 17)

33. **A.** A security registered using coordination will coordinate that registration with the registration filed with the SEC. The Securities Act of 1933 is the basis for securities registration of securities sold interstate. (Page 65)

34. **B.** Persons who have less than $25 million in assets under management must register on a state basis only. States as well as the SEC are required to enforce all antifraud regulations. (Page 8)

35. **B.** Under the Uniform Securities Act, an agent's license expires annually on December 31st unless it is renewed. (Page 38)

36. **C.** All three persons listed must provide a consent to service of process. Only broker-dealers and investment advisers are required to file financial statements and to provide updates of information. Only those broker-dealers, agents and advisers who have custody of or discretionary authority over customer securities may be required to post surety bonds. (Page 39)

37. **A.** If an agent invests money with a customer, the agent may share in profits if the broker-dealer and the customer agree in writing and if the sharing is proportionate to the agent's investment. It has nothing to do with commissions. (Page 79)

38. **B.** The term "broker-dealer" does not include a person who has no place of business in the state and who (1) effects transactions exclusively through issuers, other broker-dealers or institutions or (2) directs an offer in the state to an existing customer who is not a permanent resident of the state where the offer is received. (Page 37)

39. **A.** An individual who effects securities transactions for compensation is defined as an agent. A person representing an issuer in an exempt transaction does not fall under the definition, nor does a person who represents an issuer in effecting transactions with existing employees in which no commissions are paid. (Page 38)

40. **A.** A broker-dealer is in the business of effecting transactions in securities for its own account or for the accounts of others. Under the Uniform Securities Act, the broker-dealer must register in the state where business is transacted. (Page 37)

41. **C.** The term "investment adviser" means any person who is in the business of selling investment advice. (Page 2)

42. **D.** A qualified purchasers pool is an unregistered investment pool. Its purpose is to raise venture capital. (Page 4)

43. **D.** The Uniform Securities Act specifically excludes these four choices from the definitions of "offer and sale." (Page 29)

44. **C.** The administrator *may* require that, as a condition of registration, the agent post a surety bond, pay filing fees and take an examination that may be written, oral or both. (Page 38)

45. **B.** Although the securities are exempted from registration, the agent must register in every state where business is attempted. (Page 38)

46. **A.** Registration may be denied if the applicant willfully violates the Uniform Securities Act, is financially insolvent or has been enjoined from engaging in the securities business. If the person qualifies by virtue of training or knowledge, registration cannot be denied for lack of experience only. (Page 41)

47. **D.** Registrations expire annually on December 31st unless renewed. (Page 38)

48. **C.** Registration becomes effective after a five-day cooling-off period. (Page 66)

49. **B.** Registration by filing and coordination do not require a response from the state administrator for effectiveness. Registration by qualification, however, becomes effective only at the order of the administrator. (Page 66)

50. **B.** The Uniform Securities Act allows an exemption from registration for securities if they are sold to no more than 10 people (other than institutional investors), purchased for investment purposes and no commission is paid. (Page 72)

12 Series 65 Final Exam One

1. Each of the following is a security under the Uniform Securities Act EXCEPT

   A. common stock
   B. a futures contract
   C. a variable annuity
   D. right or warrant

2. The term "person" as defined in the Uniform Securities Act may include

   A. an individual or a partnership
   B. almost any entity
   C. an individual, a partnership, a corporation or an association
   D. an individual

3. Under which of the following circumstances would an investment adviser be exempt from registration, licensing or qualification requirements of state securities regulators?

   I. The investment adviser has no place of business in the state.
   II. The investment adviser has fewer than three places of business in the state.
   III. The investment adviser has fewer than six clients who were residents of the state in the preceding 12-month period.
   IV. The investment adviser has made fewer than five solicitations within the state in the preceding 12-month period.

   A. I and III
   B. I and IV
   C. II and IV
   D. III and IV

4. Which of the following is NOT considered an agent under the Uniform Securities Act?

   A. Vice-president of a broker-dealer who solicits clients for the firm
   B. Associate of a broker-dealer who manages the account of a single client
   C. Clerk employed by a broker-dealer
   D. Partner of a broker-dealer who engages in securities transactions for themselves and clients

5. Which of the following is included under the definition of "broker-dealer" under the Uniform Securities Act?

   A. One who effects securities transactions solely for his own account
   B. Agent
   C. Out-of-state broker-dealer that services only other broker-dealers
   D. Issuer of securities

6. Which of the following is(are) prohibited by the antifraud provisions of the Uniform Securities Act?

   I. Omission of a fact important to understanding other statements that are made
   II. Deceptive sales presentation that does not result in a sale
   III. Misstatement of a material fact

   A. I and III only
   B. II and III only
   C. III only
   D. I, II and III

7. Which of the following is considered a willful violation of the antifraud provisions of the Uniform Securities Act?

   I. Adviser Belle Charolais advises her client to invest in a new issue stock without knowing that the issue has not been properly registered.
   II. Joe Kuhl recommends that a client purchase shares in Microscam without disclosing that the company is financially unstable. The client does not make the purchase.
   III. Angus Bullwether offers for sale shares in Kelptek, which he owns.

   A. I and II only
   B. I and III only
   C. II only
   D. I, II and III

8. Which of the following activities is(are) prohibited under the Uniform Securities Act?

   I. Engaging in a practice not expressly forbidden by the act, but defined as unethical by the administrator in a rule
   II. Omitting a material fact when soliciting a client
   III. Selling recommended securities to a client from one's own account without disclosing this fact to the client

   A. I and II only
   B. I and III only
   C. II only
   D. I, II and III

9. SEC regulations stipulate that investment advisers that have custody of client's funds or securities must

   I. establish one or more bank accounts that contain only clients' funds
   II. immediately after accepting custody of funds or securities, notify the client in writing of the place and manner in which the funds and securities will be held
   III. send each client, not less than once every month, an itemized statement showing the securities and funds in custody
   IV. provide for an independent public accountant who will perform a "surprise audit" at least once each year, to verify clients' funds and securities

   A. I and II only
   B. I, II and IV only
   C. I and III only
   D. I, II, III and IV

10. Investment advisers subject to registration with a state securities regulator are exempt from registration with the Securities Exchange Commission unless the investment adviser

   I. manages at least $100 million in retirement funds subject to ERISA rules
   II. manages at least $25 million in assets for clients
   III. acts as the investment adviser for a federally registered investment company
   IV. holds customer's cash and securities and operates in a discretionary manner for wrap accounts

   A. I and III
   B. I and IV
   C. II and III
   D. III and IV

11. Under the Uniform Securities Act, the requirements for registration of an investment adviser may include which of the following?

   I. A surety bond for advisers who do not have custody of or discretion over client securities or funds
   II. Minimum financial requirements for advisers who do not have custody of client securities or funds
   III. An announcement of the application for registration in one or more newspapers in the state

   A. I and II only
   B. I and III only
   C. II and III only
   D. I, II and III

12. Under the Uniform Securities Act, who automatically becomes registered as an agent when a broker-dealer's registration becomes effective?

   A. Any partner, officer or director of the firm
   B. The individual designated on the application for registration
   C. Any individual employed by or associated with the firm who will have responsibilities as an agent
   D. No one

13. An investment adviser is currently organized as a sole proprietor, but is changing the structure of the firm to a limited partnership. This change will require the investment adviser to file

   A. a new Form ADV because the limited partnership will be a new business entity
   B. a Form ADV-S, supplementing the old form by showing the change in the nature of its business
   C. a Form ADV-W withdrawing its current filing
   D. additional documentation only if the principals responsible for management of client portfolios change

14. "Agency cross transaction for an advisory client" means that the

A. investment adviser is acting on behalf of the client in a discretionary manner to sell one security and, using the proceeds, purchase another, and is to be compensated for both transactions
B. adviser, acting as a broker for the client, effects a buy or sell transaction while simultaneously acting as broker for another party on the other side of the transaction
C. adviser, acting as a market maker, sells securities to an advisory account client from its own inventory, charging the client a markup on the securities
D. adviser buys securities for its own investment account and then advises all clients to buy the same securities in order to positively affect the value of the securities

15. The disciplinary actions that may be taken by the administrator against an investment adviser representative under the Uniform Securities Act include which of the following?

I. Restricting the performance of any activity in the advisory or brokerage business
II. Barring the rep from employment with an investment advisory firm
III. Permanent revocation of registration

A. I and II only
B. I and III only
C. II and III only
D. I, II and III

16. Under the Uniform Securities Act, in which of the following circumstances may the administrator take action against an investment advisory firm?

I. A minority shareholder with no management role in the firm cannot meet his financial obligations as they come due.
II. The administrator of another state found that the president of the firm violated the securities laws of that other state nine years ago.
III. The firm has liabilities that exceed its assets.

A. I and III only
B. II only
C. II and III only
D. I, II and III

17. All of the following are grounds for canceling an investment adviser's registration under the Uniform Securities Act EXCEPT if the adviser

A. has ceased doing business as an investment adviser
B. cannot be located after a reasonable search
C. has engaged in an unethical business practice
D. has been found by a court to be mentally incompetent

18. Disciplinary proceedings under the Uniform Securities Act generally require the administrator to provide which of the following?

I. Opportunity for a hearing
II. Written findings of facts and conclusions of law
III. Appropriate prior notice

A. I and III only
B. II only
C. II and III only
D. I, II and III

19. What is the purpose of margin requirements?

    A. To prevent excessive speculation by customers
    B. To ensure the solvency of broker-dealers
    C. To allow the individual investor to leverage investments
    D. To augment revenue of a broker-dealer

20. Each of the following is an exempt security under the Uniform Securities Act EXCEPT a

    A. stock issued by a local profit-making manufacturing corporation not listed on any exchange
    B. stock issued by a railroad regulated by the Interstate Commerce Commission
    C. bond issued by a state credit union
    D. bond guaranteed by the City of Winnipeg, Canada

21. Under the Uniform Securities Act, each of the following is a requirement for a preorganization subscription exemption EXCEPT

    A. no payment may be made by any subscriber
    B. there may be no more than 10 subscribers
    C. the offer of the security may not be advertised
    D. no commission may be paid to anyone for soliciting potential subscribers

22. Which of the following statements is true concerning the authority of the administrator to revoke an exemption under the Uniform Securities Act?

    A. The revocation may apply to a period of time prior to the date the revocation order was issued.
    B. In a proceeding to revoke an exemption, it is assumed that the exemption applies and the administrator must prove that it does not apply.
    C. The order revoking an exemption may be issued without prior notice to the persons affected.
    D. The administrator may not revoke the exemption of securities issued by a nonprofit corporation.

23. Under the Uniform Securities Act, the administrator has the authority to

    I. take evidence
    II. subpoena witnesses
    III. indict offenders
    IV. administer oaths

    A. I, II and III only
    B. I, II and IV only
    C. IV only
    D. I, II, III and IV

24. Under the Uniform Securities Act, which of the following statements is(are) true?

    I. Violators may incur a criminal penalty of a $5,000 fine or three years in jail, but not both.
    II. There is no statute of limitations on the return of criminal indictments.
    III. The administrator may issue a cease and desist order without a prior hearing.

    A. I and II only
    B. I and III only
    C. III only
    D. I, II and III

25. Under the Uniform Securities Act, which of the following negates a client's right to a civil suit for damages?

    I. The advice was given more than three years ago.
    II. The adviser has died.
    III. The client willingly signed a statement waiving the adviser's compliance with the provision of the act on which the suit is based.

    A. I only
    B. I and II only
    C. II and III only
    D. I, II and III

26. The Securities Act of 1933 was passed to provide for

    A. the registration of newly issued securities and the disclosure of information in their sale
    B. the registration of investment advisory firms and their representatives
    C. the regulation of broker-dealers and exchanges
    D. protection against "high pressure" tactics in the sale of securities

27. Under the Securities Act of 1933, which of the following is defined as a "person"?

    I. Subdivision of a government
    II. Nonprofit, charitable corporation
    III. Unincorporated amateur athletic club

    A. I only
    B. I and II only
    C. II and III only
    D. I, II and III

28. Under the Securities Act of 1933, the term "underwriter" includes any person who

    A. buys or sells securities for his own account or for the accounts of others
    B. represents an issuer in distributing a security to the public
    C. sells a security to a customer for a commission
    D. purchases a security for investment

29. Under the Securities Act of 1933, the definition of "prospectus" includes a

    I. written offer of an initial public offering
    II. verbal offer of a security
    III. tombstone advertisement for a security

    A. I only
    B. I and II only
    C. III only
    D. I, II and III

30. The definition of "accredited investor" under the Securities Act of 1933 includes

    I. securities industry professionals such as investment adviser representatives and agents
    II. institutions such as banks, insurance companies, investment companies and employee benefit plans
    III. individuals with a college degree and professional certification in the fields of finance, accounting or law

    A. I and II only
    B. I and III only
    C. II only
    D. I, II and III

31. Under the Securities Act of 1933, which of the following is(are) conditions under which sales to accredited investors are exempt?

    I. The investor is purchasing for investment.
    II. No one is receiving any remuneration on the transaction.
    III. No advertising or public solicitation takes place.

    A. I and II only
    B. I and III only
    C. III only
    D. I, II and III

32. The cooling-off period for a new issue registered under the Securities Act of 1933 extends for how many days?

    A. 5
    B. 20
    C. 30
    D. 45

33. The prospectus for a stock issued by the Tippecanoe Ferry Co. is found to contain material errors of fact. A purchaser of the security files a lawsuit to recover damages. Under the Securities Act of 1933, which of the following could NOT be named as a defendant in the lawsuit?

    A. Any of Tippecanoe Ferry's directors
    B. Adam Grizzly, a private investor who owns a small fraction of Tippecanoe Ferry's outstanding shares
    C. The underwriter of the issue
    D. Tippecanoe Ferry's chief accounting officer

34. The Securities Act of 1933 requires that, where the publisher of an investment advisory newsletter has been paid a fee by the underwriter of a new issue to print a detailed report on a security the underwriter is distributing, the publisher is required to

    A. make a reasonable investigation to confirm the facts that appear in the report
    B. state in the publication that payment was received and the amount of the payment
    C. print the word "advertisement" prominently above the report
    D. state prominently that the inclusion in the newsletter of a description of the security should not be regarded as a recommendation of the security

35. The purpose of the Securities Exchange Act of 1934 is to

    A. regulate the persons involved in the new issue market
    B. regulate the persons involved in the secondary market
    C. close loopholes in the Securities Act of 1933
    D. make securities regulation more uniform among the several states

36. Under the Securities Exchange Act of 1934, an "exchange" is a(n)

    A. disposition of a security for value
    B. organization that provides facilities for bringing together buyers and sellers of securities
    C. organization of securities professionals designed to promote fair practices in doing business with the public
    D. transaction involving a security

37. Under the Securities Exchange Act of 1934, a "market maker" is a

    A. security in high demand
    B. person who buys and sells securities for her own account or for the accounts of others
    C. dealer who holds himself out as being ready at all times to buy or sell shares of a specified security at a quoted price
    D. person who provides a marketplace to bring together buyers and sellers of securities

38. Which of the following are NOT defined as a securities information processor under the Securities Exchange Act of 1934?

I. Broker-dealer carrying out the activities customary to its business
II. New York Stock Exchange
III. Financial section of a daily national newspaper

A. I and II only
B. I and III only
C. II and III only
D. I, II and III

39. According to the Securities Exchange Act of 1934, in which of the following cases is an investment adviser exercising investment discretion?

I. When the market price of a stock is $100.42 per share, the client tells the adviser to sell it if it drops another $10 per share; the price falls to $90 per share, and the adviser sells it without further consultation with the client.
II. The client tells the adviser to purchase growth mutual fund shares and leaves the choice of the fund to the adviser.
III. The adviser determines what securities should be purchased for an account after the client sets specific investment objectives.

A. I and II only
B. I and III only
C. II and III only
D. I, II and III

40. The Securities Exchange Act of 1934 prohibits which of the following transactions?

I. A member of an exchange buys 1,000 shares of a stock on that exchange for its own account, and simultaneously sells 1,000 shares of that stock on another exchange for a higher price.
II. A member of an exchange effects a transaction for its own account in its capacity as a market maker.
III. A registered broker-dealer effects a transaction on an exchange that is not registered.

A. I
B. I and II
C. I and III
D. III

41. Under the Securities Exchange Act of 1934, a person dealing exclusively in government securities

A. is exempt from registration if she makes use of only one exchange located in her home state
B. must be registered as both a government securities dealer and a general broker-dealer
C. must be registered as a government securities dealer unless she has general broker-dealer registration
D. is exempt from federal registration requirements but not from state requirements

42. Under the Securities Exchange Act of 1934, which of the following statements are true regarding the use of credit to make securities purchases?

    I. The purpose of margin requirements is to prevent the excessive use of credit by the purchasers of securities.
    II. Credit may not be used to purchase new issues of securities.
    III. Margin requirements are set by the Federal Reserve Board.

    A. I and II only
    B. I and III only
    C. II and III only
    D. I, II and III

43. Which of the following statements is NOT true regarding the civil penalties that may be imposed for insider trading violations under the Securities Exchange Act of 1934?

    A. A civil penalty may be imposed only on a person who is registered under a securities act.
    B. The violation for which the penalty may be imposed is defined as "buying or selling securities while in possession of material, nonpublic information."
    C. The SEC may ask a court to impose a penalty of up to three times the loss avoided or profit gained on an illegal transaction.
    D. Improper supervision may cause an investment advisory firm to be liable to pay a penalty for an insider trading violation committed by one of its representatives.

44. Which of the following statements is true regarding an investment adviser's use of a full-service broker to make transactions for an account over which the adviser has investment discretion under the Securities Exchange Act of 1934?

    A. A full-service broker may be used if the charge is reasonable in relation to the advice, analyses or other services provided.
    B. A full-service broker may not be used for any transaction that could be done by a discount broker.
    C. A full-service broker may be used only if the broker is not affiliated with the adviser.
    D. Sales incentives, such as free vacations, may be taken into consideration by the adviser in determining whether to use a full-service broker.

45. Which of the following are NOT excluded from the definition of "investment company" under the Investment Company Act of 1940?

    I. Real estate investment trust
    II. Insurance company separate account
    III. Investment adviser

    A. I and II only
    B. I and III only
    C. II and III only
    D. I, II and III

46. Under the Investment Company Act of 1940, which of the following statements is NOT true regarding shares of mutual funds?

    A. They must be redeemed at their net asset value upon shareholder demand.
    B. They are issued by open-end investment companies.
    C. Their net asset value must be calculated each business day.
    D. Their sales price may be greater or less than their net asset value.

47. Under the Investment Company Act of 1940, it is legal for an investment adviser to

I. reduce a client's fee by any commissions earned on mutual fund sales to that client
II. rebate the commission on a mutual fund sale to a client who has already paid a fee for investment advice
III. keep the commission on a mutual fund sale when the client who purchased the shares has paid for investment advice

A. I and II only
B. I and III only
C. II and III only
D. I, II and III

48. Under the Investment Company Act of 1940, the SEC must issue an exemptive order before a mutual fund can

I. change its investment objective
II. employ as its investment adviser a person convicted of a felony involving the securities business
III. lend money to its investment adviser

A. I and II only
B. I and III only
C. II and III only
D. I, II and III

49. Which of the following statements is NOT true regarding a mutual fund's contract with its investment adviser under the provisions of the Investment Company Act of 1940?

A. It must be approved by a majority of the outstanding shares.
B. It must be in writing.
C. It must describe the adviser's compensation.
D. It may not be terminated except with the approval of a majority of the outstanding shares.

50. The Investment Company Act of 1940 generally prohibits affiliated persons of a mutual fund from

I. buying securities from the fund's portfolio
II. borrowing money from the fund
III. investing in shares of the fund

A. I and II only
B. I and III only
C. II and III only
D. I, II and III

51. A person who renders investment advice solely with respect to securities issued by the U.S. government

A. is exempt from state registration under the Uniform Securities Act, but must be federally registered under the Investment Advisers Act of 1940
B. is exempt from both federal and state registration requirements
C. must be registered with both the SEC and the state
D. need not be federally registered under the Investment Advisers Act of 1940, but generally must be state registered under the Uniform Securities Act

52. Under the Uniform Securities Act, which of the following is NOT included in the definition of "person associated with an investment adviser"?

A. Employee who manages client accounts for an investment advisory firm
B. Clerk in an investment advisory firm
C. Minority partner of an investment advisory firm
D. Majority stockholder of an investment advisory firm

53. Under the Investment Advisers Act of 1940, which of the following statements is NOT true with respect to an investment advisory firm that changes the fee it charges clients?

A. The firm is not required to obtain prior SEC approval of the change.
B. The change can be made only if all existing clients consent to the new arrangement.
C. The firm must promptly file an amended Form ADV with the SEC.
D. The firm must revise the disclosure brochure it provides to prospective clients.

54. Under the Investment Advisers Act of 1940, an investment adviser must

A. maintain a bond if he has custody of client securities or funds
B. appoint the SEC as his attorney for service of any legal process
C. have at least six months' experience as a representative for a registered broker-dealer
D. disclose pertinent information about himself to all prospective clients

55. Which of the following investment advisers may have their registration revoked under the Investment Advisers Act of 1940?

I. Joe Kuhl is accused by a client of violating a securities law.
II. August Polar did not properly supervise an employee who broke an SEC rule.
III. Belle Charolais is insolvent.

A. I and II only
B. I and III only
C. II only
D. I, II and III

56. Which of the following compensation arrangements is typically NOT allowed under the Investment Advisers Act of 1940?

A. Chip Bullock waives a client's fee if the client experiences a loss for the year.
B. Klaus Bruin charges a set fee regardless of how long it takes him to generate his recommendation for a given client or how well the recommendation turns out.
C. Belle Charolais varies her fee according to the amount of time she spends managing the account.
D. Karen Kodiak charges her clients a percentage of assets under management.

57. An investment adviser charges a client a flat percentage fee, computed as an annual fee and charged quarterly, for management services of the client's assets handled on a discretionary basis. What document must be filed with the SEC regarding this type of program?

A. Form ADV (Parts I and II)
B. Form ADV-E
C. Form ADV-W
D. Form ADV-H

58. Which of the following requirements must be met in order for an investment adviser to make cash payments to a solicitor under the Investment Advisers Act of 1940?

    I. Adequate disclosure must be made to the client about any affiliation between the adviser and the solicitor if the solicitation involves anything other than impersonal advisory services.
    II. The adviser must earn a majority of his income from conducting an investment advisory business.
    III. There must be a written agreement between the adviser and the solicitor.

    A. I and II only
    B. I and III only
    C. II and III only
    D. I, II and III

59. The Investment Advisers Act of 1940 permits which of the following statements to be made to a client?

    I. "The SEC has approved the registration statement for this security."
    II. "To become registered, I had to pass rigorous scrutiny by the SEC."
    III. "I am registered as an investment adviser with the SEC."

    A. I and II only
    B. I and III only
    C. III only
    D. I, II and III

60. Under the powers of the Investment Advisers Act of 1940, the SEC has the authority to

    I. take evidence
    II. subpoena witnesses
    III. set bail

    A. I and II only
    B. I and III only
    C. II and III only
    D. I, II and III

61. Violations of the Investment Advisers Act of 1940 are punishable by

    I. suspension of registration
    II. a fine of up to $10,000
    III. a prison term of up to 20 years

    A. I and II only
    B. I and III only
    C. II and III only
    D. I, II and III

62. All of the following are deemed, by law, to be providing investment advisory services for fees, and require registration as investment advisers EXCEPT a(n)

    A. attorney charging a professional athlete an hourly fee for services as a "sports representative" for services such as negotiation of contracts, development of promotional opportunities and advisory services relating to investments, tax planning, budget and money management
    B. accountant who prepares a client's taxes and advises the client on tax-advantaged investments including selecting of securities, and market timing. The accountant has a separate billing system for tax preparation and securities recommendations.
    C. registered representative who calls one of his clients to inform her that, in his opinion, one of the stocks held in her portfolio has "peaked" and should be sold immediately. The registered representative will receive a commission for the trade if the client accepts the advice.
    D. financial planner who waives her company's fees for a client based on the client's desire to purchase the securities and other services through the planner acting as a registered representative. The registered representative will receive only commissions for the transactions.

63. A financial planner manages client accounts on a "wrap-fee" basis and publishes a monthly newsletter advising clients about current and projected stock market trends. The planner has $15.5 million in client assets under management. The planner's business

A. must register with the SEC and in each state in which the adviser has more than three clients
B. is exempt from registration with the SEC, but must register with each state in which it has a place of business and/or six or more clients who are residents of the state
C. must register with the SEC, but is not required to register within the states because it has less than $25 million under management
D. is not required to register either with the SEC or the states because of the *de minimis* exemption

64. Which of the following is an investment adviser required to disclose to clients under the Investment Advisers Act of 1940?

I. Compensation received from the issuer of a security he recommends
II. Compensation he will receive on sales of insurance
III. Compensation he will receive on the securities transactions he recommends

A. I and II only
B. I and III only
C. II and III only
D. I, II and III

65. Which of the following are NOT included in the definition of "investment adviser" under the Investment Advisers Act of 1940 if their investment advice is incidental to the practice of their professions?

A. Publishers of investment newsletters
B. Pension consultants
C. Chemical engineers
D. Members of the clergy

66. Under the Investment Advisers Act of 1940, which of the following investment advisers are in violation of the act?

I. Barry Kodiak, who persuades a client to co-sign for a loan without disclosing that he is facing financial difficulties.
II. Sadie Longhorn, whose customer instructs her to buy shares in Dohspils Pharmaceuticals. DOH is experiencing financial troubles, so Sadie buys shares in Flibinite Health Care instead.
III. June Polar, who purchases shares of a new issue and hopes to cause the price of the shares to rise by recommending that all her clients purchase the stock. She does not tell clients that she owns the stock.

A. I and II only
B. I and III only
C. II and III only
D. I, II and III

67. Which of the following statements is true regarding an investment adviser's authority to place orders for a client's account under the NASAA's Statement of Policy on Unethical Business Practices?

A. The adviser is not required to obtain authorization to place orders for a client's account unless a conflict of interest is involved.
B. The adviser may, without the client's approval, place a sell order for the purpose of avoiding losses, but may not place a buy order without the client's authorization.
C. The client's verbal approval is sufficient for a specific order.
D. Written approval from the client authorizing a stated amount of a specified security is required before placing an order.

68. In which of the following situations has the adviser acted in accordance with the NASAA's Statement of Policy on Unethical Business Practices when placing an order for a client's account?

    I. The adviser obtains written discretionary authority to manage a client's account and then proceeds to restructure the entire account without further consultation with the client.
    II. The adviser obtains a client's verbal agreement that shares of GEM fund are a good buy right now, and the client gives the adviser verbal authority to determine how much of his account should be allocated to GEM shares. Without written discretionary authority, the adviser places an order for GEM shares.
    III. A client agrees with the adviser's recommendation of a particular security and the amount that should be purchased, and tells the adviser to proceed with the purchase when the timing seems best. Because the market as a whole is dropping, the adviser waits two weeks until the economy looks brighter before making the purchase. The adviser does not have written discretionary authority.

    A. I and II only
    B. I and III only
    C. II and III only
    D. I, II and III

69. From which of the following clients could an investment adviser ethically borrow money under the NASAA's Statement of Policy on Unethical Business Practices?

    I. A broker-dealer not affiliated with the adviser
    II. A bank not affiliated with the adviser
    III. An investment company not affiliated with the adviser

    A. I and II only
    B. I and III only
    C. II and III only
    D. I, II and III

70. Under the rules regarding advertisements by investment advisers, which of the following constitutes a fraudulent, deceptive or manipulative act?

I. An investment adviser runs a television advertisement including a testimonial by a well-known professional athlete whose investments have shown extremely positive results due to management by and recommendations of the investment adviser
II. An advertisement by an investment adviser in a financial periodical that cites three recommendations by the adviser to its clients in the past six months that have resulted in unusually high profits
III. A letter sent by an investment adviser to 50 prospects detailing an exclusive mathematical market timing model developed by the adviser for exclusive use of its clients in making their own buy or sell decisions on the securities recommended by the adviser that have shown good past results
IV. A newspaper advertisement by an investment adviser that offers a free financial plan to new clients who purchase the financial products and securities recommended in the plan.

A. I and II only
B. I and IV only
C. II and III only
D. I, II, III and IV

71. Under the NASAA's Statement of Policy on Unethical Business Practices, an investment adviser's fee

A. must reflect the amount of time the adviser spends managing the client's account
B. is not subject to regulatory oversight by the administrator if the client may be considered "financially sophisticated"
C. may not be based on a percentage of the client's assets under management
D. may be considered unreasonable if it is not in line with fees charged by other advisers for similar services

72. Under the NASAA's Statement of Policy on Unethical Business Practices, an investment adviser may guarantee investment results

A. if he uses a system based on objective evaluation of data, can document consistent gains using the system and discloses to clients all of the limitations and difficulties of using the system
B. as long as the basis for making guarantees is fully and accurately described in the application for registration filed with the administrator
C. if the guarantees are reasonable in view of the results other clients have obtained following his recommendations
D. under no circumstances

73. In which of the following situations has the investment adviser acted properly in disclosing confidential information about clients under the NASAA's Statement of Policy on Unethical Business Practices?

A. A prospective client asks to speak to three current clients as references. The adviser gives the prospective client the names of the three clients without consulting those clients beforehand.
B. Without the client's permission, the adviser identifies a client in an article published in a magazine whose only readers are other investment advisers. The article contains no information about the client's account.
C. A client who is running for public office is being slandered by false reports regarding her finances. When a reporter calls the adviser, the adviser corrects certain misconceptions regarding the client's financial affairs without consulting the client.
D. A client is unaware that he is under secret investigation by local police. Without consulting the client, an adviser turns files over to investigators under a court order.

74. Under the NASAA's Statement of Policy on Unethical Business Practices, an adviser would be acting improperly if she

I. allowed a client to sign an advisory contract after disclosing a potential conflict of interest to that client
II. agreed to personally make up the difference if a client's account lost money
III. failed to inquire into a client's investment objectives, financial situation and needs

A. I and II only
B. I and III only
C. II and III only
D. I, II and III

75. Which of the following transactions is prohibited by the Investment Advisers Act of 1940 as a means of determining compensation in a contract between a registered investment adviser and its client?

A. Investment adviser basing advisory fees based on a percentage of assets under management
B. Investment adviser basing its fees on a share of capital gains or capital appreciation produced in a client's account over a specified period of time
C. Financial planner charging a flat fee for completing a financial plan based on a combination of insurance and securities
D. Financial planner who offers to waive flat fees for completing a financial plan if the client accepts the plan and purchases the recommended products and securities through the planner who will receive commissions

◆ Answers & Rationale

1. **B.** Common stock and rights and warrants are specifically named as "securities" in the act. Variable annuities also are considered securities because the investment risk of these contracts falls on the contract owner; but fixed annuities or fixed life insurance products are excluded from the definition of "security." Futures contracts, in common with precious metals, collectibles and real estate, may be used as investment vehicles but are generally not considered to be securities. (Page 30)

2. **B.** The definition of "person" is not limited to any of the choices listed; for example, a person may be a political subdivision of a government. (Page 2)

3. **A.** Choices I and III are exemptions from state registration as defined in the amendment to the Investment Advisers Act of 1940. Choice I describes an adviser who does not conduct a significant business within the borders of a state and choice III is known as the *de minimis* exemption which essentially means only a few clients. Choice II is not an exemption under the law and would require registration. The amendment to the Investment Advisers Act of 1940 requires that, in order to be exempt, the adviser would have no place of business located in the state, and have had fewer than six clients who were residents of that state during the preceding 12-month period. (Page 5)

4. **D.** Employees who perform clerical or managerial functions to effect a sale are exempt from registration as agents under the Uniform Securities Act. (Page 39)

5. **A.** Answer A is part of the definition of "broker-dealer." The other answers are specifically excluded from the definition. (Page 28)

6. **D.** The antifraud provisions prohibit misstatements, omissions and all deceptive or unethical business practices. Whether a sale was made or whether money was lost by a client as a result of the fraudulent act is irrelevant. (Page 77)

7. **C.** In choice I, the adviser did not commit a willful violation because she was unaware that there was a problem with the stock's registration. The adviser's action in choice III was not a violation. In choice II, however, the adviser violated the antifraud provisions even though no sale resulted. (Page 77)

8. **D.** The antifraud provisions apply to soliciting clients as well as to providing investment advice. They require disclosures to be made to a client if the adviser will act as a principal for his own account or as a broker for another party in effecting a recommended transaction. The act gives the administrator the power to define certain practices as unethical and prohibits these practices with the same force as those spelled out in the act. (Page 77)

9. **B.** Investment advisers having custody of clients' funds or securities must establish one or more separate bank accounts; must notify clients of the particulars of the bank account and provide for an independent, annual surprise audit. The requirement of the rule for an itemized statement to clients is once every three months, although the IA may send statements more frequently. (Page 17)

10. **B.** Choices II and III describe the instances in which investment advisers subject to regulation with State Securities Regulators must also register with the SEC. The amendment to the Investment Advisers Act of 1940 exempts investment advisers subject to a state securities regulator from registration with the SEC unless they (1) manage at least $25 million in assets and (2) serve as advisers to certain federally regulated investment companies such as Open End Management Investment Companies (mutual funds). (Page 5)

11. **C.** A published announcement may be required by the administrator. The administrator

may also establish minimum financial requirements, and have different requirements for advisers who have custody or discretion from those who do not. However, the administrator may require a bond only of advisers who have custody or discretion. (Page 8)

12. **A.** Persons who have management responsibilities with the firm are automatically registered as agents when a broker-dealer becomes registered. This includes certain partners, officers and directors of the firm. It does not include persons such as registered representatives who may perform sales functions but not management functions within the firm. (Page 40)

13. **A.** Because the limited partnership will be a new business entity, the investment adviser will be required to file a new Form ADV. If the partnership continues the present business operations, it will be deemed to be registered if it files Form ADV within 30 days after the succession. (Page 8)

14. **B.** An agency cross transaction occurs when the investment adviser, acting as a broker in a transaction, sells securities for one client and buys them for another party. This may only take place with the permission of the client and after disclosure to both parties that the adviser will receive commissions from both clients. The adviser may, however, recommend the transaction to only one of the parties. (Page 20)

15. **D.** The administrator is authorized to take all of these disciplinary actions. (Page 11)

16. **C.** Violation of another state's securities laws is cause for action against an adviser. So is insolvency, defined as having liabilities in excess of assets or the inability to meet financial obligations as they come due. However, the personal financial situation of a minority, nonmanaging shareholder does not have a bearing on the financial situation of the firm; only if the individual were a partner, a sole proprietor or perhaps a majority shareholder would personal insolvency be a cause for action against the firm. (Page 23)

17. **C.** Choices A, B and D are causes for cancellation of registration—which is not intended to be punitive. Unethical business practice is a cause for disciplinary action by the administrator, court-imposed penalties, criminal prosecution and civil legal remedies. (Page 11)

18. **D.** In general, the administrator must provide appropriate prior notice, opportunity for a hearing and written findings of facts and conclusions of law. Even if an order is issued summarily—that is, made effective upon issue without prior notice—the registrant must be notified upon issue of the order and must be given the opportunity to request a hearing. (Page 11)

19. **A.** Margin requirements restrict the amount of money that a customer may borrow from a broker-dealer to finance trading activities and are designed to protect the investor from becoming too leveraged. (Page 33)

20. **A.** Securities issued or guaranteed by a railroad, a credit union and a subdivision of the Canadian government are all exempt. There is no apparent exemption for the stock in answer A—it is stock, not commercial paper or an investment contract for an employee benefit plan; the issuer is a manufacturer, not a government, federal or state bank, U.S. insurer, federal or state credit union, common carrier or public utility; the company is for-profit; and the stock is not listed on an exchange. (Page 30)

21. **C.** A preorganization subscription may be advertised. Choices A, B and D describe the three requirements for a preorganization subscription to qualify as an exempt transaction. (Page 72)

22. **C.** Summary orders—that is, orders made effective without prior notice—may be issued to revoke an exemption. An order to deny or revoke an exemption may not operate retroactively. In any proceeding, the burden of proving an exemption or an exception to a definition is on the person claiming it. The exemption for a security issued by a nonprofit corporation is one of the

exemptions the administrator is empowered to revoke. (Page 72)

23. **B.** The administrator has the power to take evidence, subpoena witnesses and administer oaths. The administrator also has the power to compel testimony and to require the production of books and records. However, while the administrator is authorized to refer violations for possible criminal prosecution, the actual powers of criminal prosecution belong to others. Indicting offenders, for example, is the function of a grand jury. (Page 35)

24. **C.** The administrator may issue a cease and desist order either with or without a prior hearing. Regarding criminal penalties, those given in choice I are correct—a $5,000 fine and three years in prison—but violators may face both. Indictments on criminal violations must be returned within five years. (Page 25)

25. **A.** The death of either the adviser or the client does not remove a cause of action for civil liability. Waivers as described in choice III are void. (Page 25)

26. **A.** The 1933 act prohibits fraud and requires full and fair disclosure with regard to the sale of new issues, but it does not regulate sales pressure. The registration of investment advisers is required by the Investment Advisers Act of 1940. The regulation of broker-dealers and exchanges comes under the Securities and Exchange Act of 1934. (Page 47)

27. **D.** As is the case with most of the securities acts, a "person" can be almost any entity, including a corporation, a partnership, an unincorporated association, a subdivision of a government, a trust that issues shares of ownership (such as a unit investment trust) or an individual. (Page 5)

28. **B.** An underwriter represents an issuer in distributing a security to the public, or buys securities from an issuer with a view to distributing them to the public. It does not buy securities with a view to holding them as investments, as in choice D. Choice A is the definition of a broker-dealer. A person whose interest in the sale of a security is limited to a commission (choice C) is specifically excluded from the definition of "underwriter." (Page 29)

29. **A.** A prospectus is a communication made in writing that offers a new issue of a security for sale. A verbal offer, therefore, would not be a prospectus. Tombstone advertisements are specifically excluded from the definition of "prospectus." Personal letters are included in the definition; however, if the letter is not preceded or accompanied by an official prospectus that contains all of the required information, the sender of the letter has violated the 1933 act. (Page 47)

30. **C.** Only banks, insurance companies, investment companies and employee benefit plans are specifically listed as "accredited investors" in the 1933 act. Lawyers, accountants, investment adviser representatives and agents are not included in the list. (Page 61)

31. **C.** To be exempt, sales to accredited investors must meet only one condition: no advertising or public solicitation may be used. (Page 61)

32. **B.** The cooling-off period is 20 days unless the SEC orders a delay. (Page 56)

33. **B.** The persons who may be sued for misstatements in a registration statement include every director or partner of the issuer, the underwriter of the issue, every expert who verified a report or valuation and everyone who signed the registration statement, which would include the chief accounting officer; persons who control a liable person may also be sued. A person who owns a fractional interest in the issuer is not liable. (Page 52)

34. **B.** Anyone paid by a marketer of a security to publish or circulate a description of the

security must disclose that payment was received and the amount of the payment. (Page 24)

35. **B.** The 1934 act regulates those involved in secondary market trading of securities: broker-dealers, exchanges, transfer agents and so on. The new issue market is regulated by the 1933 act. Because the 1934 act deals with a different aspect of the industry, choice C is not correct. Making securities regulation more uniform among the states is the purpose of the Uniform Securities Act. (Page 47)

36. **B.** Under the 1934 act, "exchange" does not refer to a transaction (choice D), but to an organization or facilities for bringing together buyers and sellers of securities. It is important to distinguish this function from other activities carried out by persons in the secondary market such as transfer agents, securities information processors or broker-dealers. Choice A is the definition of a "sale." Choice C describes a self-regulatory organization. (Page 32)

37. **C.** A market maker is a dealer who holds himself out as being willing to buy or sell a security at a quoted price on a regular and continuous basis. Choice B describes a broker-dealer. Choice D describes an exchange. (Page 29)

38. **D.** Examples of securities information processors are ticker tape services, computer quotation services and the *Pink Sheets.* Newspapers and business/financial publications of general and regular circulation (choice III) are excluded from the definition of "securities information processor." Also excluded are: self-regulatory organizations, the definition of which includes any exchange (choice II) as well as the NASD and the MSRB; television and radio stations; banks; S&Ls; and broker-dealers carrying out activities customary to their business (choice I). (Page 30)

39. **C.** "Investment discretion" is defined as the authority to determine what specific securities and quantity of securities will be bought or sold for an account. The advisers in choices II and III are making that determination. The adviser in choice I is following an order regarding an already-specified security. (Page 3)

40. **D.** Members of exchanges are generally prohibited from effecting transactions on the exchange for their own accounts, the accounts of affiliates or accounts over which they have investment discretion, but many exceptions apply. A dealer acting in the capacity of a market maker (choice II) is one such exception. Another is the simultaneous purchase and sale of stock on different exchanges to lock in a profit (choice I); this is an example of arbitrage. Other exceptions include: transactions by odd-lot dealers; stabilizing transactions; transactions to offset transactions made in error; transactions for the account of an individual, estate or trust; and conducting a "side business" in buying and selling for one's own account, as long as one's primary business is brokerage or underwriting. However, in order for a broker-dealer to lawfully effect transactions on an exchange, the exchange generally must be registered under the 1934 act. (Page 79)

41. **C.** Registration as a government securities dealer is not required if the person has general broker-dealer registration. (Page 37)

42. **D.** The 1934 act states that the purpose of margin requirements is to prevent the excessive use of credit to finance securities purchases. Margin requirements are set by the Federal Reserve Board. New issues may not be bought on margin. (Page 33)

43. **A.** The penalty may be imposed on anyone who trades on inside information, not just persons registered under the act. The other statements are correct: choice B is the definition of "insider trading"; the penalty is up to three times the profit gained or loss avoided; and an advisory firm may face a penalty for the actions of its representatives. (Page 101)

44. **A.** Use of a full-service broker to effect transactions for an account over which an adviser has investment discretion is not a breach of fidu-

ciary duty as long as the full-service broker's commission is reasonable in view of the services he provides. "Services" includes advice, analyses, research and custodial services, but the term does not cover sales incentives offered to the adviser. (Page 20)

45. **C.** Because real estate is not a security, real estate investment trusts are excluded from the definition of "investment company." Other exclusions are banks, S&Ls, broker-dealers, underwriters and issuers whose securities are owned by less than 100 persons. Also excluded are insurance company general accounts; but insurance company separate accounts and investment advisers are not excluded. (Page 82)

46. **D.** Mutual fund shares must be sold at NAV plus any sales charge; therefore, the sales price of a mutual fund share may be equal to or greater than its NAV, but it may not be less. The other statements are true: the shares must be redeemable upon demand; "mutual fund" is the common name for an open-end investment company; and the NAV must be calculated each business day. (Page 85)

47. **B.** Rebating commissions on mutual fund sales is prohibited. But the adviser may reduce the client's fee, or she may keep the commission. (Page 78)

48. **C.** It is generally prohibited for a fund to employ as its investment adviser a person convicted of a crime involving the securities industry or to loan money to its investment adviser. However, those things may be done if the SEC issues an exemptive order that applies to the particular case. Changing an investment objective requires the approval of a majority of the shareholders, but requires no action by the SEC. (Page 89)

49. **D.** A fund's agreement with its investment adviser must provide for termination by the board of directors without a vote of the outstanding shares. The other statements are true: the contract must be approved by a majority of the outstanding shares, must be in writing and must describe the adviser's compensation. (Page 91)

50. **A.** Affiliated persons, such as a fund's investment adviser, are generally prohibited from buying securities from the fund's portfolio, selling securities to it, or borrowing money or other property from the fund. However, affiliated persons are free to purchase shares of the fund and to redeem them as other shareholders do. (Page 88)

51. **D.** A person who renders advice solely with respect to securities issued or guaranteed by the U.S. government is exempt from federal registration under the advisers act but not from state registration under the Uniform Securities Act. (Page 3)

52. **B.** Employees with no investment advisory functions, such as clerks and ministerial personnel, are excluded from the definition of "person associated with an investment adviser." Persons controlled by the adviser—such as agents, registered reps and other employees who manage client accounts—are included in the definition. Also included are partners, officers and directors, as well as controlling persons; a majority stockholder would have a controlling interest in the firm. (Page 3)

53. **B.** Consent of the adviser's existing clients to a change in fee is not required. Prior SEC approval also is not required. Because fees are contained in Part II of Form ADV, a change in fee requires prompt amendment of that form with the SEC, as well as revision of the adviser's disclosure brochure. (Page 6)

54. **D.** The "brochure rule" requires disclosures of pertinent information to be made to all clients and prospective clients. There are no requirements regarding bonding, experience or consent to service of process under the advisers act. (Page 15)

55. **C.** Lack of supervision that leads to violation of a federal rule is cause for revocation of an adviser's federal registration. Regarding choice I,

there would have to be a finding by a court or an administrative authority that the adviser broke a law, not merely an accusation by a client. Insolvency is not cause for disciplinary action under the advisers act, although it is cause for action under the Uniform Securities Act. (Page 11)

56. **A.** Typically, a fee whereby payment is contingent on investment results is prohibited unless the investor is a qualified purchaser in a private investment company. Set fees, hourly fees and fees based on the percentage of assets under management are allowed. (Page 18)

57. **D.** In the situation described, the investment adviser is considered by the SEC to be sponsoring a "wrap fee" program, and must file Form ADV-H. The adviser will also be required to furnish the client with special information regarding the wrap fee. (Page 15)

58. **B.** To make payments to a solicitor, there must be a written agreement between the adviser and the solicitor. If the advice is other than impersonal advisory services, any affiliation between the adviser and the solicitor must be disclosed. If the solicitor is not affiliated with the adviser, the solicitor's compensation must be disclosed and the adviser must make an effort to ensure that the solicitor complies with SEC rules. (Page 23)

59. **C.** It is illegal to state or imply that registration of either a person or a security involves approval or qualification by the SEC or verification of facts in the registration statement. (Page 22)

60. **A.** The SEC is empowered to take evidence, subpoena witnesses, administer oaths and require the production of books and records in conducting a formal investigation. Setting bail is the function of a court. (Page 25)

61. **A.** Criminal penalties for violations of the advisers act include a $10,000 fine and five (not three) years in prison. Administrative penalties, such as revocation or suspension of registration, may also be imposed, as well as penalties imposed by self-regulatory organizations such as the exchanges and the NASD. (Page 25)

62. **B.** A registered representative of a broker-dealer advising a client regarding the purchase or sale of a stock based on its historical performance, and receiving only the normal commissions, does not fall within the legal definition of investment adviser. If, on the other hand, the registered representative and the broker-dealer had separate, definable fees (e.g. wrap fees) for assets under management, these activities and fees would require registration as investment advisers. (Page 2)

63. **B.** The description of the business of the financial planner indicates a requirement that the concern must be registered as an investment adviser. The fact that the planner has less than $25 million in assets under management exempts it from registration with the SEC. The investment adviser must, however, register with the state regulators unless it qualifies for exemptions as indicated in choice B. (Page 8)

64. **D.** Advisers must disclose compensation received on sales of securities and nonsecurities products and also compensation received from the issuer of a recommended security. (Page 24)

65. **C.** Engineers qualify for a professional exclusion if the advice they render is solely incidental to the practice of their profession. No exclusion applies to publishers of investment newsletters, pension consultants or members of the clergy. (Page 3)

66. **D.** The antifraud provisions prohibit any deceptive act by an adviser in the course of business with a client. Although the violation in choice I does not involve a securities transaction, it still represents an abuse of the adviser-client relationship and is therefore covered by the antifraud provisions. Regarding choice II, deliberately failing to follow a customer's instruction is a violation. Advisers are required to disclose trades made for their own accounts that are

designed to profit from the market impact of recommendations (choice III). (Page 23)

67. **C.** For a *specific* order, verbal authority is sufficient. An adviser may not place an order for a client's account without proper authority. (Page 77)

68. **B.** Authority to use discretion may be given verbally if the discretion relates only to the price or the time at which an order regarding a specified amount of a particular security will be executed; such is the case in choice III. The adviser in choice I obtains proper written authority. But verbal authority is not sufficient for choice II, because the adviser is using discretion to determine the amount of the security. (Page 77)

69. **A.** An adviser may borrow money from a client only if the client is a broker-dealer, a bank or other financial institution in the business of loaning funds, or an affiliate of the adviser. None of these applies to the company in choice III. (Page 77)

70. **D.** All of the examples are *prohibited and considered fraudulent, deceptive or manipulative* under the rules governing communications with the public by investment advisers. Testimonials by individuals are prohibited unless fully qualified by disclaimers. Advertisements showing specific results for selected accounts without specific offers to furnish additional information over all accounts for at least a year are forbidden. The offering of any device that, without expert advice, promises to allow the investor to predict the market is prohibited. Any advertisement or offering to the public described as "free" must be absolutely free without any "strings." (Page 78)

71. **D.** An adviser may not charge any client an unreasonable fee. A fee could be considered excessive if it were substantially higher than that charged by other advisers for performing similar services. The administrator may research the fees charged by various investment advisers for the purposes of comparison. Whether clients have agreed to the fee or have done their own "price-shopping" is irrelevant in determining if a particular adviser's fee is unreasonable. (Page 78)

72. **D.** Under no circumstances may an adviser guarantee that a client will achieve an investment result—either that a gain will be realized or that no loss will occur. (Page 79)

73. **D.** An adviser may not disclose the identity, affairs or investments of any client without the client's consent—unless required to do so by law. (Page 25)

74. **C.** Choice II describes a guarantee against loss, which is a breach of ethical conduct. Choice III also is a breach of ethical conduct because advisers have a duty to inquire into a client's investment objectives, financial situation and needs. There is no breach of ethical conduct in choice I because the adviser disclosed the potential conflict of interest before the advisory contract was signed. (Page 78)

75. **B.** The law states, "The contract may not provide for compensation to the adviser on the basis of a share of capital gains upon (or capital appreciation of) a client's funds or compensation that is a portion of a client's funds." This so-called performance-based compensation is only allowable under a very narrowly defined set of circumstances. (Page 18)

13 Series 65 Final Exam Two

1. Which of the following is NOT an offer or a sale under the terms of the Uniform Securities Act?

   A. Negotiations for a merger
   B. Contract of sale for a security
   C. Sale of a warrant
   D. Gift of assessable stock

2. Which of the following are elements in the definition of "investment adviser" under the Uniform Securities Act?

   I. There must be compensation for the services rendered.
   II. The investment advice must be in writing.
   III. The investment advice must relate to the value of securities or to a recommendation to buy or sell securities.

   A. I and II only
   B. I and III only
   C. II and III only
   D. I, II and III

3. The Investment Advisers Act of 1940 defines "investment adviser" as a person who, for compensation

   I. engages in the business of advising others either directly or through publications or writings as to the value of securities
   II. makes recommendations to clients on the advisability of investing in, purchasing or selling securities
   III. as a part of a regular business, issues or promulgates analyses of securities
   IV. as a part of a regular business issues or promulgates reports concerning securities

   A. I and III only
   B. I and IV only
   C. II and IV only
   D. I, II, III and IV

4. Which of the following statements are true of a broker-dealer as defined in the Uniform Securities Act?

   I. A broker-dealer may not also be registered as an investment adviser.
   II. A broker-dealer may be either a firm or an individual.
   III. A broker-dealer's primary business is effecting securities transactions for clients or for the broker-dealer's own account.

   A. I and II only
   B. I and III only
   C. II and III only
   D. I, II and III

5. An individual representing an issuer is NOT considered an "agent" under the Uniform Securities Act if the issuer is a(n)

   I. insurance company
   II. bank
   III. government

   A. I and II only
   B. I and III only
   C. II and III only
   D. I, II and III

6. Concerning the antifraud provisions of the Uniform Securities Act, which of the following statements is(are) true?

   I. Governmental bodies or political subdivisions are exempt from these antifraud provisions.
   II. "Fraud" is broadly defined, and includes not only deceit but also failure to make adequate disclosure.
   III. In a securities transaction, a deceitful presentation is a violation even if it does not result in a sale.

   A. I and III only
   B. II only
   C. II and III only
   D. I, II and III

7. Which of the following persons is(are) subject to the antifraud provisions of the Uniform Securities Act?

   I. A broker-dealer who advises customers on the value of securities but is compensated only in the form of commissions on sales
   II. An investment adviser representative who receives a fee directly from clients
   III. An investment adviser representative who receives no compensation directly from clients but is paid a salary by an advisory firm

   A. I and II only
   B. II only
   C. III only
   D. I, II and III

8. Which of the following is NOT required to be included in writing in an advisory contract under the Uniform Securities Act?

   A. Provision that no assignment of rights or ownership of the contract will be made without the client's consent
   B. If the firm is a partnership, provision that clients will be notified of any change in the partnership within a reasonable time after the change
   C. The names and titles of all principals in the advisory firm
   D. Provision that the adviser's compensation will not be based on capital gains except as permitted under an exemptive rule or order of the administrator

9. The antifraud provisions of the Uniform Securities Act apply to

   I. broker-dealers and their agents
   II. attorneys who provide investment advice that is incidental to the practice of law
   III. banks

   A. I only
   B. I and II only
   C. III only
   D. I, II and III

10. Performance-based fees are prohibited under the Investment Adviser's Act for all of the following EXCEPT investment advisory contracts with

    A. qualified purchaser pools
    B. open-end investment companies registered only at the state level
    C. federally registered investment companies
    D. an IA's regular general public clientele

11. Under the Uniform Securities Act, if the administrator does not deny an application for a broker-dealer's registration and no disciplinary proceeding is under way in regard to it, how long after filing of the application does registration generally become effective?

    A. 5 days
    B. 7 days
    C. 10 days
    D. 30 days

12. Unless renewed, registrations of associated persons of a broker-dealer under the Uniform Securities Act expire

    A. one year from their effective date
    B. two years from their effective date
    C. every December 31st
    D. Registrations need not be renewed.

13. Under current law, for how long must a state-registered investment adviser generally keep business records available for examination by the administrator?

    A. Indefinitely
    B. A term specified by the administrator
    C. Three years
    D. Five years

14. An administrator acting under the Uniform Securities Act may NOT require investment advisers to

    A. post a surety bond if they do not have investment discretion over client accounts
    B. promptly file a correcting amendment to any document on file with the administrator that becomes inaccurate or incomplete in any material respect
    C. furnish or disseminate any information that the administrator finds is necessary for the public interest or for the protection of investors and clients
    D. file various financial reports

15. An administrator acting under the Uniform Securities Act must do which of the following before taking any disciplinary action with regard to a registrant?

    I. Cite a cause listed in the act.
    II. Obtain the approval of the appropriate state court.
    III. Find that the action is in the public interest.

    A. I and II only
    B. I and III only
    C. II and III only
    D. I, II and III

16. Which of the following actions would be considered a willful violation of the Uniform Securities Act?

    I. An adviser recommends the purchase of a stock she believes is exempt, but later she discovers that the administrator has revoked that stock's exemption.
    II. An adviser recommends the purchase of nonexempt, unregistered stock after being incorrectly advised by a reliable source that the stock was properly registered.
    III. An adviser recommends the purchase of a stock that she knows is not properly registered, but no sale results.

    A. I and II only
    B. II and III only
    C. III only
    D. I, II and III

17. Which of the following statements are true regarding the withdrawal of a registration under the Uniform Securities Act?

    I. If a disciplinary proceeding is under way or is instituted, the administrator may determine when and under what circumstances withdrawal shall become effective.
    II. Once withdrawal becomes effective, the administrator no longer has the power to institute disciplinary proceedings against the registrant.
    III. Generally, withdrawal automatically becomes effective 30 days after the application for withdrawal is filed.

    A. I and II only
    B. I and III only
    C. II and III only
    D. I, II and III

18. A security that is exempt from the registration requirements of the Uniform Securities Act is also exempt from the

    I. civil liabilities provisions
    II. antifraud provisions
    III. requirements for filing advertising and sales literature

    A. I and II only
    B. I and III only
    C. III only
    D. I, II and III

19. Which of the following statements is true regarding the registration of securities under the Uniform Securities Act?

    A. The administrator may not require that a prospectus be delivered to every purchaser of a registered security before the security is delivered.
    B. State registration by coordination is available only if a federal registration statement has been filed under the Securities Act of 1933 in connection with the same offering.
    C. The filing of a registration statement assures the accuracy of the information it contains.
    D. Registration by coordination becomes effective on a date ordered by the administrator.

20. Which of the following is NOT an exempt transaction under the Uniform Securities Act?

    A. A sale of stock through a rights offering to existing shareholders of the issuing corporation, if no commission is paid
    B. Private placement
    C. A sale of U.S. government securities by a registered government securities dealer
    D. A sale of securities by the executor of an estate

21. Which of the following transactions are exempt from the securities registration requirements under the Uniform Securities Act?

    I. Transaction by a trustee in bankruptcy
    II. Transaction between an issuer and underwriters
    III. An isolated, nonissuer transaction
    IV. Sale to a financial institution

    A. I and III only
    B. I and IV only
    C. II, III and IV only
    D. I, II, III and IV

22. It is legal under the Uniform Securities Act for a registered investment adviser to tell a client that

    A. a registered security may lawfully be sold in that state
    B. an exempt security is not required to be registered because it is generally regarded as being safer than a nonexempt security
    C. her qualifications have been found satisfactory by the administrator
    D. a registered security has been approved for sale in the state by the administrator

23. The state securities administrator is empowered to

    I. subpoena witnesses
    II. administer oaths
    III. collect evidence
    IV. file a civil suit

    A. I and II only
    B. II and III only
    C. III and IV only
    D. I, II, III and IV

24. Which of the following statements is true regarding the civil liability of investment advisers under the Uniform Securities Act?

    A. The administrator may file a civil lawsuit to recover damages on behalf of wronged investors.
    B. The amount an advisory client may recover is limited to the amount paid for the advice, plus any loss owing to the advice, plus interest.
    C. An investment adviser may be sued up to five years after the rendering of the advice.
    D. Persons who control a civilly liable person may also be sued to recover damages.

25. Under the Uniform Securities Act, an offer is made in a state when it

    I. is broadcast by radio or television from outside the state
    II. is contained in a newspaper published outside the state
    III. originates in that state

    A. I and II only
    B. II and III only
    C. III only
    D. I, II and III

26. Under the Securities Act of 1933, the definition of "security" generally includes

    A. futures contracts
    B. exchange-listed options to buy or sell foreign currency
    C. precious metals
    D. real estate

27. As defined in the Securities Act of 1933, an "issuer" would include a(n)

    I. government entity issuing exempt securities
    II. antique dealer selling items from a collection of rare books
    III. corporation issuing securities in an exempt transaction

    A. I and III only
    B. II only
    C. I, II and III
    D. None of the above

28. Under the Securities Act of 1933, the definition of "sale" includes

    I. a preliminary agreement between the issuer and the underwriters
    II. exercising a right to convert one security into another
    III. giving a security as a bonus with a purchase
    IV. a bona fide gift of securities

    A. I and II
    B. I, II and III
    C. II and III
    D. III and IV

29. Under the Securities Act of 1933, an "omitting prospectus" may NOT

    A. contain information from the security's final prospectus
    B. be accompanied by an application
    C. urge potential investors to obtain and read the security's final prospectus
    D. contain past performance data

30. Which of the following would be required to register with the state securities regulators when issuing new securities?

    A. A mutual fund with $20 million in assets under management
    B. A company whose stock is quoted on the NASDAQ NMS (National Market System) when making a subsequent primary offering
    C. A company whose stock is traded on the AMEX, when making a new combined offering
    D. A company issuing stock only within one state and not filing a federal registration statement

31. Under the Securities Act of 1933, a registration statement for a security must be signed by

    A. a majority of the issuer's board of directors and the underwriter
    B. a majority of the issuer's board of directors only
    C. the issuer's chief executive officer and the underwriter
    D. the issuer's chief executive officer, chief financial officer, chief accounting officer and a majority of the issuer's board of directors

32. Seven Seas Sailboat Corporation will issue a new security and distribute it through a public offering. According to the Securities Act of 1933, which of the following is NOT required to be included in SSS's registration statement?

    A. The name and address of SSS's personnel manager
    B. An estimate of the proceeds that will be raised through the offering and how that money will be used
    C. The identity of the underwriter
    D. The name and address of Minnie Leveridge, who owns 11 percent of SSS's stock

33. Under the Securities Act of 1933, a civil lawsuit to recover damages incurred owing to an investor's reliance on a registration statement must be filed within how long after the sale of the security?

A. One year
B. Three years
C. Five years
D. There is no time limit.

34. Under the Securities Act of 1934, the SEC may at its discretion

I. make, amend and rescind its rules
II. arrest and detain suspected violators, subject to the observance of due process and the preservation of citizens' rights
III. conduct formal investigations of persons under its jurisdiction

A. I and III only
B. II only
C. III only
D. I, II and III

35. Which of the following fits the category of "government security" under the Securities Exchange Act of 1934?

I. Treasury bills
II. Bonds issued by the State of Indiana
III. Bonds issued by the U.S. Postal Service

A. I only
B. I and III only
C. II and III only
D. I, II and III

36. Which of the following is defined as an "equity security" under the Securities Exchange Act of 1934?

I. Warrant to purchase stock
II. Bond that may be converted into stock
III. Bond issued with a warrant to purchase stock

A. I only
B. I and III only
C. II only
D. I, II and III

37. Which of the following would NOT be deemed "associated" with a broker-dealer under the terms of the Securities Exchange Act of 1934?

A. Joe Kuhl, one of the firm's registered representatives
B. Greater Health, Inc., a tiny fraction of whose stock the firm has purchased for its own account
C. Barry Kodiak, a firm vice-president
D. Greta Guernsey, who is on the firm's board of directors but has no other connection with the firm

38. Which of the following are excluded from the definition of "transfer agent" under the provisions of the Securities Exchange Act of 1934?

I. Clearing agency that registers transfers of ownership solely with respect to options contracts it issues
II. Firm that effects shareholder requests to convert mutual fund shares on behalf of the mutual fund
III. Insurance company that registers share ownership solely with respect to variable annuity contracts it issues

A. I and II only
B. I and III only
C. II and III only
D. I, II and III

39. A broker-dealer provides fee-based investment advice as part of its business. An employee of the firm also provides fee-based investment advice outside the scope of the business. According to SEC Release 1092, who is required to register as an IA?

    A. Broker-dealer
    B. Employee
    C. Both
    D. Neither

40. SEC commissioners appointed under the Securities Exchange Act of 1934

    A. are nominated by the NASD and are elected by a committee of state securities administrators
    B. must not have any other business or employment besides their commission with the SEC
    C. must not be affiliated with a political party
    D. must have professional experience as prosecuting attorneys as well as knowledge of the securities business

41. Which of the following statements is true regarding reports required to be filed with the SEC under the provisions of the Securities Exchange Act of 1934?

    A. Institutional investment managers who exercise discretion over accounts valued at more than $100 million need not file reports if all of their clients are insurance companies.
    B. Institutional investment managers who exercise discretion over accounts valued at more than $100 million must file reports quarterly.
    C. A person who becomes the beneficial owner of a security must file a report with the state administrator within five days.
    D. A person who becomes the beneficial owner of more than 5 percent of a security registered under the 1934 act must file a report within two days.

42. Under the provisions of the Securities Exchange Act of 1934, which of the following statements is true regarding the jurisdiction of the SEC over a person who violates the rules of the Municipal Securities Rulemaking Board?

    A. The SEC has the authority to investigate the violation unless the person is a financial institution.
    B. The SEC has the authority to investigate the violation even if the person is a financial institution.
    C. The SEC has the authority to investigate the violation only if the person is a financial institution.
    D. Only the MSRB has the authority to investigate a violation of its rules.

43. Which of the following actions is prohibited under the provisions of the Securities Exchange Act of 1934?

    A. Bambi Heifer buys 100 shares of stock, changes her mind and sells it almost immediately, but then buys it back when the price starts to go up.
    B. The price of This Can't Be Sushi doubles after a favorable earnings report is released, and TCB's accountant sells all of his holdings in TCB at a large profit.
    C. Hoping to attract other speculators' interest, Gwinneth Stout buys and sells a large block of a stock she is speculating in, but she loses money on the transactions.
    D. A rep recommends a growth stock to a retiree who is seeking capital appreciation with a small portion of their investable dollars.

44. Acting under the powers granted to it by the Securities Exchange Act of 1934, the SEC may suspend all trading on an exchange

A. for 10 days, at its discretion
B. only if it has cause to believe that the suspension is necessary to prevent criminal violations that are about to occur on the exchange
C. with notification of the President of the United States
D. under no circumstances

45. Under the provisions of the Securities Exchange Act of 1934, which of the following would result in statutory disqualification from association with an NASD-member broker-dealer?

A. Loss of a civil lawsuit involving securities
B. Lack of experience in the securities business
C. Failing to register as an investment adviser and engaging in a business that requires one to be so registered
D. Court injunction against acting as an underwriter

46. The Investment Company Act of 1940 requires a unit investment trust to issue

A. shares redeemable for a stated amount on a stated maturity date
B. shares redeemable for their net asset value upon the shareholder's demand
C. shares whose selling price is based on market demand rather than on net asset value
D. shares that are sold at net asset value, with no added sales charge

47. A customer of a broker-dealer whose sole objective is income has granted discretionary authority to his agent. The agent purchases zero coupon bonds for the account. This action is

I. suitable
II. unsuitable
III. authorized
IV. unauthorized

A. I and III only
B. I and IV only
C. II and III only
D. II and IV only

48. SEC Rule 12b-1 of the Investment Company Act of 1940 allows mutual funds to

A. use testimonials in their advertisements
B. suspend redemption of shares under certain circumstances
C. charge distribution expenses against net asset value
D. charge a redemption fee when shares are redeemed, rather than a sales charge when shares are purchased

49. Which of the following statements are true regarding a mutual fund's board of directors under the Investment Company Act of 1940?

I. No more than 60 percent of the board may be interested persons.
II. A majority of the board may not be investment bankers or have connections with the fund's regular broker-dealer or principal underwriter.
III. The members of the board are elected by the majority vote of the shareholders.

A. I and II only
B. I and III only
C. II and III only
D. I, II and III

50. Under the Investment Company Act of 1940, which of the following statements is true with regard to the receipt of excessive compensation by an investment adviser?

    A. Receipt of excessive compensation is prohibited only for mutual funds that have adopted 12b-1 plans.
    B. Receipt of excessive compensation is considered a breach of the adviser's fiduciary duty.
    C. No amount of compensation may be considered "excessive" because the adviser's compensation is set out in the advisory contract approved by the shareholders.
    D. Receipt of compensation in excess of 1 percent of a mutual fund's average daily assets requires an exemptive order by the SEC.

51. Reporting requirements for mutual funds include

    A. notifying shareholders of changes in the portfolio as they occur
    B. filing an unaudited annual report with the SEC
    C. filing such information, documents and reports as the SEC may deem necessary to keep reasonably current the information and documentation in the investment company's registration statement
    D. Registered investment companies are exempt from filing reports with the SEC so long as they are registered only at the state level.

52. Which of the following would NOT be defined as an "investment adviser" under the Investment Advisers Act of 1940?

    A. Broker-dealer who manages clients' portfolios for a fee
    B. Bank that charges a fee for providing investment advice
    C. Individual who makes recommendations regarding which types of securities would meet a client's investment objectives, but who does not recommend specific securities
    D. Publisher of an investment newsletter that does not contain advice based on the individual situation of each subscriber

53. An investment adviser's agreement with clients is considered to be a "contract for impersonal advisory services." This means provision of

    I. advisory services that do not purport to meet the objectives or needs of specific individuals or accounts
    II. statistical information that contains no expression of opinion as to the investment merits of a particular security
    III. advisory services for wrap fees that include portfolio management and monthly statements
    IV. advisory services that include a comprehensive financial plan for a client with no planned personal follow-up services

    A. I and II only
    B. I and IV only
    C. II and III only
    D. I, II, III and IV

54. Which of the following statements is NOT true regarding the records that an investment adviser is required to keep under the provisions of the Investment Advisers Act of 1940?

A. Records must be maintained for a period of three years from the end of the fiscal year in which the last entry was made.
B. Advisers must keep records of transactions made for their own personal accounts.
C. Records must be kept of client accounts, recommendations made and whether the client has granted the adviser any discretionary authority.
D. Records created by computer in the ordinary course of business may be stored in electronic format.

55. Under what circumstances is the delivery of the investment adviser brochure not required?

I. The contract is with an investment company.
II. The contract is for personal advisory services.
III. The contract is for impersonal advisory services.
IV. The contract is for impersonal advisory services requiring payment of less than $200.

A. I and II
B. I and III
C. I and IV
D. II and IV

56. Under the Investment Advisers Act of 1940, which of the following statements is NOT true regarding advisory contracts?

A. The contract must generally provide that no compensation to the adviser will be based on capital gains.
B. A waiver of the adviser's compliance with any provisions of the law is considered valid if willingly signed by the client.
C. The contract must provide for assignment only with the client's consent.
D. The contract must provide for the client's notification if a change in partners occurs in an advisory firm organized as a partnership.

57. The antifraud provisions of the Investment Advisers Act of 1940

A. apply only to advisers who are registered under the act
B. prohibit fraud only in connection with securities transactions
C. prohibit the receipt of both fees and commissions on transactions that result from advisory recommendations
D. are violated if material information is not adequately disclosed to a client

58. Federal law provides that registered investment advisers may contract for performance-based fees

    I. with any client who has received a copy of the Form ADV Part II 48 hours before signing the investment advisory contract
    II. with private investment companies under the Investment Company Act of 1940
    III. any person with assets in excess of $1 million under management
    IV. any client who has received the advisory brochure, including a copy of Form ADV Part II, at the time of the execution of the advisory contract with a five-day right of recission

    A. I and II only
    B. I, II and IV only
    C. II and III only
    D. I, II, III and IV

59. Under the provisions of the Investment Advisers Act of 1940, in which of the following situations has the adviser committed fraud by not making appropriate disclosures to clients?

    I. An adviser who has investment discretion over client accounts cannot meet her financial obligations as they come due, and does not disclose this fact to her clients.
    II. An adviser who does not require prepayment of fees and does not have discretion over accounts or custody of client securities or funds, has been found by a state court to have violated a rule issued by the administrator, and does not disclose this fact to her clients.
    III. An adviser who requires prepayment of $600 in fees nine months in advance, has liabilities that exceed her assets and does not disclose this fact to her clients.

    A. I and II only
    B. I and III only
    C. II and III only
    D. I, II and III

60. Which of the following statements is true regarding the use of the term "investment counsel" by investment advisers under the Investment Advisers Act of 1940?

    A. They may use the term without restriction as long as they are registered.
    B. They may use the term only if their principal business is acting as an investment adviser and a substantial part of their business consists of providing continuous advice tailored to a client's individual needs.
    C. They may use the term only if they are attorneys.
    D. They are prohibited from using the term under any circumstances.

61. If an investment adviser employs any fraudulent device, scheme or artifice, or engages in any business practice or act to defraud or deceive others, he is liable to that person for all of the following EXCEPT

A. consideration paid for such advice
B. any loss due to such advice with interest from date of payment of consideration
C. costs and reasonable attorney's fees less amount of any income received from such advice
D. none of the above

62. Which of the following persons meet the definition of "investment adviser" under current laws?

A. The salaried business manager for a professional athlete who has discretionary authority and makes decisions regarding stock trades and transfer of funds from money market and bank accounts to funds under management
B. An accountant who, as a part of his service, advises clients for whom he prepares taxes that they may seek tax relief by investing in such vehicles as municipal bond funds
C. An engineering firm acting as a consultant to a city in the preparation of a "feasibility study" regarding the proposed issuance of a new municipal revenue bond.
D. An individual who advertises his services as "professional financial services" and counsels clients on budgeting family income, debt retirement and the re-establishment of credit

63. Which of the following is considered to be compensation for investment advice under the Investment Advisers Act of 1940?

I. An insurance agent creates a comprehensive financial plan for a client; the plan includes investment advice; the agent does not charge for the plan, but he earns a commission on the sale of a life insurance policy included in the plan.
II. An accountant charges a fee for services that in rare, isolated instances include investment advice.
III. A broker-dealer creates a comprehensive financial plan for a client; the broker-dealer receives no fee for the plan, but he earns commissions on transactions when the plan is implemented.

A. I and II only
B. I and III only
C. II and III only
D. I, II and III

64. The Investment Advisers Act of 1940 requires an adviser to be registered if

A. his advice relates solely to securities issued or guaranteed by the U.S. government
B. all of his clients are banks
C. he is the publisher of a news magazine of general and regular circulation
D. all of his clients are insurance companies

65. Under the Uniform Securities Act, all of the following information may be disclosed to the public EXCEPT

A. registration statements
B. investment adviser's application
C. financial reports
D. personal medical files

66. The exclusion for providing investment advice that is solely incidental to the practice of a profession is NOT available to which of the following under the Investment Advisers Act of 1940?

A. Real estate agents
B. Engineers
C. Teachers
D. Broker-dealers

67. Adviser Eve Grizzly always inquires into her clients' investment objectives, financial situations and needs. Under the NASAA's Statement of Policy on Unethical Business Practices, Eve is

A. obtaining the information required to fulfill her professional obligation regarding suitability
B. determining whether she has any inherent conflicts of interest with her clients
C. violating her ethical obligation regarding confidentiality of client information
D. giving herself an unethical advantage regarding how much the client can afford to spend on an advisory fee

68. In which of the following situations has the adviser NOT acted properly under the NASAA's Statement of Policy on Unethical Business Practices when placing an order for a client's account?

A. The adviser receives written notification from the executor of the estate of a recently deceased client to the effect that the executor has power-of-attorney over the client's account. The executor instructs the adviser to liquidate the entire account, and the adviser does so.
B. A client has told the adviser to sell all the shares of a particular stock if its price falls to a certain level. The stock falls to that level and, without further consultation with the client, the adviser sells all of the shares of that stock in the client's account.
C. A client's spouse calls to say that the client has suffered a stroke and is in hospital. The spouse asks the adviser to sell enough securities to raise $5,000 in cash to pay medical bills, and the adviser does so.
D. The adviser has received a letter from a client stating that while the client is on vacation the client's son will be placing orders for the account. The client's son calls with an order, and the adviser places it.

69. The test of whether trading in a client's account is excessive under the NASAA's Statement of Policy on Unethical Business Practices depends on

I. how much compensation the adviser is earning on the trades
II. how frequent the trades are in relation to the accounts of the adviser's other clients
III. whether the trading is in line with the client's investment objectives and financial resources and the character of the client's account
IV. whether the adviser has discretionary authority over the account and how often the client is notified about account activity

A. II only
B. II, III and IV only
C. III only
D. I, II, III and IV

70. To which of the following clients would a loan from an investment adviser be unethical under the NASAA's Statement of Policy on Unethical Business Practices?

I. Another investment adviser, with whom the lending adviser has no affiliation
II. Manufacturing business that appears financially sound and the financial statements of which have been audited by the adviser's CPA
III. Savings and loan institution

A. I and II only
B. I and III only
C. II and III only
D. I, II and III

71. Under the NASAA's Statement of Policy on Unethical Business Practices, which of the following statements is true regarding the use of reports prepared by others?

A. An adviser may use a report prepared by another if the source of the report is disclosed.
B. An adviser is prohibited from basing a recommendation wholly on the product of someone else's work.
C. An adviser need not disclose the source of any information used in making a recommendation to a client unless the client asks.
D. An adviser is required to disclose the source of any information used in making a recommendation to a client.

72. Which of the following statements concerning conflicts of interest are true under the NASAA's Statement of Policy on Unethical Business Practices?

I. Where a conflict of interest exists, an adviser is required to decline taking on the client.
II. A "conflict of interest" is defined as anything that may impair the impartiality of the advice being rendered.
III. For an adviser to have as an employee a registered representative of a broker-dealer falls under the definition of a "conflict of interest."

A. I and II only
B. I and III only
C. II and III only
D. I, II and III

73. Under the NASAA's Statement of Policy on Unethical Business Practices, investment advisers who advertise must comply with the rules laid out in the Investment Advisers Act of 1940; these rules include a

A. prohibition against reduced-fee "introductory" offers
B. requirement that a copy of all advertisements be sent to the SEC at the time they are disseminated to the public
C. prohibition against testimonials from clients
D. requirement that a copy of all advertisements be sent to the SEC 10 days prior to first use

74. Under the NASAA's Statement of Policy on Unethical Business Practices, which of the following are violations of the requirements governing advisers who have custody of client securities or funds?

I. An adviser deposits client funds into her own bank account, making a careful record of the amount of funds belonging to each client.
II. An adviser allows a CPA to make an unscheduled audit of all client securities and funds in the adviser's custody.
III. Once a year, an adviser sends each client a report on the securities and funds in the adviser's custody.

A. I and II only
B. I and III only
C. II and III only
D. I, II and III

75. A customer wishes to give his attorney discretionary authority to trade his account, which is being held by an IA. This is permitted

A. if the customer has given the attorney written authority
B. if the customer gives verbal permission in the presence of both the attorney and the IA
C. if the customer's account value is in excess of $1 million
D. under no circumstances

◆ Answers & Rationale

1. **A.** Negotiations for a merger are specifically excluded from the definition of "offer or sale." Any contract of sale for a security is a "sale." A warrant is a security, so the sale of a warrant is a "sale." A gift is not a bona fide gift if the recipient will be assessed later for its value; therefore, a gift of assessable stock is considered a "sale." (Page 29)

2. **B.** An investment adviser provides advice related to securities for compensation. The advice may be given either orally or in writing. (Page 23)

3. **D.** All the selections are defined in the act and require registration at the appropriate levels as an investment adviser. (Page 23)

4. **C.** Choices II and III together make up the definition of a broker-dealer (the definition refers to a "person," which may be either an individual or a firm). However, a person may be registered as both a broker-dealer and an investment adviser at the same time. (Page 28)

5. **C.** Agents represent broker-dealers or issuers. But an individual representing an issuer is not considered an agent under certain circumstances—for example, if the issuer is a government or a bank. (Page 38)

6. **C.** Choices II and III are correct statements. However, the antifraud provisions apply to any "person," which includes government bodies and their political subdivisions. (Page 77)

7. **D.** The antifraud provisions apply to anyone involved in a securities transaction or anyone who receives compensation for providing investment advice. It does not matter whether the person receives the compensation directly or indirectly, whether the person is registered or is exempt from registration or whether an exclusion from the definition of "investment adviser" applies to the person. (Page 26)

8. **C.** Choices A, B and D are specifically required to be in writing in the advisory contract. The names and titles of the firm's principals are not required. (Page 18)

9. **D.** No one is exempt from the antifraud provisions. (Page 35)

10. **A.** The National Securities Markets Improvement Act of 1996 (NSMIA) makes an exception to the general prohibition against performance fees when applied to "qualified purchaser pools." The exceptions include IA contracts with foreign clients when such arrangements are legal and customary in the client's country of residence. Performance fees are generally prohibited for the other choices. (Page 18)

11. **D.** A broker-dealer's registration becomes effective 30 days after the application is filed, unless the administrator begins a proceeding or issues a stop order before that time. Remember also that the administrator may specify an earlier date or, if an application must be amended, may extend the date to 30 days after the amendment is filed. (Page 39)

12. **C.** Registrations under the Uniform Securities Act expire every December 31st unless they are renewed. (Page 38)

13. **D.** Records must be preserved for five years. However, the administrator may prescribe a different period for certain types of records. (Page 15)

14. **A.** The question asks for what *cannot* be required by the administrator. The administrator can require a bond only if an adviser has custody or discretion. Choices B, C and D are requirements. (Page 9)

15. **B.** Disciplinary actions with respect to registration may be taken by the administrator after a finding of public interest and cause. Court

orders are required only for legal action, such as seeking an injunction or appointing a receiver over an adviser's assets. (Page 10)

16. **C.** The standard for willful violation is *knowing* that you are doing something improper, even if you do not know that a law is being broken. The advisers in choices I and II are not aware that they are doing something improper, but the adviser in choice III is aware. (Page 77)

17. **B.** Choices I and III are correct. However, even after withdrawal becomes effective automatically, the administrator has the power to institute proceedings against the registrant for one year following the date on which the withdrawal became effective. (Page 40)

18. **C.** An exempt security is exempt only from the registration requirements and the requirements for filing advertising and sales literature. Civil liability arises any time a security is sold or advice is rendered in violation of the act, regardless of whether the security is registered or exempt. There are no exemptions from the antifraud provisions. (Page 68)

19. **B.** The federal registration statement is what the state registration is coordinated with. Concerning answer A, a prospectus must be delivered *at or prior to* the time an offer is made, not after the sale or when the security is delivered. Concerning answer C, the act prohibits any statement or implication that registration involves approval or verification of facts by the administrator. Concerning answer D, registration by coordination becomes effective simultaneously with federal registration. (Page 65)

20. **C.** Choices A, B and D are all exempt transactions. In choice C, the security is exempt but the transaction is not. (Page 72)

21. **D.** All four choices describe exempt transactions. (Page 70)

22. **A.** The fact that a security is registered or is exempt from registration has no bearing on its quality, safety or merits, and it is illegal to make any statement or implication to the contrary, as is implied in choices B and D. A similar principle applies to a person's being registered or exempt from registration (choice C). Registration does not involve verification by the administrator of any information included in a registration statement or application. When a registration becomes effective, it means only that certain legal requirements have been met in regard to that security or person. Choice A is a statement that can be legally made. (Page 21)

23. **D.** The broad powers of the state securities administrator permit him to do any of these. (Page 35)

24. **D.** The investor who has been damaged, not the administrator, files the lawsuit charging civil liability. A client may recover costs and attorney's fees in addition to the amount paid for the advice, losses caused by the advice and interest. Registered persons may be sued only up to three years following the rendering of the advice. Choice D is a true statement. (Page 36)

25. **C.** An offer is made in a state when it originates in that state. An offer is also considered to be made in a state when it is directed by the offerer to that state and is received at the place to which it is directed. However, offers received via a television or radio broadcast that originated out of state or offers contained in a newspaper published out of state are specifically excluded. (Page 35)

26. **B.** Options to buy or sell foreign currency entered into on a national exchange are specifically included in the definition of "security" under the 1933 act. As under other securities acts, futures contracts, precious metals, collectibles and real estate are generally not considered securities. (Page 30)

27. **A.** An issuer is a person who issues a security, whether or not the security is exempt. The antique dealer is issuing collectibles, not securities. (Page 60)

28. **C.** Preliminary agreements between issuers and underwriters and bona fide gifts of securities are specifically excluded from the definition of "sale." When a right to convert or purchase a security is exercised, it is considered to be a sale. A security given as a bonus with a purchase is considered to be part of the purchase and, therefore, is being "sold." (Page 29)

29. **B.** An omitting prospectus may not be accompanied by an application to invest. Answers A and C are requirements that apply to an omitting prospectus: the information must come from the prospectus, and potential investors must be urged to read the prospectus before investing. The omitting prospectus also must tell potential investors how to obtain a full prospectus. Past performance data may be included, if appropriately labeled. (Page 51)

30. **D.** Under the National Securities Markets Improvement Act of 1996 (NSMI) mutual funds (registered investment companies) securities, NASDAQ NMS securities and securities listed on the NYSE or AMEX are considered "covered securities" and are therefore exempt from registration at the state level. (Page 68)

31. **D.** The underwriter's signature is not required on a registration statement; but the issuer's chief executive officer, chief financial officer and chief accounting officer and a majority of the board of directors all must sign. (Page 56)

32. **A.** A registration statement must contain, among many other things, an estimate of the proceeds and a description of the use to which they will be put, the identity of the underwriter and the identities of owners of more than 10 percent of the issuer's stock. It must also identify all of the issuer's officers and directors, their holdings of the issuer's securities and their salaries. Answer A does not describe the personnel manager as an officer or a director, so this employee need not be identified in the registration statement. (Page 48)

33. **B.** Suits may not be brought under the 1933 act more than three years after the sale of the security. (Page 36)

34. **A.** The SEC has the power to make, amend and rescind rules in administering the securities laws. The SEC may also conduct a formal investigation whenever it deems this necessary, in its discretion, to enforce the federal securities laws. In conducting a formal investigation, the SEC may administer oaths, obtain written statements, subpoena witnesses, take evidence and require the production of books and records. The SEC does not have the power, however, to arrest and detain suspects. (Page 25)

35. **B.** The 1934 act defines "government securities" as those issued or guaranteed by the U.S. government or one of its agencies. Securities issued or guaranteed by a state, county, city, etc., or by any agency of a nonfederal governmental unit, are municipal securities. (Page 28)

36. **D.** An equity security is any kind of stock—common or preferred—and any security that allows someone to acquire stock, either through a right or warrant to purchase stock or through a conversion privilege. In themselves, bonds are not equity securities but, if they are issued with a warrant to purchase stock or are convertible into stock, they fall under the definition of an equity security in the 1934 act. (Page 28)

37. **B.** An associated person of a broker-dealer includes any partner, branch manager, officer (choice C) or director of a broker-dealer, including an outside director (choice D). It also includes employees such as registered reps or agents (choice A) who are not clerks or ministerial personnel, and anyone who controls, is controlled by or is under common control with the broker-dealer. Choice B describes no such person. (Page 28)

38. **B.** Clearing agencies performing the functions of a transfer agent with respect to contracts they issue and insurance companies are specifi-

cally excluded from the definition of "transfer agent." Choice II is a transfer agent. (Page 30)

39. **C.** Both the firm and the individual are directly compensated for investment advice and are required to register as investment advisers. (Page 4)

40. **B.** SEC commissioners may have no business or employment other than their commission. They must also refrain from securities trading. However, commissioners are not elected as described in choice A, but are appointed by the president and confirmed by the Senate. Political party affiliation is a consideration, because no more than three of the five commissioners may belong to the same party. Experience as a prosecuting attorney is not a qualification. (Page 31)

41. **B.** Institutional investment managers must file reports quarterly if they exercise discretion over accounts valued at more than $100 million; whether the clients are insurance companies (choice A) is not relevant. The requirement for reports of beneficial ownership is that anyone who becomes the owner of more than 5 percent of a security registered under the 1934 act must file a report within 10 days. (Page 16)

42. **A.** The SEC is charged with administering the federal securities laws, under which the Municipal Securities Rulemaking Board (MSRB) operates; thus the SEC has jurisdiction over the MSRB. However, financial institutions come under the jurisdiction of banking regulatory authorities. (Page 32)

43. **C.** Creating the misleading appearance of trading activity to induce others to buy or sell a security (choice C) is illegal. However, simply changing one's mind (choice A) is not. It is also illegal to make false statements or to spread rumors that one knows or suspects to be untrue in order to induce trading. Trading on material information that has not yet been made public is illegal, but the accountant in choice B traded only after the favorable earnings report was *released.* (Page 78)

44. **C.** To suspend all trading on an exchange, the SEC must notify the President. (Page 32)

45. **D.** Neither loss of a civil lawsuit, nor lack of experience nor being registered as an investment adviser causes statutory disqualification from being associated with a member of a self-regulatory organization such as the NASD. However, administrative sanctions, findings of criminal wrongdoing, court injunctions and so on are causes for statutory disqualification. (Page 37)

46. **B.** Like mutual fund shares, shares in a unit investment trust are redeemable for their NAV upon the shareholder's request. (Page 83)

47. **C.** While the trade is unsuitable based on the customer's investment objectives, the customer has granted the proper written discretionary authority to the agent to make trades in his account. (Page 77)

48. **C.** Rule 12b-1 allows funds to charge distribution expenses against net assets. (Page 94)

49. **D.** All three answers are true statements, and ones that you should memorize. (Page 40)

50. **B.** An investment adviser has a fiduciary duty with respect to the receipt of compensation from the fund, and receipt of excessive compensation is considered a breach of that duty. (Page 78)

51. **C.** The National Securities Markets Improvement Act of 1996 (NSMIA) authorizes the SEC to require such information, documents and reports from investment companies the agency deems necessary to keep reasonably current the information and documentation in the investment company's registration statement. Investment companies need not inform shareholders of all changes in the portfolio immediately. Investment companies are only registered with the SEC under NSMIA. (Page 96)

52. **B.** A blanket exclusion from the definition of "investment adviser" applies to banks.

Broker-dealers are excluded only if the advice is within the scope of their brokerage business and they receive no special compensation, such as an additional fee, for that advice. Regarding choice C, advice relating to types of securities is specific enough to qualify as investment advice, even if no mention is made of particular securities. Choice D describes an exemption under the Uniform Securities Act for publishers; under the 1940 act, an investment advisory publication must have general and regular circulation to be exempt from registering as an investment adviser. (Page 2)

53. **A.** Choices I and II or any combination of the two are definitions of a "contract for impersonal advisory services." Choices II and IV are not considered impersonal. (Page 3)

54. **A.** Records must be kept for five years, not three. The other answers are true statements: advisers must keep records of their personal transactions; choice C accurately describes the records that must be kept; and records may be kept in electronic format if they are created by computer in the regular course of business. (Page 15)

55. **C.** The investment adviser is required to provide a brochure to all clients with the following exceptions: an investment company or contracting for impersonal advisory services requiring a payment of less than $200. (Page 14)

56. **B.** Waivers of the adviser's compliance with any provisions of the law are always void, even if signed willingly by the client. The other answers are true statements: except when an exemptive rule issued by the SEC applies, advisory contracts must provide for no compensation based on capital gains; they also must provide for no assignment without the client's consent and for notification in the event of a change of partners in a partnership. (Page 18)

57. **D.** The antifraud provisions prohibit a failure to disclose material information, as well as misstatements of fact and deceptive practices. An adviser is not exempt from the antifraud provisions even if she is exempt from registration. The antifraud provisions of the Advisers Act are not limited to securities transactions, as are the antifraud provisions of other federal acts; like those of the Uniform Securities Act, they apply to the entire business relationship between adviser and client. (Page 24)

58. **C.** Performance-based fees are allowable under federal law *only* for private investment companies and persons with $1 million or more under management. (Page 18)

59. **D.** An adviser's financial impairment must be disclosed to clients if the adviser has discretion or custody or requires prepayment of over $500 in fees more than six months in advance. Legal or disciplinary action taken against an adviser by a court or a regulatory authority within the past 10 years must in all cases be disclosed to clients. Note also that by requiring prepayment of over $500 in fees more than six months in advance, the adviser in choice III is required to include an audited balance sheet with Part II of Form ADV, which must be filed with the SEC and made part of the adviser's disclosure brochure. (Page 23)

60. **B.** Advisers may use the term "investment counsel" only if two conditions are met: rendering investment advice is their principal business; and a substantial part of their business is providing investment supervisory services—that is, continuous advice based on the individual needs of each client. (Page 3)

61. **D.** An investment adviser is liable if he engages in any fraudulent or deceptive activity. (Page 76)

62. **A.** By making stock trades on behalf of the client and collecting a fee, the professional athlete's business manager is defined as an "investment adviser." The accountant's services in financial advice are incidental to his profession. Neither of the other choices describe one

who, for compensation, sells investment advice. (Page 2)

63. **B.** The insurance agent in choice I is providing investment advice and is being compensated for it. It does not matter that the compensation is in the form of commissions on a nonsecurities product. Receipt of any economic benefit from any source, if received as a result of providing investment advice, meets the criterion. The broker-dealer in choice III is providing investment advice outside the scope of what would be incidental to conducting a brokerage business; the exclusion from the definition of adviser is therefore lost. Although no separate fee for investment advice is charged, the broker-dealer is receiving compensation in the form of commissions on transactions that result from providing the investment advice. In choice II, however, the compensation received for services that include investment advice only in rare, isolated instances is an exception to the compensation criterion. (Page 2)

64. **B.** Persons are excluded from the advisers act definition of "investment adviser" if their advice relates solely to U.S. government securities or if they are publishers of news or business/financial publications of general and regular circulation. Under the advisers act, advisers are exempt from registration if all of their clients are insurance companies. However, no exclusion or exemption applies to an adviser whose only clients are banks. (Page 2)

65. **D.** Information filed in an investment adviser's registration statement is considered available to the public. However, personal information is not available to the public. (Page 14)

66. **A.** A professional exclusion is not available to real estate agents. It is available to engineers, teachers and broker-dealers if the advice rendered is solely incidental to the practice of their professions. (Page 3)

67. **A.** Advisers are under a professional obligation to inquire into a client's investment objectives, financial situation and needs, and to make recommendations consistent with that information and any other knowledge the adviser may have about the client. (Page 77)

68. **C.** In choices A and D, no breach of ethical conduct occurred because written acknowledgment of third-party trading authority was properly obtained from the client (or the client's estate) prior to acting on the instructions of the third party. In choice B, the adviser is carrying out an order with respect to a specified amount of a particular security, and this requires no further authorization. In choice C, however, the adviser acted on the instructions of a third party without obtaining prior, written authority from the client. (Page 77)

69. **C.** An adviser must not induce trading in a client's account that is excessive in view of the client's investment objectives and financial resources and the character of the client's account. Other factors, such as whether the client makes money or approves each trade, or the amount of trading in other client accounts, are not relevant. (Page 77)

70. **A.** An adviser may lend money to a client only if the client is a bank or other financial institution in the business of loaning funds, or is an affiliate of the adviser. Only choice III meets those criteria. (Page 77)

71. **A.** An adviser is not prohibited from providing clients with recommendations or reports prepared by others, but the adviser must disclose the true source of the recommendations or reports. However, the disclosure requirement does not apply to the research an adviser uses in rendering investment advice. (Page 23)

72. **C.** "Conflicts of interest" are circumstances relating to the adviser or any employee that could impair the rendering of unbiased and objective advice. This includes, but is not limited to, the possibility of receiving compensation from sources other than clients' fees (such as a salary or commission from a broker-dealer) as a result

of providing investment advice. Such conflicts of interest must be disclosed to a client in writing before the investment advisory contract is signed. (Page 4)

73. **C.** Advertisements may not contain false statements, include testimonials from clients, refer selectively to past recommendations, refer to a chart or device for evaluating securities without explaining its limitations and difficulties, or offer anything "free-of-charge" if in fact there will be some requirement, however minor, for obtaining the "free" item. (Page 21)

74. **B.** Requirements for custody are the same under the USA and the Advisers Act. Client funds must be deposited in separate bank accounts, so choice I is a violation. Clients must receive statements quarterly (not yearly), so choice III is a violation. Clients must also be notified in writing of the location of their property and of any change in that location. And client securities must be properly segregated and identified. Each year, accounts must be audited by an independent public accountant in an unannounced examination, so choice II is not a violation. (Page 17)

75. **A.** An account holder may grant discretionary authority to a third party to trade her account as long as written permission has been granted. (Page 17)

14 Series 65 Final Exam Three

1. Under the civil liabilities provisions of the Uniform Securities Act, a client may sue an adviser if

   A. the client loses money due to the advice rendered
   B. the adviser is shown to be negligent
   C. advice is rendered that is in violation of the act
   D. any of the above occurs

2. Under the Securities Act of 1933, all of the following are covered EXCEPT

   A. fair disclosure of all pertinent information
   B. blue-sky laws
   C. due diligence
   D. requirements for prospectuses

3. Which of the following statements is NOT true regarding rules issued by the administrator, under the provisions of the Uniform Securities Act?

   A. The rules must be published.
   B. The provisions of the act have the same weight as rules.
   C. The administrator may not issue rules that duplicate those issued by the SEC.
   D. The rules must be in the public interest.

4. Which of the following may NOT be stated by an issuer selling securities to the public (either directly or through an underwriter) that have been registered under the Securities Act of 1933?

   I. "The SEC has passed on the adequacy of the information provided in the prospectus."
   II. "The SEC has approved the accuracy of the information contained in the prospectus."
   III. "The SEC has studied the merits of the securities as an investment."
   IV. "The securities have been approved by the SEC."

   A. I, II and IV only
   B. I and III only
   C. III and IV only
   D. I, II, III and IV

5. The National Securities Markets Improvement Act of 1996 amends the Securities Act of 1933 to preempt state regulation of securities transactions with certain "qualified purchasers." This exempts securities transactions with which of the following from state regulatory oversight?

   I. A bank or trust company investing for its own account
   II. A money manager who has discretion over an account valued at more than $100 million
   III. The investment adviser of a mutual fund making purchases and sales for the fund
   IV. An individual investor who has more than $10 million invested in the markets

   A. I, II and III only
   B. I and III only
   C. II and III only
   D. I, II, III and IV

6. The key purpose of the Securities Act of 1933 is described by which of the following phrases?

   A. Insures that minimum standards of investment merit for new issue securities will be met
   B. Prevents fraud in the trading of securities
   C. Is designed to prevent excessive speculation in securities
   D. Provides that purchasers of new issue securities receive full disclosure of pertinent information

7. An offer under the Uniform Securities Act is considered to have been made in a state when it

   A. is received within the state via a television broadcast that originated outside that state
   B. originates within the boundaries of that state
   C. is received within the state via a newspaper published within the state, but which has more than two-thirds of its circulation outside the state
   D. is received within the state via a newspaper published outside the state

8. Securities that are sold to the public must be registered under the Securities Act of 1933 under which of the following circumstances?

   A. The total value of the issue exceeds $1 million.
   B. The U.S. Justice Department, upon request, directs that the security be so registered.
   C. The securities are sold on an intrastate basis.
   D. The securities are sold in interstate commerce through the mails or other channels.

9. Which of the following is excluded from the definition of "investment adviser" under the Investment Advisers Act of 1940?

   I. Any bank that does not hold itself out to the public as an investment company
   II. An engineer whose rendering of investment advice is solely incidental to the practice of engineering
   III. Anyone whose advice relates solely to U.S. government securities

   A. I and II only
   B. I and III only
   C. II and III only
   D. I, II and III

10. Under the Investment Company Act of 1940, which of the following does NOT fit the definition of a management company?

I. Face-amount certificate company
II. Unit investment trust
III. Closed-end investment company
IV. Open-end investment company

A. I and II
B. I and IV
C. II and III
D. III and IV

11. A "unit investment trust" is defined by the Investment Company Act of 1940 as a(n)

A. separate account established and managed by an insurance company
B. investment contract that represents an obligation to pay a determinable sum at a fixed date in the future
C. investment company that issues redeemable securities, each of which represents an undivided interest in the securities in a fixed portfolio
D. issuer who acquires investment securities whose value exceeds 40 percent of the value of the issuer's total assets

12. Which of the following would NOT define a person as being in the business of providing investment advice under the provisions of the Investment Advisers Act of 1940?

A. Providing a complete range of financial services, but with advice on investments constituting only a minor component in the overall range of services
B. Providing specific investment advice only on rare, isolated, unusual occasions
C. Advertising advice on investing
D. Receiving a small, separate fee for investment advice

13. Amusement Technology, a diversified open-end investment company, invested 5 percent of its total assets in General Gizmonics, Inc. The market soared and, because of phenomenal appreciation, GIZ securities now make up 8 percent of Amusement Technology Fund's total assets. In accordance with the Investment Company Act of 1940, Amusement Technology Fund

A. does not have to sell GIZ shares, but cannot buy more GIZ shares and still advertise itself as a diversified company
B. must sell GIZ shares only if the 8 percent investment represents more than 10 percent of GIZ's outstanding voting securities
C. must sell out its holdings in GIZ completely
D. must sell enough of GIZ securities to reduce its holdings in GIZ to 5 percent of its total assets

14. Under the Investment Advisers Act of 1940, a person who provides investment advice does so for compensation if she receives

I. a commission on the sale of an investment-related product
II. any economic benefit
III. a single fee for a broad range of financial services

A. I and II only
B. I and III only
C. II and III only
D. I, II and III

15. When a registered IA employs a solicitor to prospect for clients, in addition to providing the names of the solicitor and the investment adviser, the firm must execute a written agreement with the solicitor that

    I. describes the solicitation activities to be engaged in by the solicitor on behalf of the IA and the compensation to be paid by the IA to the solicitor
    II. indicates a willingness by the solicitor to perform his duties under the agreement in a manner consistent with the instructions of the IA and the Investment Advisers Act
    III. indicates that the solicitor is aware of his personal requirements for registration as an advisory solicitor under appropriate federal statutes
    IV. requires that the solicitor, at the time of any solicitation, provide the client with a current copy of the investment adviser's disclosure brochure

    A. I and II
    B. I, II and III
    C. I, II and IV
    D. I, III and IV

16. Under the Investment Company Act of 1940, an affiliated person of an investment company includes a

    I. member of the fund's board of directors
    II. person who holds 5 percent of the fund's shares
    III. company under the control of the investment company
    IV. member of the immediate family of the fund's investment adviser

    A. I and II only
    B. I, II and III only
    C. III and IV only
    D. I, II, III and IV

17. A person can claim a registration exemption as an "investment adviser" under the amended Investment Advisers Act of 1940 if they

    I. charge a fee separate from that for their professional services for the provision of investment advice
    II. manage less than $25 million in assets
    III. provide advice on government issues only
    IV. have insurance companies as a client base

    A. I and II only
    B. I and III only
    C. II, III and IV only
    D. I, II, III and IV

18. Under the Investment Company Act of 1940, an investment company that is NOT classified as either a face-amount certificate company or a unit investment trust would be classified as a(n)

    A. closed-end company
    B. open-end company
    C. management company
    D. mutual fund

19. Which of the following disclosures is an investment adviser required to make to clients under the provisions of the Investment Advisers Act of 1940?

I. The amount of any compensation that will be earned on transactions executed through the broker-dealer with whom the adviser is affiliated
II. That, in implementing a plan for a client, the adviser intends to act as a representative of a broker-dealer with whom he is affiliated
III. That clients have the right to execute recommended transactions through broker-dealers other than the one with whom the adviser is affiliated

A. I and II only
B. I and III only
C. II and III only
D. I, II and III

20. As defined in the Investment Company Act of 1940, which of the following statements is NOT true with regard to a unit investment trust?

A. The overall responsibility for the fund rests with the investment adviser.
B. The transfer agent may limit sales to current unit holders.
C. It invests in a portfolio that is designed to meet a stated objective.
D. No management fee is charged.

21. According to the Investment Company Act of 1940, which of the following statements is NOT true of a closed-end investment company?

A. It can buy back its own shares.
B. It can be described as a type of management company.
C. Its shares are sold in the secondary market at the market price plus a commission.
D. It may be referred to as a mutual fund.

22. Under the Investment Company Act of 1940, which of the following statements are true when used in reference to an open-end investment company?

I. It redeems shares at any time.
II. It may leverage common shares by issuing bonds.
III. It may constantly issue new shares.

A. I and II only
B. I and III only
C. II and III only
D. I, II and III

23. What is the maximum percentage of a corporation's voting securities that a diversified mutual fund may hold under the provisions of the Investment Company Act of 1940?

A. 5 percent
B. 10 percent
C. 50 percent
D. 75 percent

24. As defined in the Investment Company Act of 1940, which of the following would be considered to be affiliated persons of an investment company?

I. Corporation in which the investment company has a 22 percent ownership
II. Customer who owns 5 percent of the investment company's shares
III. Amusement Technology Fund's independent investment adviser
IV. Treasurer of the Amusement Technology Fund

A. I and II only
B. I and III only
C. III and IV only
D. I, II, III and IV

25. Under the Investment Company Act of 1940, an investment company may enter into a contract with its investment adviser up to a maximum time of

A. one year
B. two years
C. three years
D. five years

26. If the SEC suspends trading on the New York Stock Exchange, which of the following must be notified?

A. President of the United States
B. Federal Reserve Board
C. Comptroller of the Currency
D. Issuers of listed securities

27. ALFA Financial Services charges a fee for its services in managing several diversified mutual funds. Under the Investment Company Act of 1940, which of the following would be included in the services ALFA supplies?

I. Attempting to meet the investment objectives of the fund
II. Analyzing market conditions and deciding when securities in the portfolio should be bought or sold
III. Changing investment objectives in order to maximize potential gain for the shareholders
IV. Ensuring that the fund portfolio meets the legal diversification requirements

A. I and II
B. I, II and IV
C. I and III
D. II, III and IV

28. Which of the following BEST describes a 12b-1 fee, as set forth in the Investment Company Act of 1940?

A. A back-end load paid by an investor upon redeeming mutual fund shares
B. An annual expense of a mutual fund, used to defray the cost of marketing and distributing fund shares
C. A front-end load paid by an investor buying shares through a broker-dealer
D. An annual expense of a mutual fund, incurred by trading securities in the fund's portfolio

29. According to the Investment Company Act of 1940, a fund's contract with its investment adviser must be approved by a majority vote of the

A. NASD district committee
B. board of directors of the fund and the shareholders
C. board of governors of the NASD
D. SEC

30. According to the Investment Company Act of 1940, in a regulated, diversified open-end investment company, which of the following functions are performed by the investment adviser?

I. Changing the fund's investment objectives
II. Investigating the tax status of potential investments
III. Ensuring that the fund invests in such a manner as to retain its diversified status
IV. Attempting to fulfill the fund's investment objective by means of careful investing

A. I and III
B. I, III and IV
C. II, III and IV
D. II and IV

31. Under the Investment Company Act of 1940, shares held in a mutual fund's portfolio may be liquidated by the investment adviser

    A. only with the consent of the board of directors and a majority vote of the shareholders
    B. as long as the liquidation is within the guidelines set forth by the fund's objective
    C. only with the consent of a majority vote of the shareholders
    D. only with the consent of the board of directors

32. According to the USA, which of the following are exempt from registration as an agent?

    I. U.S. government representative
    II. Corporate issuer's representative
    III. Broker-dealer's representative
    IV. Bank officer

    A. I and III only
    B. I and IV only
    C. II and IV only
    D. I, II, III and IV

33. An investment adviser advertises a computer-based formula for making buy and sell decisions. Under the Investment Advisers Act of 1940, which of the following disclosures is required?

    I. How long the adviser has used the formula
    II. Degree of difficulty involved in applying the formula
    III. Limitations of using the formula
    IV. Recommendations based on the formula for the previous year

    A. I and IV only
    B. II and III only
    C. II, III and IV only
    D. I, II, III and IV

34. Under the Investment Advisers Act of 1940, which of the following changes to an investment advisory contract require(s) the client's consent?

    I. The vice-president of a management company leaves to work for another advisory firm, but will retain his 1 percent equity interest.
    II. Two advisory firms merge to provide a larger investment base for their respective clients.
    III. An advisory firm's board decides to hire Porter Stout and, as part of the compensation agreement, offers Mr. Stout a 10 percent equity interest in the firm.
    IV. The president of an advisory firm dies and is replaced on an interim basis by the chairman and CEO, who is a majority stockholder.

    A. II only
    B. II and III only
    C. III and IV only
    D. I, II, III and IV

35. Which of the following is exempt from registration with a state as an investment adviser under current law?

    I. Active fee-based financial planner that has no place of business in the state and, during the preceding six-month period, has executed advisory contracts with less than 10 clients
    II. Investment advisory firm that has client assets under management exceeding $30 million
    III. Portfolio manager for an open-end management investment company with assets exceeding $17.5 million
    IV. Financial advisory firm compensated by "wrap fees," managing total client assets totaling more than $10 million

    A. I and II
    B. I and IV
    C. II and III
    D. II and IV

36. Which of the following is(are) required to register in the state as an investment adviser?

    I. Lotta Leveridge, author of the Gracious Adviser Investment Newsletter mailed to 1,000 monthly subscribers nationwide
    II. Gwinneth Stout, who has only clients that are investment companies and banks in the state
    III. An investment advisory firm that opens an office in the state with less than $25 million in assets under management
    IV. Fleecem Runn Skippe Advisers, a newly formed investment advisory firm, which has $25 million in assets under management

    A. I and II only
    B. I and III only
    C. III only
    D. I, II, III and IV

37. An IA is permitted to borrow money from a client if the

    A. client is in the business of lending money
    B. rate of interest charged does not exceed the prime rate
    C. proceeds of the loan are used in the IA's business
    D. client gives written permission

38. According to the NASAA's Statement of Policy on Unethical Business Practices, which of the following is considered unethical for an investment adviser?

    I. Exercising discretionary authority in setting up the initial investment accounts for a new client's account after obtaining oral authority from the client
    II. Exercising discretionary authority in trading securities for an account that has been under management for three years after obtaining oral authority from the client
    III. Without oral or written discretionary authority, selling 3,000 shares of TIP as directed by a client at a price that the adviser determines is the best that the client can get
    IV. Selling 3,000 shares of TIP at a price the adviser determines is the best the client can get, without oral or written discretionary authority

    A. I, II and IV
    B. I and III
    C. I and IV
    D. II and III

39. Under current law, a person would be required to register as an investment adviser in a state under which of the following circumstances?

    I. The person effects transactions exclusively with issuers of securities in that state while maintaining no office therein.
    II. The person has directed offers to six individuals in that state within the past 12 months, even though he has no place of business within the state.
    III. The person manages less than $25 million in assets.
    IV. The person deals exclusively with broker-dealers in that state but maintains no place of business within the boundaries of the state.

    A. I and IV only
    B. II and III only
    C. II, III and IV only
    D. I, II, III and IV

40. Investment advisers must meet which requirements for registration under the Uniform Securities Act?

    I. Pass one or more written or oral examinations as required by the administrator.
    II. File a consent to service of process along with the registration application.
    III. Disclose in the registration application information required by the administrator relevant to the adviser's business
    IV. Publish an announcement of having filed an application for registration with the administrator in one or more newspapers published in the state of registration.

    A. I only
    B. II and III only
    C. II, III and IV only
    D. I, II, III and IV

41. Under the USA, which of the following would need to be registered as a security?

    A. Gold or silver ingots
    B. A fractional interest in a mining development program
    C. Stock issued by a bank
    D. Fixed annuity

42. A person is registering in the state as an investment adviser. Under the Uniform Securities Act, the state may require information regarding the firm's

    I. employees' qualifications and business histories
    II. financial condition, including the requirement to file its most recent balance sheet
    III. custody arrangements of customer funds
    IV. plans for a fee schedule of charges that it will assess clients for services rendered, including how the firm plans to calculate its fees and on what basis the fees are to be paid

    A. II only
    B. II, III and IV only
    C. III and IV only
    D. I, II, III and IV

43. Max Leveridge filed an application under the Uniform Securities Act to withdraw his registration as an investment adviser. Withdrawal of Max's registration becomes effective

    A. 30 days from Max's date for registration as an investment adviser
    B. 30 days from the date Max's application for withdrawal is filed with the administrator
    C. 30 days from the date of Max's application for withdrawal
    D. 60 days from the date Max's application is filed with the administrator

44. A person has applied for registration as an agent under the Uniform Securities Act. The administrator has summarily postponed the registration. As a result of the postponement, the administrator must

I. provide for a hearing on the reason(s) for the postponement within 15 days of receipt of a written request
II. notify the applicant in advance of the postponement
III. provide a written report of the reasons for the postponement
IV. notify the applicant's employer in advance of the postponement

A. I and II only
B. I, III and IV only
C. III and IV only
D. I, II, III and IV

45. Any disciplinary action taken by the administrator under the Uniform Securities Act must follow procedures provided under the act. These procedures include the

I. provision for a hearing on the action after receipt of a written request for a hearing
II. provision that a written order describing the violation be sent to the party involved in the dispute prior to any action being taken by the administrator
III. prompt notification to the applicant of the action taken
IV. prompt notification of the applicant's employer if the action concerns an investment adviser representative

A. I and II only
B. II and III only
C. III and IV only
D. I, II, III and IV

46. Angus Bullwether has terminated his employment with Greide S. Goode Advisory Services, Inc. as an agent and has accepted a position with Fleecem Runn Skippe Investment Advisers in the same capacity. Under the Uniform Securities Act, Angus's change in employment means that

A. Fleecem Runn Skippe must promptly notify the administrator of Angus's employment as an agent with the firm
B. Greide S. Goode must promptly notify the administrator of Angus's termination with the firm
C. Greide S. Goode, Fleecem Runn Skippe and Angus must notify the administrator of Angus's termination and reemployment
D. Greide S. Goode and Fleecem Runn Skippe must promptly notify the administrator of Angus's termination and employment, respectively

47. Filing a consent to service of process as part of registration as an investment adviser under the Uniform Securities Act means any legal notice served on the

A. administrator is legally binding on the administrator
B. adviser is legally binding on the administrator, as if the notice had been served on the administrator personally
C. adviser is legally binding on the adviser
D. administrator is legally binding on the adviser, as if the notice had been served on the adviser personally

48. Records required to be kept under the provisions of the Uniform Securities Act include

I. any records as prescribed by the administrator
II. customer account records and correspondence
III. business ledgers
IV. memoranda regarding the internal business practices of an advisory or brokerage firm

A. I and III only
B. II, III and IV only
C. II and IV only
D. I, II, III and IV

49. Which of the following are requirements imposed for investment advisers who have custody or possession of clients' funds or securities?

I. All securities for each client must be strictly segregated and marked to identify the particular client.
II. Securities held for the client in the street name may be held along with other clients' securities and securities of the IA if Form ADV Part II describes the accounting methods used by the investment adviser.
III. Investment advisers must maintain a bank account for client funds that contains only client funds, with the account maintained in the name of the IA as agent or trustee for the account.
IV. Investment Advisers must file a Form ADV-E with the SEC at least annually.

A. I and III
B. II and III
C. II and IV
D. I, III and IV

50. An administrator may require a surety bond for all of the following EXCEPT

A. issuer
B. agent
C. IA
D. broker-dealer

51. Which of the following practices are considered prohibited practices by investment advisers?

I. The distribution of statements, prepared by a campaign manager in a promotional campaign for a newsletter, which provided incorrect and exaggerated information regarding the IA's background and experience
II. A statement by an IA's newsletter which indicates that the 39 Week Moving Average of the Dow Jones Industrial Average may be used in and of itself to determine when to buy and sell mutual fund shares without giving sufficient cautionary warnings
III. Publishing articles in the IA's newsletter recommending clients purchase securities and omitting disclosure of the IA's purchase of those securities shortly before their recommendation in the newsletter
IV. Sending a notice of assignment to clients without informing them that no assignment may be made without their consent

A. I and IV only
B. II and III only
C. II, III and IV only
D. I, II, III and IV

52. Under the Uniform Securities Act, prior to taking any disciplinary action against a registered investment adviser, the administrator must first find that the action is

A. in the public interest
B. appropriate considering the violation
C. supportable by the state court system
D. within the purview of the statutes and procedures mandated by the SEC

53. The administrator, acting under the provisions of the Uniform Securities Act, may deny an investment adviser's application for registration based upon

I. misleading information in an application for registration
II. lack of experience in the business as the sole basis for denial
III. failure to pay the application fee for registration
IV. failure to meet minimum net capital requirements mandated by state law

A. I only
B. I and III only
C. III and IV only
D. I, II, III and IV

54. According to the Uniform Securities Act, the administrator is NOT permitted to order a registration canceled under which of the following circumstances?

A. Angus Bullwether, a registered investment adviser, has suffered irreversible brain damage and has been adjudged mentally incompetent.
B. Karen Kodiak has no experience as an investment adviser.
C. Lotta Leveridge, a registered investment adviser, is convicted of a securities misdemeanor.
D. Dullard Advisors is permanently barred from the securities business by the SEC.

55. Under the Securities Act of 1933, a prospectus must include which of the following items?

I. Whether the underwriter intends to stabilize the issue if necessary
II. A statement indicating the SEC has not approved nor disapproved the issue
III. Disclosure of pertinent information concerning the issuer's financial situation
IV. The effective date of the registration

A. I and II only
B. I, III and IV only
C. III and IV only
D. I, II, III and IV

56. Of the following, which does NOT meet the definition of providing investment advice as a business outlined in SEC Release IA-1092?

A. Management consultant who has not provided investment advice to clients other than to tell a couple of small business clients who had invested their surpluses in speculative securities that they should find something less risky
B. Financial planner who provides only nonspecific investment advice as part of his fee-based services but who makes specific securities recommendations to his clients in his capacity as a registered representative for a broker-dealer
C. Attorney who advertises the availability of investment advice
D. Accountant who charges clients an additional fee for providing investment advice

57. Under the Securities Act of 1933, a registered representative whose firm is in the process of underwriting a stock issue that is currently in registration is allowed to

A. accept an indication of interest from a customer
B. perform a private transaction for a customer
C. promise a specific number of shares to a customer
D. accept an order for the stock

58. Under SEC Release IA-1092, which of the following constitutes providing investment advice for compensation?

I. An insurance agent develops a financial plan for clients, at no charge, providing generic investment and savings information. The agent is compensated only by commissions on his insurance sales.
II. An insurance agent develops a financial plan for clients, at no charge, analyzing life insurance and mutual fund investments. The agent is compensated only by commissions on his insurance sales.
III. A broker-dealer provides financial strategies and recommends specific securities. The broker-dealer is compensated only by commissions on securities transactions.
IV. A financial planner develops financial plans, at no charge, containing specific investment advice and referring clients to the ALFA Securities brokerage company in order to follow the plans. The planner receives a referral fee from ALFA Securities.

A. I and III
B. I and IV
C. II and III
D. II and IV

59. The Securities Act of 1933 applies to which securities market?

A. Third
B. Fourth
C. Primary
D. Secondary

60. Under the Securities Act of 1933, a registered representative is prohibited from which activities in connection with the sale of a new issue and prior to the effective date of the registration statement for that issue?

I. Confirming the sale of the security to a customer
II. Soliciting indications of interest for the security
III. Soliciting orders for the stock

A. I and III only
B. II and III only
C. I and II only
D. I, II and III

61. According to the USA, an IA must keep records relating to customers for a minimum of

A. three years
B. five years
C. seven years

62. According to the Securities Act of 1933, what is the time limit for sending a prospectus for an initial public offering to customers?

A. 30 days
B. 60 days
C. 90 days
D. 120 days

63. Violations of the Uniform Securities Act may result in

A. imprisonment for no less than three years
B. a $5,000 fine with a maximum of up to three years in jail
C. having a receiver appointed over an adviser's assets
D. all of the above

64. When the SEC reviews a prospectus and registration statement prepared under the Securities Act of 1933, the SEC

A. passes on the merits of a particular security covered by the registration statement
B. does not approve securities registered with it and offered for sale
C. guarantees the adequacy of the disclosures made in the prospectus
D. guarantees the accuracy of the disclosures made in the prospectus

65. Under the provisions of the Securities Act of 1933, which of the following statements are accurate concerning the offering of non-exempt securities to the public?

I. The SEC must pass on the truthfulness of the information in the prospectus.
II. A registration statement must be filed with the SEC.
III. A prospectus is provided to all potential purchasers, and any sale without such a prospectus is illegal.
IV. A tombstone advertisement must be published or otherwise publicly displayed before any offering of new issue securities can be made.

A. I, II and IV only
B. II and III only
C. III and IV only
D. I, II, III and IV

66. An investor wishes to open a discretionary account at a broker-dealer. The first thing that the agent for the account should do is

A. verify that there is cash in the account
B. obtain authority verbally
C. obtain authority in writing
D. Agents are not permitted to exercise discretion.

67. Which of the following is an unlawful activity for a broker-dealer under the Securities Exchange Act of 1934?

A. Stating a belief that a security's price will rise
B. Stating a belief that a security's price will fall
C. Stating that a security's registration has been declared effective by the SEC
D. Artificially creating the impression of market activity

68. An investment adviser is exempt from registration under the Investment Advisers Act of 1940 if

A. all of the adviser's clients are banks
B. the adviser does not hold herself out to the public as being an investment adviser, and she has fewer than 15 clients, of whom none is an investment company
C. all of the adviser's clients reside in the same state and the adviser renders advice on exchange-listed securities only
D. all of the adviser's clients are investment companies

69. Under the Securities Exchange Act of 1934, which of the following is(are) regulated or mandated by the act?

    I. The setting of margin requirements by the Federal Reserve Board
    II. Operation of exchange and OTC markets
    III. Creation of the SEC
    IV. Full and fair disclosure on new offerings

    A. I, II and III
    B. II, III and IV
    C. III
    D. IV

70. The SEC, acting under the provisions of the Investment Advisers Act of 1940, may suspend or revoke an adviser's registration, censure an adviser or place limits on an adviser's business activities for

    I. being enjoined by a state court against engaging in the commodities business
    II. failing to properly supervise the activities of employees whose behavior leads to violations of securities rules
    III. omitting material information from a document required to be filed with the SEC

    A. I and II only
    B. I and III only
    C. II and III only
    D. I, II and III

71. Under the Investment Advisers Act of 1940, which of the following firms may use the term "investment counsel"?

    A. A principal part of the firm's business consists of investment advisory activities.
    B. A substantial part of the firm's business consists of investment supervisory services.
    C. The firm's principal business is investment advice and a substantial part of the business is investment supervisory services.
    D. The firm's principal business is impersonal investment advice.

72. Which act requires publicly traded corporations to issue annual reports?

    A. Securities Exchange Act of 1934
    B. Trust Indenture Act of 1939
    C. Securities Act of 1933
    D. Investment Company Act of 1940

73. The Securities Exchange Act of 1934 has to do with which of the following?

    I. Issuance of financial reports by corporations
    II. Issuance of government securities
    III. Trading of government securities
    IV. Trading of corporate securities

    A. I and III
    B. I, III and IV
    C. II, III and IV
    D. II and IV

74. Which of the following is NOT a redeemable security under the provisions of the Investment Company Act of 1940?

A. Security that pays out each investor's proportionate share of the company's assets
B. Security that is sold on an exchange at the current market price
C. Common stock issued by an investment company
D. Any stock issued by an open-end investment company

75. Which of the following statements is(are) true regarding an affiliated firm that is paid to solicit clients for an investment adviser under the provisions of the Investment Advisers Act of 1940?

A. The relationship between the affiliate and the adviser must be disclosed to prospective clients.
B. There must be a written agreement between the affiliate and the adviser regarding solicitation.
C. Neither A nor B is true.
D. Both A and B are true.

◆ Answers & Rationale

1. **C.** Legal action by a client against an adviser under the USA's civil liabilities can be brought only in a case involving the sale of a security that is deemed to have violated the act. Improper advice (such as the omission of material facts) violates the act. A decline in market value or adviser negligence are not violations. (Page 36)

2. **B.** Blue-sky laws concern the registration of securities with the states. The 1933 act deals only with the registration of securities at the federal level. (Page 47)

3. **C.** Once the SEC issues a set of rules, they are binding and apply to all registered representatives and broker-dealers in all states. A state administrator's rules are valid only in that state, and the USA deals with the registration of securities at the state level. (Page 35)

4. **D.** An issuer may not make any of these claims. The SEC does not approve or disapprove securities. It reviews registrations for omission of material facts and clarity of information and to make certain that all supporting documentation is included. (Page 49)

5. **D.** All responses define "qualified purchasers" under the law. Qualified purchasers are those individuals whose net worth and investments make them, along with institutions, "sophisticated investors." (Page 4)

6. **D.** The purpose of the 1933 act is to make certain that investors are given as much full disclosure of important and pertinent financial information on a security as possible before they invest any money. (Page 47)

7. **B.** Under the USA, a television or newspaper advertisement is considered an offer only in the state where the broadcast or publication originated—the advertisement is not considered an offer in any other state. A national publication, such as the one described in choice C, is the exception to this rule. (Page 34)

8. **D.** The 1933 act regulates new security issues (both debt and equity) that are sold through the mails or any other instrument of interstate commerce. (Page 48)

9. **D.** All three of these choices are excluded from the definition of "investment adviser" under the 1940 act. Also excluded are (1) publishers of any bona fide newspaper, newsmagazine or business or financial publication of general and regular circulation and (2) brokers or dealers whose giving of investment advice is incidental to the conduct of their business, provided they receive no special compensation for the advice. (Page 2)

10. **A.** Although all four choices are investment companies, only closed-end and open-end investment companies fall under the 1940 act's definition of "management company." Management companies manage a portfolio of securities. Face-amount certificate companies and unit investment trusts are not managed. An investor in a UIT owns shares representing a beneficial interest in the underlying mutual fund or securities. (Page 84)

11. **C.** A UIT essentially functions as a type of holding company for investors. First, the portfolio manager purchases the securities, and then redeemable shares of interests in the portfolio are sold to investors. (Page 83)

12. **B.** The criteria for being categorized as an investment adviser is any person who: provides investment advice; is in the business of providing investment advice; and is compensated for providing the investment advice. The person in choice B does not meet all three criteria; therefore, the advice he gives would most likely be considered incidental. (Page 24)

13. **A.** The fund met its diversification limit when it invested 5 percent of its assets in General Gizmonics. The fact that market performance

pushed up its percentage share of the company's ownership is immaterial. However, the fund is prohibited from buying more GIZ stock. (Page 85)

14. **D.** If any compensation is received for giving investment advice, the advice is considered to have been given for compensation under the 1940 act. (Page 2)

15. **C.** A solicitor must be retained under a written agreement and must agree to follow the IA's instructions and abide by federal law. The solicitor must provide the IA's brochure at each solicitation. The agreement to abide by federal law is necessary because the solicitor is *not a registered person.* (Page 22)

16. **B.** An affiliated person is any person in a position to control the activities of an investment company. This category includes 5 percent shareholders, companies partly or wholly owned by the fund, the board of directors and officers of the investment company and the investment adviser. A member of the immediate family of an affiliated person is considered an interested person; such a person is in a position only to influence the activities of the investment company. (Page 92)

17. **C.** Under the amended 1940 act, persons exempt from federal registration include those persons (1) managing less than $25 million in assets, (2) providing advice on government issues only and (3) maintaining a client base of insurance companies only. (Page 5)

18. **C.** There are three types of investment companies: UITs; face-amount certificate companies; and management companies. Open-end and closed-end companies are subcategories of management companies. (Page 82)

19. **D.** Advisers must disclose their total compensation, which includes fees and commissions. They must disclose all business affiliations; and they must inform clients that they have discretion when it comes to using a broker-dealer for buying or selling securities. (Page 19)

20. **A.** This statement is incorrect because a UIT functions as a holding company. (Page 83)

21. **D.** Only open-end funds can be referred to as "mutual funds." Although closed-end fund shares are bought and sold in the secondary market after the initial distribution, nothing prevents a closed-end fund from buying back its shares. (Page 84)

22. **B.** An open-end investment company must be prepared to redeem shares at any time based upon the shareholder's written request. By definition, open-end funds are continually offering new shares and are prohibited from issuing anything other than common stock. The fund itself may invest in bonds if the prospectus permits it to do so. (Page 84)

23. **B.** No more than 10 percent of a corporation's voting securities (common stock) can be owned by a management company. (Page 85)

24. **D.** An affiliated person includes: any corporation in which the fund holds more than 5 percent of its outstanding securities; anyone who owns 5 percent or more of the fund's voting securities; all officers, directors, partners and employees of the fund; and the fund's investment adviser. These rules are designed to prevent someone from using the control they have over a fund's operations to their own personal benefit. (Page 92)

25. **B.** The fund's investment adviser is initially appointed for a maximum of two years. Thereafter the contract is approved annually by a majority vote of the directors and shareholders. (Page 91)

26. **A.** The SEC may suspend trading on any exchange if it believes the action to be in the public good and if notice is given to the President of the United States. (Page 32)

27. **B.** The fund's adviser would have to ensure that the fund's investment objectives are met. In addition, because mutual funds are

actively managed, portfolio securities are bought or sold to meet the fund's stated objective. As part of the adviser's job, he would have to analyze the current market and make adjustments to the portfolio. Some securities could be at a bargain price, thereby representing a good buying opportunity. Other securities could have reached a price level where some profit-taking would be justified or competitive factors could change the stock's value. Because the adviser is making investment decisions, it would have to ensure that the fund meets the diversification requirements. (Page 90)

28. **B.** A 12b-1 fee is charged under the Investment Company Act of 1940, which allows a fund to collect a small percentage of net asset value from its shareholders and use the money to defray the expense of acting as a distributor of its own shares. (Page 94)

29. **B.** The investment adviser's contract must be approved annually by a majority vote of the fund's board of directors and/or its shareholders. (Page 91)

30. **C.** The investment adviser cannot change the fund's investment objectives. Changing the objectives can be done only after approval by the board of directors and the shareholders. The other three choices are all functions of the adviser. (Page 90)

31. **B.** The adviser is responsible for the day-to-day operations of the fund, including buying and selling securities. The adviser can sell any security provided the liquidation is within the fund's guidelines outlined in the prospectus. For example, if a certain percentage of assets must always be invested in cash or cash equivalents, the adviser could not liquidate some of these assets and reduce the percentage to a point at which it violated the fund's objectives. With the other three choices, the time involved in voting would make selling decisions unwieldy. (Page 90)

32. **B.** An individual acting as an agent who sells government bonds is not defined as an agent, nor are bank officers and employees. (Page 38)

33. **B.** An advertisement containing a formula for making investment decisions must also prominently disclose its limitations and the difficulty of using it. (Page 18)

34. **B.** The question deals with the assignment of an advisory contract or a controlling interest in an advisory contract. Specifically excluded are changes in control based on the death of a partner or other member of an investment adviser (choice IV). There is no transfer of control in choice I but there is in choices II and III. (Page 18)

35. **C.** Choice I is not exempt. This adviser does not meet the national de minimis standard which is: No place of business in the state and during the preceding 12-month period has had fewer than six clients who are residents of that state. Choice II is exempt from state registration. IAs managing more than $25 million in client assets are registered only at the federal level. Choice III is exempt from state registration under the National Securities Markets Improvement Act of 1996 (NSMIA). Choice IV is not exempt. NSMIA '96 requires registration with the states of IAs managing less than $25 million. (Page 5)

36. **C.** An investment adviser must register in that state if it has less than $25 million in assets under management. The registration exemption for few solicitations applies only to firms having no place of business in the state. Publishers of financial publications with paid subscribers are also exempt, as are advisers whose clients are institutions (such as banks or trust companies). (Page 8)

37. **A.** If the IA's client is a financial lender, such as a bank, the IA is permitted to borrow money. Otherwise, this is a prohibited practice. (Page 77)

38. **A.** Discretionary authority must be in writing. The adviser cannot unilaterally decide to sell shares without some form of approval by the customer. (Page 77)

39. **B.** Persons having no place of business in a state are generally limited to directing less than six offers to residents of that state before being required to register. All investment advisers having a primary place of business in the state and managing less than $25 million in assets must register (choice III). (Page 5)

40. **B.** As part of the registration procedure, an investment adviser files a consent to service of process along with the state registration application. An application for registration must contain whatever information the administrator requires relevant to the adviser's business. There is no requirement to publish the filing of an application. An investment adviser may be required to pass a written or oral examination. (Page 8)

41. **B.** An investment in mining programs typically represents an ownership interest in a limited partnership. These investments are defined as securities and need to be registered. Stock issues by banks and insurance companies are also defined as securities but are exempt from registration. Precious metals are not securities. (Page 30)

42. **B.** The state administrator has the authority to ask for information regarding a firm's financial condition, whether the firm will have custody of customer funds, and the firm's fee schedule. (Page 17)

43. **B.** Under the USA, a termination becomes effective 30 days after receipt of the notice by the state administrator. Choice C is ambiguous because the date of the application can be different from both when it is sent to the administrator and when it is received by the administrator. Under the Investment Advisers Act of 1940, a termination becomes effective after 60 days. (Page 11)

44. **D.** The USA requires that an administrator provide the persons affected with notice of his actions to deny, suspend or revoke registration. The administrator also must provide for a hearing and disclose the reasons for the action. (Page 11)

45. **D.** The USA requires that the administrator follow these procedures when intending to take disciplinary action against someone registered in the state. (Page 11)

46. **C.** In those cases where an individual changes employment from one firm to another, all of these three persons—the agent, the old employer and the new employer—must notify the state administrator. (Page 40)

47. **D.** Once a consent to service of process has been filed by an applicant, any complaint presented to the administrator has the same force and validity as if it had been served personally on the applicant. (Page 9)

48. **D.** Under the USA, all records relating to the firm's business must be maintained by the firm for possible review by the administrator. These records must be kept easily accessible for three years by a broker-dealer and for five years by an investment adviser. (Page 15)

49. **D.** Choices I, III and IV are all direct requirements of the SEC for IAs having possession of clients' funds or securities. Choice II is incorrect. Strict segregation of client and IA securities must be practiced at all times. Failure to practice segregation is a prohibited act known as commingling. (Page 17)

50. **A.** The administrator has no authority to require bonding for an issuer of securities. (Page 39)

51. **D.** All the practices described have been specifically prohibited by the SEC and have resulted in sanctions for the companies and individuals involved. (Page 21)

52. **A.** An administrator may deny, suspend or revoke any registration if he deems that the order would be in the public interest and that the applicant, registrant or issuer of a security is guilty of any of a specified list of offenses. (Page 10)

53. **B.** Filing a misleading registration application and failing to pay application filing fees are grounds for a state administrator to deny registration. Lack of experience cannot be the sole reason to deny registration. There are no net capital requirements for advisers. (Page 10)

54. **B.** Lack of experience cannot be the sole reason for denying an applicant's registration. (Page 10)

55. **D.** A prospectus must include all of the information given in the choices. In an initial public offering, if the underwriters suspect that stabilizing transactions may be needed, they must disclose this in the prospectus. The SEC disclaimer must be clearly printed on all prospectuses. In a new issue, the prospectus must include pertinent financial information in order for investors to decide whether to purchase the securities. They need to know whether the company is financially sound. The effective date of the registration is required in order to let investors know that the prospectus contains relatively recent information. (Page 49)

56. **A.** The management consultant's advice to clients is more personal opinion than providing investment advice as a business. In the other three choices, investment advice is being offered as part of the individual's regular business. Lawyers, accountants, engineers and teachers are generally not considered investment advisers provided the advice is incidental to their regular profession. (Page 23)

57. **A.** The 1933 act permits registered representatives to accept indications of interest only for a security that is in the registration process. (Page 49)

58. **D.** An insurance agent who develops a financial plan for clients and analyzes mutual funds crosses the line into being considered an investment adviser. The fact that he does not sell mutual funds does not prevent him from being considered an investment adviser. The agent in choice I is giving generic advice. The financial planner in choice IV writes financial plans with specific investment recommendations and then refers clients to a broker-dealer in order for the recommendations to be executed. Broker-dealers are not considered investment advisers. (Page 23)

59. **C.** The 1933 act requires the full and fair disclosure of all material information regarding the issuing of new securities. (Page 55)

60. **A.** The only activity that the 1933 act allows registered representatives to do while a security is in the registration process is to solicit indications of interest. (Page 49)

61. **B.** Any required records must be maintained for a minimum of five years. (Page 15)

62. **C.** SEC rules dictate that for initial public offerings a prospectus must be made available to investors for the first 90 days from the effective date of the offering. (Page 50)

63. **B.** The maximum monetary fine for individuals found violating the USA is $5,000 with a maximum of three years in jail. (Page 25)

64. **B.** The SEC analyzes each registration statement for omission of material facts and clarity of information and to make certain that all supporting documentation is included. The SEC does not approve securities that have been registered with it, and this disclaimer is printed clearly on the front of each prospectus. (Page 49)

65. **B.** The SEC does not pass on the truthfulness of the information in the registration statement. It analyzes the statement for omission of material facts and clarity of information and to make certain that all supporting financial docu-

mentation is included; but this is not the same as saying that the SEC claims that everything in the registration statement is true. Before a new offering to the public can be made, a registration statement must be filed. A prospectus must be provided to all potential investors. Although many firms place tombstone advertisements, there is no requirement to do so. (Page48)

66. **C.** Discretionary authority must be granted in writing by the owner of an account. (Page77)

67. **D.** The Securities Exchange Act of 1934 regulates the secondary market. Its provisions prohibit a broker-dealer from engaging in manipulative and deceptive devices in relation to the trading of securities, such as misleading investors with the false appearance of active trading in a security. A broker-dealer may analyze securities and recommend transactions based on her beliefs. Stating that the SEC has cleared a certain issue of securities for sale is not a violation of the Securities Act of 1933. (Page79)

68. **B.** Only choice B fits the exemption requirements for filing as an investment adviser under the 1940 act. The other three choices describe exemptions under the Uniform Securities Act. (Page5)

69. **A.** The Securities and Exchange Act of 1934 created the Securities and Exchange Commission, and it authorized the Federal Reserve Board to set margin requirements. New offerings are regulated by the 1933 act. (Page33)

70. **D.** In general, the regulatory authorities have a wide range of power when it comes to disciplining anyone in the securities industry. Being enjoined by a court to stop selling commodities, failing to provide proper supervision, or omitting material information in a document filed with the SEC are all grounds for an adviser to be censured or for his activities in the industry to be limited. (Page 10)

71. **C.** For a firm to call itself an "investment counsel," it must have both a principal business consisting of investment advisory activities and a substantial business in investment supervisory services. Investment supervisory service is continuous, ongoing investment advice specific to the needs of an individual customer. (Page 3)

72. **A.** The 1934 act requires public companies to file periodic financial reports, with an annual report being one of the requirements. (Page32)

73. **B.** The 1934 act requires public companies to file periodic financial reports. Government agencies and municipalities are not public companies. In addition, the 1934 act deals with the trading of all securities in the secondary market, regardless of who the issuer of the security is. (Page31)

74. **B.** A redeemable security is one that can only be redeemed from the issuer. If a security can be sold on an exchange in a transaction between a willing buyer and a willing seller, it is not a redeemable security. (Page 84)

75. **D.** This relationship would have to be disclosed to investors in the prospectus. A written agreement must also exist between the affiliate and the adviser, and this agreement would have to be voted on by the shareholders at least once every two years. Mutual funds are the best example of this type of arrangement. (Page 22)

15 Series 65 Final Exam Four

1. According to the Securities Exchange Act of 1934, the SEC has enforcement and jurisdiction powers over violations of the securities rules and regulations of which of the following?

    I. MSRB
    II. Exchanges
    III. The states
    IV. NASD

    A. I, II and III only
    B. I, II and IV only
    C. III and IV only
    D. I, II, III and IV

2. Which entity regulates the extension of credit in the securities industry?

    A. Federal Reserve Board
    B. New York Stock Exchange
    C. Municipal Securities Rulemaking Board
    D. Comptroller of the Currency

3. Under the Investment Advisers Act of 1940, which of the following may appear on a registered investment adviser's stationery?

    A. Randy Bear, RIA, CFP
    B. Randy Bear, Registered Investment Adviser
    C. Randy Bear, Approved Investment Adviser
    D. Randy Bear, Designated Investment Adviser

4. Which of the following is NOT exempt from registration as an investment adviser under the Investment Advisers Act of 1940?

    A. Bank
    B. Broker-dealer
    C. Doctor
    D. Engineer

5. According to the Uniform Securities Act, which of the following investment advisers who have custody of and exercise discretion over customer funds and securities would be required to post a surety bond?

    A. Adviser who has posted a surety bond covering other transactions
    B. Adviser who meets minimum financial requirements but does not hold funds in excess of those minimum requirements
    C. Dual-registered adviser who meets the net capital and surety bond requirements
    D. Adviser who meets minimum financial requirements and holds funds in excess of those minimum requirements in an amount equal to the required surety bond

6. In which of the following situations would the investment adviser be in violation of the discretionary account authorization rules as set forth in the Uniform Securities Act?

   A. A customer buys 1,000 shares of Datawaq and tells his adviser to limit the loss, without specifying a particular price; when the stock has declined 20 percent, the adviser sells 500 of the shares.
   B. A customer places an order to sell 1,000 shares of Datawaq at the market, and the adviser sells the shares that day for a loss.
   C. A customer places an order to buy 1,000 Datawaq shares whenever the adviser thinks the price is right; the adviser buys the shares at the open, which turns out to be the high price of the day.
   D. A customer places an order first thing in the morning to sell 1,000 Datawaq, telling the adviser he really needs the money; the adviser does not put in the order until the end of the day because he thinks the market will then give him a better price.

7. Who decides changes in investment policy for a managed investment company?

   A. Shareholders
   B. Board of directors
   C. SEC
   D. Investment adviser

8. The Investment Advisers Act of 1940 requires investment advisers to deliver a brochure

   A. on request
   B. to those investors who invest less than $50,000
   C. to those investors who invest more than $50,000
   D. with offering documents

9. The Securities Act of 1933 requires that a prospectus for a new offering be made available to

   A. the general public
   B. members of the SEC only
   C. appropriate persons on presentation of a subpoena
   D. the general public on written request only

10. Under the Investment Advisers Act of 1940, a testimonial for an investment adviser from a celebrity who uses the adviser's service may be employed

    A. under no circumstances
    B. only if no compensation is made to the celebrity
    C. only if the celebrity is compensated adequately
    D. only if the celebrity agrees in writing

11. Under the Uniform Securities Act, an investment adviser may use the name of a customer in sales literature or advertising material under which of the following circumstances?

    A. The customer is compensated adequately.
    B. The amount of the customer's compensation is revealed in the literature or advertisement.
    C. The customer consents to such use.
    D. There is no restriction on such activity.

12. An investment adviser is convicted of securities fraud and is sentenced to one year in jail. Upon conviction, what is the maximum penalty that can be assessed under the Investment Advisers Act of 1940?

    A. $0; any additional penalty would be considered double jeopardy
    B. $5,000
    C. $10,000
    D. $20,000

13. In order for a new securities issue to qualify as an intrastate offering under the Securities Act of 1933, all of the following must be true EXCEPT

    A. all of the investors must be residents of the state
    B. the underwriter must be registered in the state
    C. the president of the issuing company must be a resident of the state
    D. the issuer must conduct at least 80 percent of its business in the state

14. According to the Investment Advisers Act of 1940, an investment adviser is prohibited from borrowing money from which of the following?

    A. Affiliate adviser
    B. Bank that charges compensation for investment advice
    C. Client
    D. Broker-dealer

15. Which of the following would be exempt from registration under the Uniform Securities Act?

    I. Government securities
    II. Common stock of a national bank
    III. Debt issue of Calgary, Alberta, Canada
    IV. Security listed on the Chicago Stock Exchange

    A. I and II only
    B. I, II and III only
    C. III and IV only
    D. I, II, III and IV

16. Which of the following securities issuers would NOT be subject to having its registration denied, revoked or suspended by a state administrator under the Uniform Securities Act?

    I. Nonprofit corporation
    II. Railroad or other interstate carrier
    III. Investment company with assets of more than $1 million
    IV. Unit investment trust

    A. I and II
    B. I, II and III
    C. II and III
    D. III and IV

17. Under the Investment Company Act of 1940, which of the following would NOT be required to issue redeemable securities?

    I. Open-end investment company
    II. Closed-end investment company
    III. Unit investment trust
    IV. Business development company

    A. I and II
    B. I and III
    C. II and III
    D. II and IV

18. The antifraud provisions of the Securities Act of 1933 cover which of the following?

    I. Federal securities fraud
    II. State securities fraud
    III. Common law deceit (Case law)
    IV. Breach of contract

    A. I and II
    B. I, II and III
    C. I and III
    D. II, III and IV

19. According to the Investment Company Act of 1940, which of the following statements may an investment adviser make regarding an investment in mutual funds?

    I. "I recommend that you read the prospectus to find out if this fund's objective matches yours."
    II. "A mutual fund's return is not guaranteed, so the value of your investment may go up or down."
    III. "Because their portfolios are diversified, mutual funds are one of the safest investments around."
    IV. "If this fund's performance is down this month, I recommend that you move your money to a similar fund that's doing better."

    A. I and II
    B. I, III and IV
    C. II and III
    D. II and IV

20. Max Leveridge, president of Millon, Billon, Dillon & Co. Investments, has achieved a 25 percent return for each of his customers each year for the last 10 years. Without violating the Uniform Securities Act, Max can make which of the following statements?

    A. "Millon, Billon customers are guaranteed at least a 10 percent return on their money each year."
    B. "Millon, Billon customers are guaranteed against losing money in any year."
    C. "Millon, Billon guarantees that it will outperform its competition."
    D. "Millon, Billon customers are guaranteed prompt, attentive service for all of their investment needs."

21. Which of the following securities issuers would NOT be subject to having its registration denied, revoked or suspended by a state administrator under the Uniform Securities Act?

    I. Nonprofit corporation
    II. Exchange-listed security
    III. Savings and loan association
    IV. Federal credit union

    A. I and II only
    B. I, II and IV only
    C. III and IV only
    D. I, II, III and IV

22. Under the Uniform Securities Act, the administrator may deny, revoke or suspend the registration of an investment adviser for all the following causes EXCEPT

    A. insolvency
    B. inexperience
    C. unqualified by training or education
    D. failure to supervise

23. Tex Longhorn is an accountant. Under which of the following conditions is he required to register as an investment adviser, according to SEC Release IA-1092?

    I. He charges an additional fee for providing investment advice to an existing accounting client.
    II. More than 25 percent of his business consists of investment advisory activities.
    III. He holds himself out to the public as an investment adviser.
    IV. Investment adviser activity is incidental to his business.

    A. I, II and III
    B. I and III
    C. II
    D. III and IV

24. Under the Uniform Securities Act, which of the following statements are true of the termination of an investment adviser's registration?

    I. Termination becomes effective 30 days after receipt of the termination notice.
    II. Termination may be postponed if a suspension or revocation proceeding is pending.
    III. After the termination becomes effective, the administrator retains the right to revoke or suspend registration for one year.
    IV. Other civil or criminal action may be taken without time limit.

    A. I and II only
    B. I, II and III only
    C. III and IV only
    D. I, II, III and IV

25. Which of the following statements are true concerning the Uniform Securities Act?

    A. The administrator may enter an order against an investment adviser solely on the basis of lack of experience.
    B. The administrator may provide for an oral examination of the investment adviser.
    C. An investment adviser can be considered qualified on the basis of his experience as a broker-dealer or agent.
    D. An investment adviser must attest that his partners also are qualified as investment advisers.

26. Under the Uniform Securities Act, the definition of a sale or an offer to sell includes all of the following EXCEPT a(n)

    A. offer of a right to subscribe to a class of securities other than the class originally purchased
    B. gift of assessable stock
    C. pledge of a security for a loan
    D. warrant issued by a company for stock issued by another company

27. According to the Uniform Securities Act, the definition of "security" includes all of the following EXCEPT a(n)

    A. collateral trust certificate
    B. investment contract in a profit-sharing plan
    C. voting trust certificate
    D. endowment contract

28. The burden of proving an exemption from registration under the Uniform Securities Act lies with the

    A. buyer
    B. seller
    C. broker-dealer or investment adviser
    D. person claiming the exemption

29. An offer or sale of a preorganization certificate or subscription is exempted under the Uniform Securities Act in which of the following circumstances?

    I. No commission is paid.
    II. A registration statement has been filed.
    III. The number of subscribers does not exceed 10.
    IV. No payment is made by a subscriber.

    A. I and II only
    B. I, III and IV only
    C. II, III and IV only
    D. I, II, III and IV

30. Under the Uniform Securities Act, the statute of limitations for filing a lawsuit based on investment advice that has been rendered runs for how many years?

    A. Two
    B. Three
    C. Five
    D. Seven

31. Under the Uniform Securities Act, an investment adviser may base a recommendation to a customer concerning the purchase of a security on which of the following?

 I. Length of time that the customer has followed the adviser's recommendations
 II. His authority to act for the customer
 III. Financial capability of the customer
 IV. Investment objectives of the customer

 A. I and II
 B. II and III
 C. II, III and IV
 D. III and IV

32. In order to comply with the Investment Advisers Act of 1940, an investment adviser who takes custody of customer funds and securities must do all of the following EXCEPT

 A. clearly segregate customer funds and securities
 B. send an itemized list of funds, securities and their placement to the customer every six months
 C. tell the customer where and how the funds and securities are located
 D. send quarterly statements to their customers

33. Under the Investment Advisers Act of 1940, if an investment adviser holds custody of customer funds and securities, which of the following statements is true?

 I. The funds and securities must be segregated.
 II. The location of the funds and securities and the manner in which they are stored must be clearly and frequently reported.
 III. The adviser may be subject to higher financial and surety bond requirements.
 IV. The adviser may not engage in activities in regard to those funds and securities that are more favorable to the adviser than to the customer.

 A. I and II only
 B. I and III only
 C. II and III only
 D. I, II, III and IV

34. Under the Uniform Securities Act, which of the following would NOT be considered sales literature and advertising in State A?

 I. Radio or television advertisements originating in State A
 II. Radio or television advertisements originating in State B and broadcast to residents of State A
 III. Newspapers and magazines originating in State A
 IV. Newspapers and magazines originating in State B and mailed to residents of State A

 A. I and III only
 B. I, III and IV only
 C. II and IV only
 D. I, II, III and IV

35. An investment adviser uses its past record of stock selections in an advertisement. According to the Investment Advisers Act of 1940, this is permissible if it

I. includes a statement that historical returns are not an indicator of future performance
II. discloses the business background of the adviser
III. states the suitability of the recommendations for a particular investment objective
IV. includes both successful and unsuccessful recommendations for the past year

A. I and II
B. I and IV
C. II and III
D. II and IV

36. Which of the following is an improper activity under the Uniform Securities Act?

A. An investment adviser charges a customer a fee that is different from the fee charged another customer for a similar service.
B. A dealer charges a commission on sales of a security it has held for six months in its inventory.
C. An investment adviser charges a customer a fee for advice leading to the sale of a security, receives a commission on the sale and discloses the amount of the commission to the customer.
D. An investment adviser collects a commission on the sale of insurance products that he recommended.

37. Which of the following persons is required to register as an investment adviser, according to SEC Release IA-1092?

A. Joe Kuhl recommends that any person with substantial assets allocate portions to securities, insurance and real estate.
B. Belle Charolais is a registered representative of a broker-dealer and receives a commission when a customer implements one of her securities recommendations.
C. Tex Longhorn is an real estate agent and occasionally gives investment advice incidental to his real estate practice.
D. A newspaper publisher prints a weekly column featuring securities recommendations and analysis of market performance.

38. According to the Investment Advisers Act of 1940, which of the following are NOT permitted in an investment advisory contract?

I. Exculpatory provisions stipulating that the customer waives rights guaranteed in law
II. Provisions for payment based on a percentage of capital gains and market appreciation
III. Stipulation that no fees are to be assessed if the account realizes no profit
IV. Provisions for custody of customer funds and securities

A. I and II
B. I, II and III
C. I, II and IV
D. III and IV

39. An investment adviser recommends securities and receives compensation based on both a fee for the advice and commissions from the securities sold. To comply with the Investment Advisers Act of 1940, he must inform the customer of which of the following?

    I. The fact that the securities could be purchased from another broker-dealer
    II. The compensation received from the securities sale
    III. His roles as agent for the broker-dealer and as investment adviser
    IV. The compensation he receives as adviser

    A. I and II only
    B. I and III only
    C. II, III and IV only
    D. I, II, III and IV

40. Under the Investment Advisers Act of 1940, all of the following could be considered compensation to an investment adviser EXCEPT

    A. commission received on the sale of a universal life insurance policy
    B. payment received for the sale of an exempt security
    C. margin deposit received for a stock purchase
    D. shares of common stock received as a bonus for the sale of warrants

41. According to the Investment Advisers Act of 1940, an investment adviser may keep records in which of the following formats?

    I. Computer disks
    II. Computer tapes
    III. Microfiche
    IV. Paper

    A. I only
    B. I and IV only
    C. II and III only
    D. I, II, III and IV

42. Which of the following is NOT considered a violation of the Investment Advisers Act of 1940, requiring an investment adviser to furnish material information?

    A. In an offer to sell that results in a sale, the seller omits a material fact.
    B. In an offer to sell that results in a sale, the buyer omits a material fact.
    C. In an offer to purchase that results in a sale, an uninvolved third party omits a material fact.
    D. In an offer to purchase that does not result in a sale, the seller omits a material fact.

43. After filing a registration statement under the Securities Act of 1933, and assuming that no stop orders have been issued, sale of the offering may begin after how many days?

    A. 20
    B. 30
    C. 60
    D. 90

44. Under the Investment Advisers Act of 1940, an investment adviser may use a testimonial from a former client in an advertisement

    A. if no compensation is paid
    B. if a disclaimer is used
    C. without restriction
    D. under no circumstances

45. Which of the following are subject to the antifraud provisions of the Securities Act of 1933?

I. Sale of treasury securities
II. Sale of exchange-listed securities
III. Purchase of bankers' acceptances
IV. Purchase of OTC securities by a trust department that handles assets of $2,000,000

A. I and II only
B. I and III only
C. II and III only
D. I, II, III and IV

46. If an individual acquires securities and the result is an ownership of 5 percent or more of the securities of that issuer, the buyer must notify the SEC within how long of the purchase?

A. 24 hours
B. 48 hours
C. 5 business days
D. 10 business days

47. According to the Investment Advisers Act of 1940, which of the following persons may use the title "investment counsel"?

I. Insurance broker who occasionally engages in the business of rendering investment advice
II. Investment adviser whose principal business is rendering investment advice
III. Investment adviser whose business consists of less than 25 percent investment supervisory services
IV. Investment adviser whose business is substantially investment supervisory and related services

A. I and III
B. I and IV
C. II and III
D. IV

48. Under the Uniform Securities Act, which of the following would NOT be a violation of discretionary authority?

A. Buying securities in a cash account without the consent of the customer
B. Buying securities in a joint margin account without the spouse's consent
C. Selling securities from a custodial account with only the custodian's consent
D. Selling securities from a corporate account with a limited power of attorney

49. Under the Uniform Securities Act, all of the following are exempt from registration as investment advisers EXCEPT a(n)

A. bank providing advice on general types of securities
B. investment adviser rendering advice to fewer than 15 persons in a 12-month period
C. investment adviser with no place of business in the state and whose clientele is limited to investment companies
D. investment adviser who manages more than $25 million in assets

50. Under the Uniform Securities Act, all of the following are exempt from state registration as investment advisers EXCEPT an adviser

A. rendering investment advice to less than 6 persons in a single state in a 12-month period
B. to investment companies registered under the Investment Company Act of 1940
C. to an employee plan with assets of $1 million
D. rendering investment advice to fewer than 15 persons in a 12-month period

51. Max Leveridge renders investment advice to Karen Kodiak relating to unlisted securities. According to the Investment Advisers Act of 1940, which of the following statements regarding Max is NOT true?

A. Max would need to be registered as an investment adviser if his advice related to specific securities.
B. Max would not need to be registered as an investment adviser if his advice was incidental to the sale of securities.
C. Max would need to be registered as an investment adviser if in selling securities he was compensated for his advice.
D. Max would not need to be registered as investment adviser if he was not compensated for his advice, regardless of his sale of securities.

52. According to the Investment Advisers Act of 1940, which of the following persons would need to be registered as an investment adviser?

A. Bank giving advice to its trust accounts for a fee
B. Broker-dealer advising specific customers on nonspecific securities
C. Accountant providing advice on securities related to his advisory business and receiving no compensation for the advice
D. Chemist charging a fee for securities advice relating to his profession

53. Under the Investment Advisers Act of 1940, which of the following persons must be registered as an investment adviser?

A. Registered representative who provides advice within the scope of his employment with a broker-dealer
B. Registered representative who provides advice beyond the scope of his employment with a broker-dealer
C. Broker-dealer whose registered representative provides advice within the scope of his employment
D. Broker-dealer whose registered representative provides advice beyond the scope of his employment

54. Max Leveridge, a registered investment adviser, has custody of the funds and securities of Joe Kuhl. Under the Investment Advisers Act of 1940, Max is permitted to

A. collateralize customer securities for a loan
B. send Joe a statement once a year
C. use customer securities to guarantee Joe against loss on a loan
D. place segregated customer funds in an interest-bearing account in escrow

55. According to the Investment Advisers Act of 1940, all of the following are characteristics of an investment advisory contract EXCEPT that the contract

A. must be in writing
B. details the services to be provided
C. provides for assignment of the contract when necessary to benefit the customer
D. states the formula for computing the fee and the amount of any prepaid fee

56. Under the Investment Advisers Act of 1940, an investment adviser must disclose which of the following to a customer if she is charging a fee for her advisory services?

    I. Amount of commission received for the sale of an endowment life policy
    II. Amount of commission received for the sale of commodity futures
    III. Amount of payment received from the sale of securities
    IV. Amount of payment made to purchase securities for the customer's account

    A. I only
    B. I, II and III only
    C. II and IV only
    D. I, II, III and IV

57. Under the Investment Advisers Act of 1940, all of the following persons are considered to be in the business of providing investment advice EXCEPT a(n)

    A. accountant or attorney who advertises advisory services
    B. broker-dealer that provides advisory services for each of its managed accounts
    C. broker-dealer that provides nonspecific securities advice
    D. business manager who is paid for managing his client's assets

58. Under the Investment Advisers Act of 1940, which of the following practices would an investment adviser be prohibited from engaging in even if she has disclosed the practice in writing to the customer?

    A. Providing advice to the customer and receiving compensation for the resulting sale of products
    B. Employment with a broker-dealer and service as an investment adviser
    C. Using advice she provides to customers regarding securities transactions as a basis for her own investment account trades
    D. Putting her own interests before those of the customer

59. Which of the following persons must be registered as an investment adviser under the Investment Advisers Act of 1940?

    A. Bank providing general securities information in research reports
    B. Broker-dealer providing securities advice to its customers only
    C. Broker-dealer providing securities advice through market letters
    D. Publisher providing specific securities recommendations through research reports

60. A customer directs her representative to execute an unsolicited trade. Later, it is discovered that the customer was acting on inside information. Under the Insider Trading Act, which of the following may be held liable?

    A. Representative
    B. Customer
    C. Both representative and customer
    D. Neither representative nor customer

61. Your customer purchased securities from you that were issued and sold in violation of the state's registration regulations. You were unaware of the violation at the time of the transaction and have notified your customer of the problem. Under the Uniform Securities Act, your customer can file for rescission of the transaction within how many years?

    A. One
    B. Two
    C. Five
    D. Seven

62. Under the Investment Advisers Act of 1940, which of the following persons would NOT have to register as an investment adviser?

    A. Person whose only customers are investment companies
    B. Financial planner who does not give advice about exchange-traded securities and whose customers are all residents of the same state as the adviser
    C. Person whose only customers are savings and loan institutions and bank trust departments
    D. Financial planner who gives advice only about securities that qualify for the blue chip exemption and whose customers are all residents of the same state as the adviser

63. Under the Investment Advisers Act of 1940, a person who does NOT hold himself out as an investment adviser could provide investment advice to how many persons and still qualify for the de minimis exemption?

    A. Four
    B. Nine
    C. Fourteen
    D. Sixteen

64. Under the Uniform Securities Act, what is the maximum criminal penalty an agent could be given for engaging in fraud and deceit in the sale of unregistered, nonexempt securities?

    A. $5,000 fine and one year in prison
    B. $5,000 fine and three years in prison
    C. $10,000 fine and one year in prison
    D. $10,000 fine and three years in prison

65. Under the Investment Advisers Act of 1940, which of the following is required to register as an investment adviser?

    A. Accountant who is paid a fee to assess the value of a fixed annuity
    B. Attorney who occasionally gives investment advice incidental to her law practice
    C. Teacher who instructs his class on the theory of stock selection
    D. Broker-dealer that charges customers additional fees for financial planning services

66. According to the Uniform Securities Act, surety bonds are intended to be used for which of the following purposes?

    A. To protect an adviser against charges of fraud
    B. To provide a source of funds for legal fees in the event of a lawsuit
    C. To provide customers with protection against extreme market losses
    D. To provide customers with protection against broker-dealer bankruptcy

67. Under the Investment Advisers Act of 1940, which of the following books and records must be kept for the life of the advisory firm and for which provisions must be made for passing them on to any successor firm?

    A. Journals
    B. Blotters
    C. Customer complaints
    D. Articles of incorporation

68. According to the Uniform Securities Act, a registered representative who enters transactions in a customer's account that are excessive in either size or frequency is likely to be guilty of

    A. skimming
    B. churning
    C. hypothecation
    D. wash sales

69. Which of the following securities or issuers are exempt from the antifraud statutes of the Securities Act of 1933?

    I. U.S. government securities primary dealers
    II. Municipal securities
    III. Banks and bank issues

    A. I and II
    B. I and III
    C. II and III
    D. None of the above

70. Which of the following actions by a registered rep would be considered an unethical practice under the Uniform Securities Act?

    A. Recommending to a customer securities that result in major losses in the customer's account
    B. Splitting commissions with a sales assistant who is registered and works for the same firm but who has had no dealings with customers
    C. Not entering a sell order for a security when its price is falling, the customer having signed a power of attorney giving the registered rep discretionary authority
    D. Failing to tell a customer that the investments being recommended are proprietary securities offered by the registered rep's firm when the investments are performing better than comparable securities offered by other firms

71. Which of the following statements is true regarding the registration of an investment adviser?

    I. Investment advisers who are properly registered with the SEC do not need to register with the state.
    II. Investment advisers who are properly registered with the state do not need to register with the SEC.
    III. Investment advisers who are properly registered with the SEC must give notice and pay filing fees in the states in which they conduct business.
    IV. Investment advisers who are properly registered with the SEC may have to give notice to the states for those who act as investment adviser representatives.

    A. I and II only
    B. I, II and III only
    C. II and III only
    D. I, II, III and IV

72. Commercial paper is exempt from the Uniform Securities Act's registration requirements if it is issued with a maturity within how many days?

    A. 90
    B. 180
    C. 270
    D. 365

73. Persons who are considered *professional investors* as defined in the Uniform Securities Act may qualify for which of the following?

    A. Manual exemption
    B. Blue chip exemption
    C. Registration exemption
    D. Transaction exemption

74. Which of the following are considered to be securities information processors, as defined in the Securities Exchange Act of 1934?

I. *The Pink Sheets*
II. *The Wall Street Journal*
III. Consolidated Ticker Tape
IV. Customer statements

A. I and II
B. I and III
C. II and III
D. III and IV

75. The Investment Advisers Act of 1940 does NOT prohibit which of the following provisions in investment advisory contracts?

A. Assignment of the contract at the discretion of the adviser and with notification of the customer
B. Sharing arrangements based on capital gains
C. Guarantees that losses will be reimbursed at a 50 percent rate
D. Changes in the management of the investment advisory firm, provided that reasonable notice is given to customers

◆ Answers & Rationale

1. **B.** The Securities and Exchange Commission has jurisdiction over the self-regulatory organizations (such as the MSRB and the NASD) and over the registered stock exchanges. The SEC now has preemptive authority over state securities administrators. (Page 32)

2. **A.** The Federal Reserve Board sets the rules for extending credit and delegates the enforcement of them to the SEC. (Page 33)

3. **B.** An investment adviser may not use the initials "RIA" in such a way as to imply that he has attained a certain level of education or qualification. The adviser may inform customers that he is registered as an investment adviser, but may not give the misleading impression that he has received the approval of the state administrator or the SEC. (Page 22)

4. **C.** Banks, broker-dealers, certain publishers, teachers, lawyers, accountants and engineers whose giving of investment advice is incidental to the practice of their profession are exempt from registration as investment advisers. (Page 3)

5. **B.** All investment advisers who have custody of customer funds or securities must post a surety bond, or must hold in a separate account funds equal to a required surety bond in addition to their minimum financial requirement. (Page 9)

6. **A.** The customer's request was not specific enough to allow the adviser to make that type of decision. Without a written discretionary authorization, an adviser may decide only time and price. (Page 20)

7. **A.** Changes in investment objectives are subject to approval by a majority vote of the outstanding shares of an investment company. (Page 89)

8. **A.** The act of 1940 requires the registered adviser to deliver a brochure to all new clients, to deliver or offer to deliver a brochure to all existing clients at least once each year and to deliver a brochure to any client who makes a written request for one. (Page 14)

9. **A.** The act of 1933 requires an issuer to make a copy of a prospectus available without restriction to anyone who wishes to see it. (Page 47)

10. **A.** Investment advisers are prohibited from using celebrity testimonials. (Page 21)

11. **C.** The customer's consent is necessary, and the use of the name must not constitute a testimonial. (Page 21)

12. **C.** Upon a person's conviction for securities fraud, the SEC can assess a penalty of up to $10,000, five years in prison or both. (Page 25)

13. **C.** Rule 147 does not require the officers of an issuer to be residents of the state. (Page 63)

14. **C.** Investment advisers are prohibited from borrowing funds or securities from clients or from lending funds or securities to clients. (Page 77)

15. **D.** All of the securities listed are considered exempt under the Uniform Securities Act. (Page 69)

16. **A.** Securities of nonprofit corporations and common carriers are exempt under the act. (Page 69)

17. **D.** The stock of closed-end investment companies is traded on an exchange or over the counter. Business development companies are not required to issue redeemable securities. (Page 84)

18. **B.** Breach of contract is considered a civil violation, not a fraudulent one. (Page 63)

19. **A.** Recommendations regarding mutual funds should address suitability and should state the risks involved. An adviser should not claim that mutual funds are safe, although diversification is a useful technique for minimizing the risk of loss in a single security. Recommending short-term trading among mutual funds with similar investment objectives is a prohibited practice known as switching; the investor will probably incur heavy sales charges that outweigh any gains. (Page 77)

20. **D.** Investment advisers are prohibited from guaranteeing client accounts, investment performance and minimum gains. (Page 21)

21. **D.** All of the issuers listed are exempt from the provisions of the Uniform Securities Act. (Page 68)

22. **B.** An inexperienced adviser is permitted the time to gain experience and expertise in the field. (Page 10)

23. **A.** A person working as a teacher, engineer, lawyer or accountant may render investment advice without registering as an investment adviser if the advice is incidental to his business. If the person provides investment advice more frequently than on rare and isolated occasions, that person is required to be registered. A person who advertises himself to the public as an investment adviser, or a person who receives any form of compensation for investment advice, must also be registered. (Page 23)

24. **B.** Statutes of limitations are not waived by the Uniform Securities Act. (Page 11)

25. **B.** The administrator may provide for an oral test of the investment adviser candidate. (Page 9)

26. **C.** The definition of a sale or an offer to sell does not include a bona fide pledge or loan. (Page 29)

27. **D.** Insurance contracts, endowment contracts and annuity contracts are excluded from the definition of "security." (Page 30)

28. **D.** The person claiming the exemption bears the burden of proving that he qualifies for that exemption. (Page 72)

29. **B.** An offer or sale of a preorganization certificate is exempt if it meets the following conditions: (1) no commission or other remuneration is provided for soliciting prospective subscribers, (2) the number of subscribers does not exceed 10 and (3) no payment is made by any subscriber. (Page 72)

30. **B.** No person may sue under the Uniform Securities Act more than three years after the advice has been given or two years after the discovery of the violation. (Page 36)

31. **D.** Recommendations to a customer must be based on the customer's financial status, financial needs, investment objectives, investment knowledge and ability to handle risk. (Page 77)

32. **B.** There is no requirement to send an itemized list of funds and securities to any party. Investment advisers are required to provide quarterly statements to their clients. (Page 17)

33. **D.** All of the choices listed are required of an investment adviser who has custody of customer funds or securities. (Page 17)

34. **C.** Newspapers, magazines and radio and television programs fall under the jurisdiction of the state in which they originate and must abide by that state's statutes. An advertisement in any of these mediums is not considered an offer in any state other than the state of publication. (Page 34)

35. **B.** An adviser may advertise its past recommendations if the advertisement includes all recommendations for at least the past year and states that the reader should not assume that future recommendations will equal or exceed the

adviser's past performance. The business background of the adviser, and the suitability of the recommendations, are not required as part of an advertisement. (Page 21)

36. **B.** A dealer acts as a principal in transactions and can charge a markup on the securities but not a commission on the transaction. (Page 78)

37. **C.** The exclusion from investment adviser status is limited to lawyers, accountants, teachers and engineers. Only these professionals may provide investment advice incidental to their professions without registering as an investment adviser. General allocation recommendations are not considered investment advice, and a newspaper may publish nonspecific investment recommendations without registering. A registered representative of a broker-dealer may recommend securities in the normal course of business if no additional compensation is received. (Page 3)

38. **B.** The investment advisory contract must contain provisions describing the custody and safekeeping arrangements for any customer funds or securities. (Page 18)

39. **D.** The investment adviser is required to disclose all significant facts to the customer. Failure to disclose these or any other significant facts would be considered fraudulent. (Page 4)

40. **C.** The deposit a customer makes to meet a margin requirement belongs to the customer and is not part of the adviser's compensation. (Page 2)

41. **D.** An investment adviser may maintain records in any format as long as they are readily accessible to the administrator. The adviser must maintain the equipment necessary to make the records available for examination. (Page 15)

42. **C.** Offers and sales create disclosure liabilities only for the parties involved. An uninvolved third party should remain uninvolved and has no bearing on the status of the offer. (Page 78)

43. **A.** The SEC's cooling-off period runs for 20 days unless either a stop order has been issued or the SEC has extended the cooling-off time limit. (Page 56)

44. **D.** Advertisements distributed by investment advisers may not include testimonials concerning the investment adviser or any advice provided. (Page 21)

45. **D.** There are no exemptions from the antifraud provisions of the act of 1933. (Page 63)

46. **D.** When an investor becomes a control person, the SEC requires notification within 10 business days. (Page 62)

47. **D.** In order for a person to use the title "investment counsel," her principal business must consist of acting as an investment adviser and a substantial part of her business must consist of rendering investment supervisory services. (Page 3)

48. **C.** The custodian of an account, and not the beneficial owner, is the person who has the authority to make investment decisions for the account. (Page 3)

49. **B.** To qualify for the national (state) de minimis exemption, the investment adviser would have to limit his clientele to less than six persons during any 12-month period. (Page 8)

50. **D.** Under the Uniform Securities Act, investment advisers who offer investment advice to less than six persons in a state are exempt from registration in that state under the de minimis exemption. It is the Investment Advisers Act of 1940 that allows exemption from registration as investment advisers for persons who do not hold themselves out as investment advisers and who give investment advice to fewer than 15 persons in total, regardless of the state in which those persons live. (Page 5)

51. **A.** If the securities are unlisted and not admitted for unlisted trading on a national exchange, Max would not need to be registered as an investment adviser. (Page 5)

52. **D.** Chemists are not among the professions that are exempt from investment adviser registration. (Page 3)

53. **B.** The broker-dealer would not need to register as an investment adviser if an employee gives advice outside the scope of the rep's employment. The broker-dealer has not granted permission to give investment advice and has not accepted liability for the advice. (Page 24)

54. **D.** The escrow account can be an interest-bearing account. (Page 17)

55. **C.** Investment advisory contracts cannot be assigned without the express written permission of the customer. (Page 18)

56. **B.** The amount of the payment the customer makes towards a securities purchase is regulated by Reg T and is not something the adviser needs to disclose. Under the act of 1940, the disclosure brochure must disclose the fees and services an adviser offers. (Page 4)

57. **C.** A broker-dealer that provides investment advice that is solely incidental to the conduct of its business as a broker-dealer and that receives no special compensation for the advice does not have to register. (Page 3)

58. **D.** An investment adviser may never put her own interests before those of her customers. (Page 77)

59. **D.** The publisher is offering *specific* advice and does not qualify for the exemption offered to publishers of general-interest newspapers and magazines whose giving of investment advice is incidental to the normal content of their publications. (Page 2)

60. **C.** Under the provisions of the Insider Trading Act, the customer and the rep may both be held liable for insider trading. The customer is liable for acting on nonpublic information, but the rep may also be held responsible for failing to note if the customer was a corporate insider and thus might have had access to inside information. (Page 101)

61. **B.** If there was no fraud involved, your customer has two years from the date of notification or three years from the transaction, whichever comes first, in which to take action. (Page 36)

62. **B.** Under the Investment Advisers Act of 1940, investment advisers who limit their advice to securities that are not listed or traded on a national securities exchange and whose customers are all residents of the same state as the adviser are exempt from registration. (Page 5)

63. **C.** Under the act of 1940, the de minimis exemption applies to those persons who do not hold themselves out to the public as investment advisers and who provide advice to fewer than 15 persons. (Page 5)

64. **B.** The maximum criminal penalty for the use of fraud and deceit in the sale of unregistered, nonexempt securities is a fine of $5,000 and three years in prison. (Page 36)

65. **D.** If a person, including a broker-dealer, receives any financial gain from rendering investment advice, he must register as an investment adviser. The other persons described are exempt from the 1940 act's registration requirements. (Page 2)

66. **D.** Surety bonds are required as a means of providing customers with protection against a broker-dealer's or adviser's bankruptcy. (Page 9)

67. **D.** A firm must keep its articles of incorporation (or partnership agreements), books containing the minutes of board meetings, and firm

stock certificate records for the lifetime of the firm, and must make provisions for the passing on of these documents to any successor firm. (Page 15)

68. **B.** *Churning* is defined as entering transactions in a customer's account that are excessive in either size or frequency. (Page 77)

69. **D.** No securities or issuers are exempt from the antifraud provisions of the act of 1933. (Page 60)

70. **D.** Failing to disclose that the investments being recommended are underwritten by the registered rep's own firm would be considered an omission of a material fact, in violation of the Uniform Securities Act. (Page 78)

71. **D.** The amended act of 1940 exempts investment advisers from state registration if they manage more than $25 million in assets. Federally registered advisers must give notice and pay state filing fees to practice within the given state. State administrators may also require federally registered investment advisers to give notice for any of their reps. (Page 5)

72. **C.** Commercial paper that is issued with a maturity of 270 days or less is exempt from the registration requirements of both the Securities Act of 1933 and the Uniform Securities Act. (Page 70)

73. **D.** Transactions with professional and institutional investors are considered exempt transactions. (Page 71)

74. **B.** A securities information processor is a person who is in the business of providing continuous information about securities prices and transactions. A newspaper, though it may report on securities prices regularly, is not considered to be in the business of providing continuously updated information. Customer statements are required disclosure documents provided periodically to customers. (Page 30)

75. **D.** The investment adviser is permitted to make changes in the firm's management provided he gives reasonable notice to the firm's customers. (Page 6)

16 Series 66 Final Exam

1. Each of the following is a security under the Uniform Securities Act EXCEPT

   A. common stock
   B. a futures contract
   C. a variable annuity
   D. right or warrant

2. Which of the following would be included under the definition of "broker-dealer" under the Uniform Securities Act?

   A. One who effects securities transactions solely for their own account
   B. Agent
   C. Out-of-state broker-dealer that services only other broker-dealers with no place of business in this state
   D. Issuer of securities

3. Under the Uniform Securities Act, which of the following is NOT considered a person?

   A. Custodian
   B. Minor
   C. Municipality
   D. Corporation

4. According to the Uniform Securities Act, which of the following are considered sales?

   I. Gift of an assessable stock
   II. Gift of an ordinary stock
   III. Security given as a bonus for purchasing a bond
   IV. Offer of securities

   A. I and II
   B. I, II and IV
   C. I and III
   D. II, III and IV

5. A partner in an issuing company effects transactions in the company's registered, nonexempt securities and receives a commission. Under the Uniform Securities Act, the partner is considered a(n)

   A. agent
   B. broker-dealer
   C. investment adviser
   D. issuer

6. All of the following are included in the Uniform Securities Act's definition of investment adviser representative (supervised person) EXCEPT an employee who

   A. performs clerical duties
   B. solicits prospective customers
   C. makes investment recommendations
   D. manages customer accounts

7. An investment adviser describes a security as "guaranteed by the U.S. government." Under the Uniform Securities Act, this means that the

   A. adviser promises that the security is a bona fide issue of the U.S. government
   B. customer is always able to sell the security at a profit
   C. U.S. government is responsible for making principal and interest payments
   D. U.S. government promises that the security is suitable for the customer

8. Chip Bullock is an accountant who recommends securities to his clients in the course of his accounting practice. The clients pay Chip a minimal hourly rate for the recommendations. Under the Uniform Securities Act, Chip is

   A. not included in the definition of an investment adviser because he is an accountant
   B. not included in the definition of an investment adviser because he receives an hourly rate instead of a commission
   C. included in the definition of an investment adviser because he is compensated for giving investment advice
   D. included in the definition of an investment adviser because accountants are not among the professionals excluded from the definition

9. Under the Uniform Securities Act, all of the following are excluded from the definition of investment adviser EXCEPT

   A. investment adviser rep
   B. bank
   C. broker-dealer
   D. issuer

10. Under the Uniform Securities Act, all of the following are excluded from the definition of broker-dealer EXCEPT

    A. bank
    B. issuer
    C. agent
    D. accountant

11. If it is in the public interest to do so, the state administrator may deny the registration of a person under the Uniform Securities Act for all of the following reasons EXCEPT

    A. the applicant is not qualified owing to lack of experience
    B. a willful violation of the Uniform Securities Act has taken place
    C. the applicant is financially insolvent
    D. the applicant is temporarily enjoined from engaging in the securities business

12. Which of the following statements is true regarding a state administrator's authority under the Uniform Securities Act?

    A. The administrator has authority over any transaction made in his state.
    B. The administrator has subpoena power within his state.
    C. The administrator may suspend an agent's license based solely on the public's best interest.
    D. The administrator must determine the state from which payment is made and to which securities are delivered.

13. An agent in Alabama directs a solicitation to a customer who lives in Connecticut while the customer is temporarily in Indiana. The customer does not accept the offer until he arrives back in Connecticut. According to the Uniform Securities Act, the administrators of which states have jurisdiction?

A. Alabama and Connecticut
B. Alabama and Indiana
C. Indiana and Connecticut
D. Alabama, Connecticut and Indiana

14. Disciplinary proceedings under the Uniform Securities Act generally require the administrator to provide which of the following?

I. Opportunity for a hearing
II. Written findings of facts and conclusions of law
III. Appropriate prior notice

A. I and III only
B. II only
C. II and III only
D. I, II and III

15. Civil liabilities available to the buyer of a security which was sold by means of any untrue statement or omission of a material fact include all of the following except

A. consideration paid for the security
B. interest from date of payment and costs
C. damages calculated based upon original purchase price less the sales price plus 12 percent interest from date of purchase
D. reasonable attorney's fees

16. A broker-dealer can execute a transaction for a client who is away from home if it is registered in the state in which the client permanently resides or the client was present for how many days?

A. 10
B. 20
C. 30
D. 45

17. Which of the following securities issuers would NOT be subject to having its registration denied, revoked or suspended by a state administrator under the Uniform Securities Act?

I. Nonprofit corporation
II. Exchange-listed security
III. Savings and loan association
IV. Federal credit union

A. I and II only
B. I, II and IV only
C. III and IV only
D. I, II, III and IV

18. Under the NSMIA, state securities administrators are required to do which of the following?

A. Regulate the securities registration and offering process for registered investment companies
B. Forward all filing fees received from issuers, broker-dealers and agents to the SEC
C. Enforce all antifraud provisions within their boundaries
D. Impose state law on broker-dealers with respect to financial responsibility and reporting requirements in all cases

19. As defined in the Uniform Securities Act, all of the following are part of the registration by filing procedure EXCEPT that

    A. companies must have attained a specific level of earnings for the prior three-year period
    B. a copy of the offering circular or prospectus must be filed
    C. if not denied, registration becomes effective after 30 days
    D. a statement must list the name(s) of the underwriter(s) and describe the terms of the offering

20. According to the Uniform Securities Act, which of the following statements are true regarding the registration of securities by coordination?

    I. The cooling-off period for the states is 10 days.
    II. The cooling-off period for the SEC is 20 days.
    III. The registration becomes effective in the state only after the state's cooling-off period.
    IV. The registration becomes effective at the state level in conjunction with the SEC if the administrator has not entered an order to deny it.

    A. I, II and IV only
    B. I and III only
    C. III and IV only
    D. I, II, III and IV

21. The SEC is now responsible for

    A. improvement and oversight of market efficiency
    B. competition in the securities industry
    C. capital formation
    D. all of the above

22. Which of the following requirements are common to the registration of agents, state-registered investment advisers and broker-dealers under the Uniform Securities Act?

    I. All must file, along with their application, a consent to service of process.
    II. The registration for all is two years in length.
    III. All may be required to pass a written exam.
    IV. All may be required to post a surety bond.

    A. I and III
    B. I, III and IV
    C. II, III and IV
    D. IV

23. Under the Uniform Securities Act, which of the following is responsible for notifying the administrator when an agent of a broker-dealer changes his place of employment?

    A. Agent
    B. Former employer
    C. New employer
    D. The agent, the former employer and the new employer

24. A person would be required to register as a broker-dealer under the NSMIA and the USA under which of the following circumstances?

    I. The person has no place of business in the state but has directed offers to clients with more than 30 days' temporary residency.
    II. The person has no place of business in the state and deals exclusively with broker-dealers in that state.
    III. The person has no place of business in the state and effects transactions exclusively with issuers of securities in that state.
    IV. The person has a place of business in the state.

    A. I, II and IV only
    B. I and IV only
    C. II and III only
    D. I, II, III and IV

25. According to the Uniform Securities Act, when a broker-dealer's registration is revoked, which of the following occur(s)?

    I. The registrations of agents of that firm are no longer in effect.
    II. The registration of agents of that firm are still in effect.
    III. The agent's registration is held in escrow until the broker-dealer gets out of jail.
    IV. One of the agents must be appointed the new broker-dealer.

    A. I
    B. I and III
    C. II
    D. II and IV

26. Which of the following statements are true of a broker-dealer as defined in the Uniform Securities Act?

    I. A broker-dealer may not also be registered as an investment adviser.
    II. A broker-dealer may be either a firm or an individual.
    III. A broker-dealer's primary business is effecting securities transactions for clients or for the broker-dealer's own account.

    A. I and II only
    B. I and III only
    C. II and III only
    D. I, II and III

27. A broker-dealer's registration under the Uniform Securities Act is effective how many days after the application is filed?

    A. 10
    B. 20
    C. 30
    D. 45

28. Under the Uniform Securities Act, all of the following information must be included in an investment adviser's disclosure brochure EXCEPT

    A. services offered and fees charged
    B. affiliations with financial services firms
    C. performance history of customer accounts
    D. balance sheet

29. According to the Uniform Securities Act's rules for an investment adviser who has custody of customer assets, which of the following statements are true?

    I. The administrator must give written approval before the adviser may hold customer assets in custody.
    II. Customer assets must not be commingled with assets of the investment adviser.
    III. An adviser who has discretion over customer accounts faces a higher surety bond requirement than an adviser who has custody.
    IV. Every three months, the adviser must send an itemized account statement to each customer whose assets are held in custody.

    A. I and II only
    B. II and IV only
    C. III and IV only
    D. I, II, III and IV

30. According to the USA, an IA must keep records relating to customers for a minimum of

    A. three years
    B. five years
    C. seven years
    D. ten years

31. According to the NSMIA and the USA, investment advisers are required to maintain all of the following records EXCEPT

    A. order tickets for transactions in exempt securities
    B. written communications regarding recommendations
    C. copies of customer account statements
    D. advertising materials relating to exempt securities

32. An investment adviser recommends that a customer purchase shares of Mountain Brewing, saying that the company has "graduated to the level of quality acceptable to the New York Stock Exchange." According to the Uniform Securities Act, the adviser's statement is

    A. permitted because the NYSE sets stringent earnings requirements for listed stocks
    B. permitted because an investment adviser may recommend listed stocks without restriction
    C. not permitted because it is misleading to imply that an exchange-listed security is approved by the exchange
    D. not permitted because the transaction is not suitable for the customer

33. An agent wants to make a short and efficient presentation to several clients about a security she is recommending. The agent deliberately sorts out material facts regarding the security. Under the Uniform Securities Act, the agent has

    A. committed a violation because she has not considered each client's individual objectives
    B. committed a violation because every known fact about the security must be discussed
    C. committed a violation because she must state every fact a prudent investor would need to consider
    D. acted in accordance with antifraud provisions

34. A person who sells securities in violation of the Uniform Securities Act is civilly liable for which of the following?

    I. Principal
    II. Interest
    III. Court costs
    IV. Attorney's fees

    A. I, II and IV only
    B. I and III only
    C. II and III only
    D. I, II, III and IV

35. Which of the following statements is true regarding the antifraud provisions of the Uniform Securities Act?

    A. The only securities exempt from the provisions are those regulated by federal authority.
    B. The only exempt securities are those issued by national governments or political subdivisions of countries that maintain diplomatic relations with the United States.
    C. The only exempt securities are those that are properly registered under blue-sky laws.
    D. No securities are exempt from the antifraud provisions of the act.

36. Which of the following actions would NOT be considered unlawful under the Uniform Securities Act?

    A. An agent makes an untrue statement of a material fact.
    B. An agent omits a material fact because she knew she did not have time to cover everything in a short presentation.
    C. An agent deliberately fails to follow a customer's instructions.
    D. An agent actively solicits orders in unregistered exempt securities.

37. According to the Uniform Securities Act, which of the following statements is true of an agent who deliberately gives a fictitious quote to a customer?

    A. He is guilty of a felony.
    B. He has committed a fraudulent and misleading act.
    C. He must execute at that price.
    D. He is committed to selling or buying 100 shares at that price.

38. An agent of a broker-dealer who willfully violates the Uniform Securities Act is subject to which of the following?

    I. Civil liabilities
    II. Criminal penalties
    III. Suspension, denial or revocation of registration as an agent by the administrator

    A. I only
    B. I and II only
    C. III only
    D. I, II and III

39. An investment adviser arranges a trade on behalf of a customer. According to the Uniform Securities Act, which of the following statements is(are) true?

    I. The adviser must disclose that it is acting as an agent in this transaction.
    II. The adviser must disclose that it is acting as a principal in this transaction.
    III. The customer must consent to the transaction in writing.
    IV. The transaction described is prohibited for investment advisers.

    A. I and III
    B. II
    C. II and III
    D. IV

40. If convicted of a willful violation of the Uniform Securities Act, an agent may be subject to a maximum of

    I. imprisonment for five years
    II. a fine of $5,000 and/or imprisonment for three years
    III. a fine of $10,000
    IV. disbarment

    A. I
    B. I and III
    C. I, III and IV
    D. II

41. Under the Uniform Securities Act, an agent may NOT make which of the following statements to a customer?

    A. "This security is registered with the state."
    B. "This security is cleared by the administrator."
    C. "This security is approved for sale by the administrator."
    D. "This security is exempt from registration."

42. An agent discovers that he has sold to a customer an unregistered nonexempt security that he thought was exempt. Under the Uniform Securities Act, if the agent offers to buy it back, which of the following statements is(are) true?

    I. The customer may accept the offer, but still may sue.
    II. This is legal and is called *rescission.*
    III. The offer also must include interest.
    IV. This cannot be done under any circumstances.

    A. I
    B. II
    C. II and III
    D. IV

43. An agent executes a transaction that the customer knows is illegal, but is willing to enter into anyway and signs a waiver. Under the Uniform Securities Act, the agent is relieved of

    A. civil liabilities
    B. criminal penalties
    C. administrative censure
    D. none of the above

44. Which of the following activities is(are) prohibited under the Uniform Securities Act?

    I. Engaging in a practice not expressly forbidden by the act, but defined as unethical by the administrator in a rule
    II. Omitting a material fact when soliciting a client
    III. Selling recommended securities to a client from one's own account without disclosing this fact to the client

    A. I and II only
    B. I and III only
    C. II only
    D. I, II and III

45. Under the Uniform Securities Act, which of the following negates a client's right to file a civil suit for damages?

    I. The advice was given more than three years ago.
    II. The adviser has died.
    III. The client willingly signed a statement waiving the adviser's compliance with the provision of the act on which the suit is based.

    A. I only
    B. I and II only
    C. II and III only
    D. I, II and III

46. The SEC can deny a person a license in which of the following circumstances?

    I. The person has a criminal record.
    II. The person has served jail time of one year or more.
    III. The person has lost a civil lawsuit within the last year.
    IV. The person was convicted of a crime but was given probation.

    A. I and II
    B. I and III
    C. II and III
    D. III and IV

47. Concerning the antifraud provisions of the Uniform Securities Act, which of the following statements is(are) true?

    I. Governmental bodies or political subdivisions are exempt from these antifraud provisions.
    II. "Fraud" is broadly defined, and includes not only deceit but also failure to make adequate disclosure.
    III. In a securities transaction, a deceitful presentation is a violation even if it does not result in a sale.

    A. I and III only
    B. II only
    C. II and III only
    D. I, II and III

48. Which of the following persons is(are) subject to the antifraud provisions of the Uniform Securities Act?

    I. Broker-dealer who advises customers on the value of securities but is compensated only in the form of commissions on sales
    II. Investment adviser representative who receives a fee directly from clients
    III. Investment adviser representative who receives no compensation directly from clients but is paid a salary by an advisory firm

    A. I and II only
    B. II only
    C. III only
    D. I, II and III

49. Which of the following actions would be considered a willful violation of the Uniform Securities Act?

    I. An adviser recommends the purchase of a stock she believes is exempt, but later she discovers that the administrator has revoked that stock's exemption.
    II. An adviser recommends the purchase of nonexempt, unregistered stock after being incorrectly advised by a reliable source that the stock was properly registered.
    III. An adviser recommends the purchase of a stock that she knows is not properly registered, but no sale results.

    A. I only
    B. II and III only
    C. III only
    D. I, II and III

50. It is legal under the Uniform Securities Act for a registered investment adviser to tell a client that

    A. a registered security may lawfully be sold in that state
    B. an exempt security is not required to be registered because it is generally regarded as being safer than a nonexempt security
    C. her qualifications have been found satisfactory by the administrator
    D. a registered security has been approved for sale in the state by the administrator

51. Which of the following advisory fee structures is NOT allowed to be charged under the Uniform Securities Act?

    A. Fees based on a percentage of the change in value of funds from year to year
    B. Fees based on a fixed dollar schedule for funds under management, with payment tied to account performance
    C. Fees based on a fixed dollar schedule tied to the value of funds under management
    D. Fees based on a percentage of the aggregate value of funds under management

52. A customer asks an agent for a valuation of his securities portfolio. Because the agent does not want to induce the customer to panic and sell his shares at a loss, the agent inflates the value of the stock. Under the Uniform Securities Act, this action is

    A. permitted because the agent determined that selling the securities was not suitable
    B. permitted because the agent was not recommending a transaction
    C. not permitted because the agent must not deceive the customer by misstating a material fact
    D. not permitted because the agent must not attempt to influence the market value of a security

53. June Polar puts together a recommendation for a customer. She is unexpectedly called out of town and asks another agent at her firm to meet with the customer and present the recommendation. When the other agent makes the presentation, he omits some of the material facts. According to the Uniform Securities Act, this is

    A. permitted if the recommendation pertains to an exempt security
    B. permitted if the second agent was unaware of the omission
    C. permitted if the second agent receives no compensation for presenting the recommendation
    D. not permitted under any circumstances

54. An investment adviser owns a large block of Kelptek stock. A customer places an order for 100 shares of Kelptek. In compliance with the antifraud provisions of the Uniform Securities Act, the adviser

    A. must disclose that it will act as a principal in the transaction
    B. must act as an agent in the transaction because it must maintain its stock position
    C. must refuse the order because there is a conflict of interest
    D. may execute the transaction without taking further action

55. The Securities Act of 1933 was passed to provide for

    A. the registration of newly issued securities and the disclosure of information in their sale
    B. the registration of investment advisory firms and their representatives
    C. the regulation of broker-dealers and exchanges
    D. protection against "high pressure" tactics in the sale of securities

56. Under the NSMIA and the USA, "sophisticated investors" are defined as

A. qualified purchasers
B. persons who have full-time jobs
C. country club members
D. persons with a financial education degree or three years industry experience

57. Microscam, Inc. will issue a new security and distribute it through a public offering. According to the Securities Act of 1933, which of the following is NOT required to be included in Microscam's registration statement?

A. Name and address of Microscam's personnel manager
B. Estimate of the proceeds that will be raised through the offering and how that money will be used
C. Identity of the underwriter
D. Name and address of Max Leveridge, who owns 11 percent of Microscam's stock

58. Under the Securities Act of 1933, the SEC may at its discretion

I. make, amend and rescind its rules
II. arrest and detain suspected violators, subject to the observance of due process and the preservation of citizens' rights
III. conduct formal investigations of persons under its jurisdiction

A. I and III only
B. II only
C. III only
D. I, II and III

59. Which of the following fits the category of "government security" under the Securities Act of 1933?

I. Treasury bills
II. Bonds issued by the State of Indiana
III. Bonds issued by the U.S. Postal Service

A. I only
B. I and III only
C. II and III only
D. I, II and III

60. Under the Securities Act of 1933, all of the following are covered EXCEPT

A. fair disclosure of all pertinent information
B. blue-sky laws
C. due diligence
D. requirements for prospectuses

61. Securities that are sold to the public must be registered under the Securities Act of 1933 under which of the following circumstances?

A. The total value of the issue exceeds $1 million.
B. The U.S. Justice Department, upon request, directs that the security be so registered.
C. The issue is sold in more than three states.
D. The securities are sold in interstate commerce through the mails or other channels.

62. In accordance with the Securities Act of 1933, a registered representative is prohibited from which activity(ies) in connection with the sale of a new issue and prior to filing a registration statement for that issue?

    I. Confirming the sale of the security to a customer
    II. Soliciting indications of interest for the security
    III. Soliciting orders for the stock

    A. I and III only
    B. II only
    C. III only
    D. I, II and III

63. The purpose of the Securities Exchange Act of 1934 is to

    A. regulate the persons involved in the new issue market
    B. regulate the persons involved in the secondary market
    C. close loopholes in the Securities Act of 1933
    D. make securities regulation more uniform among the several states

64. Under the Securities Exchange Act of 1934, which of the following statements are true regarding the use of credit to make securities purchases?

    I. The purpose of margin requirements is to prevent the excessive use of credit by the purchasers of securities.
    II. Credit may not be used to purchase new issues of securities.
    III. Margin requirements are set by the Federal Reserve Board.

    A. I and II only
    B. I and III only
    C. II and III only
    D. I, II and III

65. Under the USA, who has licensing authority over the investment adviser representatives (supervised persons)?

    A. State
    B. Federal
    C. NYSE
    D. NASD

66. SEC commissioners appointed under the Securities Exchange Act of 1934

    A. are nominated by the NASD and are elected by a committee of state securities administrators
    B. must not have any other business or employment besides their commission with the SEC
    C. must not be affiliated with a political party
    D. must have professional experience as prosecuting attorneys as well as knowledge of the securities business

67. Under the provisions of the Securities Exchange Act of 1934, which of the following would result in statutory disqualification from association with an NASD-member broker-dealer?

    A. Loss of a civil lawsuit involving securities
    B. Lack of experience in the securities business
    C. Failing to register as an investment adviser and engaging in a business that requires one to be so registered
    D. Court injunction against acting as an underwriter

68. The Securities Exchange Act of 1934 has to do with which of the following?

    I. Issuance of financial reports by corporations
    II. Issuance of government securities
    III. Trading of government securities
    IV. Trading of corporate securities

    A. I and III
    B. I, III and IV
    C. II, III and IV
    D. II and IV

69. Regarding SEC commissioners appointed under the Securities Exchange Act of 1934, which of the following statements is true?

    A. Commissioners are appointed to the SEC by the president of the United States.
    B. Political affiliation is not an important criterion for appointment as an SEC commissioner.
    C. Two SEC commissioners constitute a quorum and can enact legislation with the signature of the president of the United States.
    D. An SEC commissioner can engage in any business activity as long as that business activity is disclosed.

70. Which of the following is(are) excluded from the definition of "transfer agent" under the provisions of the Securities Exchange Act of 1934?

    I. Clearing agency that registers transfers of ownership solely with respect to options contracts it issues
    II. Firm that effects shareholder requests to convert mutual fund shares on behalf of the mutual fund
    III. Insurance company that registers share ownership solely with respect to variable annuity contracts it issues

    A. I and II
    B. I and III
    C. II
    D. II and III

71. Which of the following statements is NOT true regarding a mutual fund's contract with its investment adviser under the provisions of the Investment Company Act of 1940?

    A. It must be approved by a majority of the outstanding shares.
    B. It must be in writing.
    C. It must describe the adviser's compensation.
    D. It may not be terminated except with the approval of a majority of the outstanding shares.

72. SEC Rule 12b-1 of the Investment Company Act of 1940 allows mutual funds to

    A. use testimonials in their advertisements
    B. suspend redemption of shares under certain circumstances
    C. charge distribution expenses against net asset value
    D. charge a redemption fee when shares are redeemed, rather than a sales charge when shares are purchased

73. Under the NSMIA, which of the following are true about management investment companies?

    I. They are exempt from state regulation.
    II. They are exempt from state registration.
    III. They are federally registered only with the SEC.
    IV. They are federally regulated only by the SEC.

    A. I, II and III only
    B. I, II and IV only
    C. I, III and IV only
    D. I, II, III and IV

74. Which of the following statements are true regarding a mutual fund's board of directors under the Investment Company Act of 1940?

    I. No more than 60 percent of the board may be interested persons.
    II. A majority of the board may not be investment bankers or have connections with the fund's regular broker-dealer or principal underwriter.
    III. The members of the board are elected by the shareholders.

    A. I and II only
    B. I and III only
    C. II and III only
    D. I, II and III

75. As defined by the Investment Company Act of 1940, an investment company that is not classified as either a face-amount certificate company or a unit investment trust would be classified as a(n)

    A. closed-end company
    B. open-end company
    C. management company
    D. mutual fund

76. Under the Investment Advisers Act of 1940, which of the following investment advisers is considered to have custody of client securities or funds?

    A. Bea Kuhl requires payment of fees six months in advance.
    B. June Polar can write checks on the client's account for the sole purpose of paying custodial fees to the bank that has custody of that client's securities.
    C. Klaus Bruin requires a full year's advisory fee to be paid in advance.
    D. Hugh Heifer has the authority to place orders for a client's securities account.

77. Which of the following statements is NOT true regarding the records that an investment adviser is required to keep under the provisions of the Investment Advisers Act of 1940?

    A. Records must be maintained for a period of three years from the end of the fiscal year in which the last entry was made.
    B. Advisers must keep records of transactions made for their own personal accounts.
    C. Records must be kept of client accounts, recommendations made, and whether the client has granted the adviser any discretionary authority.
    D. Records created by computer in the ordinary course of business may be stored in electronic format.

78. The antifraud provisions of the Investment Advisers Act of 1940

    A. apply only to advisers who are registered under the act
    B. prohibit fraud only in connection with securities transactions
    C. prohibit the receipt of both fees and commissions on transactions that result from advisory recommendations
    D. are violated if material information is not adequately disclosed to a client

79. An agency cross transaction may NOT be effected in which of the following circumstances?

A. The same investment adviser recommended the transaction to both seller and buyer.
B. Different investment advisers recommended the transaction to the seller and buyer.
C. The investment adviser recommended the sale and the buyer's offer was unsolicited.
D. The investment adviser recommended the purchase and the seller's offer was unsolicited.

80. A federally registered investment adviser is exempt from registration under the amended Investment Advisers Act of 1940 if

A. all of the adviser's clients are banks
B. the adviser does not hold herself out to the public as being an investment adviser, and she has fewer than 15 clients, of whom none is an investment company
C. all of the adviser's clients reside in the same state and the adviser renders advice on exchange-listed securities only
D. all of the adviser's clients are investment companies

81. A broker-dealer provides fee-based investment advice as part of its business. An employee of the firm also provides fee-based investment advice outside the scope of the business. According to SEC Release 1092, who is required to register as an IA?

A. Broker-dealer
B. Employee
C. Both
D. Neither

82. Which of the following is NOT included in the definition of "investment adviser" under SEC Release IA-1092?

A. Economist who regularly renders investment advice in the course of her business
B. Bank that is not an investment company
C. Registered representative who provides investment advice outside the scope of his employment with a broker-dealer but who receives no compensation besides commissions on the transactions
D. Attorney who charges a separate fee for investment advice and can document that less than half of her income is derived from providing investment advice to clients

83. Which of the following individuals satisfy the definition of "investment adviser" under SEC Release IA-1092?

I. Financial planner who advises clients on whether municipal bonds, common stock or money-market funds are most appropriate for their situation, but who does not make recommendations regarding particular securities within those groups
II. Insurance agent who makes general recommendations about allocating financial resources to savings accounts, real estate and securities, but whose specific advice is related solely to, and whose income depends solely on, sales of insurance policies
III. Accountant who advertises the availability of investment advice

A. I and II only
B. I and III only
C. II and III only
D. I, II and III

84. Which of the following is considered to be compensation for investment advice under SEC Release IA-1092?

I. An insurance agent creates a comprehensive financial plan for a client; the plan includes investment advice; the agent makes no charge for the plan, but he earns a commission on the sale of a life insurance policy included in the plan.
II. An accountant charges a fee for services that in rare, isolated instances include investment advice.
III. A broker-dealer creates a comprehensive financial plan for a client; the broker-dealer receives no fee for the plan, but he earns commissions on transactions when the plan is implemented.

A. I and II only
B. I and III only
C. II and III only
D. I, II and III

85. Under the NSMIA and the USA, who has jurisdiction for the supervision of investment advisers who manage $25,000,000 or more in client assets?

A. SEC
B. State administrator
C. NYSE
D. NASD

86. The exclusion for providing investment advice that is solely incidental to the practice of a profession is NOT available to which of the following, under SEC Release IA-1092?

A. Real estate agents
B. Engineers
C. Teachers
D. Broker-dealers

87. Attorneys and accountants can claim an exclusion from the definition of "investment adviser" under SEC Release IA-1092 if

I. they charge a fee separate from that for their professional services for the provision of investment advice
II. they advertise that they are available to provide investment advice
III. the advice is incidental to the practice of their profession
IV. the advice is a small part of their total business but they do charge a specific fee for the advice

A. I, II and IV
B. I and III
C. II
D. III

88. Which of the following would NOT define a person as being in the business of providing investment advice under the provisions of SEC Release IA-1092?

A. Providing a complete range of financial services, but with advice on investments constituting only a minor component in the overall range of services
B. Providing specific investment advice only on rare, isolated, unusual occasions
C. Advertising advice on investing
D. Receiving a small, separate fee for investment advice

89. Which of the following disclosures is an investment adviser required to make to clients under the provisions of SEC Release IA-1092?

A. Amount of any compensation that will be earned on transactions executed through the broker-dealer with whom the adviser is affiliated
B. That, in implementing a plan for a client, the adviser intends to act as a representative of a broker-dealer with whom he is affiliated
C. That clients have the right to execute recommended transactions through broker-dealers other than the one with whom the adviser is affiliated
D. All of the above

90. Of the following, which does NOT meet the definition of providing investment advice as a business, as set forth in SEC Release IA-1092?

A. Management consultant who has not provided investment advice to clients other than to tell a couple of small business clients who had invested their surpluses in speculative securities that they should find something less risky
B. Financial planner who provides only nonspecific investment advice as part of his fee-based services but who makes specific securities recommendations to his clients in his capacity as registered representative for a broker-dealer
C. Attorney who advertises the availability of investment advice
D. Accountant who charges clients an additional fee for providing investment advice

91. Which of the following constitutes providing investment advice for compensation, according to SEC Release IA-1092?

I. An insurance agent develops a financial plan for clients, at no charge, providing generic investment and savings information. The agent is compensated only by commissions on his insurance sales.
II. An insurance agent develops a financial plan for clients, at no charge, analyzing life insurance and mutual fund investments. The agent is compensated only by commissions on his insurance sales.
III. A broker-dealer provides financial strategies and recommends specific securities. The broker-dealer is compensated only by commissions on securities transactions.
IV. A financial planner develops financial plans, at no charge, containing specific investment advice and referring clients to the Boring Securities brokerage company in order to follow the plans. The planner receives a referral fee from Boring Securities.

A. I and III
B. I and IV
C. II and III
D. II and IV

92. Which of the following statements is true regarding an investment adviser's authority to place orders for a client's account under the NASAA's Statement of Policy on Unethical Business Practices?

A. The adviser is not required to obtain authorization to place orders for a client's account unless a conflict of interest is involved.
B. The adviser may, without the client's approval, place a sell order for the purpose of avoiding losses, but may not place a buy order without the client's authorization.
C. The client's verbal approval is sufficient for a specific order.
D. Written approval from the client authorizing a stated amount of a specified security is required before placing an order.

93. From which of the following clients could an investment adviser ethically borrow money under the NASAA's Statement of Policy on Unethical Business Practices?

I. Broker-dealer not affiliated with the adviser
II. Bank not affiliated with the adviser
III. Investment company not affiliated with the adviser

A. I and II only
B. I and III only
C. II and III only
D. I, II and III

94. Under the NASAA's Statement of Policy on Unethical Business Practices, an adviser would be acting improperly if she

I. allowed a client to sign an advisory contract after disclosing a potential conflict of interest to that client
II. agreed to personally make up the difference if a client's account lost money
III. failed to inquire into a client's investment objectives, financial situation and needs

A. I and II only
B. I and III only
C. II and III only
D. I, II and III

95. Under the NASAA's Statement of Policy on Unethical Business Practices, investment advisers who advertise must comply with the rules laid out in the Investment Advisers Act of 1940; these rules include

A. a prohibition against reduced-fee "introductory" offers
B. a requirement that a copy of all advertisements be sent to the SEC at the time they are disseminated to the public
C. a prohibition against testimonials from clients
D. all of the above

96. Gwinneth Stout has been following the recommendations of another agent in her office because of the other agent's impressive performance record. As soon as the other agent recommends a particular security, Gwinneth recommends it to all of her clients too. According to the NASAA's Statement of Policy on Unethical Business Practices, Gwinneth's activity is

    A. prohibited because the other agent's recommendations are confidential
    B. prohibited because she failed to determine if the recommendation was suitable for her clients
    C. prohibited because it tends to induce excessive trading in the security
    D. permitted as long as she discloses the source of the recommendation

97. An agent sells his client 10 U.S. government bonds due to mature in 30 years. According to the NASAA's Statement of Policy on Unethical Business Practices, which of the following statements may be made?

    A. "There is no way you can lose money on the safest security on earth."
    B. "The bonds are guaranteed as to principal and interest payments by the U.S. government."
    C. "The full faith and credit backing of the U.S. government means virtually no chance of loss."
    D. "The U.S. government guarantees that principal and interest payments will keep pace with inflation."

98. An agent gets a phone call from the wife of a customer. The wife wants to sell $25,000 worth of securities and use the proceeds as a down payment on a house. The account is in her husband's name, but she says he told her to sell the securities. The agent knows the couple to be happily married. To comply with the NASAA's Statement of Policy on Unethical Business Practices, he should

    A. call the husband immediately and confirm the order
    B. sell as instructed
    C. get permission from his principal
    D. tell the couple that the purchase of a house is a bad investment

99. Which of the following statements is true regarding the use of material facts under the NASAA's Statement of Policy on Unethical Business Practices?

    A. To omit them is fraudulent and unethical.
    B. Because all material facts cannot be presented, it is up to the agent to decide which to use.
    C. Restrictions apply only to sales, not solicitations.
    D. The agent is the final arbiter on what is material and what is not.

100. An agent hears a rumor concerning an investment and uses the information to influence a customer who has hesitated to make the purchase. According to the NASAA's Statement of Policy on Unethical Business Practices, which of the following statements is true?

A. Because the agent made it clear that it was a rumor, this is not a violation.
B. Because the customer knew it was a rumor and therefore could not be reliable, this is not a violation.
C. Because rumors are not considered to be inside information, this is not a violation.
D. Under no circumstances would this be allowed.

◆ Answers & Rationale

1. **B.** Common stock and rights and warrants are specifically named as "securities" in the act. Variable annuities also are considered securities because the investment risk of these contracts falls on the contract owner. Futures contracts, in common with precious metals, collectibles and real estate, may be used as investment vehicles but are generally not considered to be securities. (Page 30)

2. **A.** Choice A is part of the definition of "broker-dealer." The other choices are specifically excluded from the definition. (Page 37)

3. **B.** Minors cannot enter into contracts and therefore are not considered legal persons. (Page 2)

4. **C.** "Sale" is defined as a contract or transaction for value. Because an assessable stock may have value or require a payment made by the recipient, the gift is considered a sale. A warrant is both an offer and a sale. Gifts of stock are not sales, and choice IV is an offer, not a sale. (Page 29)

5. **A.** Being a partner of an issuer does not automatically make you an agent unless you actively participate in the underwriting process and receive a commission for sales efforts. (Page 28)

6. **A.** Clerical duties are not included in the definition of investment adviser representative (supervised person). (Page 3)

7. **C.** A security can be described as guaranteed by the U.S. government if the government is responsible for making payments. This does not mean that the customer will always make a profit. The issuer of a security does not determine if the security is suitable for the customer; the suitability determination is the responsibility of the adviser recommending the security. (Page 29)

8. **C.** An accountant who gives advice incidental to his professional practice is not included in the USA's definition of an investment adviser. However, if the accountant provides advice in the course of business and receives compensation for providing investment advice, the exclusion no longer applies. (Page 3)

9. **D.** The USA's definition of an investment adviser excludes an investment adviser rep, a bank and a broker-dealer acting within the scope of its normal business. The definition does not provide an exclusion for issuers. (Page 2)

10. **D.** The USA's definition of "broker-dealer" excludes banks, issuers and agents. Accountants are not excluded from the definition of broker-dealer. However, they are allowed an exclusion from the definition of investment adviser if they render advice incidental to their professional practice. (Page 37)

11. **A.** An administrator may not deny, suspend or revoke registration solely on the basis of lack of experience. (Page 41)

12. **A.** The Uniform Securities Act gives the state administrator jurisdiction (the scope of the act) over transactions originated in, directed to or accepted in the administrator's state. An administrator may suspend any registration if two things are true: (1) it is in the public interest and (2) one of the specific offenses listed has been committed. (Page 34)

13. **D.** The administrator in any state to or from which an offer is made has jurisdiction over the offer. (Page 34)

14. **D.** In general, the administrator must provide appropriate prior notice, opportunity for a hearing and written findings of facts and conclusions of law. Even if an order is issued summarily—that is, without prior notice—the registrant must be notified upon issue of the order and must be given the opportunity to request a hearing. (Page 35)

15. **C.** Damages can be recovered, but the amount recoverable includes cost and 6 percent annual interest. (Page 36)

16. **C.** A broker-dealer is exempt from state registration if an existing client has less than 30 days' temporary residency in another state. (Page 37)

17. **D.** All of the issuers listed are exempt from the provisions of the Uniform Securities Act. (Page 38)

18. **C.** Under the NSMIA and the USA, administrators are required to enforce all antifraud provisions. Also, under the NSMIA, investment companies are exempt from state registration. Broker-dealers who are exempt from state registration are not subject to the state's reporting requirements. (Page 5)

19. **C.** Registration by filing becomes effective concurrently with federal effectiveness. The state's cooling-off period under registration by filing is five days. (Page 66)

20. **A.** The federal 1933 securities act requires that securities offered to the public be registered with the SEC. The registration statement becomes effective on the 20th calendar day following the date the statement is received by the SEC (assuming the SEC does not find any deficiencies or misrepresentations). During the 20-day cooling-off period between the filing date and the effective date, indications of interest from the public for shares may be taken. When the registration becomes effective, shares in the new issue may be reconfirmed and actual orders taken. On the federal level, the registration must be on file with the SEC for 20 days. On the state level, it must be on file with the administration for at least 10 days. (Page 65)

21. **D.** Under the NSMIA, the SEC will now oversee the improvement and oversight of market efficiency, competition in the securities industry, and capital formation. The SEC is still responsible for acting in the public's best interest. (Page 32)

22. **B.** Broker-dealers, agents and state-registered investment advisers must file a consent to service of process with their initial applications for registration. The consent to service gives the administrator rights over the applicants. Each applicant may be required to pass an exam and post a surety bond. Federally registered investment advisers must give notice and pay filing fees in the states they conduct business. (Page 8)

23. **D.** All three parties must notify the administrator. (Page 40)

24. **B.** The term "broker-dealer" does not include a person who has no place of business in the state and who (1) effects transactions exclusively through issuers, other broker-dealers or institutions or (2) directs an offer in the state to an existing customer who has less than 30 days' temporary residency in the state where the offer is received. (Page 37)

25. **A.** An agent's license is effective only as long as that agent is associated with a registered broker-dealer. (Page 41)

26. **C.** Choices II and III together make up the definition of a broker-dealer (the definition refers to a "person," which may be either an individual or a firm). However, a person may be registered as both a broker-dealer and an investment adviser at the same time. (Page 37)

27. **C.** Under the Uniform Securities Act, broker-dealer registrations are effective on the 30th day after the application is filed. Broker-dealer registrations under federal law are effective after 45 days. (Page 39)

28. **C.** The investment adviser brochure discloses important information about the adviser's business. Performance figures for customer accounts need not be included in the brochure. Fees, affiliations with other investment-related

institutions and financial information are required disclosures. (Page 14)

29. **B.** Customer assets held in custody by an investment adviser must be segregated. The adviser must send a statement every three months to customers whose assets are held in custody. The administrator does not approve custodial accounts; if there is no rule prohibiting custody, the administrator must be notified that the adviser has custody. Advisers with custody of customer assets have a higher surety bond requirement than advisers with discretionary authority. (Page 17)

30. **B.** Any required records must be maintained for a minimum of five years. (Page 15)

31. **D.** Investment advisers are required to maintain records of customer transactions, customer accounts and investment recommendations, among other records. Advertising materials need not be kept; state-registered advisers may be required to file with the administrator advertising materials pertaining to nonexempt securities. (Page 16)

32. **C.** The agent should have pointed out that the Exchange listing requirements are, in many cases, quantitative, not qualitative. Acceptance for listing by the New York Stock Exchange does not necessarily reduce the risk of loss to the client. The agent's statement is misleading and, therefore, prohibited. (Page 78)

33. **C.** The violation described is the agent's failure to present all material facts regarding a security recommendation. The antifraud provisions of the USA do not require the disclosure of all known facts, but the agent must disclose the facts essential to making a sound investment decision. (Page 78)

34. **D.** The person illegally selling the securities is liable for the purchase price of the securities plus interest from the date of purchase, costs and reasonable attorney's fees. (Page 36)

35. **D.** Neither exempt securities nor exempt transactions are exempt from the antifraud provisions. (Page 69)

36. **D.** Securities that do not require registration under the Uniform Securities Act are exempt securities. Although the securities are exempt, the agent who makes the solicitation and his broker-dealer must be registered. (Page 77)

37. **B.** "Fraud" is a deliberate attempt to deceive another person. (Page 77)

38. **D.** Violations of securities laws are subject to criminal penalties, civil liabilities and denial, suspension or revocation of registration. (Page 41)

39. **A.** An investment adviser must disclose the capacity in which it will act with regard to a client transaction. The client must then give written consent to the transaction. (Page 20)

40. **D.** Under the act, the maximum penalty is a fine of $5,000 and/or three years in jail. Keep in mind that these penalties may be in addition to other penalties. (Page 36)

41. **C.** The state administrator does not *approve anything*. The other statements are statements of fact and are permitted. (Page 73)

42. **C.** As long as the agent sold the security with no intent to defraud, rescission may be offered. Rescission is the return of the customer's money, plus interest, less any income received from the investment. (Page 36)

43. **D.** Regardless of what the customer signs, the agent is responsible for executing an illegal transaction. The agent is liable for criminal, civil and administrative action. (Page 36)

44. **D.** The antifraud provisions apply to soliciting clients as well as to providing investment advice. They require disclosures to be made to a client if the adviser will act as a principal for his own account or as a broker for another party

in effecting a recommended transaction. The act gives the administrator the power to define certain practices as unethical and prohibits these practices with the same force as those spelled out in the act. (Page 78)

45. **A.** The death of either the adviser or the client does not remove a cause of action for civil liability. Waivers as described in choice III are void. (Page 36)

46. **A.** The SEC will now deny licensure to those persons with a criminal record who have served jail sentences of one year or more. (Page 6)

47. **C.** Choices II and III are correct statements. However, the antifraud provisions apply to any "person," which includes government bodies and their political subdivisions. (Page 77)

48. **D.** The antifraud provisions apply to anyone involved in a securities transaction or anyone who receives compensation for providing investment advice. A person's compensation structure or registration status does not exclude them from the antifraud provisions. (Page 75)

49. **C.** The standard for willful violation is *knowing* that you are doing something improper, even if you do not know that a law is being broken. The advisers in choices I and II are not aware that they are doing something improper, but the adviser in choice III is aware. (Page 77)

50. **A.** The fact that a security is registered or is exempt from registration has no bearing on its quality, safety or merits, and it is illegal to make any statement or implication to the contrary, as is implied in choices B and D. A similar principle applies to a person's being registered or exempt from registration (choice C). Also remember that registration does not involve verification by the administrator of any information included in a registration statement or application. When a registration becomes effective, it means only that certain legal requirements have been met in regard to that security or person. Choice A is a statement that can be legally made. (Page 21)

51. **A.** Fees that are based on a share of capital gains or appreciation in an account are prohibited. Fees based on the value of assets under management are acceptable. (Page 18)

52. **C.** In any dealings with the public, an agent may not commit an act of deceit. Giving the customer false information about a security's value is dishonest and unethical. It does not, however, constitute manipulation of the market in that security. (Page 78)

53. **D.** An agent making a recommendation to a customer is responsible for presenting all of the material facts. The responsibility is not affected by the type of security being discussed or the agent's compensation. (Page 78)

54. **A.** The antifraud provisions of the USA require an investment adviser to disclose before the completion of the transaction whether it will act as a principal or as an agent. The customer must then give written consent. The adviser is not required to refuse the order. (Page 20)

55. **A.** The 1933 act prohibits fraud and requires full and fair disclosure with regard to the sale of new issues, but it does not regulate sales pressure. The registration of investment advisers on a state or federal level by the amended Investment Advisers Act of 1940. The regulation of broker-dealers and exchanges comes under the Securities and Exchange Act of 1934. (Page 48)

56. **A.** A "qualified purchaser" falls into one of the following categories: (1) individuals with $5 million in investments, (2) trusts sponsored by qualified purchasers, (3) family-owned businesses with $5 million or more in investments or (4) any person who has discretion over no less than $25 million in investments. (Page 4)

57. **A.** A registration statement must contain, among many other things, an estimate of the proceeds and a description of the use to which they

will be put, the identity of the underwriter and the identities of owners of more than 10 percent of the issuer's stock. It must also identify all of the issuer's officers and directors, their holdings of the issuer's securities and their salaries. Choice A does not describe the personnel manager as an officer or a director, so this employee need not be identified in the registration statement. (Page 48)

58. **A.** The SEC has the power to make, amend and rescind rules in administering the securities laws. The SEC may also conduct a formal investigation whenever it deems this necessary, in its discretion, to enforce the federal securities laws. In conducting a formal investigation, the SEC may administer oaths, obtain written statements, subpoena witnesses, take evidence and require the production of books and records. The SEC does not have the power, however, to arrest and detain suspects. (Page 32)

59. **B.** The 1934 act defines "government securities" as those issued or guaranteed by the U.S. government or one of its agencies. Securities issued or guaranteed by a state, county, city, etc., or by any agency of a nonfederal governmental unit, are municipal securities. (Page 28)

60. **B.** Blue-sky laws concern the registration of securities with the states. The 1933 act deals only with the registration of securities at the federal level. (Page 48)

61. **D.** The 1933 act regulates new security issues (both debt and equity) that are sold through the mails or any other instrument of interstate commerce. (Page 48)

62. **A.** The only activity that the 1933 act allows registered representatives to do while a security is in the registration process is to solicit indications of interest. (Page 49)

63. **B.** The 1934 act regulates those involved in secondary market trading of securities: broker-dealers, exchanges, transfer agents and representatives. The new issue market is regulated by the 1933 act. Because the 1934 act deals with a different aspect of the industry, choice C is not correct. Making securities regulation more uniform among the states is the purpose of the Uniform Securities Act. (Page 31)

64. **D.** The 1934 act states that the purpose of margin requirements is to prevent the excessive use of credit to finance securities purchases. Margin requirements are set by the Federal Reserve Board. New issues may not be bought on margin. (Page 33)

65. **A.** Supervised persons are under the jurisdiction of the state administrators. Representatives of state-registered investment advisers must register separately with the states. Federally registered advisers may have to provide notice regarding their reps to the states. (Page 7)

66. **B.** SEC commissioners may have no business or employment other than their commission. They must also refrain from securities trading. However, commissioners are not elected as described in choice A, but are appointed by the president and confirmed by the Senate. Political party affiliation is a consideration, because no more than three of the five commissioners may belong to the same party. Experience as a prosecuting attorney is not a qualification. (Page 33)

67. **D.** Neither loss of a civil lawsuit, nor lack of experience, nor being registered as an investment adviser causes statutory disqualification from being associated with a member of a self-regulatory organization such as the NASD. However, administrative sanctions, findings of criminal wrongdoing and court injunctions are causes for statutory disqualification. (Page 37)

68. **B.** The 1934 act requires public companies to file periodic financial reports. Government agencies and municipalities are not public companies. In addition, the 1934 act deals with the trading of all securities in the secondary market, regardless of who the issuer of the security is. (Page 31)

69. **A.** Commissioners are appointed to the Securities and Exchange Commission by the President, and may be appointed for a number of reasons. To assure independence, no more than three members of the Commission may be from the same political party. (Page 31)

70. **B.** Clearing agencies performing the functions of a transfer agent with respect to contracts they issue and insurance companies are specifically excluded from the definition of "transfer agent." Choice II is a transfer agent. (Page 30)

71. **D.** A fund's agreement with its investment adviser must provide for termination by the board of directors without a vote of the outstanding shares. The other statements are true: the contract must be approved by a majority of the outstanding shares, must be in writing and must describe the adviser's compensation. (Page 91)

72. **C.** Rule 12b-l allows funds to charge distribution expenses against net assets. (Page 94)

73. **D.** Under the NSMIA, management investment companies are now exempt from state registration and regulation. The SEC will register and oversee registered investment companies (funds). (Page 86)

74. **D.** All three statements are true. (Page 90)

75. **C.** There are three types of investment companies: UITs, face-amount certificate companies and management companies. Open-end and closed-end companies are subcategories of management companies. (Page 82)

76. **B.** An adviser who has the authority to have funds dispersed from a client's bank account, as described in choice B, is considered to have "custody." Neither receipt of advisory fees—whether or not they are prepaid—nor investment discretion are considered "custody." (Page 4)

77. **A.** Records must be kept for five years, not three. The other choices are true statements: advisers must keep records of their personal transactions; choice C accurately describes the records that must be kept; and records may be kept in electronic format if they are created by computer in the regular course of business. (Page 15)

78. **D.** The antifraud provisions prohibit a failure to disclose material information, as well as misstatements of fact and deceptive practices. An adviser is not exempt from the antifraud provisions even if she is exempt from registration. The antifraud provisions of the Adviser's Act are not limited to securities transactions, as are the antifraud provisions of other federal acts. Like those of the Uniform Securities Act, they apply to the entire business relationship between adviser and client. (Page 76)

79. **A.** In an agency cross transaction, the investment adviser arranges the transaction for an advisory client and another person. However, the adviser can recommend the transaction to only one person. The advisory client must provide written consent prior to effecting an agency cross transaction. (Page 20)

80. **B.** Under federal law, investment advisers are exempt from registration if they have fewer than 15 clients. (Page 5)

81. **C.** Both the firm and the individual are directly compensated for investment advice and are required to register as investment advisers. (Page 11)

82. **B.** A blanket exclusion applies to any bank that is not an investment company. Economists are not one of the professionals to whom an exclusion applies. Broker-dealers and their representatives lose their exclusion from the definition of "investment adviser" if they provide advice beyond what is incidental to conducting a brokerage business. Attorneys or accountants who charge a separate fee for investment advice lose their exclusion from the definition, regardless of

the percentage of income derived from their investment advisory activities. (Page 2)

83. **B.** In choice I, the financial planner's advice regarding different types of securities is specific enough to qualify as investment advice. Regarding choice III, attorneys and accountants lose their exclusion from the definition of "investment adviser" if they advertise or if they charge a separate fee for investment advice. But in choice II, the insurance agent's general recommendation to allocate resources to different types of financial vehicles is not specific enough to qualify as investment advice. (Page 23)

84. **B.** The insurance agent in choice I is providing investment advice and receiving compensation for it. Receipt of any economic benefit from any source, if received as a result of providing investment advice, meets the criterion. The broker-dealer in choice III is providing investment advice outside the scope of what would be incidental to conducting a brokerage business; the exclusion from the definition of adviser is therefore lost. Although no separate fee for investment advice is charged, the broker-dealer is receiving compensation in the form of commissions on transactions that result from providing the investment advice. In choice II, however, the compensation received for services that include investment advice only in rare, isolated instances is an exception to the compensation criterion. (Page 2)

85. **A.** Persons who manage $25 million or more in client assets must be registered with the SEC. These persons fall under the direct supervision of the SEC. (Page 8)

86. **A.** A professional exclusion is not available to real estate agents. It is available to engineers, teachers and broker-dealers if the advice rendered is solely incidental to the practice of their professions. (Page 3)

87. **D.** Under the 1940 act, persons giving investment advice that is *incidental* to their professions are not considered investment advisers. If they receive a fee for their advice, they lose this exclusion and are considered investment advisers. Registration on a state or federal level would be based upon assets under management. (Page 3)

88. **B.** The criteria for being categorized as an investment adviser is any person who: provides investment advice; is in the business of providing investment advice; and is compensated for providing the investment advice. The person in choice B does not meet all three criteria; the advice he gives would most likely be considered incidental. (Page 24)

89. **D.** Advisers must disclose their total compensation, which includes fees and commissions. They must disclose all business affiliations; and they must inform clients that they have discretion when it comes to using a broker-dealer for buying or selling securities. (Page 23)

90. **A.** The management consultant's advice to clients is more personal opinion than providing investment advice as a business. In the other three choices, investment advice is being offered as part of the individual's regular business. Lawyers, accountants, engineers and teachers are generally not considered investment advisers provided the advice is incidental to their regular profession. (Page 23)

91. **D.** An insurance agent who develops a financial plan for clients and analyzes mutual funds crosses the line into being considered an investment adviser. The fact that he does not sell mutual funds does not prevent him from being considered an investment adviser. The agent in choice I is giving generic advice. The financial planner in choice IV writes financial plans with specific investment recommendations and then refers clients to a broker-dealer in order for the recommendations to be executed. The broker-dealer is not considered an investment adviser because the firm does not charge a specific fee for its investment advice. (Page 23)

92. **C.** For a *specific* order, verbal authority is sufficient. An adviser may not place an order for a client's account without proper authority. (Page 79)

93. **A.** An adviser may borrow money from a client only if the client is a broker-dealer, a bank or other financial institution in the business of loaning funds or an affiliate of the adviser. None of these applies to the company in choice III. (Page 77)

94. **C.** Choice II describes a guarantee against loss, which is a breach of ethical conduct. Choice III also is a breach of ethical conduct because advisers have a duty to inquire into a client's investment objectives, financial situation and needs. There is no breach of ethical conduct in choice I because the adviser disclosed the potential conflict of interest before the advisory contract was signed. (Page 77)

95. **C.** Advertisements may not contain false statements, include testimonials from clients, refer selectively to past recommendations, refer to a chart or device for evaluating securities without explaining its limitations and difficulties, or offer anything "free-of-charge" if in fact there will be some requirement, however minor, for obtaining the "free" item. (Page 21)

96. **B.** The agent is recommending the purchase of a security without reasonable grounds for the recommendation. The agent is probably also guilty of recommending security transactions without regard to clients' individual financial situations or investment objectives. (Page 77)

97. **B.** Assuring clients that they will make a profit is a prohibited practice. Besides, it is all too possible to lose money (interest rate risk) on fixed-income securities when interest rates go up. (Page 78)

98. **A.** The agent may accept orders only from the customer, unless third-party trading authorization has been obtained. (Page 77)

99. **A.** Material facts are facts essential for making an investment decision. To omit them is fraudulent or deceitful. (Page 78)

100. **D.** The use of information that has no basis in fact is strictly prohibited. The use of rumors is misrepresentation and a violation of the Uniform Securities Act. (Page 77)

Appendix

Form ADV, Part II

OMB APPROVAL	
OMB Number:	3235-0049
Expires:	April 30, 2000
Estimated average burden hours per response......	9.01

FORM ADV
Part II - Page 1

Uniform Application for Investment Adviser Registration

Name of Investment Adviser:						
Address:	(Number and Street)	(City)	State)	(Zip Code)	Area Code: ( )	Telephone Number:

This part of Form ADV gives information about the investment adviser and its business for the use of clients. The information has not been approved or verified by any governmental authority.

Table of Contents

Item Number	Item	Page
1	Advisory Services and Fees	2
2	Types of Clients	2
3	Types of Investments	3
4	Methods of Analysis, Sources of Information and Investment Strategies	3
5	Education and Business Standards	4
6	Education and Business Background	4
7	Other Business Activities	4
8	Other Financial Industry Activities or Affiliations	4
9	Participation or Interest in Client Transactions	5
10	Conditions for Managing Accounts	5
11	Review of Accounts	5
12	Investment or Brokerage Discretion	6
13	Additional Compensation	6
14	Balance Sheet	6
	Continuation Sheet	Schedule F
	Balance Sheet, if required	Schedule G

(Schedules A, B, C, D, and E are included with Part I of this Form, for the use of regulatory bodies, and are not distributed to clients.)

Potential persons who are to respond to the collection of information contained in this form are not required to respond unless the form displays a currently valid OMB control number.

FORM ADV
Part II- Page 2

Applicant:	SEC File Number: 801-	Date:

Definitions for Part II

Related person — Any officer, director or partner of applicant or any person directly or indirectly controlling, controlled by, or under common control with the applicant, including any non-clerical, non-ministerial employee.

Investment Supervisory Services — Giving continuous investment advice to a client (or making investments for the client) based on the individual needs of the client. Individual needs include, for example, the nature of other client assets and the client's personal and family obligations.

1. A. **Advisory Services and Fees.** (check the applicable boxes)

For each type of service provided, state the approximate % of total advisory billings from that service. (See instruction below.)

Applicant:

- ☐ (1) Provides investment supervisory services .... ____%
- ☐ (2) Manages investment advisory accounts not involving investment supervisory services .... ____%
- ☐ (3) Furnishes investment advice through consultations not included in either service described above .... ____%
- ☐ (4) Issues periodicals about securities by subscription .... ____%
- ☐ (5) Issues special reports about securities not included in any service described above .... ____%
- ☐ (6) Issues, not as part of any service described above, any charts, graphs, formulas, or other devices which clients may use to evaluate securities .... ____%
- ☐ (7) On more than an occasional basis, furnishes advice to clients on matters not involving securities .... ____%
- ☐ (8) Provides a timing service .... ____%
- ☐ (9) Furnishes advice about securities in any manner not described above .... ____%

(Percentages should be based on applicant's last fiscal year. If applicant has not completed its first fiscal year, provide estimates of advisory billings for that year and state that the percentages are estimates.)

B. Does applicant call any of the services it checked above financial planning or some similar term? .... Yes ☐ No ☐

C. Applicant offers investment advisory services for: (check all that apply)

- ☐ (1) A percentage of assets under management
- ☐ (2) Hourly charges
- ☐ (3) Fixed fees (not including subscription fees)
- ☐ (4) Subscription fees
- ☐ (5) Commissions
- ☐ (6) Other

D. For each checked box in A above, describe on Schedule F:

- the services provided, including the name of any publication or report issued by the adviser on a subscription basis or for a fee
- applicant's basic fee schedule, how fees are charged and whether its fees are negotiable
- when compensation is payable, and if compensation is payable before service is provided, how a client may get a refund or may terminate an investment advisory contract before its expiration date

2. **Types of Clients** — Applicant generally provides investment advice to: (check those that apply)

- ☐ A. Individuals
- ☐ B. Banks or thrift institutions
- ☐ C. Investment companies
- ☐ D. Pension and profit sharing plans
- ☐ E. Trusts, estates, or charitable organizations
- ☐ F. Corporations or business entities other than those listed above
- ☐ G. Other (describe on Schedule F)

Answer all items. Complete amended pages in full, circle amended items and file with execution page (page 1).

FORM ADV Part II- Page 3	Applicant:	SEC File Number: 801-	Date:

3. **Types of Investments.** Applicant offers advice on the following: (check those that apply)

A. Equity Securities
- ☐ (1) exchange-listed securities
- ☐ (2) securities traded over-the-counter
- ☐ (3) foreign issuers

☐ B. Warrants

☐ C. Corporate debt securities (other than commercial paper)

☐ D. Commercial paper

☐ E. Certificates of deposit

☐ F. Municipal securities

G. Investment company securities:
- ☐ (1) variable life insurance
- ☐ (2) variable annuities
- ☐ (3) mutual fund shares

☐ H. Unites States government securities

I. Options contracts on:
- ☐ (1) securities
- ☐ (2) commodities

J. Futures contracts on:
- ☐ (1) tangibles
- ☐ (2) intangibles

K. Interests in partnerships investing in:
- ☐ (1) real estate
- ☐ (2) oil and gas interests
- ☐ (3) other (explain on Schedule F)

☐ L. Other (explain on Schedule F)

4. **Methods of Analysis, Sources of Information, and Investment Strategies.**

A. Applicant's security analysis methods include: (check those that apply)

(1) ☐ Charting

(2) ☐ Fundamental

(3) ☐ Technical

(4) ☐ Cyclical

(5) ☐ Other (explain on Schedule F)

B. The main sources of information applicant uses include: (check those that apply)

(1) ☐ Financial newspapers and magazines

(2) ☐ Inspections of corporate activities

(3) ☐ Research materials prepared by others

(4) ☐ Corporate rating services

(5) ☐ Timing services

(6) ☐ Annual reports, prospectuses, filings with the Securities and Exchange Commission

(7) ☐ Company press releases

(8) ☐ Other (explain on Schedule F)

C. The investment strategies used to implement any investment advice given to clients include: (check those that apply)

(1) ☐ Long term purchases (securities held at least a year)

(2) ☐ Short term purchases (securities sold within a year)

(3) ☐ Trading (securities sold within 30 days)

(4) ☐ Short sales

(5) ☐ Margin transactions

(6) ☐ Option writing, including covered options, uncovered options or spreading strategies

(7) ☐ Other (explain on Schedule F)

Answer all items. Complete amended pages in full, circle amended items and file with execution page (page 1).

FORM ADV
Part II - Page 4

Applicant:	SEC File Number: 801-	Date:

5. Education and Business Standards.

Are there any general standards of education or business experience that applicant requires of those involved in determining or giving investment advice to clients? .... Yes ☐ No ☐

(If yes, describe these standards on Schedule F.)

6. Education and Business Background.

For:

- each member of the investment committee or group that determines general investment advice to be given to clients, or
- if the applicant has no investment committee or group, each individual who determines general investment advice given to clients (if more than five, respond only for their supervisors)
- each principal executive officer of applicant or each person with similar status or performing similar functions.

On Schedule F, give the:

- name
- year of birth
- formal education after high school
- business background for the preceding five years

7. Other Business Activities. (check those that apply)

☐ A. Applicant is actively engaged in a business other than giving investment advice.

☐ B. Applicant sells products or services other than investment advice to clients.

☐ C. The principal business of applicant or its principal executive officers involves something other than providing investment advice.

(For each checked box describe the other activities, including the time spent on them, on Schedule F.)

8. Other Financial Industry Activities or Affiliations. (check those that apply)

☐ A. Applicant is registered (or has an application pending) as a securities broker-dealer.

☐ B. Applicant is registered (or has an application pending) as a futures commission merchant, commodity pool operator or commodity trading adviser.

C. Applicant has arrangements that are material to its advisory business or its clients with a related person who is a:

☐ (1) broker-dealer

☐ (2) investment company

☐ (3) other investment adviser

☐ (4) financial planning firm

☐ (5) commodity pool operator, commodity trading adviser or futures commission merchant

☐ (6) banking or thrift institution

☐ (7) accounting firm

☐ (8) law firm

☐ (9) insurance company or agency

☐ (10) pension consultant

☐ (11) real estate broker or dealer

☐ (12) entity that creates or packages limited partnerships

(For each checked box in C, on Schedule F identify the related person and describe the relationship and the arrangements.)

D. Is applicant or a related person a general partner in any partnership in which clients are solicited to invest? .... Yes ☐ No ☐

(If yes, describe on Schedule F the partnerships and what they invest in.)

Answer all items. Complete amended pages in full, circle amended items and file with execution page (page 1).

FORM ADV
Part II - Page 5

Applicant:	SEC File Number: 801-	Date:

9. **Participation or Interest in Client Transactions.**

Applicant or a related person: (check those that apply)

☐ A. As principal, buys securities for itself from or sells securities it owns to any client.

☐ B. As broker or agent effects securities transactions for compensation for any client.

☐ C. As broker or agent for any person other than a client effects transactions in which client securities are sold to or bought from a brokerage customer.

☐ D. Recommends to clients that they buy or sell securities or investment products in which the applicant or a related person has some financial interest.

☐ E. Buys or sells for itself securities that it also recommends to clients.

(For each box checked, describe on Schedule F when the applicant or a related person engages in these transactions and what restrictions, internal procedures, or disclosures are used for conflicts of interest in those transactions.)

10. **Conditions for Managing Accounts.** Does the applicant provide investment supervisory services, manage investment advisory accounts or hold itself out as providing financial planning or some similarly termed services *and* impose a minimum dollar value of assets or other conditions for starting or maintaining an account? .... Yes ☐ No ☐

(If yes, describe on Schedule F.)

11. **Review of Accounts.** If applicant provides investment supervisory services, manages investment advisory accounts, or holds itself out as providing financial planning or some similarly termed services:

A. Describe below the reviews and reviewers of the accounts. **For reviews**, include their frequency, different levels, and triggering factors. **For reviewers**, include the number of reviewers, their titles and functions, instructions they receive from applicant on performing reviews, and number of accounts assigned each.

B. Describe below the nature and frequency of regular reports to clients on their accounts.

Answer all items. Complete amended pages in full, circle amended items and file with execution page (page 1).

FORM ADV
Part II · Page 6

Applicant:	SEC File Number: 801-	Date:

12. Investment or Brokerage Discretion.

A. Does applicant or any related person have authority to determine, without obtaining specific client consent, the:

(1) securities to be bought or sold? .... Yes ☐ No ☐

(2) amount of the securities to be bought or sold? .... Yes ☐ No ☐

(3) broker or dealer to be used? .... Yes ☐ No ☐

(4) commission rates paid? .... Yes ☐ No ☐

B. Does applicant or a related person suggest brokers to clients? .... Yes ☐ No ☐

For each yes answer to A describe on Schedule F any limitations on the authority. For each yes to A(3), A(4) or B, describe on Schedule F the factors considered in selecting brokers and determining the reasonableness of their commissions. If the value of products, research and services given to the applicant or a related person is a factor, describe:

- the products, research and services
- whether clients may pay commissions higher than those obtainable from other brokers in return for those products and services
- whether research is used to service all of applicant's accounts or just those accounts paying for it; and
- any procedures the applicant used during the last fiscal year to direct client transactions to a particular broker in return for products and research services received.

13. Additional Compensation.

Does the applicant or a related person have any arrangements, oral or in writing, where it:

A. is paid cash by or receives some economic benefit (including commissions, equipment or non-research services) from a non-client in connection with giving advice to clients? .... Yes ☐ No ☐

B. directly or indirectly compensates any person for client referrals? .... Yes ☐ No ☐

(For each yes, describe the arrangements on Schedule F.

14. Balance Sheet. Applicant must provide a balance sheet for the most recent fiscal year on Schedule G if applicant:

- has custody of client funds or securities; or
- requires prepayment of more than $500 in fees per client and 6 or more months in advance

Has applicant provided a Schedule G balance sheet? .... Yes ☐ No ☐

Answer all items. Complete amended pages in full, circle amended items and file with execution page (page 1).

Glossary

accredited investor As defined in Rule 502 of Regulation D, any institution or individual meeting minimum net worth requirements for the purchase of securities qualifying under the Regulation D registration exemption.

An accredited investor generally is accepted to be one who:

- has a net worth of $1 million or more; or
- has had an annual income of $200,000 or more in each of the two most recent years (or $300,000 jointly with a spouse) and who has a reasonable expectation of reaching the same income level in the current year.

administrator (1) A person authorized by a court of law to liquidate the estate of an intestate decedent. (2) The official or agency administering the securities laws of a state.

advertisement Any material designed for use by newspapers, magazines, radio, television, telephone recording or any other public medium to solicit business. The firm using advertising has little control over the type of individuals being exposed to the advertising. *See also* sales literature.

advertising prospectus An investment company prospectus that includes the fund's performance data, as well as standardized information contained in the summary prospectus.

advisory board Under the Investment Company Act of 1940, a board that advises an investment company on matters concerning its investments in securities, but that does not have the power to make investment decisions or take action itself. An advisory board must be composed of persons who have no other connection with, and serve no other function for, the investment company.

affiliate Any person directly or indirectly owning, controlling or holding, with power to vote, 10 percent or more of the outstanding voting securities of another person; also, any officer, director or partner of another entity for which such person acts in such capacity.

When used with respect to a member or sponsor, "affiliate" means any person who controls, is controlled by or is under control with such member or sponsor and includes:

- any partner, officer or director (or any person performing similar functions) of such member or sponsor, or a person who beneficially owns 50 percent or more of the equity interest in, or who has the power to vote 50 percent or more of the voting interest in, such member or sponsor; or
- any person who beneficially owns or has the right to acquire 10 percent or more of the equity interest in, or who has the power to vote 10 percent or more of the voting interest in, such member or sponsor, or a person who beneficially owns 50 percent or more of the voting interest in, or who has the power to vote 50 percent or more of the voting interest in, such member or sponsor.

agent (1) An individual acting for the accounts of others; also, any person licensed by a state as a life insurance agent. (*Syn.* broker) (2) A securities salesperson who represents a broker-dealer or an issuer when selling or trying to sell securities to the investing public. This individual is considered an agent whether he actually receives or simply solicits orders. In other words, an agent is anyone who receives an order while representing a broker-dealer.

assignment (1) A document accompanying or part of a stock certificate that is signed by the person named on the certificate for the purpose of transferring the certificate's title to another person's name. (2) The act of identifying and notifying an account holder that an option held short in that account has been exercised by the option owner.

associated person of a member (AP) Any employee, manager, director, officer or partner of a member broker-dealer or another entity (issuer, bank, etc.) or any person controlling, controlled by or in common control with that member is considered an associated person of that member.

blue-sky To qualify a securities offering in a particular state.

blue-sky laws The nickname for state regulations governing the securities industry.

broker (1) An individual or a firm that charges a fee or commission for executing buy and sell orders submitted by another individual or firm. (2) The role of a broker firm when it acts as an agent for a customer and charges the customer a commission for its services.

broker-dealer (1) An individual or a firm that charges a fee or commission for executing buy and sell orders submitted by another individual or firm. (2) The role of a broker firm when it acts as an agent for a customer and charges the customer a commission for its services.

The term "broker-dealer" is defined in the Uniform Securities Act so that it can be determined who must register in the state as a broker-dealer. If the person does not fall under the definition of "broker-dealer" as defined by the law, the registration process is not necessary.

The following persons are not classified as broker-dealers:

- agents (registered representatives);
- issuers;
- banks, savings institutions or trust companies;
- persons who have no place of business in the state and who: (a) effect securities transactions in the state exclusively through the issuers of the securities, other broker-dealers or financial institutions (banks, savings institutions, trust companies, insurance companies and investment companies) or (b) directs an offer in this state to an existing customer who has less than 30 days' temporary residency in the state where the offer is received.

dealer The role of a brokerage firm when it acts as a principal in a particular trade. A firm is acting as a dealer when it buys or sells a security for its own account and at its own risk and then charges the customer a markup or markdown. Any person who is engaged in the business of buying and selling securities for her own account either directly or through a broker, and who is not a bank, is considered a dealer. (*Syn.* principal)

discretion The authority for someone other than the beneficial owner of an account to make investment decisions for that account regarding the security, the number of shares or units and whether to buy or sell. Decisions concerning only timing and price do not constitute "discretion."

exempt security A security exempt from the registration requirements (although not from the antifraud requirements) of the Securities Act of 1933 (e.g., U.S. government and municipal securities).

exempt transaction A transaction exempt from registration and advertising requirements under the Uniform Securities Act. Examples of exempt transactions include:

- isolated nonissuer transactions;
- nonissuer transactions in outstanding securities (normal market trading);
- transactions with financial institutions (banks, savings institutions, trust companies, insurance companies, pension or profit-sharing plans, broker-dealers, etc.);
- unsolicited transactions;
- fiduciary transactions;
- private placement transactions;
- transactions between an issuer and its underwriters; and
- transactions with an issuer's employees, partners or directors if no commission is paid directly or indirectly for the soliciting.

Exemption from the act's registration and advertising requirements does not mean that a transaction is exempt from the act's antifraud provisions.

fidelity bond *See* surety bond.

fiduciary A person legally appointed and authorized to represent another person and act on her behalf.

fraud The deliberate concealment, misrepresentation or omission of material information or the truth to deceive or manipulate another party for unlawful or unfair gain.

government security An obligation of the U.S. government, backed by the full faith and credit of the government, and regarded as the highest grade or safest issue (i.e., default risk-free). The U.S. government issues short-term Treasury bills, medium-term Treasury notes and long-term Treasury bonds.

guaranteed Securities that have a guarantee, usually from a source other than the issuer, as to the payment of principal, interest or dividends.

inside information Material and nonpublic information obtained or used by a person for the purpose of trading in securities.

insider Any person who has nonpublic knowledge (material information) about a corporation. Insiders include directors, officers and stockholders who own more than 10 percent of any class of equity security of a corporation.

institutional account An account held for the benefit of others. Examples include banks, trusts, pension and profit-sharing plans, mutual funds and insurance companies.

institutional investor A person or an organization that trades securities in large enough share quantities or dollar amounts that it qualifies for preferential treatment and lower trade costs (commissions). Institutional investors are covered by fewer protective regulations because it is assumed that they are more knowledgeable and better able to protect themselves.

investment adviser Any person who, for compensation (a flat fee or a percentage of assets managed), offers investment advice. For investment companies, the adviser has the day-to-day responsibility of investing the cash and securities held in a mutual fund's portfolio. The adviser must adhere to the objectives as stated in the fund's prospectus. This definition includes persons who issue written reports or analyses for compensation. The term "investment adviser" does not include:

- institutions such as banks, savings institutions or trust companies;
- professionals such as lawyers, accountants or teachers whose performance of these services is solely incidental to the practice of their profession;
- broker-dealers that offer investment portfolio advice as part of their business of being broker-dealers and that receive no special compensation for that service;
- publishers of any financial publication of general, regular and paid circulation; however, a person who sells subscriptions to investment advisory publications (market letters) is considered an investment adviser under the Uniform Securiti _ Act;
- persons whose investment advice relates only to U.S. government securities and certain municipal securities; and
- persons having no place of business within the state and whose activities are limited to (a) professional clients (institutions) or (b) a very few solicitations or sales to clients other than those mentioned above. For instance, some states limit this activity to less than six clients in any 12 consecutive months.

The term "investment adviser" also excludes any person that the state administrator of the Uniform Securities Act decides not to include.

investment adviser representative Any partner, officer, director or other individual employed by or associated with an investment adviser who (1) gives investment advice or makes recommendations, (2) manages client accounts or portfolios, (3) determines which investment recommendations or advice should be given, (4) offers or sells investment advisory services or (5) supervises employees involved in any of these activities.

Investment Advisers Act of 1940 Legislation passed by Congress that requires all investment advisers to register as such with the SEC and to abide by the Investment Advisers Act of 1940 and all other applicable federal acts.

investment company A company engaged primarily in the business of investing and trading in securities, including face-amount certificate companies, unit investment trusts and management companies.

Investment Company Act of 1940 Congressional legislation enacted to regulate investment companies that requires any investment company in interstate commerce to register with the SEC.

issuer (1) The corporation or municipality that offers its securities for sale; also, the creator of an option (the issuer of an over-the-counter option is the option writer, and the issuer of a listed option is the Options Clearing Corporation). (2) According to the Uniform Securities Act, any person who issues or proposes to issue any security.

When a corporation or municipality raises additional capital through an offering of securities, that corporation or municipality is the issuer of those securities. An issuer transaction also is called a *primary transaction.*

There are two exceptions to the basic definition of "issuer." In the case of voting-trust certificates or collateral-trust certificates, the term "issuer" refers to the person who assumes the duties of depositor or manager. There is considered to be no issuer for certificates of interest or participation in oil, gas, or mining titles or leases where payments are made out of production.

market maker (principal) A dealer willing to accept the risk of holding securities to facilitate trading in a particular security(ies).

municipal security A debt security issued by a state, a municipality or another subdivision (such as a school, a park, or a sanitary or some other local taxing district) to raise money to finance its capital expenditures. Such expenditures might include the construction of highways, public works or school buildings.

net capital Liquid capital (cash and assets readily convertible into cash) maintained by a broker-dealer.

nonissuer A person other than the issuer of a security. In a nonissuer securities transaction, for example, the issuer is not one of the parties in the transaction, and the transaction therefore is not, according to the law, directly or indirectly for the benefit of the issuer.

When the Uniform Securities Act refers to a *nonissuer transaction,* it is referring to a transaction in which the proceeds of the sale go to the selling stockholder. For example, a trade of 100 shares of RCA on the New York Stock Exchange is a typical nonissuer transaction. Most nonissuer transactions also are called *secondary transactions.*

offer (1) An indication by an investor, a trader or a dealer of a willingness to sell a security or commodity. (2) Under the Uniform Securities Act, every attempt to solicit a purchase or sale in a security for value.

person An individual, a corporation, a partnership, an association, a fund, a joint stock company, an unincorporated organization, a trust in which the interests of the beneficiaries are evidenced by a security, a government or a political subdivision of a government.

private investment company An unregistered investment company whose investment objective is to raise capital for business ventures. Qualified purchasers are eligible to invest in private investment companies.

private placement An offering that complies with Regulation D (Rule 505 and Rule 506); generally, the offer of an unregistered security to no more than 35 nonaccredited investors or to an unlimited number of accredited investors. The Uniform Securities Act's private placement provision allows an exemption from full state registration for a security that is sold in that state to no more than 10 nonaccredited investors.

prospectus The legal document that must be given to every investor who purchases registered securities in an offering. It describes the details of the company and the particular offering. (*Syn.* final prospectus)

qualified purchaser A sophisticated investor who invests in a private investment company. This includes:

- an individual with $5 million or more invested;
- a family-owned business with $5 million or more invested;
- a trust established by qualified purchasers; and
- a company that invests on a discretionary basis a minimum of $25 million in investments.

registered representative For NASD registration and exam and licensing purposes, refers to all associated persons engaged in the investment banking and securities business. This includes:

- assistant officers (who are not principals);
- individuals who supervise, solicit or conduct business in securities; and
- individuals who train people to supervise, solicit or conduct business in securities.

Anyone who is not a principal and not engaged in clerical or brokerage administration is subject to registration and exam licensing as a registered representative—except for foreign associates. (*Syn.* account executive, stockbroker)

registration by coordination A security is eligible for blue-sky registration by coordination in a state if the issuer files for registration of that security under the Securities Act of 1933 and files duplicates of the registration documents with the state administrator. The state registration becomes effective at the same time the federal registration statement becomes effective.

registration by filing A security is eligible for blue-sky registration by filing in a state if the issuer files for registration of that security under the Securities Act of 1933, meets minimum net worth and other requirements, and notifies the state of this eligibility by filing certain documents with the state administrator. The state registration becomes effective at the same time the federal registration statement becomes effective.

registration by qualification A security is eligible for blue-sky registration by qualification in a state if the issuer files registration documents for that security with the state administrator; meets minimum net worth, disclosure and other requirements; and files appropriate registration fees. The state registration becomes effective when the administrator so orders.

registration statement Before nonexempt securities can be offered to the public, they require registration under the Securities Act of 1933. The registration statement must disclose all pertinent information concerning the issuer and the offering. This statement is submitted to the SEC in accordance with the requirements of the 1933 act.

sales literature Any written material used to help sell a product and distributed by the firm in a controlled manner.

Securities Act of 1933 The federal legislation requiring the full and fair disclosure of all material information about the issuance of new securities.

Securities and Exchange Commission (SEC) The commission, created by Congress to protect investors, that enforces the Securities Act of 1933, the Securities Exchange Act of 1934, the Trust Indenture Act of 1939, the Investment Company Act of 1940, the Investment Advisers Act of 1940 and other securities laws.

Securities Exchange Act of 1934 The federal legislation establishing the Securities and Exchange Commission that regulates securities exchanges and over-the-counter markets and that protects investors from unfair and inequitable practices.

securities information processor A person who is in the business of providing information about securities transactions or quotations on a current and continuing basis. The information may be published on paper (such as in the *Pink Sheets*) or it may be disseminated through a computer network. Specifically excluded from the definition are persons who handle such information on a regular basis in the course of their business activities but who are not "in the business" of doing so.

security Under the act of 1934, any note, stock, bond, investment contract, debenture, certificate of interest in profit-sharing or partnership agreement, certificate of deposit, collateral trust certificate, preorganization certificate, option on a security or other instrument of investment commonly known as a *security*.

Also categorized as securities are interests in oil and gas drilling programs, real estate condominiums and cooperatives, farmland or animals, commodity option contracts, whiskey warehouse receipts, multilevel distributorship arrangements and merchandising marketing programs.

The accurate determination of what is a security is crucial to registered representatives conducting their activities in compliance with state securities laws. In general, "security" can be defined as any piece of securitized paper that can be traded for value, except an insurance policy or a fixed annuity. As established by the federal courts, the basic test for determining whether a specific investment falls within the definition of "security" is whether the investor invests his money in a common enterprise and is led to expect profits from the managerial efforts of the promoter or a third party.

self-regulatory organization (SRO) An entity that is accountable to the SEC for the enforcement of federal securities laws, as well as for the supervision of securities practices, within an assigned field of jurisdiction. Eight SROs function under the oversight of the Commission. Selected jurisdictions include the:

- New York Stock Exchange (NYSE). All matters related to trading in NYSE-listed securities and the conduct of NYSE member firms and associated persons.
- National Association of Securities Dealers (NASD). All matters related to investment banking (securities underwriting), trading in the over-the-counter market and the conduct of NASD member firms and associated persons.
- Municipal Securities Rulemaking Board (MSRB). All matters related to the underwriting and trading of state and municipal securities.
- Chicago Board Options Exchange (CBOE). All matters related to the writing and trading of standardized options and related contracts listed on that exchange.

sell The act of conveying ownership of a security or other property for money or other value; every contract to sell a security or an interest in a security. Sales include the following:

- Any security given or delivered with, or as a bonus for, any purchase of securities is considered to have been offered and sold for value.
- A gift of assessable stock is considered to involve an offer and sale.
- Every sale or offer of a warrant or right to purchase or subscribe to another security is considered to include an offer of the other security.

Sales do not include bona fide pledges or loans, or stock dividends if nothing of value is given by the stockholders for the dividend.

surety bond (1) A bond required by NYSE Rule 319 for all employees, officers and partners of member firms to protect clients against acts of misplacement, fraudulent trading and check forgery. (2) The blanket surety bond that indemnifies against losses due to check forgery, lost securities or fraudulent trading that every member firm required to join the Securities Investor Protection Corporation (that is, any firm doing business with the public) must purchase and maintain. (*Syn.* fidelity bond)

transfer agent A person or an organization responsible for recording the names of registered stockholders and the number of shares owned, seeing that the certificates are signed by the appropriate corporate officers, affixing the corporate seal and delivering the securities to the transferee.

underwriter The entity responsible for marketing stocks, bonds, mutual fund shares and so on.

Index

Accredited investor, 28, 61
Additional issue market, 55
Administrator, 3, 34, 35
Advertisements, 21-22, 34-35
  materials, 15
  for new issue, 50-51
  with prospectus, 95
Advice, analyses concerning securities, 24
Advisers
  custody of customer funds and securities, 16
  disclosure, 97
  operating investment supervisory or management services, 16
Affiliated person, 62, 91-92
Aftermarket sales, by prospectus, 50
Agency cross transactions, 20
Agent, 28
  registration, 38
Amendments to records, 17
Antifraud regulations, 63-64
Application
  registration, 38-39
  state registration, 8-9
Ask, 84
Assignment, 3
Associated person, 28

Bank, 3
Banking Act, 46-47
Bid, 84
Blue-sky laws, 34, 45, 54
Board of directors, 90
Bonding, of directors, employees, 95
Borrowing, 77
Brochure rule, 14-15
Broker-dealer, 28
  federal registration of, 37
  federal and state laws regarding, 43
  state registration of, 37-40
Burden of proof of exemption, 5
Business activities, 14-19
Business-related records, 16
Business standard, 24

Canadian firms, agents, 42
Cancelation of registration, 11
Capacity, disclosure of, 76
Cash payment, client solicitation, 22-23
Charitable organization securities, 69
Chinese Wall doctrine, 101
Civil penalties, 25, 36, 102
Claims and opinions, couched as facts and conclusions, 21
Client solicitation, cash payment for, 22-23
Closed-end investment company, 84
Collection procedures, 102-103
Combined distributions, 56
Commercial paper, 70
Commingling, 78
Common carrier securities, 69
Communication
  prohibitions, 22
  untruths in, 52
Company's present PE, 58
Compensation, 24
  restrictions, 18
Conditional exemption, 18-19
Confidentiality of investigations, 25
Conflict of interest, 24, 78
Consolidation, 145
Contemporaneous traders, 102
Continuous public offering securities, 87
Contract, 78, 91
Contract terms, 18
Control, 62, 102
Cooling-off period, 48, 56-57
Covered securities, 68
Crash of 1929, 46-47
Credit, extension of in securities industry, 33
Criminal penalties, 25, 36, 79, 102-103
Custodian, 93
Custody, 16, 17
Customer
  custody of funds, securities, 17
  payment, 59
  protection, 78
  services agent, 93

Deceptive name, 87
Deficiency letter, 56
Delivery
  by dealer, 50
  of disclosure brochure, 14
De minimis exemption, 5
Denial
  of exemption, 72
  of registration, 10-11, 41-42
Directors, 95
Disbursement, of proceeds, 59
Disclosure
  additional requirements, 96-97
  of advisers, 97
  brochure, 14
    contents, 14
    exceptions, 14
  of capacity, 76
  conflicts of interest, 24
  financial and disciplinary information, 23

of legal action, 76
wrap fee brochure, 15
Discretionary account transactions, 20
Discretionary authority, 77
Dishonest business practice, 77
Diversified investment company, 85
Document preparation, 56
Due diligence, 57

Effective date, 58
Employee pension plan, 70
Employees, 95
Employment, 40
changes in, 40
Enforcement, Uniform Securities Act, 26
Equity security, 28
Excessive trading, 77
Exemptions
Canadian firms, agents, 42
denial, revocation of, 72-73
federal registration of broker-dealer, 37
state registration of agent, 38
state registration of broker-dealer, 37
Exempt issuers, 60
Exempt securities, 60, 64, 69-70
Exempt transactions, 60-63, 70-72

Face-amount certificate company, 82-83
Federal laws, investment adviser, 12-13
Federal registration
exemptions from, 60-64
of new issues, 47-51
Fees, 78
Fiduciary, 3-4, 71
Final prospectus, 49, 58
Financial highlights, 96
Financial institutions' securities, 69
Financial reports, 17, 96
Financial requirements, 9, 39
Firm registration, 40
Foreign authorities assistance, 79
Foreign government securities, 69
Foreign securities, 62
Foreign securities authority, 4
Form ADV, 6, 303-310
Form ADV-W, 6
48-hour rule, 50

Free service, offers of, 21
Fund performance, 96

Glass-Steagall Act of 1933, 46-47
Government securities dealer, 29
Government security, 28
Guaranteed, 29

Hot issue, 58

IA. *See* Investment adviser
Identification, sales literature, 21
Impersonal advisory service, 3
Indication of interest, 49
Information
availability of, 25
distributed to investors, 95-97
Initial public offering (IPO), 55
Insider trading rules, 101-102
Insider Trading and Securities Fraud Enforcement Act of 1988, 100-103
Institutional investor, 29
Insurance company advisory exemption, 5
Insurance company securities, 69
Interested person, 91-92
Interlocking directorate, 90
Intrastate adviser exemption, 5
Intrastate offerings, 63
Investigations, 35
Investment adviser (IA), 90-91
brochure rule, 14-15
business activities of, 14-19
ethical behavior of, 76-79
federal registration of, 5-7
federal and state laws regarding, 12-13
forms filed by, 12
person considered, 23
registration of, 2-4
registration form, public access to, 25
state registration of, 8-13
status, 23-24
Investment adviser representative, 3, 8
Investment adviser representative registration, 7
Investment Advisers Act, 1, 17, 25
Investment advisory contracts, 17-19
Investment banker, 53
Investment banking, 53

Investment company
functions, activities of, 88-89
management of, 90-97
offerings, 82-85
purpose, 82
registration, 86-89
types of, 82-85
Investment counsel, 3
Investment recommendations, 77-79
Investment supervisory service, 3
IPO, 55
Isolated nonissuer transactions, 70
Issuer, 29, 54
Issuer transactions, 71
Issuing corporation, 55

Judicial review, registration denial, suspension, 11

Legal action
disclosure of, 76
registration, 11
Legended stock, 61
Legislative reaction, Crash of 1929, 46-47
Lettered stock, 61
Local adviser exemption, 5
Losses avoided, 102

Maloney Act, 47
Management investment company, 84
Margin, 33
Market maker, 29
Market manipulation, 78
Material facts, 78
Material misstatements, 6
Merger, 145
Misleading name, 87
Misrepresentations, 52
Municipal securities, 69
Mutual fund, 84-85
organization of, 94
shares on margin, 88

NASAA, 4, 8
NASD, 54
Nasdaq-quoted securities, 70
National Association of Securities Dealers (NASD), 54
National Securities Markets Improvement Act (NSMIA), 1

New issue
advertising, 50-51
market, 55
participants in corporate, 53-54
pricing, 58
regulation, overview of, 46-52
state registration of, 65-73
Nonaccredited investors, 61
Nondiversified investment company, 85
Nonissuer transactions, outstanding securities, 70-71
Nonpublic information, misuse of, 103
Nonregistered foreign securities, 62
North American Securities Administrators Association (NASAA), 4, 8
Notification requirements, registration denial, suspension, 11
NSMIA, 1

Offer, 29-30
Offering
circular, 61
recent, 58
types of, 55-56
Offers of free service, 21
Open-end investment company, 84-85

Participants in corporate new issue, 53-54
Pegging, 59
Pension plan, 70
Person, 2, 23, 28
Pledges, 71
Preliminary prospectus, 48-49
Preorganization certificates, 72
Prepayment of fees, 17
Price-earnings ratio, 58
Primary offering, 55
Private investment company, 4
Private placement, 61, 71-72
Profits gained, 102
Profit-sharing plan, 70
Prospectus, 47-51, 88, 95
untruths in, 52
in use after nine months, 50
Proxy statement, 63
Public access to investment adviser registration form, 25
Public offering, 86-88
Publicly traded fund, 84
Public utility securities, 69

Qualification examinations, 39-40
Qualified purchaser, 4
Qualified purchasers pool, 18

Reclassification, 145
Recordkeeping, 15-17
Red herring, 48-49
Redeemable securities, 85
Reg T, 33
Registration
agent, 38
Canadian firms, agents, 42
cancelation of, 11
denial, suspension, revocation, 10-11, 41-42, 68
exchanges and corporations, 32-33
federal, 5-7
of broker-dealer, 37
exemptions, 5-6, 60-64
of new issues, 47-51
firm, 40
investment adviser, 2-4
investment company, 86-89
investment company securities, 88
judicial review, 11
legal action, 10
length of, 38
notification requirements, 11
SEC procedure, 6-7
state
of broker-dealer, 37-38
exemptions, 8
of new issues, 65-73
procedures, 38-40
withdrawal from, 6, 11
Registration by coordination, 54, 65-66
Registration by filing, 54, 66
Registration by qualification, 54, 66-67
Registration statement, 48
changes in, 89
prospectus, 88
untruths in, 52
Regulation, new issue, 46-52
Regulation A, 61
Regulation D, 61
Regulation T, 33
Religious organization securities, 69
Reorganization, 62-63
Reporting requirements, 15-17
Rescission, right of, 36
Responsibilities, those who pass examination, 40
Restricted securities, 62
Restrictions, 92
on operations, 88-89
Revocation, of exemption, 72
Rule 144, 62
Rule 144a, 62
Rule 145, 62-63
Rule 147, 145
Rule 415, 56
Rule 427, 50
Rule 506, 61

Sales literature, 21-22
Sales materials, 15
Sales representative, 28
Sales volume restrictions, 62
Savings plan, 70
SEC. *See* Securities and Exchange Commission
Secondary offering, 55
Securities, 30
information processor, 30
listed on national stock exchanges, 69-70
selling, 59
trading regulation, 28-30
types of, 65-67
Securities Act of 1933, 31, 46
antifraud regulations, 63-64
civil liabilities under, 52
Securities and Exchange Commission (SEC), 31, 53
enforcement, 25
expansion of role, 32
investigations, 101
jurisdiction of, 32
registration and, 32-33
procedure, 6-7
public offering, 86-88
Release IA-1092, 23-24
review, 49-50
Securities Exchange Act of 1934, 31-33, 47, 63-64
Securities Investor Protection Act of 1970, 100-103
Securities Investor Protection Corporation (SIPC), 100

Securities markets, 55
Security, 30
Sell, 29-30
Selling group prohibitions, 51
75-5-10 test, 85
Shareholders' right to vote, 89
Shelf offering, 56
Short-swing profits, 102
Simplified registration, 42
SIPC, 100
Small offerings, 61
Sources, 78
Split offering, 56
Stabilizing, 59
State laws, 54
  investment adviser, 12-13
State registration
  application, 8-9, 38-39
  exemptions from, 68-72
  financial requirements, 9
  procedures, 67-68
  regulations, restrictions, 9-10
  responsibilities of those who pass exam, 9-10
  surety bonds, 9
State securities laws, 34
Statute of limitations, 36, 52, 102
Sticky issues, 59
Stock selection records, using past, 21
Stop order, 48
Subpoenas, 35
Suitability, 77-79
Supervised person, 3, 8
Surety bonds, 9, 39
Syndicate, forming, 56

TCPA, 103
Telephone Consumer Protection Act of 1991 (TCPA), 103
Testimonials, 21
Third-party authority, 77
Tombstone, 51
Transactions, 20-26
  by certain persons, 71
  covered by Rule 145, 63
  with financial institutions, 71
Transfer agent, 30, 93
Transfer of assets, 145
Trust Indenture Act of 1939, 47

Underwriter, 29, 54, 94
  selling group prohibitions, 51
Underwriting
  corporate securities, 53
  group, 84
  process, 53-59
  time line for, 56-59
Unethical business practice, 77-79
Uniform Securities Act (USA)
  administration of, 34-36
  enforcement of, 26
  penalties under, 36
  scope of, 34-35
  state securities administrators, 35
  state securities laws, 34
U.S. government securities, 68
Unit investment trust, 83-84
Unlawful representations, 73
Unsolicited orders, 71
Untruths
  prospectuses and communications, 52
  registration statements, 52
USA. *See* Uniform Securities Act

Validity, investment advisory contracts, 19

Withdrawal, from registration, 11
Wrap fee brochure, 15
  definition, 15
  disclosure, 15
  sales and advertising materials, 15
Written disclosure statement, 14
Written supervisory procedures, 101

Notes

Notes